ARCHANGELS
ARCHAEOLOGY

"Logic!" said the Professor half to himself. "Why don't they teach logic at these schools? There are only three possibilities. Either your sister is telling lies, or she is mad, or she is telling the truth. You know she doesn't tell lies and it is obvious that she is not mad. For the moment then and unless any further evidence turns up, we must assume that she is telling the truth."

C.S. Lewis, *The Lion, the Witch and the Wardrobe*

ARCHANGELS & ARCHAEOLOGY

J.S.M. Ward's Kingdom of the Wise

Geoffrey Ginn

sussex
ACADEMIC
PRESS
Brighton • Portland • Toronto

2 4 6 8 10 9 7 5 3 1

First published in 2012 by
SUSSEX ACADEMIC PRESS
PO Box 139
Eastbourne BN24 9BP

and in the United States of America by
SUSSEX ACADEMIC PRESS
920 NE 58th Ave   Suite 300
Portland, Oregon 97213-3786

and in Canada by
SUSSEX ACADEMIC PRESS (CANADA)
8000 Bathurst Street, Unit 1, PO Box 30010, Vaughan, Ontario L4J 0C6

British Library Cataloguing in Publication Data
A CIP catalogue record for this book is available from the British Library.

Library of Congress Cataloging-in-Publication Data
Ginn, Geoffrey A. C.
Archangels & archaeology : J.S.M. Ward's kingdom of the wise / Geoffrey A.C. Ginn.
p. cm.
Includes bibliographical references (p.   ) and index.
ISBN 978-1-84519-492-5 (h/b : alk. paper) —
ISBN 978-1-84519-493-2 (p/b : alk. paper)
   1. Ward, J. S. M. (John Sebastian Marlow), 1885–1949. 2. Spiritualists—England—Biography. I. Title. II. Title: Archangels and archaeology.
BF1283.W28G56 2012
130.92—dc23
[B]

2011040266

MIX
Paper from
responsible sources
FSC
www.fsc.org   FSC® C013056

Typeset and designed by Sussex Academic Press, Brighton & Eastbourne.
Printed by TJ International, Padstow, Cornwall.
This book is printed on acid-free paper.

Contents

List of Illustrations

All photographs are courtesy of the Abbey Museum of Art and Archaeology (AMAA), and used with permission. Figure 13 is courtesy of Anna Ferguson Architect, and Figure 22 is reproduced with permission from Mirrorpix.

Preface

How many historians profess to be in psychic contact with departed spirits, and have visions of archangels? How many museum curators regard their artefact collections as divinely ordained for the purpose of explaining an imminent Christian apocalypse? How often do we find a man with a scholarly historical imagination turning increasingly to the mystical, and dedicating his life to the fusion of history and the occult that was the result? If we agree that these are unusual confluences, it follows that a life on these lines has intrinsic interest. John Sebastian Marlow Ward was indeed an antiquarian with a difference, and this book tells his curious and remarkable story in full for the first time.

A child of the Victorian era and its relentless modernity, John Ward was fascinated by the relics of history and studied them – from brass rubbings and medieval architecture to handicrafts, weaponry, ceramics, artworks and the paraphernalia of secret societies – with a scholarly dedication leavened by an irrepressible, boyish enthusiasm. He earned prominence during the 1920s as a scholar of the history and ritual of Freemasonry, with a prodigious knowledge of occult traditions: his unconventional approach to the subject inspired many readers even as his speculative style left many fellow-researchers unimpressed. The treasure trove of antiquities and historical curiosities he assembled in a lifetime of collecting, meanwhile, aimed to sketch out the cultural evolution of the great civilizations in world history. It was first displayed to public acclaim in London in the 1930s, and its remnants are now in a small but dynamic Australian museum where Ward's quirky and compelling objects continue to enthral and educate visitors.

But these interests were accompanied by a private mysticism that, ultimately, enveloped and transformed his outlook and convictions. At the end of the Great War, Ward's accounts of his own clairvoyant communication with departed spirits joined the flood of spiritualist works that rose in response to wartime grief and mourning. Later, with the onset of increasingly urgent psychic visions, he plunged into an ecclesiastical underworld of fringe sects, irregular bishops and Christian millenarianism as the 1930s tumbled toward another European catastrophe. The community he and his followers established – the Confraternity of the Kingdom of Christ, with around a dozen members living in a communal abbey – fused doctrines of reincarnation and karmic justice with conventional Christian theology as they announced an imminent world-historical crisis that would climax in the return of Christ the King. In time Ward's community embraced an 'Orthodox Catholicism' replete with a heritage of church ritual that was re-interpreted for their modern pentecostal mission.

Paradoxically, the innovative history museum Ward developed as part of his Abbey of Christ the King was extraordinarily popular when thrown open to the public in 1934. The Abbey Folk Park united Ward's scholarly enthusiasms with his millenarian conviction that the collapse of western civilization was imminent. As its director he achieved a national profile. But this achievement crumbled to dust when Ward was disgraced unfairly in a sensationalised High Court case in 1945. As a shattered Europe began its recovery from the devastation of war, he contemplated the ruin of his life's work.

His career thus follows a classically tragic arc: from youthful antiquarian, to the mature scholar, to full-blown mystic and eccentric religious leader and finally to his own decline and fall from public grace at the High Court in 1945 as Allied forces stormed into Hitler's Berlin. His journey makes fascinating and unexpected links in cultural history: from the occult revival to the interwar heritage movement, from Spiritualism to Freemasonry and on to a synthesis of Christianity with eastern doctrines of reincarnation. His Orthodox Catholicism was infused with mystical visions of an enthroned Christ to salvage England and her Empire. Ward's extraordinary life and career demonstrates how these religious, intellectual and cultural themes – so often treated in isolation – came together in one man's life in the turbulent decades of the early twentieth century.

✳   ✳   ✳

Ward may be an obscure figure, but his legacy has been further veiled in intrigue and speculation as researchers of various kinds have tackled his story. In the absence of any authoritative biography the wildest speculations flourish and prosper, especially in today's shadow-world of the internet, where Ward's not inconsiderable achievements are at the mercy of slipshod research and recycled innuendo. Francis King, the influential scholar of the occult, described Ward briefly as "a bogus Bishop . . . who had written some quite good but far-fetched books on masonry, and who ran a peculiar religious-cum-occult community called The Abbey of Christ the King . . ."[1] King's superficial and dismissive comment is characteristic of the many fragmentary sketches of Ward's life and work. Peter Anson's *Bishops at Large*, published in the 1960s, was the first to present any substantial account, and while this is broadly accurate, it too is abbreviated and largely unsympathetic.[2] Most of the fragmentary versions of Ward's life in circulation can be traced to Anson. Among recent scholars, Philip Heselton and Joanne Pearson have made do with the limited source material available to them: although both are genuinely interested in Ward's achievements and significance and seek to place him in context as an important but neglected presence in the modern occult revival, their studies have lacked the historical detail that would enable such a placement to occur.[3] Pearson, in particular, makes a case for Ward's significance in shaping the terms of modern Wicca's debt to earlier traditions of heterodox Christianity, but lacks the evidence to fully elaborate this theme. Likewise, Tony Baker's account of Ward's Masonic career is fulsome but restricted to the published documents.[4]

This book, by contrast, has been written with the benefit of access to the library of the Abbey Museum of Art and Archaeology and the archives of the Confraternity of the Kingdom of Christ in Caboolture, Australia. Interviews with those members of the Confraternity who knew Ward personally brought memories and anecdotes into the picture. Ward's books, lectures and articles, newspaper and magazine reports of his various public activities, the records of Masonic libraries and archives, Anglican diocesan records and other official sources have been systematically integrated into the analysis presented here. Ward's life story has its own peculiar twists and turns, fully documented for this first time in this book, that can now be understood in their historical and biographical contexts to a far greater extent than has previously been possible.

At the peak of his career, from the middle years of the Great War to the defeat of Nazi Germany, Ward occupied two realms that present quite different challenges and opportunities for the historian. The first, a public realm, saw his developing career as an economic analyst, Director of the Abbey Folk Park and Father Superior of his monastic order in which he aspired to a broad stage for his research interests and religious mission. He had taken a similar posture during his two decades as an active Freemason and Masonic scholar: a love of publicity, debate and controversy was ever in him. Consequently he enjoyed some prominence in the national press between 1934 and 1940, and again (under less agreeable circumstances) in 1945. But simultaneously he occupied a cloistered and private realm, dominated by his psychic experiences that in time were embodied in the pious devotions of his Confraternity. This dimension of his life, with its roots in intensely subjective, ineffable experiences that resist external verification, has been far more difficult to chart historically. How can we be sure the whole paraphernalia of mystical enlightenment, his claims to visionary psychic insight and so on, was not mere invention, a cynical ploy to boost his mystique and standing in the eyes of the world and of his followers?

My response has been to wonder, repeatedly, whether John Ward was sincere in his belief that his visions were authentic. My conclusion is that he probably was, simply because there is no evidence of deliberate fraudulence and much circumstantial evidence of his sincerity. His belief system, even if more elaborate than most, needs to be appreciated historically: he was far from being the only Englishman or woman of his period to profess an experience of psychic episodes. He was not the only spirit medium to feel he had received messages from disincarnate personalities and entities he regarded as 'higher beings'. Nor was he the only Englishman to seek a common creative principle that might fuse the religious traditions of East and West. But the elaborate religious mission Ward constructed from these disparate experiences and insights *was* distinctive, even if it drew deeply on the major spiritual and esoteric currents of his day. And this is perhaps the essential value of his biography: far from being an isolated crank and eccentric, Ward's experiences and outlook provide a point of entry into the undercurrents of spiritual life that rippled beneath the conventional exterior of British society in this period. Although never an avowed Theosophist, he had much in common with that subtle, far-reaching movement. He arguably helped define later patterns of speculative Freemasonry, and seems, elusively, to have shaped the emergence of Wicca and its rejuvenation of esoteric ritual for a democratic age. Few self-proclaimed mystics of Ward's era established so impressive a house of worship as the Abbey Church at New Barnet; surely none achieved as unique a legacy as the Abbey Folk Park.

Ward's career thus echoes those of countless other mystics, visionaries, psychics and sensitives throughout human history who have registered anomalous experiences, interpreted a calling in them, and thus pursued the often erratic course of the religious leader. Certainly, we should not be surprised when their manner and perspective on life is odd. The philosopher William James acknowledged that such individuals, beset by an "acute fever" of unusual religious insight, are often literally "geniuses in the religious line". James understood that men and women of this kind are unlikely to be conventional:

> Even more perhaps than other kinds of genius, religious leaders have been subject to abnormal psychical visitations. Invariably they have been creatures of exalted emotional sensibility. Often they have led a discordant inner life, and had melancholy during part of their career. They have known no measure, been liable to obsessions and fixed ideas; and frequently they have fallen into trances, heard voices, seen visions, and presented all sorts of peculiarities which are ordinarily classed as pathological. Often, moreover, these pathological features in their career have helped to give them their religious authority and influence.[5]

As a historian, then, I have sought to make sense of an unusual but evocative career by placing Ward in his context and composing a coherent narrative from the fragmentary documents of a life in flux between the mundane and transcendent. If parts of the story remain elusive, I leave it to others better qualified and more esoterically-minded to determine the ultimate sources and value of his spiritual beliefs. The pages that follow are predicated on a (not uncritical) acceptance of Ward's sincerity as a religious visionary. My interest was hooked by his effervescent historical curiosity, which had a counterpart in the tireless explorations that made up his spiritual quest. I have been intrigued at how those two preoccupations came to shape and infuse each other, and so fascinated by the unfolding trajectory of his ultimately tragic career.

Acknowledgements

To Michael Strong, Director of the Abbey Museum of Art and Archaeology, belongs the credit for the initiation and continued encouragement of this study. Father Peter Strong of the Orthodox Catholic Church in Australia, and the Reverend Mother Superior of the Confraternity of the Kingdom of Christ both provided generously of their time, documentary information and memories of J. S. M. Ward. Father George Cuffe also read draft and provided valuable comments. Research assistance and advice from Edith Cuffe at the Abbey Museum library was extremely valuable.

Prior biographical research by the late Prof. Richard Stephens plotted out the main lines of Ward's life, his various occupations and places of residence. Masonic research by Dr Tony Baker was generously made available to this study, and original research in the United Kingdom was carried out by the author under a University of Queensland staff research grant in February 2004. A period of study leave from the University of Queensland in the second half of 2005 allowed the project to develop considerably. I should also thank Dr Deborah Brown, whose intervention to secure for me a reduced teaching load for 2011 was extremely timely in that I was able to finish the book.

Some of the evidence and arguments in the chapters that follow first appeared in articles for the *Journal of the History of Collections* and *Crossroads*, and my thanks go to the editors of both journals for permission to utilise that material here. I also have particular thanks for people who have generously commented on draft papers and chapters as the elements of this book took shape. Papers delivered at the first Alternative Expressions of the Numinous conference at the University of Queensland in 2006, at the religious history stream of the Australian Historical Association conference in Perth in 2010, and a number of departmental research seminars in the intervening period elicited many insightful observations from colleagues. I am particularly indebted to comments and suggestions received from Philip Almond, Bob Milns, Tim Parkin, John Moorhead, Peter Spearritt, Joanna Timms, Janet Thomas, Joseph Azize, Helen Farley and Melissa Ballanta at these sessions. Gregory Tillett, Gillian Gear and Philip Heselton suggested particular sources and lines of enquiry, and comments received after the three papers delivered on aspects of Ward's life to meetings of the Friends of the Abbey Museum were also very helpful. The lively questions and discussions that followed each of those papers were simply the best dialogue I could have hoped for in revising and improving my work. Finally, friends and family went the extra yard in actually reading chapter drafts, and so a large and appreciative thank-you to Farve, Glenda, Matt, Malcolm and George in distant Melbourne. Margaret Higgs made many marvellous observations as the book took shape, and then valiantly chased down errant commas and capitals when we at last got to the proof-reading stage.

Many academic historians used to thank their wives for typing the manuscript. Anna has had far more important things to do as Eleanor and Henry appeared, hurtled through their toddler years and went across the road to school, but her love and support amid the manifold wonders of family life and architectural practice have been unfailing. Her site plan of the Abbey Folk Park (Figure 13) should be the first page you consult in reading this book.

GEOFFREY A.C. GINN
University of Queensland
September 2011

To my history teacher,
Dr John Volep

and my father,
who first put the words
'adventure', 'learning' and 'delight'
together for me

1

Recollecting the Child

Public humiliation, no matter how unfair, takes a grievous toll. In the spring of 1946, the Reverend Father J. S. M. Ward, Archbishop of Olivet in the Orthodox Catholic Church of England, made a final and wrenching decision. Jeered by the popular press, his mental capacities questioned, edging close to bankruptcy and with his health failing, Ward and his little band of followers prepared to leave England forever.

As the rest of his neo-medieval Confraternity busied themselves elsewhere in the big old house, Ward emptied the shelves of the library on the upper floor of their Abbey in New Barnet, north of London. It was a dispiriting task. A local dealer took the best of the books away in a small lorry. Books on the occult, mysticism, Freemasonry and secret societies,

1 The Confraternity of the Kingdom of Christ departs their Abbey of Christ the King for Cyprus, 8 June 1946. Father Ward at centre holding cat. *AMAA 3 WD 1/1.*

Spiritualism, Theosophy, anthropology and folklore, Eastern philosophy, a collection he had assembled for decades. Others had been tossed out the windows, strewn on the lawn and left disorderly for another trip to the rubbish dump. Meanwhile the precious jewellery, ceramics, prehistoric tools and medieval weapons, lamps, icons, stained glass panels, the relics large and small of the Abbey's unique social history museum were carefully packed into timber crates and tea chests, marked and numbered for the sea journey to Cyprus.

A last photograph taken early on the morning of the departure captures their mingled emotions. The younger members of the Abbey – Sister Mary, Father Peter, Sister Ursula, Father Ignatius and the others – are lively and excited. Father Ward with his wife at the centre of the group, nursing the cat they were leaving behind, seems more circumspect. He was departing with feelings that were deeply mixed. Sister Terese, the oblate at the centre of the lurid 'Sister Terese Enticement Case' that had thrust the Abbey into the harsh spotlight of national tabloid attention, remained hidden as she prepared to leave the country under a false name and passport.

From New Barnet to Southampton, embarking on the *Athlone Castle* to Port Said, and on to a farmhouse above a curving, sandy beach near Limassol on Cyprus, the Confraternity of the Kingdom of Christ took themselves into self-imposed exile. Spurned by his countrymen, his 'Message to the Nation' ignored in a dour, austere England recovering from devastating war, Father Ward and his Confraternity found refuge on an island washed by the tides of history: Minoan, Hellenic, Roman, Byzantine, Ottoman.

They bought a farmhouse and there re-established their Abbey. By day Father Ward busied himself with religious services, the work of the farm, sorting what remained of his collection and organising his papers. Life was filled with goats and chickens, repairs to the sheds and fences, visits to local ruins, services, reading, prayer and ample contemplation. On hot afternoons or in the quiet evenings he set aside time to compose his memoirs. The story of Ward's extraordinary life was set down in a series of notebooks embellished with illuminated capitals and decorated margins, a record for the community as they dedicated their lives to the work he had begun.

The surviving volumes of Ward's unfinished autobiography record his childhood memories in immense detail. His spelling, as always, was atrocious but in all other respects it was labour diligently performed with his characteristic zest. It was a statement of the social and psychological foundations of his being, a therapy to his battered ego in the aftermath of courtroom humiliation, and a document for posterity as his Confraternity faced the uncertain years ahead.

✸   ✸   ✸

Beyond the reaches of his memory, Ward's life began at the very edge of the British world. Lashed by hurricanes, its sparse townships and villages scattered about the low-lying coast and hilly interior, British Honduras was an isolated Caribbean outpost of Queen Victoria's empire. Wedged between Guatemala and Mexico and facing into the Bay of Honduras towards Cuba, it was a centre of the mahogany and sugarcane trade and was formally claimed by Great Britain in 1862 after several centuries of Spanish sovereignty and a shorter period of unrest. As one account puts it, "the British Government drew the logical deduction from the abandonment of Spanish sovereignty in America and the final stabilisation of the frontiers of British Honduras, and decided . . . to convert what had originally been a British settlement in Spanish territory into a colony".[1] Its Protestant minority was ministered to by expatriate Englishmen like Herbert Ward, who stepped ashore at Belize, the major township, with his pregnant wife Alice in mid-1885. Approaching thirty, Ward had completed his degree at Oxford before taking Holy Orders in the Church of England. Now they busied themselves with accommodation, unpacking luggage and settling into the weekly routine at St Mary's, Belize. The couple's first son, John Sebastian Marlow Ward, was born just three days before Christmas.

Little is known of the circumstances of John's infancy, although it is clear that his mother did not enjoy Belize's humid climate and tropical setting. By 1888, the family had returned to England where Herbert assumed a lowly curacy at St Andrew's, West Kensington (now Fulham Fields). This was a solid and respectable suburb on London's western fringe, with a large, High Victorian brown-brick church erected in the mid-1870s. The Wards lived at nearby Perham Road, where John's younger brother Reginald was born in September 1888. Apart from a period during 1894 and 1895 when they shifted to Leicester while Herbert was Diocesan Inspector of Schools, the family remained in the modest and comfortable middle-class surrounds of Perham Road as the boys – known familiarly as Jack and Rex – grew older.

Despite the exotic setting of his birth, the circumstances of utter normality that marked J. S. M. Ward's upbringing present only a few clues to explain the psychological drama and spiritual foment of his later life. To begin with, his father's choice of parish reflected a religious moderation that would not be characteristic of his elder son. Herbert Ward was one of four curates assisting the vicar at St Andrew's, a Mr Hilliard who favoured a moderate but expressive Anglicanism. As Ward put it, it sat half-way – both geographically and theologically – between the elaborate 'high' ritualism of the nearby St Matthias at Earl's Court, and the equally extreme 'low' austerity and evangelism of St Mary's in Hammersmith Road.[2] St Andrew's shared the conventional Low Church ceremonial of the latter but its clergy leaned (in Ward's recollection at least) towards the High Church doctrine of the former. Hilliard was an active and energetic vicar, who encouraged a great range of social activities centred on the church and its parish institutions. His services were popular, and during the Wards' time there the congregation was growing such that two extensions were required to increase the church's capacity. Parish bazaars, charity activities and a full calendar of church festivals that kept his father busy made up the immediate social environment of John Ward's childhood.

His parents conformed precisely to the social duties and obligations expected of a respectable middle-class curate on a modest income. Household expenditure was never lavish; there were no seaside holidays or extravagant toys. Economy measures were often imposed to cover unexpected medical bills when the two boys fell ill, and Ward remembered one occasion in early 1897 when his Christmas money from a distant uncle was nearly appropriated by his parents for domestic needs. But Perham Road was comfortable enough, his father's parochial duties were not overly demanding, and his mother maintained the household with appropriate frugality and decorum.

Small pleasures were seized. One was the Sunday 'Church Parades' in Hyde Park during the warmer months. According to Ward's memoirs, his mother would sweep out of their church in West Kensington at noon, with Jack in his best Eton suit and leaving her younger son in the care of a maid. The two travelled by omnibus to Hyde Park Corner, hunting to secure an empty park bench so that Mrs Ward could join in a characteristically Victorian social ritual. The aristocratic mansions of Park Lane, Berkeley Square and Mayfair emptied as a steady stream of gleaming carriages – broughams, landaus and victorias – and perambulating gentlemen and ladies on the long path beside Rotten Row offered themselves, for an hour or two, as the great open-air set-piece of London society. "Up and down this short stretch they paraded", remembered Ward,

> and you could on a fine Sunday see in the parade everybody who was anybody, while in the seats which bordered the parade were massed . . . everybody who was nobody, closely studying the fashions and whispering to each other that yonder was the Duchess of Marlborough talking to Lord and Lady X; or that is Mr Arthur Balfour, a rising statesman, one of the Cecils, my dear and such a charming man – a phrase meant to imply that the speaker was a personal friend of the statesman, which she almost certainly was not.[3]

'Celebrity-spotting' at this stately display of prestige and fashion provided women of the respectable middle classes, perched decorously at its margins, with a window into the glamorous world of plutocratic society. Mrs Ward, her son remembered, "was just as keen as any of the onlookers to spot the notables and was quite good at the game . . . She seemed to recognise nearly every distinguished person including many foreigners, such as the French Ambassador and his wife". As he grew older, Jack came to understand the source of his mother's apparently remarkable familiarity with the haughty beings of this high-born, alien world. Like many wives of respectable clergymen, shopkeepers, and lowly professional men across London and the provincial towns, Alice Ward devoured the illustrated magazines for women that emerged in mass-market publishing late in the nineteenth century. Her particular favourite was *The Gentlewoman*, a weekly devoted "mainly to two themes, fashions and court gossip, both well illustrated with steel engravings of drawings by our correspondent, 'A Lady of Fashion' [with] reports on social functions, including sometimes the Church Parade itself and illustrated . . . with clever and easily recognisable sketches of the notables she mentioned."[4]

Few activities reveal more about the Wards' social standing and outlook. Mrs Ward was certainly not influential, wealthy or fashionable, but she aspired with other women of her social class to be a worthy echo of the gentility and good taste of well-bred 'Society'. Indeed Mrs Ward's careful scrutiny of the social elite, even if largely drawn from the pages of a popular magazine and time spent as an onlooker at the edge of Hyde Park, marked her in her own circle of acquaintances as a woman of sensibility, with an informed interest in refined matters such as the marriage market, political personalities of the day and contemporary fashion. Her respectability and good sense were unquestionable, and were displayed in the modest comfort and orderliness of her home, the care she paid to social duties, the starched collars that encased her sons' necks in public, and the education they received when the time for schooling arrived. Jack started as a pupil at Colet Court School, a preparatory school for St Paul's School, Hammersmith, in 1895.

A life of solid respectability in West Kensington fuelled her son's taste for imaginative escapism outside the classroom. A vacant lot in a nearby street became an impromptu recreation ground for the local children and their games, where Ward orchestrated running battles and grand campaigns inspired by his youthful reading. Special outings such a night at the circus or local pantomime, trips by penny steamer on the river or efforts to sail model boats in the round pond at Kensington Gardens were keenly anticipated treats that rarely disappointed. He had a boyish fascination with transport: the local omnibus services, their routes and fares and even the internal arrangements of seats and fixtures are lovingly detailed in his reminiscences.

He was also an avid reader of juvenile fiction. By the age of ten he was a regular at the local public library, devouring "several volumes a week when I could get them and when I could not re-reading those I had". His tastes were characteristic of his age and the last decades of Victoria's reign:

The Swiss Family of Robinson was my favourite, I read it no less than nine times. Next came Robinson Crusoe, but only the part which dealt with his life on the desert island. After these two favourites came Fernimore [sic] Cooper with his tales of the Red Indians, such as The Last of the Mohacans [sic], The Pathfinder and the Prairie. A year or so later Rider Hagard's [sic] Adventure Stories and Henty's historical novels dominated my literary horizon . . . [5]

To compensate for the lack of family holidays Herbert Ward often took his boys to the landmark museums, galleries and exhibition halls found across the face of Victorian London. These visits to South Kensington, the British Museum, the Crystal Palace at Sydenham and other great collections inspired a life-long love of collections and curious objects, museum displays and visual spectacle. "Of course I liked the stuffed lions and tigers", Ward remembered of his first visit to the Natural History Museum at South Kensington,

> but strange to say my favourite cases were those which showed how birds and beasts changed their coats in winter to snow white, from those they had in summer, and cases which showed how some animals tried to match their surroundings. There was one other showcase which stands out clearly in my memory. It was one depicting albino animals and birds and in the midst was a snow-white peacock.[6]

Science and art museums were worthy and educational, but the young John Ward was just as fascinated by the great exhibition halls and temporary shows of Victorian London. The great greenhouses at Kew Gardens, for example, stood out in his memory. The Palm House was particularly impressive with its tall palms and lily pond: "Father loved that 'Greenhouse'", Ward wrote, "because it reminded him of British Honduras; Mother hated it and would seldom enter it, for the same reason".[7] He was also impressed by the grand scale, the glass and iron of the Crystal Palace, standing splendidly at Sydenham amid the outer suburbs of South London. He loved the "series of huge prehistoric monsters" cast in cement arrayed in front of it, especially when lit by fireworks at night. But most of his time in the Crystal Palace was spent in the small courts and displays off the main aisle in the building's interior. "These contained", he recalled, "clever reconstructions (probably in plaster) of examples of architecture of all periods and countries. I remember most clearly an ancient Egyptian 'court', a Roman room, with frescoes copied from a room at Pompeii, and a mediaeval building. More dimly I recollect there was an example of Indian architecture and other courts depicting other styles."[8]

Even more enthralling was the vivid spectacle of the Earls Court Exhibitions, so enthralling in his memory, in fact, that he devoted two entire chapters of his memoir to them. "Shall I ever succeed in making my readers realise how much the old Earls Courts meant to us and why?" he wondered. "I fear not, but I can only do my best and say that through the roseate spectacles of youthful memory those exhibitions still look up as the most delightful places to visit and the hours spent there as among the happiest and most exciting in my life."[9] The Earls Court Exhibitions of Ward's childhood were annual shows, which felt partly like a travelling fair, partly like pleasure gardens and partly like an extremely life-like and invigorating popular museum. Now largely forgotten, they were the brainchild of the Hungarian émigré and theatrical entrepreneur Imre Kiralfy, who in Ward's opinion "combined the qualities of a born artist and a first class organizer – a rare combination". Kiralfy's son attended school with Ward and distributed precious season tickets to his appreciative friends, a passport (for Ward at least) to a marvellous and breath-taking 'fairyland' of delight that tremendously influenced the vibrant displays of his own history museum in New Barnet nearly forty years later.

Evidently inspired by the success of the Royal Colonial and Indian Exhibition of 1886, and with keen commercial instincts honed by success in America and work with P. T. Barnum on his grand spectacular *Nero, or, The Destruction of Rome*, Kiralfy commenced his firm London Exhibitions Ltd. in 1895, by which time he had already been active at Earls Court for several years.[10] He gained leases for three irregular vacant lots at the intersection of the Midland and District railways with the West London extension, surrounded by busy commercial streets, linked by covered arcades and bridged walkways to create an exhibition ground, an enclosure insulated from the dreary humdrum of everyday London. In Ward's memory, passing through the North End Road entry into the Exhibitions with his 10/6 season ticket was like a crossing a threshold into fantasy.

> On passing through the turnstiles you found yourself in a long dark shabby passage or shed made of rusty corrugated iron sheets and at the end of the tunnel was bright sunlight by day or the twinkle of countless coloured fairy lights if it was night. Another minute and you had passed out of the dismal passage into a brightly lit scene which seemed . . . a fragment of Fairyland.[11]

Ward's recollections of this "enchanted land" and its attractions crackle with the effervescent delight of his boyhood visits. It was dominated by large permanent features like the false mountain range with its switchback railway and a large artificial lake surrounded by stagey architectural buildings used for performances and displays. Landscaped gardens, bandstands, rotundas and painted backdrops defied the tight dimensions of the available space, a "clever combination of scenery, buildings and real trees and shrubs", Ward wrote, that "produced an illusion of spaciousness which in itself constituted a large part of the charm of the place".[12] The 1895 *Official Guide* encouraged the visitor to "notice that his illusion is not disturbed by the sight of outside buildings, these being entirely excluded from view by painted scenery, which, as it were, shuts him out from London, and leaves him to luxuriate midst Indian scenes".[13] Spectators paid five shillings to float in 'Majestic', a hydrogen balloon, admiring the view with telescopes and binoculars, while others waited in the Elysia gardens for a vacant car in the steam-driven Great Wheel that loomed up as a local landmark over Kiralfy's 'fairyland'. Commercial booths with shooting galleries and slot machines were scattered about, with sideshow attractions from the 'Maze of Mirrors' to Pepper's Ghost, menageries and jugglers. In the entrance arcade between the pillars of a classical oval court, stallholders sold fancy goods, perfumes, sweets, cheap jewellery and toys.

The artificial lake was a favourite haunt for the two Ward boys. It was surrounded by a stone balustrade and a broad walk linking a series of buildings and exhibition halls forming the area known as 'Queen's Court'. At one end of the lake two rocky islands were fabricated in timber and plaster, "high and mountainous with steep cliff-like sides descending to a shallow gravel beach" and accessible by narrow footbridges. Paths led through passageways and grottoes and made their way to the look-out point at the summit of the island. The boys found the islands and their secretive tunnels irresistible:

> Of course it was not long before we knew by heart every passage and cave. Then the demon of adventure lured us on to further exploration. We climbed over the guardrails off the beaten track onto the rocky sides of the islands. The paths were made of wood and strongly built so as to bear any reasonable weight and then covered with sand, but the rocks were only canvas fastened to light wood scaffolding and then covered with plaster and painted to look like rock.
>
> It speaks well for the strength of plaster and canvas that it bore unflinchingly the weight of two hefty youngsters, 10 years and 8 years old respectively . . . occasionally we were spotted by an attendant and ordered down, but that only added spice to the adventure. We kept a sharp look-out for attendants – they wore a smart distinctive uniform – and immediately we hid behind a jutting rock or dived into a nearby opening in the cliff.[14]

A 'Mysterious Subterranean River' under the mountain range was another fond memory, and his recollections of it capture neatly his delight in visual effects that remained throughout his life. In the semi-darkness, visitors boarded a small boat with the sound of rushing water in their ears. It bumped along a dark tunnel of canvas and plaster painted to appear like rock:

Gradually the darkness became diffused with a faint glow which grew brighter and suddenly the 'rock wall' on the left hand fell back to reveal a party of gnomes at work at a forge. The figures were in the round and made of painted plaster. Quickly the boat whirled past the scene into the dark tunnel and again there was a ruddy glow and this time a scene appeared on the right hand: it was gnomes mining for gems, there were piles of rubies, sapphires and diamonds and which flashed and gleamed in the strange eerie light, despite the fact that they were only made of glass. Still the boat whirled and the Palace of the Gnome King came into view: seated on a throne of gleaming stalamite [*sic*], with gleaming crystal pillars and walls, his throne room flashed and gleamed with all the colours of the rainbow. On and still on the river wound and twisted revealing fresh scenes and sometimes notes of queer yet fascinating music would be heard.[15]

Feature exhibitions drew fresh visitors to Earls Court each year. Given the groundswell of popular imperialism in Britain in the mid-1890s, those of 1895 and 1896 had an Empire theme with a particular focus on India. Inspired "by the thought of the absorbing and ever-increasing interest with which everything relating to India is regarded by all Englishmen, both from its political history and its great commercial importance", Kiralfy's firm "had the desire . . . to vividly present to the British public as perfect a picture as possible of its oriental splendour and magnificence, and of the everyday life of the Queen's Indian subjects".[16] The India and Ceylon exhibition of 1896 "holds an outstanding position in my memory", Ward wrote, largely because of its success in achieving these aims but also because his whole family received season tickets and so visited the site many times over.[17]

Kiralfy's centrepiece in these years was a reconstructed Indian village, a remarkable attempt to evoke the spatial and cultural experience of Britain's far-flung colonial possessions in the heart of London. Entered through the Maidan Gate in a mock city wall, the village had a series of narrow streets and courtyards, containing shops of timber and plasterwork for a colourful array of trades, crafts and produce. Ward considered it "an excellent reproduction of a small Indian town with its native shops with open fronts where you could see many of the lesser handicrafts being performed before your eyes".[18] Close to the centre was a working mosque, claimed as one of only two existing in the country at this time, but Ward could not remember a Hindu temple, which seemed a strange oversight. As well as elephants, camels and Indian cattle the village had a resident population of seventy artisans, musicians and performers, employed through the agency of an Oxford Street importer of Indian arts and brought to London for the duration of the Exhibition. Punjabi silk-weavers and Burmese *mahouts* lent colour and human interest to the scenery. "In a strictly Government Exhibition", the

Exhibition's official report observed, "such a thing would be nearly impossible, but . . . not being hampered by official restrictions [Kiralfy's firm] were enabled to place before the people of England, a life-like and most realistic panorama of the daily avocations of the teeming millions of our fellow-subjects in British India".[19] The Indian City, with its workshops, tea house and native livestock wandering picturesquely "through the mimic Town as was their wont in that strange land beyond the sea",[20] became a favourite haunt of Kipling-esque officers and retired civil servants who likewise sauntered its streets exchanging pleasantries in dialect with the craftsmen and shopkeepers.

As a boy, Ward was intoxicated by this vision of the exotic East, offered to his eager gaze in the attractions of this stage-managed 'virtual museum'. Fragments of memory remained particularly sharp to him as a grown man: the pots of the corn merchant overflowing with seed, the taciturn metalsmith hammering away at brassware trinkets and figurines glinting in the fitful English sunlight. A jeweller made salt cellars and pepper pots, and filigree silver and brass charms inlaid with a crushed turquoise mosaic. A nearby potter worked his wheel with his foot. The rough cotton fabrics of the tailor rolled down the steps of his shopfront, and scraps of scented sandalwood littered the wood-carver's shop, where inlaid boxes were piled up for sale and delicate ebony elephants were worked from chunks of black timber. Another shop sold Indian textiles, embroidered mats, prayer rugs, brawls bowls and pitchers, and "countless brass objects, from Hindoo gods to quaint teaspoons made to resemble a scorpion. I bought one of these for my *Museum*", he wrote in his memoirs, "and have it still. There were lovely old seventeenth-century helmets and shields inlaid with silver and gold which I greatly coveted but could not afford; weapons of all sorts and quaint little sandalwood boxes of which after pinching and saving I managed to purchase a specimen."[21]

"That village", he concluded, "was to us a never-failing source of joy and twenty years later when in 1915 I visited South India, I was deeply impressed by the accuracy with which the village had been reproduced. In Madura and Siringham [sic] . . . I saw Indian shops precisely resembling those I had seen at Earls Court in 1895 and 1896."[22]

✱   ✱   ✱

His father's position at St Andrews was secure but lowly. Like any long-serving curate, by 1897 Herbert Ward was ready for more rewarding responsibilities and a more substantial living as a vicar. When his former tutor at Oxford wrote to offer a vacancy at Wath-upon-Dearne, near Rotherham in the South Yorkshire coalfield, there was only short family discussion before the decision was taken to accept it. The living of £340 per year was a considerable improvement on Herbert's income at West Kensington. Young Jack would remain a pupil at Colet Court, and take up lodgings with the family of a school friend. Gordon Wells' parents kept a tall, spacious house on North End Road where Jack moved at his parents' departure for their country parsonage in November 1897.

He felt the separation keenly, and remembered gorging on sweets to drown his misery "as an adult might try and drown his sorrows in drink."[23] Although Dr and Mrs Wells were kindly and thoughtful enough, there were inevitable adjustments and frictions involved as he settled into an unfamiliar family routine. His visits to other friends in the neighbourhood of Perham Road were curtailed. While Jack's friendship with Gordon continued, his older brother Gerald proved to be hot-tempered and difficult to get along with. Although not exactly unhappy, he still yearned for the end of each school term when he could spend the vacation with his family. Autobiographical fragments detail the journey to Sheffield by train to meet his father, then by hired carriage to Rotherham and at last to the stone vicarage in Wath-upon-Dearne, where his mother and brother waited at the door. Standing in three acres, with its own outhouses, vegetable garden and meadows, the slate-roofed vicarage was an evocative relic of an older, rural England now increasingly threatened by the coal mines and redbrick suburban cottages nearby. Enough of its historic associations remained to stoke his antiquarian imagination:

> There was not really much actual flower garden [around the vicarage] but banks of tall trees, strategically planted so as to shut out views of other buildings, a large tennis lawn and the paddock. This was the site of the mediaeval Vicarage, built early in the 15th century, which had been surrounded by a moat, now dry but traceable in part and which I later tried to excavate. It was demolished in 1793 when the Georgian Vicarage was built.[24]

Ward's love of historical and natural curiosities had by this time produced quite a collection of treasures and keepsakes, and a large empty room in the vicarage's attic served as his first museum. Here during his holidays he spent hours working on display cases and shelves lit by sunshine falling through the large bull-eye window in the gable of the roof. Historical oddments from his fossicking were the first displays, while his natural history section commenced with the arrangement of three stuffed bullfrogs in clumps of dried grass stained green; these were soon joined by two stuffed birds bought for him by his mother at a house sale. The shelves filled up with an egg collection he had nurtured over the years and a crop of seashells donated by his father that had come to him from a seafaring uncle. Representative pieces from the family's heirloom china were likewise coaxed from his mother.[25]

This was the beginning of a habit of collection and display, bordering on the obsessive, that remained with Ward for the rest of his life.

But there were days of robust outdoor activity as well. He and Rex haunted the rambling old stables and carriage shed that stood in the grounds, and a log hut was erected nearby to continue the adventurous games and make-believe they had enjoyed together in Perham Road. "We had to crawl into it on our hands and knees", Ward recalled, "but we packed all the interstices between the logs with straw, somehow got the roof watertight and covered the floor with straw which we found in the stable loft. Whether it snowed or rained we were, to use a vulgar but popular expression of the time, 'as snug as two bugs in a rug'".[26] On the Easter holidays that followed they grew more ambitious in erecting a Dark Age fort around a stone wall that enclosed the vicarage's compost heap. Jack's antiquarian instincts were precocious, even at the age of little more than twelve:

> At one end of the wall was a willow tree at the opposite end was a gate into the vegetable garden. Here, despite mild protests from Father who warned us that the leaf mould would be required for the garden, we built our fort by driving a double row of stakes into the ground and then lacing willow wands and boughs of trees between them. The entrance was in the outer bailey and was closed by means of short planks slip[ped] between stout upright posts and the only entrance to the keep was through the bailey and was similarly closed with planks which could easily slide in and out. We also made wooden swords, shields and spears (ie broom handles). I spent quite a long time cutting a large heavy wooden axe from a log of pear wood. Ultimately we built a battering ram, consisting of a heavy tree trunk slung by ropes from a wooden frame . . . We spent many days in exciting battles to storm the fort, taking it in turns to be the defender. Some times we would persuade the servants to form the attacking force but more often we had to play by ourselves, [and] a good deal of our time had to be spent in repairing the breach we ourselves had made in the stockade.[27]

After complications arose with the Wells family, Jack was billeted from October 1898 with another family acquaintance, a Miss Kilroy, an Anglo-Irish spinster from a military family living alone in genteel poverty on Ravenscourt Park Road. She seems to have been fond of him, appreciating both his company and the weekly board paid by his parents, and he returned her affection in remaining there until his final year of school.

✳   ✳   ✳

For all their conventionality, these childhood influences and experiences impressed certain values on the young J. S. M. Ward. The most important of them shaped his outlook powerfully, and continued to direct his energies and interests throughout his adult life. His slight build, short-sightedness and quick intelligence made him a natural scholar rather than a sportsman, but this tendency was perhaps reinforced by the uneven domestic arrangements of his childhood. It seems likely that his separation from his family saw him seek emotional refuge in his studies and hobbies. Although socially quite outgoing, we sense that he was homesick and often lonely, and that the solace he found in books and objects imprinted habits of scholarly application and perseverance that in time defined his personality.

Ward's upbringing also imbued him with a deep commitment to the ideals and arrangements of the British Empire. At home, both parents supported Lord Salisbury's Unionist-Conservative Government, elected on a pro-Empire platform in 1895. At school, Ward and his classmates attended their books under a wall chart depicting a world with Britain at its centre, its broad and far-flung colonial territories tinted red, linked by steamer routes and telegraph lines. They were taught ideals of duty, respect for justice, and the providential destiny of the British to govern as firm but benevolent rulers of regions and peoples regarded as 'primitive'. They devoured stories of imperial conquest and adventure in their spare time. English patriotism and pride in the British Empire, to an impressionable boy of Ward's era, were two sides of a single coin. Travelling to school, for instance, Jack chose his place on the Kensington omnibus carefully, preferring to sit with other like-minded boys immediately behind the Union Jack fluttering on a little staff at the front of the vehicle.

In this vein, another attraction at Kiralfy's Earls Court that captured Ward's affections was the spectacular 'Naval Battle' display of 1897 in the Empress Theatre, one of the main permanent halls of the exhibition. This was a martial *tour de force* that synchronised with the popular mood of Victoria's jubilee year; the Ward boys carefully saved their pennies to visit the show again and again. The audience took their seats in darkness, in front of model warships floating gently on an indoor lake in front of a large diorama of a harbour town. As daylight gently broke, an effect provided by a light and colour show against the backdrop, the little fleet of cruisers, torpedo boats and destroyers rocked smoothly at anchor or on the quayside. A miniature cruiser, clearly an enemy marauder, rushed in from the wings firing into the peaceful scene until, with "a terrific roar and [as] the theatre filled with dense clouds of smoke and our nostrils were assailed by the acrid smell of gunpowder", the defenders began firing salvoes in return which intensified as the entire enemy fleet came into view. Ward's memory of the ensuing battle captures the alacrity of his youthful reaction:

Soon both fleets were fiercely engaged. Salvo followed salvo and soon

13

these began to tell. A large cruiser was apparently hit in the funnel which fell over the side and left a great hole in the deck through which grey clouds of smoke and steam poured up. Next there was a violent explosion in the water and a destroyer went down stern first, hit either by a torpedo or blown up by a mine and the top masts of several ships were blown away and then a battleship turned over and sank. Thereupon several of the defenders fled and were speedily followed by the rest of the fleet, still firing. As the attacking ships started in pursuit the land batteries in the forts opened fire and the victorious fleet stopped its pursuit, formed in line parallel to the shore, salvo after salvo into the city. Slowly the guns in the forts ceased firing one by one. Then a dull glow appeared in the city, first in one place and then it was followed by others . . . [28]

And so on; beneath the military bombast Ward's memories pulsed with his youthful enthusiasm for the drama and pageantry of Empire. He also remembered October 1899 and the commencement of the Boer War, and joining with his school-fellows the cheering crowds to send off the City of London Volunteers to South Africa. In a similar mood he and a schoolfriend decided one afternoon to visit the bulletin board outside the War Office in Whitehall. They expected to see cheering crowds and announcements of dashing engagements on the battlefield, but instead there were lists of casualties and weeping groups of women. "Burton and I stole quietly away," he remembered, "and we decided never to go there again. We had had our first glimpse of war as it really is, robbed of all pomp and glamour, and we kept that resolution."[29] The memory stuck in his mind but failed to shake his sense of the moral justice – the historical inevitability – of Britain's imperial mission on the world historical stage.

Also important was Ward's dutiful Christianity, which may have been learnt under his father's tutelage but was enriched by a lively curiosity. Both were reflected in one childhood memory, when shortly after the death of their pet cat, he was struck by an inevitable theological question: did animals have souls? Was Pussy in heaven? His father's reaction as Ward remembered it neatly captures the religious environment of Ward's home life.

Father hesitated, torn between his habitual affection for all animals and his desire not to resuscitate our grief on the one hand, and on the other by his theological training. After quite a long pause during which no one, not even Mother, dared to breathe, he said slowly and as if talking to himself:

"I don't think the question has even been authoritatively decided by the Church. I am fully aware that individual theologians both Protestant and Catholic have taken for granted that animals have not immortal souls as men have, but unless the matter has be[en] considered by any Council of the Church I do not consider we are bound to accept their views. If I am right in this belief, namely that the Universal Church has never formally denied that animals may have immortal souls, then we are free to believe what we consider is reasonable."[30]

In adulthood Ward's religious curiosity spurred him to enquiries and conclusions that were unusual to the point of eccentricity. The reasonable, even-handed moderation demonstrated by his father encouraged his son in later life towards ever more elaborate insights into the metaphysics of the afterlife and the soul's journey beyond the grave. He left the comfortable Anglican orthodoxy of his childhood far behind as he turned for insight to a great diversity of spiritual and quasi-religious traditions: Spiritualism, Theosophy, Occult Freemasonry, Eastern mysticism and Orthodox ritualism among them. This was a mixed bag, but in Ward's eyes at least they shared a common foundation in an open-minded religious curiosity fostered by his upbringing. "Truth to tell", Ward wrote in defending his eclectic interests, "the author learnt the foundations of his faith from a most excellent father, a clergyman of the Church of England, who saw to it that he understood what the Church stood for without leaning too much to any extreme party."[31]

From his father's influence and this childhood environment Ward distilled an unshakeable faith in a loving and omniscient God, and in the Christian church's historical mission to humanity. He was fascinated by religious doctrine as a rich, complex source of human knowledge, and in-trinsically curious about the nature of the Divine: what precisely was it that suffused, as religion promised, both the everyday world and the Hereafter and provided meaning to the cosmos? The passage of Ward's adult life threw up a set of elaborate answers to this eternal question.

A similar curiosity infused Ward's fascination with past times and antiq-uities. His imagination stimulated by his reading and museum visits, Ward developed a youthful passion for history. The vivid historical and imperial *tableaux* he so relished at Earls Court kindled something elemental in him, and translated easily to success in the schoolroom. He absorbed the litany of dates, battles and monarchs served up by his history teachers with a quick and keen intelligence. At his first school he was unexpectedly placed top of the history class, a moment that "had a profound impression on my whole future at school".

I realised in a flash that History was 'my subject' and I was henceforth always first each term, not only at Colet Court but also the whole time I was at Merchant Taylors. I might be bad at languages and worse at math-ematics but in History I knew I could be top if I worked, and work I did.

It was partly that I loved the subject but partly also that I felt it was 'my subject' and was determined not to let anyone beat me.[32]

Ward's historical imagination was also sparked by rambles amid London's historic streets and buildings, especially in the neighbourhood of the Merchant Taylors' School in the old Charterhouse buildings near Farringdon where he commenced in April 1899. Along with a schoolfriend named Wallace, whose father was also an Anglican clergyman, Ward often spent Wednesday afternoons at the British Museum, from where Wallace introduced him to the pleasures of urban rambling amid the sights and sounds of 'Old London'. Their first excursion together began at Cloth Fair, the evocative street of crooked townhouses and shops built by Elizabethan clothiers and drapers attending Bartholomew's Fair. The magnificent medieval edifice of St Bartholomew the Great, at nearby West Smithfield, also captivated their imagination. "The success of our visit to Cloth Fair and St Bartholomew's fired our enthusiasm", Ward wrote, "and Wallace and I spent many happy half holidays exploring ancient London. Sometimes I would discover a new place of interest and sometimes it would be my chum."[33]

On their first outing, stepping through an arch into Cloth Fair, the boys "saw before us a narrow lane flanked on either side by fine half-timbered houses, whose upper storeys overhung the street . . . I gasped with surprise", Ward recalled nearly fifty years later. The moment impressed itself on his memory:

> We wandered up and down the street studying the old buildings which were, alas, rather shabby and dilapidated, and they were worse inside than out judging by the glimpses we obtained through open doors. It was in short a slum, but what a picturesque slum. What it needed was a careful restoration by a competent architect and it would have become one of the archaeological treasures and show places of London. I thought so then and even dreamed and planned how I would do it when I grew up and became wealthy, but long before I was old enough to start an agitation in its favour it had been allowed to collapse and now every house has vanished.[34]

The parish church of St Bartholomew the Great was even more impressive. Originally an Augustinian Priory church founded in 1123 and dissolved in the sixteenth century, its cloisters and outbuildings sold off and the main chapel turned over to the local Anglican parish, the "vast, dark and Romanesque"[35] old church was still genuinely majestic. The massive Norman pillars and arches filled him, Ward recalled, with "awe and reverence". His youthful passion brimmed in his memory in the language of romantic love: "This, even in its mutilated state, was far grander and more impressive than any other church I knew; even my beloved church at Wath faded into insignificance. I fell to St Bart's at once and have remained true to that first love ever since. Again and again I would return to it, go over old ground and explore the fresh discoveries."

In visits to the old church in the years that followed the two budding antiquarians watched avidly as the elderly verger and other parish volunteers chipped away to complete the restoration work first begun in the mid-1860s and resumed in 1885. There was much to do: the adjoining cloisters had been excised from the original St Bartholomew's Priory in the sixteenth century and used as stables. The Chapter House had been used as a common warehouse and had suffered extensive fire damage. Rubbish had been dumped in the crypts, a transept had been used as blacksmith's forge, and another chapel used as a factory before it was restored as the Lady Chapel to the main body of the church in 1896.[36]

By the time Ward began his visits the parish had bought back the stables and other surviving structures around the church, and volunteers had organised themselves to assist the verger in the renovation work. Fragments of ornamental stone were collected together from the rubbish, doorways and fireplaces were unbricked, and shards of illuminated glass were pieced together. The verger showed them a trestle table scattered with carved pieces of stone during their first visit. "How we pored over those interesting relics of the past", Ward remembered fondly, "and on seeing how I loved every little bit, the old man, on a subsequent occasion, found two or three pieces which had been left in the courtyard near the crypt door and gave them to me."[37] These were treasured by the young antiquarian, and occupied pride of place in his museum in the attic at Wath-upon-Dearne.

Thirty years later, when Ward established his own neo-medieval abbey at New Barnet, two of these fragments were built into the eastern wall of his Abbey Church. Two others, precious personal relics of his youth, were packed up along with the remains of Ward's lifelong collection for the journey to Cyprus.

2

History, Marriage and the Afterlife

Busy with his studies and his blooming interest in antiquities, John Ward didn't leave Merchant Taylors' School until he was nearly nineteen years old. He sat the entrance exams for Cambridge University, and delighted his family by winning an open scholarship to Trinity Hall to read history and English literature. His scholarship was valued at £40 per year, supplemented by an annual grant of £30 supplied by the Merchant Taylor's Company to scholarship winners from his school. He could look forward to a relatively comfortable few years at his Cambridge college.

Ironically, given Ward's family background and his father's career in the church, Trinity Hall was the "least clerical of all the colleges".[1] Founded in 1350 for students of canon and Roman law, it had traditionally been associated with clerical laymen who had avoided ordination altogether. During the latter part of the nineteenth century its undergraduate numbers had grown rapidly so that it was considered among the more lively middle-sized Cambridge colleges and no longer merely a lawyerly enclave.[2] Little of its medieval origins were visible, but the college's elegant Tudor library and the serenity of its lawns and courtyards evoked timeless scholarship, contemplation and the life of the mind. Ward settled happily at Trinity Hall as he completed the two parts of the History tripos in 1907 and 1908,[3] and graduated BA with Honours in 1908.

Arriving so early in the new century Ward found himself at the epicentre of a range of exciting developments at Cambridge, especially in his chosen studies in history and literature. Since the reform of the syllabus in 1885, historical studies at Cambridge balanced between the demands of a generalist liberal education and a more modern emphasis on the specialist skills of evidence-based historical research. The dry and factual constitutional history promoted by J. R. Seeley in the 1860s was still taught, but a new and more inquisitive era of historical exploration had dawned. Rather than simply learning by rote, Ward and his fellow students were encouraged by specialised courses of study to advance the frontiers of historical knowledge

18

through their own careful and critical research in original sources. Despite attempts by modernisers such as J. B. Bury to further reform the syllabus in this direction during Ward's undergraduate years, the 'clashing ideals' of the two approaches characterised historical study at Cambridge until the First World War.[4]

But beyond fragmentary college records we have little direct evidence of Ward's Cambridge years. His memoirs terminated before reaching that period of his life, and no personal documents such as letters or scrapbooks survive. From what we can glean, however, it seems his college tutor, a fellow by the name of Thornely, thought highly of him and perhaps encouraged his historical interests directly.[5] Daily life revolved around lectures, tutorials and essays, accentuated by intensive self-directed reading. The Tripos candidate was expected to read widely outside the strict examination texts of his chosen topics, and it seems likely that Ward responded avidly to this challenge. The cryptic tutorial records at Trinity Hall record his progress by Easter 1906: he passed low in the second class in Political Economy and his special period, and low in the first class in Ancient or Medieval History. The verdict: "altogether a second [class], about half-way down".[6]

2 John Ward (seated) and his brother Rex in 1906, the year Ward commenced at Cambridge. *AMAA 3 WA 1/1.*

We can be fairly certain he dedicated most of his time to his studies, although he joined a rowing team at one point, and recalled running along the riverbank to follow boat races on the Cam. But otherwise he took little interest in the carousing and boisterous sports of fellow undergraduates. He was the studious type, and especially so under the influence of the powerful enthusiasms that remained with him throughout his life. History was first in his affections, but English literature came a strong second. The two came together in his friendship with Charles Previté-Orton, then a fellow-undergraduate some years his senior. A Cambridge fixture, who remained at St John's College for forty-two years rising to be Professor of Medieval History, college librarian and bulwark of the Cambridge history school, Previté-Orton was remembered by another friend as possessing "an inner life so cultivated and serene that it did not seek though it welcomed sympathy". [7] He communicated some of this in dedicating a June 1906 poem to his young friend at Trinity Hall. It began:

> Ward, whence comes Poetry and whence Romance?
>   What is this charm upon us and the power
>   Wherewith they hold us in dream-girdled trance,
> That timeless wonder of a lonely hour
>   When the world fades to mist, and false or true
>   Gives place to that which time cannot devour?

The poem reviewed the many and varied charms of great English literature to ask why the passing whimsies of poetry exercised such a pull on the human imagination. The answer, Previté-Orton suggested in characteristically Romantic terms, lay in the unique insights available only to an authentically poetic sensibility. The ordinary man "paces out eternity the slave/ Of his own hamper'd being, there confined/ And tether'd," but the poet

> Feels not that rigorous border to his mind,
> And gropes in the beyond, and, thence inspired,
> Some echo on his silver horn can wind.

It was an astute dedication, because for his part John Ward never erected a "rigorous border to his mind". Indeed through his adult life he pursued contrary impulses that continually enlarged his horizons as he groped beyond the boundaries of ordinary sense and comprehension. His curiosity was intrinsically antiquarian, as we have seen, but in time it passed through the youthful Romanticism of his undergraduate years and matured as an adventurous enquiry into the mysteries of transcendental reality.

"Here has poetry her power", Previté-Orton concluded, for "she sings the song that we would sing, she dreams the dreams we wish, whose sleep comes not with charmed wings."[8] His example seems to have encouraged Ward's own literary ambitions, and in 1907 he was awarded Trinity Hall's Latham Prize for an essay on a literary topic. No trace of his essay or its subject survives, but we can be fairly sure it followed the conventional academic practice of the day. Other Latham Prizes were awarded to Trinity Hall scholars in 1906–07, for example, were for essays examining Shakespeare's *The Tempest*, Bacon's Essays, and Seeley's *Ecce Homo*.[9]

✻ ✻ ✻

At Cambridge, aged twenty, Ward was also initiated as a Freemason. This was a routine step for many respectable young men of the Edwardian middle class, particularly those anticipating careers in the professions and public service. Membership in a lodge established a network of acquaintances and introductions that could prove extremely valuable. But Ward embraced Freemasonry with an enthusiasm that was quite exceptional, reading avidly in Masonic texts and commencing independent research into Masonic tradition and other aspects of esoteric symbolism.[10] His imagination was seized by the antiquarian mystique of Freemasonry's archaic and evocative rituals, their origins lost in time and historical obscurity. He was attracted by the esoteric mysteries that beckoned to the Masonic student as he worked through the lore of the three basic Masonic degrees, and then, perhaps, into the arcane 'higher degrees' that promised increasingly profound insights into human spirituality. The combination of antiquarianism and spiritual enlightenment that Ward found in Freemasonry was a potent one, which irrevocably transformed his youthful interests into a lifetime's work of enquiry.

He joined the Isaac Newton University Lodge (No. 859) in March 1906, perhaps on the invitation of its Worshipful Master, J. R. Roxburgh, whom Ward would have known at Trinity Hall. The lodge had been established in 1861 and harboured ambitions to become a 'University of Freemasonry'. It numbered many esteemed Cambridge graduates among its members, and held a special dispensation to initiate undergraduates like Ward who, under normal circumstances, were below the age of twenty-one and therefore not eligible. Lodge meetings, installations and dinners were held at the Masonic Hall on Corn Exchange Street, erected in the early 1890s and noted for its magnificently ornate ceiling. Here lodge members gathered regularly, their distinctive attire glinting with Masonic regalia:

> It was the custom for members of the [Isaac Newton] Lodge to wear modified court evening dress, consisting of ordinary evening dress coat with knee breeches, silk stockings and court shoes with plain buckles, but

with black waistcoats, thus conforming to usual Masonic practice in this respect unlike their sister Lodge, Apollo at Oxford, whose members wore white waistcoats. Isaac Newton [Lodge], however, added one piece of sartorial display, for its officers wore a pale blue garter buckled below the right knee.[11]

Self-conscious in his finery and doubtless relishing the occasion, John Ward was formally initiated at a lodge meeting on 29 May 1906 and gained his first degree – that of the 'Entered Apprentice' – at the end of October that year. As his attendance continued through his Cambridge years and his interest in Freemasonry deepened, he took the 3rd Degree in the Craft and Royal Arch and was also exalted in his lodge's Euclid Chapter in March 1907.[12] This progression required active attendance and participation: like other young Freemasons, Ward was taught the secrets and principles of the brotherhood "through a series of ritual dramas, rather like prewritten plays" that gradually cohered into a systematic body of knowledge.[13] He found his Masonic studies and rituals so rewarding that he remained an active member of Isaac Newton Lodge until December 1911, well after his graduation, and an enthusiastic Freemason until 1930.

What did Ward find in Freemasonry? The veiled world of the Masonic brotherhood has long been the subject of speculation, intrigue and innuendo. While Freemasonry's welfare and charitable functions are well-recognised and its internal history has been pored over by generations of Masonic scholars, the movement itself, its history and purposes, remains for most people largely opaque.

As a modern fraternal movement, Freemasonry crystallised in metropolitan London in the early decades of the eighteenth century. Its first members claimed diverse and obscure origins for their 'Ancient and Honourable Fraternity of Free and Accepted Masons', including most directly the fraternal lodges of medieval stonemasons. Lodges of operative stonemasons had been commonplace in medieval Europe, existing outside the regular guild arrangements to accommodate itinerant stonemasons who moved about to take up work. The company of the lodge provided an agreeable 'home away from home', where benefits could be shared and operatives' trade skills protected. These operative masons, it was later claimed, developed traditions of secret signs and rituals necessary to recognize fellow-masons and ensure the preservation of their trade secrets. Others claimed even deeper origins for the mysterious rites of modern Freemasonry, and as its adherents grew in number and influence so did the extent of their claims for its deep antiquity and significance. Some traced the Craft's origins to medieval sects or the cults of classical Rome, while others went so far as to locate its source in the esoteric teachings of ancient religions of various kinds. Freemasonry, it was claimed, was in its essence a system of ancient knowledge, with a profound message of spiritual insight cloaked in its mysterious symbolism and ritual.

Whatever the truth of these distant antecedents, it is clear that a newer, non-operative or 'speculative' masonry emerged in the latter part of the seventeenth century as men – many not even workmen – enrolled in the existing lodges, swore oaths and were initiated. Their interests tended towards Enlightenment philosophy, lively cosmopolitanism and gentlemanly sociability. To what extent this had a direct link with the older 'operative' Masonic associations is open to considerable debate. Certainly the development of speculative Freemasonry needs to be seen in its broader context, as "there was considerable experimentation with different kinds of voluntary association in the later Stuart period . . . one finds parallel attempts to convert textile gilds into benefit clubs and growing upper-class patronage of bell-ringing bands, turning them into fashionable societies."[14] Many speculative masons accepted into fraternities came from the middle classes and gentry; some were *habitués* of the learned societies and gentlemen's clubs of Restoration and Hanoverian Britain. These were often exclusive and semi-secretive, where topics from cosmology and natural philosophy to the emerging empirical sciences were avidly discussed. Men of more modest capabilities and interests – tradesmen, professionals, soldiers – were also attracted to the conviviality of regular meetings in agreeable company. Few records remain to document the process clearly, but as such groups met regularly and assumed a formal and permanent character they adopted (or adapted for their own purposes) the practices, symbolism and outward forms of the earlier stonemasons' lodges.

In time, these newcomers – the so-called 'free and accepted masons' – were establishing lodges of their own, often in the complete absence of any 'operative' members at all. By the early eighteenth century, the new lodges were proliferating even as the older operative lodges became more scarce. At a basic level, the lodge structure offered a model for formalised membership and internal procedure that was well-suited to urbane fraternalism. Members were bound to each other as 'brothers', and met regularly to perform the duties required by their fraternal obligations. These centred on the performance of rituals designed to create and maintain the community of the lodge, the election of office bearers and consideration of new members, and the instruction of initiates. The lodge also offered an atmosphere of hoary antiquity, dignifying lodge meetings as a continuation of time-honoured ritual and its members as custodians of traditional wisdom. At this deeper level, the ritual and symbolism of masonry – arising from the technical expertise of the operatives in stonecutting, measurement, levelling and construction – appealed to dutiful brethren who imagined themselves pillars of society, dedicated to scrupulous conduct, fair and level dealing, and bonded together in fraternity. Such vivid traditions and allegories attracted members to the new speculative lodges from among the propertied and educated classes of London and its environs at the beginning of the eighteenth century.

Speculative Freemasonry thus emerged with a middle-class and occasionally aristocratic character, its members typically drawn from the educated professions, upper tradesmen, and officers in the military. Joining a Masonic lodge was "one of the fashionable things to do".[15] A meeting of several London lodges in a Covent Garden tavern in 1716 resolved to assemble annually on St John's Day, and as one historian comments, "it appears that the desire for improved social arrangements and greater opportunities for conviviality thus lies at the root of the modern movement."[16] A year later, in June 1717, four separate lodges numbering a little over 100 members agreed to unite and form a 'Premier Grand Lodge' for London, electing a Grand Master as their presiding authority. By the early 1720s this new organisation had accepted the affiliations of more than fifty lodges, adopted the title Grand Lodge of England and issued the first *List of Lodges* and a constitution setting out rules and regulations for proper Masonic administration. "Whatever the background", concludes Clark, "there can be no question that after 1717 the London grand lodge performed a key role in promoting the advance and organization of English freemasonry, setting a pattern quickly copied in Ireland and Scotland through the establishment of their own grand lodges."[17] Freemasonry spread into Europe, merging into an underground Enlightenment culture of speculative philosophy, fraternal sociability and esoteric learning that helped sustain egalitarian notions of civic participation. The first lodges for Englishmen abroad appeared in Gibraltar and Calcutta in the 1720s, and thereafter followed British colonial expansion into North America and settlements in India and the Pacific as "Masonic fraternalism . . . helped preserve and extend British power in both its material and ceremonial forms".[18]

While some were attracted by Freemasonry's antiquarian and esoteric character, it seems clear the majority of early Freemasons were attracted by their lodge's fraternal and sociable aspects. In an increasingly class-bound and status-conscious society, Freemasonry offered a social outlet where the gentry, titled nobility, the emerging middle class, tradesmen, shopkeepers and even the occasional working man could meet and mingle as fellow masons. Military men, ambitious commercial types and upwardly-mobile professionals (doctors, lawyers, journalists) also sought the conviviality of all-male company in regular lodge meetings. Women were excluded from membership, and no doubt many early Freemasons – married men or bachelors – sought little more than a relaxed and amenable masculine social environment. But the lodges' fraternal and charitable activities were always enclosed within an essential, defining function: the preservation and continuation of a Masonic heritage allegedly grounded in an ancient and secretive knowledge. At its essence, the Craft perpetuated "a morality peculiar to itself, veiled in allegory and cloaked in traditional ritual and symbol. The trade secrets of the operative masons became the esoteric secrets of the speculative masons."[19]

By Ward's time Freemasonry also provided an important thread in the social and administrative life of the late-Victorian and Edwardian British Empire. As members travelled and lodges were formed with military deployments, merchant activity and colonial bureaucracy, the spread of Freemasonry occurred in step with British territorial acquisitions during the eighteenth and nineteenth centuries. The formation of lodges accelerated with the flood of British emigrants overseas in the nineteenth century and the heightened 'new imperialism' of the period 1870–1914, so that overseas lodges affiliated with the United Grand Lodge of England rose in number from 271 out of a total of 941 in 1862 to 905 (out of some 3,743) in 1914.[20] Meanwhile, locally-affiliated lodges, and others linked to the Scottish and Irish Grand Lodges had also grown strongly in Britain's colonies and imperial territories.

The networks of lodge membership and Masonic fraternity provided *entrée* to a social clique, access to persons of influence, and a club-like atmosphere that was apolitical and non-sectarian. Lodges preserved a sense of home and its values. Senior colonial officials from high commissioners and governors, senior military men and colonial statesmen were more often than not practicing Freemasons, and further down the social scale traders, commercial agents and soldiers also found Masonic membership to be advantageous in the outposts of Empire. Their lodges provided small highlights of comradeship and sociability in the often dull routine of colonial administration, and active membership was an important stepping stone in colonial advancement. Paradoxically, despite its strict internal hierarchy, a Masonic lodge provided a setting where differences of birth, wealth, religion and social status – so important in the class-ridden arrangements of Victorian Britain – could be temporarily transcended. It was also a vehicle for patriotism, national identity and empire loyalty, and thus colonials in South Africa, Canada, Australia and New Zealand proved enthusiastic Freemasons. Even more so than sporting endeavours like cricket and football, Freemasonry flourished in the miniature colonial societies that developed wherever British territorial or commercial interests spread. It "promoted a set of enlightened, liberal-minded, tolerant, but authoritarian and disciplined, values among soldiers as well as traders, and it acted as a central focus of social activity for Britons overseas, often bringing together groups with no other common interest".[21] Certainly, proponents of Empire such as Rudyard Kipling waxed fulsomely on the imperial sinews of fraternity and fellowship, and their importance in the business of securing and maintaining Britain's dominions overseas. By the end of Victoria's reign, indeed, Freemasonry "was playing a significant role in the 'imperialist' movement that sought to unify the empire under the symbol of the crown and make the empire, especially the settlement colonies, a source of strength to Britain".[22]

But the opportunities presented by an active Freemasonry often went beyond merely camaraderie and social networking. Indeed, at the beginning of the twentieth century, Freemasonry was one of the very few formalised, established vehicles available to Englishmen attracted to the study of esoteric tradition. This aspect is likely to have been uppermost in the mind of the twenty-year old John Ward, waiting nervously outside the Isaac Newton Lodge room at Cambridge on the night of his initiation in 1906. His youthful interests in antiquarian 'survivals' had drawn him to Freemasonry; in turn, the Craft would make him an esoteric scholar. By the mid-1920s, twenty years after his initiation into the Masonic brotherhood, J. S. M. Ward had become one of Britain's best-known and most provocative scholars of Freemasonry and occult tradition.

❋   ❋   ❋

He was looking for answers to questions that had agitated many before him. Throughout human history, scholars of the great esoteric traditions have sought to "penetrate the surface meaning [of things in general] in order to reach a secret and superior knowledge", as Joscelyn Godwin puts it.[23] The European west has a particularly rich esoteric tradition, traceable from classical roots to medieval alchemists, Renaissance astrologers, seventeenth-century Rosicrucians and *illuminati*, through to Victorian spiritualists and the New Age mystics of today. Neo-Platonism, astrology, numerology, pantheism, fertility rites and a modern emphasis on clairvoyance and psychic perception have shaped the historical forms and patterns of Western occultism. Despite vast differences of time, place and cultural setting, from the magus of classical antiquity to suburban Wicca, students of esoteric illumination share an intense, almost devotional, immersion in the arcane learning of their creeds.

The culture of late Victorian and Edwardian Britain, in which John Ward matured into young adulthood, had a particularly rich esoteric underground. He didn't directly encounter this alluring world of ritual magic, occult scholarship and speculation until beginning his Masonic research around 1906, but his early love of historical relics and antiquities proved an ideal preparation. This passion made him, in many ways, a cultural conservative in the strict sense of the term. It primed his interest in arcane forms of knowledge and survivals of ancient systems of human wisdom.

Despite Britain's rapid modernisation through the nineteenth century, the study of occult traditions continued to attract curious minds and questing souls. In part this was because older modes of thinking were being systematically eradicated by the rapid developments of modern life. Extraordinary advances in technology, the primacy of science and the increasing dominance of secular and materialistic values (what the sociologist Max Weber called the 'disenchantment of the world') had all made enormous inroads into older beliefs and patterns of life. Urban development and modern communications eroded rural isolation and the folk beliefs of past generations. As daily life became more rational and materialistic, as technology and applied science demonstrated human mastery of the natural and physical world, such older patterns of thinking were discredited. In the critical sciences, metaphysics was no longer a tool to explore the true and infinite nature of the cosmic order. Darwinian biology reduced the great story of life and the possibility of ultimate truth and meaning to little more than a brutish struggle for survival. Superstition, religious fundamentalism and folk beliefs in the supernatural faded in the cold light of rational analysis, while scepticism and doubt emerged as the characteristic modern attitudes in an age of Weberian disenchantment.

Weber's phrase thus captures a general truth about the rational, technocratic modern temper in the European west. But it also ignores the very vivid survivals (and re-inventions) of ancient systems of knowledge and insight that persisted amid the modernisation of the European mind. Most visible in the British experience were the divisive convulsions suffered by mainstream Anglicanism over the central problem of tradition and ritual in Christian worship, beginning with the High Church Tractarian movement of the 1830s, moving through the Gothic Revival in ecclesiastical architecture and climaxing in the 1874 anti-ritualist Public Worship Regulation Act. Deep sectarian tensions arose because a Protestant suspicion of Catholic 'hocus-pocus' fuelled opposition to Anglican ritualism, just as "a revival and rediscovery of ritual practice in the nineteenth and twentieth centuries [occurred] in reaction to the perceived dearth of ritual in an overly-rational Protestantism".[24] Yet the Anglo-Catholic revival, for all its political contentiousness, demonstrated that time-honoured, semi-mystical rites and ceremonies had a consolatory quality for the faithful. Part of the attraction was the pure aestheticism of evocative ritual, but inscrutable Latin phrases recited and sung, signs inscribed in holy oil, gestures and genuflections offered a psychological haven of comfort and permanence in a cold and functional world.

Historians of the nineteenth century's occult movements are likewise keen to point out that metaphysical speculation and a desire for cosmic illumination lingered despite the intolerant environment of rational modernity. In fact, the Victorian interest in the occult seems itself a response to the period's acute experience of modernity. For James Webb, human consciousness endured a crisis in the modernising world of Western Europe in the nineteenth century, resulting in a "flight from reason", a "revulsion from the methods of thought and action that were responsible for the insecurity of Western man. Because these were seen as rationalism and materialism, the reaction . . . took the form of a rejection of Reason, a resurrection of faith and the spontaneous generation of causes of an exalted or mystical nature. . . . "[25] Old-fashioned superstition, primitive faith and 'irrationality', in other words, held on, and not simply as a fashionable conceit among the daring bohemians of the *fin-de-siècle*. It had a much deeper, more entrenched presence in nineteenth-century consciousness and spirituality. Webb describes the broad *milieu* well:

> The Establishment culture of late 19th-century Europe – based on capitalism, individualism, and the pursuit of profit – was confronted with a selection of idealisms whose kingdoms were not of this world, whose categories of thought were apocalyptic, were based on visions of absolute values and drew sustenance from traditions of thinking that have, through historical accident, remained rejected through the course of European history. This Underground of rejected knowledge, comprising heretical religious positions, defeated social schemes, abandoned sciences, and neglected modes of speculation, has as its core the varied collection of doctrines that can be combined in a bewildering variety of ways and that is known as the occult.[26]

Strange new sects, utopian communities and charismatic cults *à la mode* blossomed accordingly in the modern, urbanised landscape of the industrial west. Many inhabited the rural fringe in a deliberate flight from the centres of urban modernity, as in the New Forest of rural England and the Pentecostal and Shaker communities of the American frontier. But outwardly bizarre practices mushroomed in respectable drawing rooms of British towns and cities too, where crystal-gazing, divination by tarot, numerology and palmistry attracted devotees in considerable numbers. Popular Spiritualism was a particularly powerful expression of this 'flight from reason', as séances and contact meetings offered by mediums and clairvoyants drew crowds of adherents eager to discover a deeper meaning to human existence in the face of a materialistic universe. Spirit messages – from table raps, ouija boards and messages delivered by automatic writing and mediums in trance – seemed to offer tangible insights into the passage of the human soul after death and the nature of the infinite that lay beyond ordinary human experience.

Many spiritualists looked to alternative religious traditions to clarify such matters, and found guidance in Theosophy and other variations on Eastern religion as interpreted by *savants* such as Madame Blavatsky and Annie Besant. Among the literary elite, the occult science of the Theosophical Society based on the 'Secret Doctrine' revealed to Blavatsky by Tibetan masters added the spice of Eastern mysticism to this mix from the late 1870s, especially following the formation of the society's London Lodge in 1883. Interest in Buddhism grew, exemplified by the runaway success of *The Light of Asia* (Edwin Arnold's blank-verse life of the Buddha published under this title in 1879, and quickly running through over a hundred editions) that appealed to western readers fashionably attuned to the transcendental mysteries of karma and rebirth.[27] William James' *The Varieties of Religious Experience*, published in 1902, also popularised notions of reincarnation and spiritual evolution. The mystical traditions of the East, from Sufism in Islam to the enlightened paths of Buddhism and the Hindu pantheon, were power-fully seductive to many in the industrialised west, and were becoming increasingly familiar concepts as the nineteenth century came to a close.

Rippling and diverse, these undercurrents climaxed in a *fin-de-siècle* occultism exemplified by the ritual magic, or 'practical occultism', of the Hermetic Order of the Golden Dawn founded among London's literary bohemians in the late 1880s. It was dominated by Samuel Liddell Mathers, translator of Kabbalistic texts and "one of the most brilliant amateur scholars of his generation",[28] and attracted adepts such as the poet W. B. Yeats, the occult writer A. E. Waite, Oscar Wilde's wife Constance, the Irish patriot Maud Gonne (briefly), James M. Barrie, Aleister Crowley and later the celebrated writer on Christian mysticism Evelyn Underhill who, like her predecessors, was drawn to the spiritual mystique of the magical traditions synthesized in the Order's rituals. Dozens of other Rosicrucian and Theosophist groups arose through this period, small enclaves of research and ritual practice that developed members' interests in a range of esoteric tra-ditions from the Jewish Kabbalah to the Hermetic texts and eastern mysticism as the so-called 'Theosophical Enlightenment' gathered pace. Like Catholic ritualism and Oscar Wilde's flamboyant homosexuality, occultism was a sign of the times that was regarded by respectable society with a deep suspicion.[29] Nevertheless with its currents spreading into the period's literature, visual arts and graphic design, *fin-de-siècle* occultism managed to be intriguing, fashionable and exciting all at once.

Although Freemasonry was not generally seen as occult, initiates were able to use its lodge meetings and reading groups to pursue esoteric topics and interests. Consequently, active Freemasons were in the vanguard of the occult revival at the end of the nineteenth century. William Wynn Westcott, a doctor of medicine, London coroner, Hermetic scholar and active Mason, pursued the heterodox fringes of conventional Freemasonry with great zeal. After securing Masonic initiation in the early 1870s, he pursued his esoteric interests through a host of obscure ritualistic orders including the Rite of Swedenborg (established in England in 1876 on American foundations), the Royal Order of Knights of Eri and the Order of the Red Cross of Constantine. He suspended his medical career in the late 1870s to study

Kabalistic philosophy and Hermeticism, through which he found a vehicle in the *Societas Rosicruciana in Anglia* (SRIA), the English Rosicrucian body founded in the mid-1860s. Westcott was admitted to SRIA in 1880, and was elected its General Secretary in 1883 and Supreme Magus (effectively its honorary president) in 1891. Membership of the SRIA was limited to Master Masons and so its activities ranged far beyond the usual concerns of mainstream Freemasonry in pursuit of cosmic revelation through the study of the Kabalah and the doctrines of Hermes Trismegistus.[30] As Westcott explained in welcoming attendees to the society's Jubilee Festival in 1919, the Rosicrucian project had been revived in England

> to provide for Freemasons a means of instruction in the more recondite meanings and the symbolism of the rituals of Masonic Orders, of the myths of ancient nations, and of the Sacred Mysteries of the past. It was also intended, by mutual efforts to throw light upon the mystic ideas which lie at the bases of ancient art, sculpture and architecture, as well as to give information regarding the curious theosophic and philosophic systems which have flourished in past times. I refer especially to the Kabalah of the Hebrew Rabbis, to the legendary lore of the Egyptian Pharaohs and the tenets of the Gnostics of the early Christian centuries. Lastly, there was the intention to investigate the possibility of increasing the power of intuition and of extending the present human faculties, especially of sight and of hearing, with a view of gaining increased powers to be used for benevolent ends.[31]

Thus the esoteric antiquarianism embraced by curious Freemasons could move beyond mere study to embrace the practical implications of psychic powers. Westcott took this step himself as a founding figure in the Hermetic Order of the Golden Dawn, the famed 'practical occultists' noted above that embodied the intellectual fashion for ritual magic in the *fin-de-siècle*. Although the Golden Dawn was non-Masonic and even admitted women, all three of its founding figures were active in esoteric Freemasonry and English Rosicrucianism. It is clear, then, that Freemasonry had occult potential, even if most Freemasons were not dedicated to or even interested in occult pursuits. By the time of Ward's initiation into the Craft in 1906, the developments sketched in above had coalesced as a solid foundation for the studies in esoteric tradition that now beckoned to him. Its promise was well encapsulated by Westcott: 'The secrets of Occultism are like Freemasonry; in truth they are to some extent the secrets that Freemasonry has lost.'[32]

At the same time the new sciences of anthropology and ethnography, then rising to eminence in academic circles, endowed the study of esoteric tradition with a new intellectual respectability. In its own way, as a social function of Empire, Freemasonry served to encourage ethnographic and cultural research, particularly among those Englishmen abroad (as John Ward was soon to be) with an interest in primitive religion, mysticism and the occult. Certainly, his interest in esoteric knowledge, comparative ethnography and the universal principles that underlay Masonic lore blossomed in the years that followed when, as an 'enlightened' Englishman and an inquisitive Freemason, he took up Kipling's 'White Man's Burden' as a servant of Empire.

❋   ❋   ❋

Soon after graduating Ward took up a position teaching history and literature at Reigate Grammar School, Surrey, from mid-1908 through at least to the end of 1910. He also married his cousin, Eleanor Caroline Lanchester, on 18 December 1908 at the Weybridge parish church.

They had met during a family holiday, but little else is known of their initial attraction to each other and the family's attitude to their marriage. Carrie was the daughter of Henry Lanchester, a Brighton architect married to Ward's aunt Octavia. She was one of eight children; her younger brother Frederick went on to prominence in British engineering circles as the inventor of a revolutionary petrol engine in the 1890s and founder of the Lanchester Motor Company in Birmingham.[33] For all the advantages gained, Ward later regretted their decision to marry. Carrie was nearly twenty years his senior, and although the two were good companions it seems they shared few interests in any deeper or more profound sense. Carrie's impatience with her husband's spiritual interests, in particular, proved fatal to the marriage.

Early in their marriage the Wards rented a cottage known as 'The Whym' in Gomshall on the North Downs, and it seems Ward travelled the eight miles to his school in Reigate daily by train. A pretty Home Counties village, Gomshall boasted local beauty spots such as the wooded downlands of Setley Heath to the north, the 'Silent Pool' shielded by beech trees close to Albury Downs to the west, and the woodlands of Abinger and high Leith Hill to the south-east. A daughter Blanche was born in October 1909, and the family later moved to Sheffield where Ward taught history at King Edward VII School.

Even with his teaching responsibilities and young family John Ward found time to research and publish two books between 1910 and 1912. His *Outline Notes on English History* for use by fellow-schoolmasters was intended as a supplement to the usual school textbooks. Ward hoped the text would also be useful to pupils sitting the various Scholarship, Matriculation and Junior Examinations and Pupil Teacher Certificates. Although providing only a basic chronological outline of key topics, his lecture notes hinted at

Ward's teaching philosophy in an era when school history suffered from the rote learning of dry facts and dates. He suggested that illustrations, photographs and postcards on architecture, furniture and other aspects of social life helped to capture the interest of his pupils. Local visits and literary readings could also be useful:

> Further illustrations should be supplied by visits to any old buildings in the neighbourhood, and by the reading of extracts from contemporary writers. By these means the History lesson will be made bright and inter-esting, and at the same time the outline of facts so essential for Exams will be easily assimilated.[34]

This was heartfelt advice, because by this time the interests kindled by his childhood rambles through old London and in visits to the great museums had flared into a lifelong fascination with archaeological relics and historical artefacts. Ward was particularly absorbed in the history and stylistic variations of the brass memorials found in the medieval parish churches of the English countryside. Creating impressions of the brasses by rubbing cobblers wax over ceiling paper was a hobby that attracted many devotees among Victorian and early twentieth-century antiquarians. The Oxford rooms of undergraduate medievalists like William Morris in the 1840s and 1850s, for example, were hung with rubbings. Ward was an avid collector, and built up a personal collection of over 1,500 brass rubbings from his visits to historic churches in various parts of England. A quarter of these were later donated to the important national collection at the Victoria and Albert Museum.[35] By 1912 Ward was sufficiently well-versed on the subject of English monu-mental brasses to publish a comprehensive guide on the subject with Cambridge University Press. According to the author's earnest preface, it was intended as "a cheap and handy manual which will give the ordinary man in the street a fair idea of the classes into which they may most readily be grouped, and at the same time furnish him with such essential details as will enable him to distinguish instinctively the salient points of the subject, and assimilate them to the full".[36]

✻   ✻   ✻

In late 1913 an extraordinary series of psychic experiences intruded quite suddenly into the quiet and unpretentious life of this provincial schoolmaster, antiquarian and brass rubbing collector.

One night in early December he and Carrie retired to bed as usual. But he had a disturbed night's sleep, and dreamt vividly of the death of his uncle and father-in-law, Henry Lanchester. The clarity of the dream was striking. "The vision began with a message that he had died suddenly", he later reported, "and went on with the funeral, at which I was present. The sensations of grief, and the remarks and actions of the other mourners, were vividly impressed on my mind." Awakening the following morning, he discussed the dream with his wife. They planned to visit her parents at their home in Lindfield near Haywards Heath, but Carrie fell ill and so they missed seeing her father at Christmas that year. Within a month of the vision, on 5 January 1914, the Wards were notified by telegram that Carrie's father had died suddenly that day, the morning of his eightieth birthday. "All the sensations of grief that I had felt in my dream were repeated exactly", Ward wrote, "as were the incidents of the funeral. Even his face in the coffin looked like the one I had seen in my dream; it differed considerably from his face when alive."[37]

In the months that followed, Ward's dreams followed an extraordinary pattern, and seemed to resolve as a sequence of clear and direct spirit messages from his departed father-in-law. He found them profoundly convincing, lucid and logical in their internal details, providing extraordinary insight into life after death. These experiences, which Ward recorded diligently and later published in book form, rocked the conventional rhythm of his previously quiet and unassuming life. Utterly convinced by the messages and their content, he firmly embraced the central tenets of Modern Spiritualism: that human beings possessed a spiritual essence that was immortal, which transcended the limitations of the earthly, physical world at the moment of bodily death and passed to an equally real existence on higher planes of reality. After a pause during the transition itself, consciousness continued uninterrupted so that disembodied communications from the spirit plane, such as those he felt he had received from Henry Lanchester, might be sent and received as psychical messages across the void.

Many of Ward's contemporaries held similar convictions, of course, because by 1914 Spiritualism had infused British religious and social life. The late Victorians and Edwardians were fascinated by the idea of communication from beyond the grave, from spirit messages and telepathy to 'raps' and physical manifestations such as telekinesis and spirit photography. For many, such glimpses of an afterlife provided consolation in periods of personal grief. But the deeper implications of Spiritualism provided for others a startling confirmation of the metaphysical teachings of conventional religion. Despite widespread scepticism and opposition in scientific and ecclesiastical circles, Spiritualism answered a religious need in a society where indifference to dogmatic Christianity was widespread. Organised Spiritualist churches appeared in the cities and major towns, professional mediums advertised for private sittings and a commercial publishing industry thrived, dedicated to 'spirit photography' and the testimony of prominent mediums.

For many, Spiritualism opened a door onto an inner spiritual world that seemed to echo the pantheistic teachings presented in Eastern faiths and philosophies and popularised through Theosophy and its many variants. Ward's interest in such matters, however, did not remain simply a question of intellectual curiosity. The startling experiences of December 1913 and into January 1914 propelled him from the comfortable conventions of Anglican orthodoxy to an active pursuit of the essential nature of metaphysical reality. He came to embrace a personal mysticism that profoundly re-directed his life's work.

To begin with, Ward appears to have been quite baffled by the insights and messages he received in the dream state. As he became convinced by their veracity, and thus more comfortable receiving communications of this sort, a different view evolved. He was never, as he later put it, "a medium plying for hire",[38] but he decided that the communications he was receiving had a purpose. His father-in-law had made contact from beyond the grave, Ward believed, to explain the afterlife, its arrangements and principles as a means of redemption for his (Lanchester's) agnostic insouciance when alive. "It is entailing much labour on me [to contact you]", Lanchester's spirit informed him, "but I do it gladly, for thereby I am making amends for my slackness on earth. Believe me, you too will benefit; but above all, I hope the world may deign to learn something from what I am trying to communicate."[39] With this imperative firmly lodged in his mind, Ward found it impossible to ignore his trance visions and their implications.

A week after Henry Lanchester's sudden death, Ward dreamt vividly of an encounter with him. As he explained in the foreword to *Gone West*, published in 1917, a dream on Monday January 12 was so compelling that he wrote it down the following morning.

> I dreamt I saw Uncle like, and yet unlike, he was before he died; something between what I remember him as before, and what he looked like after death. He said: 'I have been trying to speak to Carrie, but can't, so I have come to you. Tell her I am alive, more alive than before I died; that I am mentally clearer than I was for some time before I died. But here I have had to set to work to learn, as if I were a child again, much of what I should have learnt on earth. I am with those who did just believe, but had not much real belief. Tell Carrie this.'[40]

As Ward described it his father-in-law wanted to "convey to me an account of life beyond the grave. He discovered that I was mediumistic – a fact of which I was unaware, although I have for many years been keenly interested in the occult." For weeks after he experienced similarly vivid dreams each Monday evening. They continued on from each other in a coherent narrative that Ward found utterly convincing.

'HJL' first appeared in Ward's dream visions as an isolated figure; a disembodied, floating spirit in a dark vacuum keen to welcome his son-in-law and establish their dialogue. He was dressed in normal clothes and his physical appearance was unchanged from that which Ward remembered. By concentrating his mind, HJL explained, he was able to 'connect' telepathically with living people such as Ward who were psychically receptive. He wanted to make contact, he explained, in order to "tell them of this life, so that they may try and prepare themselves for it, so that they need not go through the elementary lessons which I had to learn."[41] He had first contacted Ward in an attempt to comfort Carrie in her sorrow, but stayed in touch to supply "a connected account of our life over here".[42] Six weeks after his first spirit communication, during a trance vision on 16 February 1914, Ward was encouraged by HJL to open his eyes, and:

> Then it seemed as if my eyes were opened and behold, I was in the most lovely country. The light was of the kind one sees on a summer evening. Over the distant horizon the red glow of sunset was just visible, tingeing the hill-tops and reflected in the water of many streams and lakelets. We were standing side by side in an avenue of trees, tall and splendid.
>
> I saw H.J.L. quite plainly. He was not dressed in the clothes I had seen him in when he appeared clairvoyantly, i.e. earthly, but in long flowing robes of white which seemed as if they were really part of his body in some mysterious way. A soft faint light seemed to come out from his body, impossible to describe.
>
> Looking again at the landscape, it seemed to me to contain everything beautiful of natural scenery. The view grows wider; I perceive lakes and snow-capped mountains, rushing rivers, and lo, beyond all, the sea.[43]

As he accompanied his father-in-law and other spirits about this psychic landscape of 'Afterdeath', filled with buildings, gardens, trees and pathways much like those of the physical world but entirely composed of 'thought-forms', they told him of their experiences and what they had learnt since departing their earthly existence. His account at times conflates the banal with the transcendent: at one point, Ward encounters a group of other spirits on his way to meeting HJL. "'Who are you, and are you dead?'" they ask. "'You do not look quite like one of us, and yet if you are not dead, how came you here?' I replied: 'No, I'm not dead, but somehow I have developed in such a way recently since my father-in-law died that I am able to come and visit him here and even carry away a remembrance of what I see.'"[44]

Ward was convinced that the communications he received under these unusual circumstances were authentic insights into transcendental dimensions of human experience for several reasons. He was struck by the unusually strict coherence of his visions, the fact that the narrative always recommenced where it had left off the week before, and the fact that they "remained firmly impressed upon my mind until they were written down" unlike conventional dreams. Perhaps most persuasive was the classic test of the spirit medium:

> These visions contained veridicable facts entirely unknown to me, which nevertheless proved to be true on investigation. Some of these facts were of a personal and private character, known only to the dead man and one living person, and the latter admitted their truth. Further, there were certain references which, to the writer, were unintelligible, but were recognised by the living person to whom they were related (as requested).[45]

Many mediums, clairvoyants and spiritualist authors of Ward's day were revealed under investigation to be frauds and impostors. The Society for Psychical Research was founded in 1882 by Cambridge scientists and philosophers to investigate the paranormal phenomena associated with modern spiritualism, and its critical approach subjected many claims to piercing scientific scrutiny. With the SPR's encouragement a rational scepticism took hold as the dominant intellectual response to the outlandish phenomena reported at séances and other spiritualist gatherings. Many among Ward's contemporaries dismissed spiritualist claims out of hand as inherently ludicrous and unworthy of serious attention; a cynical exploitation of the bereaved in their vulnerability. The acceptance of spirit messages at face value seemed to confirm the gullibility of a credulous, semi-educated public.

But John Ward, for his part, professed a firm belief in the reality and veracity of the spirit communications he had experienced. In truth we simply do not know whether he imagined, invented or exaggerated these psychic episodes. The experiences he reported were private and unrepeatable, and thus inherently resistant to independent verification then or now. We do know that he recounted his visions to his wife, and that she was willing to corroborate the facts as he reported them to her. We also know he edited and re-worked the content of his dream visions for publication, and like all authors we can assume he was determined to sell books. Perhaps Ward's biblical cadences – his fondness for terms like 'lo', 'behold' in depicting the psychic vistas of the afterlife, for instance – is a clue that at a very basic level he regarded his insights as revelations, and was perhaps a little too willing to suspend his critical doubts in order to announce them to the world at large. It is impossible to be certain, in other words, that he never 'fudged' the record of his experiences in order to render them more persuasive, detailed or convincing.

But we should not leap to condemn him at a deeper level based on our own sense of whether clairvoyance is plausible or not, and what its implications might be. Medical science has sought to explain anomalous psychic experiences by invoking a range of pathologies and disorders, including schizophrenia and frontal lobe epilepsy. But there is no trace in Ward's biography of any mental instability or periodic incapacity that prevented his normal social functioning as a responsible adult. His psychic episodes, that is to say, were quite unlike the involuntary seizures that characterize the mentally ill. Quite to the contrary, he reported that he developed an ability to control his episodes temporally, beginning with the ability to 'will himself' into a state of psychic receptivity in preparation for his regular contact with Lanchester's spirit on Monday evenings.

Ward shared a dilemma with others who have experienced similarly anomalous and challenging psychic episodes. The objective fact of Lanchester's messages could never be proven to the world at large; but nor could they be denied to himself. If we are to make sense of Ward's biography and his life's work, perhaps the ultimate truth of these experiences is actually less significant than the strength and sincerity of his conviction that they had in fact occurred just as he understood them. Always rational, and always driven by a boundless curiosity, Ward was no stubborn materialist in the face of his own direct experience that insisted that a metaphysical sphere of conscious existence (and the spirit beings that moved in it) lay somehow behind or beyond the commonplace reality of his everyday life. We are then drawn to consider what they meant, or appeared to mean, to Ward in his context. The veracity of his own direct experience meant that he accepted absolutely not just the validity of these spirit messages and the visions that followed, but also the accuracy of the information that was in this way revealed to him. The experience itself was so profoundly *real*, so utterly convincing, that it was deeply persuasive in all its details.

What do these dream narratives tell us? Certainly, they are not typical historical sources. They are unverifiable and intensely subjective, and by their very nature resistant to ordinary critical treatment. At one end of a possible spectrum of responses we might accept them at face value as profound expressions of ineffable transcendental experience, that Ward like other *savants* only resolved with difficulty into meaningful prose. At the opposite end we might dismiss them as calculated fictions he simply made up to impress his readers, project an identity of spiritual profundity and thereby sell books. It is however possible to take a middle ground, if we accept that Ward did indeed have unusual psychic experiences, a position that seems reasonable given his otherwise rational and reliable demeanour. He felt obliged to put these episodes into words: describing the setting as he experienced it visually, identifying his participants as conversational participants delivering lines as in a play, in order to synthesise these elements as a smooth narrative flow. They might make best sense to us, in other words, when regarded as a set of stories, composed to express the meaning and coherence (as Ward understood them) of the anomalous experiences that began in January 1914. His narrative presentation of these experiences offers important insights into the outlook and values Ward was willing to profess in public.

A later chapter considers more fully the account of 'Afterdeath', its cosmic implications and larger themes of spiritual and moral progress that Ward presented in his two spiritualist books of 1917 and 1919. But for the moment it is enough to recognise that these events were a watershed in Ward's life. He was convinced he had received detailed intimations of transcendental reality that were normally hidden to commonplace human perception. He became convinced there was an intimate connection between the psychic phenomena he had experienced directly and the great mystical traditions of human spirituality. The human consciousness might work its way from the appreciation of isolated phenomena, to fragments of insight, and from there to a higher and more complete understanding of the true and occluded nature of the cosmos. Sir Arthur Conan Doyle, another convinced spiritualist of Ward's day, developed this broader theme:

> the whole of this system, from the lowest table-rap up to the most inspired utterance of a prophet, is one complete whole, each link attached to the next one, and that when the humbler end of that chain was placed in the hand of humanity, it was in order that they might, by diligence and reason, feel their way up it until they reached the revelation which waited in the end. Do not sneer at the humble beginnings, the heaving table or the flying tambourine, however much such phenomena may have been abused or simulated, but remember that a falling apple taught us gravity, a boiling kettle brought us the steam engine, and the twitching leg of a frog opened up the train of thought and experiment which gave us electricity.[46]

Commencing with HJL's spirit messages in early 1914, John Ward felt his way up the chain until he arrived at a unified religious conviction that was not fully pronounced until some fifteen years later. But to begin with his concerns were limited to conventional 'mediumship' and the account he had received of life after death. "As to what opinion the reader will form of the present work I know not", Ward concluded his opening statement to *Gone West*, "but, for myself, I have been profoundly impressed with the reality and the reasonableness of what I have seen and what the spirits have related of Life beyond the Grave."[47] This conviction provided an unshakeable basis for his spiritual beliefs thereafter, especially when his trance visions took a new, more urgent direction in the late 1920s. By then, Ward's voracious studies in esoteric and occult matters had enlarged his conception of the veiled realm of transcendental reality. After two decades of private reading and scholarship and after his papers on Freemasonry and Secret Societies were published by the *Encyclopaedia Britannica*, he was regarded as one of the greatest living authorities on occultism and esoteric knowledge.[48] When lecturing on the subject of 'Life after Death' in early 1929, he asked rhetorically about the source of his own knowledge on the subject. His simple answer has the ring of utter conviction: "I will reply boldly, 'By the only way in which any man can acquire knowledge and by the only authority which any can be expected to accept, by knowledge gained through experience.'"[49]

3

To the East

In 1914, nearly thirty years old and an experienced schoolmaster, Ward was appointed headmaster of the Diocesan Boys School in Rangoon, Burma. As the armies of Europe mobilized and were flung into battle, he was travelling with his young family through the Suez Canal. Transport ships passed by in the opposite direction, "packed with sunburnt men in khaki . . . the garrisons of Hong-kong and Singapore hastening to France", as he later recalled.[1] With the nations of Europe turning ferociously upon each other, drawing into the death-struggle the resources and manpower of their colonial empires, Ward turned to embrace the East.

Although in Burma for little more than a year, Ward's time there was highly significant for him on several fronts. The exuberant imperialism of his childhood matured into a more considered and circumspect outlook. His attitudes continued to reflect certain commonplace assumptions of the day, but to his credit he shunned the crass racial ideologies that helped justify European imperialism to favour a more open-minded sense of cultural differ-ence and equivalence. His eager fascination with Burmese ethnography, in particular, gave a new aspect to his interest in antiquities, folklore, heritage and culture. His passion for Freemasonry deepened as he realized the poten-tial of a comparative anthropological approach to the study of Masonic rituals and traditions. Finally, his exposure while in Burma to Eastern cosmology and religious mysticism, and especially ideas of spiritual evolu-tion and reincarnation, complemented the metaphysical insights he had received from his spirit guides since HJL first made contact in January 1913. Our source material dealing with this period is slender and confined to patchy memoirs and a handful of published articles, but in each of these respects we sense that Ward's colonial sojourn profoundly enlarged his outlook.

He probably arrived in Rangoon with the same generalised expectations noted in a guide book to Burma published in 1905. Burma, R. Talbot Kelly wrote, was "rich in physical beauties, adorned by many monuments of extreme antiquity and interest, and inhabited by a people admitted by general consent to be both picturesque and lovable".[2] Ward carried a copy of this book with him in 1914 and perhaps he shared its disappointment with the low-lying mud-flats of the mouth of the Irrawaddy, fringed by scrubby jungle and untidy grass. It was only as the gleaming dome of the Shwe Dagon Pagoda came into view, golden above the dirty haze of Rangoon and the turbid waters of the river, that the scenery was enlivened and the visitor's sense of expectation seemed likely to be satisfied. The busy river vessels hinted at the exotic life of the place, especially the "quaintly shaped boats of the Burmans – strange craft, whose graceful lines and richly carved sterns seem to reflect the minds of a people who love beauty and are content to be happy".[3]

Ward developed similar views of the Burmese, their manners and culture during his brief and busy time in the Far East. He reflected on what he had learnt of the Burmese character soon after returning to London in 1916:

> The Burman, even when fully grown, is somewhat of a child, but a delightful child as a rule. He is clean and loves to dress in beautiful silk 'lungis' or skirts. He is kind-hearted and hospitable, charitable and generous to a degree, light-hearted, happy, and fond of a joke. He has his faults of course – which of us has not? He sometimes loses his temper, and then is rather too fond of settling his quarrel with his 'dah' or sword. Perhaps, too, he is not as hard-working as his cousin the Chinaman! Perhaps he objects to working hard so that others may grow rich. Yet with all he is very lovable, and there is much that is good to be learnt from this race that lives in the most easterly of our Indian provinces.[4]

Such romantic conceptions of British subjects in the colonial territories of the East were, of course, implicit to the essentially paternalistic imperialism endorsed by British authorities and public opinion in this heyday of empire. Natives imagined as child-like needed the steady guiding hand of the western colonial administrator, at least until the necessary lessons of progress and modern civilization had been learnt. Ward shared such values stanchly to the extent that he remained a lifelong supporter of Britain's colonial mission. A testament to this was his *Poems of the Empire*, short verses for younger readers published after Ward's return to England that expressed his unblushing imperialism and patriotism without irony or ambivalence. Dedicated to "the colonial born and all who love the Empire" and inspired by the rollicking yarns of the popular collection *Epic Tales of Empire,* his collection included poems on 'The King Emperor', Clive of India, the Union Jack and other similar topics that were designed to stir imperial sentiment. "Poems on the Empire," he informed his readers, "are all too scarce, and it is with the hope of inspiring both old and young, and leading them to realise that the various parts of the Empire are as intimately linked with the [home] country as are the various counties thereof, that I have endeavoured to sing in verse these romantic stories which have made our

Empire great."[5] Thus the instinctive, patriotic imperialism of his childhood was strengthened by Ward's Burmese experiences. Years later, in October 1947, when he heard of plans to grant Burma independent statehood, he could not contain his dismay. "It's a great shame," he wrote in his diary in a heartfelt statement of his Empire sensibilities, "and the first deliberate step by the British Socialist Government towards breaking up the British Empire. Think of all the British lives sacrificed during this last war to recover Burma and now it is being deliberately thrown away."[6]

Ward's post at the Diocesan Boys School, where he took up his duties in late 1914, presented an opportunity to guide the destiny of the young colonials under his charge, and he took his responsibilities seriously during his short term as headmaster. Most of the boys were of British or Eurasian parentage, studying to prepare for positions in the Indian Civil Service. He taught classes assisted by a small staff of English expatriates, with some Burmese and Eurasian teachers. The rambling buildings needed care and maintenance, and early in his term Ward commenced a School Improvement Fund. By the end of 1915 renovation work on the old buildings was underway and a new gymnasium and dormitory had opened.

The grim business of war intruded when Burmese recruits were called for the British offensive against Turkish Mesopotamia. As a patriotic headmaster, Ward did not dissuade a group of his pupils aged between fifteen and eighteen from eagerly volunteering for active service. Many subsequently died or were captured in the siege of Kut-al-Amara on the Tigris river from December 1915 to April 1916, the great catastrophe of the British campaign in Mesopotamia. "Archer [a favourite student] was one of them", he later recorded.

> I had a letter from him in a Turkish prison camp when I was back in England. I arranged for gifts of food to be sent to him through the Red Cross, but I heard no more, whether he died or his letters were suppressed by the Turkish Censor I do not know. I wrote several times but had no reply.[7]

✳ ✳ ✳

Rangoon during the Great War was a bustling, cosmopolitan river port, its trade and commerce dominated by Chinese merchants. Although Britain enjoyed territorial sovereignty, Europeans made little impression on the daily life and activity of the sprawling, diverse city. Neat wide streets, fringed by trees and studded with temples and gardens, were set out in a grid against the busy wharves and warehouses of the river frontage. Market areas, bazaars, shops and businesses flourished in the vivacious town centre. "[I]n the streets, ablaze with coloured costume", wrote Talbot Kelly, "the dominant types are Hindus, Tamils, Madrassees, Cingalese, and Chinese. The Burman seems crowded out here . . . even the police in the streets are drawn from that fine body of men the Sikhs, while all the 'chuprassies' or Government messengers are natives of India."[8] The Chinese were especially prominent, and dominated much of the commercial activity of the wharves, warehouses and shopping streets. Ward remembered Rangoon's Chinese quarter, with its temples and shops with lovely carved wooden fronts made by craftsmen in Singapore.

Further out along drives shaded by tamarind and banyan trees, some respite from the bustle and activity was gained in the residential cantonments favoured by the British colonial elite. Stucco villas and bungalows housed the leading merchants, administrators and professionals of Rangoon, their houses attended by servants, maids and cooks, and their lawns and flower beds manicured by native gardeners. Traditional Burmese villages could be found nearby, in pockets where traditional trades and life patterns continued relatively unchanged by European domination. Pagodas, shrines and temples – especially the great 'pyramid of fire', Shwe Dagon – rising over the trees lent dignity and magnificence to the skyline. Also close by, however, were the unkempt neighbourhoods of the lowest caste of Rangoon's workers, crowded with rudimentary shacks of palm leaf matting, corrugated iron and bare dirt floors. Here Rangoon's dock coolies, 'gharry wallahs', 'dhobies' (washermen) and lesser servants led lives of crushing toil on the lowest rungs of colonial society.

Ward and his family settled quickly into this lively setting of colonial privilege, commercial bustle and native colour, moving into a spacious new home and purchasing a four-wheeled gharry. He enjoyed a degree of social status as the headmaster of an important school, and accordingly he and Carrie found themselves elevated above the modest social rank they had held in England. According to Talbot Kelly, Rangoon's Anglo-Indian elite commenced their days early with a light breakfast before walking or riding in the cool of the day: "by 9 a.m.", he suggested, "a cool verandah with a lounge chair under a 'punkah' is a refuge to be desired". A long siesta and afternoon tea was followed by another promenade, when "Rangoon betakes itself to tennis or Dalhousie Park, where, at a rendezvous not inaptly named 'Scandalpoint', the Volunteer band plays well enough to render the promenade and gossip attractive." A working schoolmaster such as Ward was more pressed for time than this, but doubtless he and Carrie participated in Rangoon's version of the elegant, aimless evening rituals of the Anglophone colonial world. At sunset the resident British tended to gather at the Gymkhana Club, a destination for cards, billiards, reading and conversation in the cool of the evening.[9] Other Rangoon social institutions such as the Boat Club on the lake in Dalhousie Park, the Pegu Club, the various Masonic lodges and services clubs, and of course private gatherings and garden parties, provided an outlet for colonial expatriates to mingle and relax.

Ward acclimatized quickly, helped by the membership of a local Masonic lodge that he immediately took up and his interest in local ethnography and antiquities. He became friendly with one antique dealer, an elderly Yorkshireman and colonial knockabout named Hirst, who had recovered from bankruptcy several times and was a recognised authority on Burmese antiques. Ward was a frequent visitor to Hirst's Rangoon curio shop, purchasing statuettes and carvings, comparing collectibles and lending an ear to the proprietor's vivid stories of colonial collecting.[10] From here, and other shops like it, his considerable collection of Eastern antiquities began to take shape, including rare and precious items of Indian and Tibetan origin. In the latter case, for instance, Ward's collection of ceremonial teapots, prayer wheels, deity figures and ritual 'devil-daggers' from Tibet was assembled from 1915, including a wonderfully ornate ceremonial apron, carved from human bone fragments and now in the collection of the World Museum, Liverpool.[11]

It is not surprising that his collecting and ethnographic interests blossomed in the exotic setting provided by colonial Burma. Shrines and temples were abundant, and fascinating scenes of religious observance were played out before him at regular intervals. The annual Shi'ite festival of Ashura during Muharram, for example, provided an enthralling diversion for him over several days in November 1915. Processions, ceremonies and demonstrations by Rangoon's Islamic community filled the streets in commemoration of the martyrs Hussain and Hasan ibn Ali, killed in the struggle over Mohammed's succession. He ventured into the streets to follow the spectacle closely, and later recorded his observations with the breathless alacrity of the amateur anthropologist:

> There was a huge procession carrying torches and bearing the full-sized reproductions (in bamboo and paper) of the [two martyrs'] tombs. As the procession moved through the streets the men (no women were present) chanted wild dirges and beat their chests, tore their garments and threw dust on their heads . . . As the drums rolled, the crowd grew more and more excited and hurled into the air blazing torches and discharged blank cartridges form antiquated guns. The torches fell anywhere in the crowd and were caught up and again hurled into the air to fall on the heads of the closely packed crowd. How no one was set on fire I really do not know. Every now and then men armed with swords and shields converge in mock battles, clashing sword on each others' swords or shields. This was supposed to represent the battles between the two parties and it was done to weird rhythmic step and was really a kind of dance.[12]

Other evenings brought displays of firewalking by devotees in a patch of open ground near one of Rangoon's mosques, and further processions climaxing in the immersion of the model tombs into a series of large bathing tanks. "The ceremony", he commented, "has undoubtedly incorporated many pre-Moslem features and appear to be derived from the heathen cult of Tammuz – the dying god." "I had to pay for witnessing the Mahorhan Festival", he concluded ruefully, "for I caught a bad dose of Dengue fever from the crowd. It was like a bad attack of old-fashioned influenza and lasted 10 days. Still it was worth it!!"[13] Another time a Burmese teacher from his school took him to a village some distance from the city, where the body of a Buddhist monk was being prepared for cremation. To Ward's initial puzzlement, the occasion was marked by gaiety and celebration. The deeper religious significance of the moment, however, helped to explain the curious festival mood.

> Near the village a number of booths had been erected, mostly made of palm matting, and near them was the funeral stand. This was a tall structure about 30 ft. high built in a series of terraces and surmounted by a pagoda-shaped canopy. Here lay the body of the monk which had been removed from its coffin. He had been dead a year and some kind of embalming process had been employed but not too successfully. The funeral stand was made of a bamboo framework covered with paper and the paper sides were decorated with paintings by a Burmese artist. Presently the monk's empty coffin was carried round by a number of men and all the unmarried girls crowded round it and tried to touch it amid much laughter and joking. My companion told me that those girls who touched the coffin would get married within the year. He could not explain why the touching of the coffin of a man vowed to celibacy would lead to matrimony but such was the belief.

"Nowhere was there any sign of grief for the dead man", Ward wrote in reflecting on the events years later, "on the contrary it was a festal occasion." His colleague's explanation of the Buddhist creed lingered in his memory. By living a life of devotion, the Burmese believed, a true monk "had learnt to dry up 'desire' and therefore there was nothing to drag him back to earth". He had attained *Nikban* or 'nirvana' upon his death, "and thus achieved the object of his last life on earth, the Breaking of the Wheel of Rebirth. He had, in short, entered eternal bliss and peace."[14]

Within a few months he had collected a set of Burmese folk stories, which he collated and re-told for children in a publication issued in England in 1916. The collection revealed a simple delight in fables and story-telling that remained with him throughout his life, overlaid by a deepening appreciation of the function of myth as a vehicle for moral and spiritual parable. "I have gathered [the folktales] from many sources and people," he wrote in the book's introduction. "Some are just folk-tales told round the village fire or on the pagoda platform at night, and listened to with bated breath."[15] But he was quite aware of the larger significance the stories enjoyed in a cultural or religious context:

> Others have become the themes of plays – or, as the Burman calls them, 'pwes'. These I have often seen being enacted up and down the country by bands of strolling players in gorgeous costumes and painted faces. Others again, religious in tone and having a moral meaning attached to them, were related by venerable 'hpoonghis' or monks. The same stories, generally in a more elaborate form, are found in the sacred books of Buddhism, and these are perhaps the noblest of all.[16]

The volume closes with two small but significant pieces that testified to Ward's growing appreciation of Buddhist conceptions of life and meaning. They may not be especially skilful poetry, but they neatly illustrate Ward's budding sense of spiritual growth through overcoming the obstacles of life, a moral progress that might transcend the material reality of one's bodily death and continue in lifetimes beyond. In one poem, Ward re-tells the parable of Buddha and the Tiger to emphasise its central message that suffering and strife in the material world is fleeting and impermanent, that serves a deeper purpose when subsumed into the struggle for spiritual wisdom. The second, a poetic statement of the 'Fourfold Way,' likewise urges a renunciation of desire and the material urgings of self. Through his Burmese experiences, it seems, Ward was able to grasp aspects of Buddhist doctrine that tallied with his own metaphysical outlook in thought-provoking ways. From this point forward, Ward's spiritual life involved an effort to entwine such concepts into his own framework of belief and, in the process, to reconcile them with the conventional Christianity of his upbringing.

The first stanza of Ward's simple verse 'Buddha and the Tiger' presents a landscape of ferocious, relentless nature. In the blazing heat a mother tiger, maddened by thirst and hunger, searches the drought-blasted forest in search of nutrition for her young cubs. The foliage was "brown and perished, and even the burnt-up sods/ Proclaimed to the pitiless heavens the curse of the angry Gods". She meets Buddha, the *Bodhisat*, in the figure of a wise old man pondering the mysteries of history and human existence; in Ward's phrases, "on many strange matters of life, and death, and age,/ On youth and birth and re-birth, and the piled-up aeons of time,/ Since life as we mortals know it emerged from primordial slime." The sight of the Buddha calms the tigress, and they talk. She begs for guidance to capture prey for her young; he bows his head to consider the implications. "There is nought around that draws breath", he concludes, "And e'en if there were, is it right I should bring another to death?" Instead he offers his own body to the tiger.

So, sister, I give you my flesh, and from this life will depart

On another journey to wend, as often in lives before,
On the long, long path to Neikban I passed in days of yore.

The tigress has taken the food which the Blessed One has given,
Has torn his carcass apart, and bone from bone has riven;

His Spirit is standing by, and smiles as the famished beast
Stays for awhile its hunger and shares the long-sought feast

With its famished cubs. Earth quakes with wild surprise
At a deed of such loving-kindness, that even the brazen skies

Tremble, and tears of pity fall on the shriveled earth,
While the Great One passes once more through the throes of
    another birth.

And high in the Nat King's realm speaks the voice of Thagyia-min,
"The day of His coming draws nearer, who shall rescue the world
    from sin;

For another life is sped, and a further milestone passed
On the road to attainment of Buddha, and the final rest at last."[17]

'The Fourfold Way' similarly presented a simple moral and invocation. He asked why did life hold such pain, "sordid strife", grief and sorrow? The answer lay in the Buddhist insight that "Desire entangles all mankind/ If your wish you do not gain / Grief and suffering cloud your mind." The re-nunciation of shallow desires prompted by egotism and petty material wants was the key to a spiritual enlightenment that could bring inner peace. "Desire and Self" were the great adversaries against which a soul in search of peace must struggle; "Lose desire, and all your woes / From your troubled mind shall cease." The last stanza underlined the ethical code that accompanied this insight:

Love all creatures, take the vow,
Think no evil, know that thou

Art nothing, and above thyself sublime
Shalt rise to heights beyond the reach of time.[18]

As poetry the two pieces are fairly unsophisticated, but again we find in them a neat statement of Ward's interests at this time. His anthropological curiosity, shading into a romantic fascination with folklore, historical pageant and curiosities of language and material artefact, is vividly present. His feel for drama and narrative flow is also here, an attachment that could sometimes deteriorate into melodrama and mawkish effects but which, at its best, gave Ward's writings their verve and vigour. The most sincere element, perhaps, is Ward's enthusiastic promotion of an Eastern cosmology, in which he found important correlations with his own clairvoyant insights and the moral and ethical implications of being and transcendence they implied. Importantly, as his reference to "The day of His coming draws nearer, /who shall rescue the world from sin" makes clear, in Ward's mind there was no inconsistency between the transcendental insights of Eastern religion (uncovered, as it were, by his anthropological curiosity) and the essential teachings of Christianity that had been deeply implanted by his upbringing and family background. The oblique introduction of Christian themes – specifically the anticipation of Christ's earthly incarnation – into a Buddhist parable is thus a clue to the larger synthesis of eastern and western systems of belief that Ward attempted later in life. A positioning of the western Christian revelation within the mystical cosmology of Oriental spirituality became essential to Ward's personal faith as his sense of humanity's universal spiritual heritage gradually took shape.

✳ ✳ ✳

Freemasonry provided the other governing passion of Ward's time in Burma. He was admitted to the Rangoon Lodge (No. 1268) on 28 January 1915, and was soon elected its Secretary, the first time he had held such an office. The brethren of the lodge met in their impressive stone-built New Masonic Hall, erected by the Star of Burma Lodge to replace the city's aging teak temple. It was administered by the District Grand Lodge and used by several separate lodges. Ward attended many meetings and installations in this building as his studies in Masonic ritual deepened during 1915.

Freemasonry in colonial Rangoon had been intrinsic to British empire-building since the mid-nineteenth century. Masonic lodges for soldiers, traders and expatriate Englishmen had been active in Burma since 1847, when the Philanthropy Lodge No. 542 was founded at Moulmein under the Provincial Grand Lodge of Bengal, which in turn traced its origins to the 1720s. After the end of the Second Burmese War in 1852, a number of other lodges appeared as English colonial dominion was extended throughout the province: Star of Burma No. 614 (1853), Astraea and Arracan Lodges (c.1855–1856), Victoria in Burma No. 832 (Rangoon, 1860; initially affiliated to the Provincial Grand Lodge of Madras), and the Lodge of the Isles and the Greenlaw Lodge at Toungoo (both constituted 1866).[19] This proliferation of individual lodges resulted in the formation of the District Grand Lodge of Burma in 1868. Ward's Rangoon Lodge No.1268 was constituted shortly afterwards on 31 May 1869 and counted around thirty members by the turn of the century.[20] When Ward joined in 1915, the number is thus likely to have been not much more than fifty.

But with the thrilling intimations of his Cambridge Masonic studies fresh in his memory, Bro. Ward was not simply hoping to network with insular fellows yearning for the nostalgia of home, like so many English Freemasons stranded abroad. On the contrary, he visited as many lodges as possible while living in Burma and on occasional visits to India as a matter of principle.[21] He took his Mark Degree while in Rangoon, and Masonic records indicate he attended the half-yearly meeting of the District Grand Lodge of Burma as a visitor on 28 July 1915.[22]

What was the character of Freemasonry in Burma during Ward's tenure? Its patriotic and imperial character inevitably stiffened during the fiercest fighting of the Great War in faraway Europe. Fraternal bonds among ex-patriate Masons were simultaneously heightened and tested by the peculiar challenges of wartime. Some Burmese lodges struggled to continue as brethren returned for active service in the Middle East or on the Western Front, and those that remained were united in their firm patriotic sentiments. Ward visited one of Rangoon's Scottish lodges on one occasion and was deeply moved by a rendition of *The Flowers of the Forest* sung in honour of the fallen. "Never shall I forget its influence that night", he later wrote,

> so long as I live I shall remember that scene in the Masonic Hall in Rangoon, with the brilliant tropic moon shining through the open windows, and the men at the table seated motionless as death, while the smell of the frangipani changed to the scent of the heather, and the noise of native tom-toms to the skirl of bagpipes on the hills of bonny Scotland.[23]

International hostilities lent a special resonance to each lodge's charitable and fraternal obligations, and the Masonic ideal of universal brotherhood was sorely tested in a world of nationalistic prejudice. It is likely that Ward was listening, for example, when the Deputy District Grand Master for Burma, Wor. Bro. A. Blake, referred in January 1916 to the suspension of relations with German lodges as "a severe test indeed . . . a grand crisis undreamt of in our Masonic lifetime. The three principles we cherish most viz: – Brotherly Love, Relief and Truth have been set at naught." He recognized that Masons had a patriotic duty because with their "love of liberty, freedom and truth we cannot allow nations to domineer[,] forgetting God and ignoring man". Closer to home, each had a solemn duty to the war effort.

> He is a wise man who prophesies even approximately the time when this terrible war shall cease and therefore we cannot tell to what extent our charitable funds may be called upon. But when the end will come there

will be many demands on the Craft for a fuller exemplification of its benevolence than has ever been made. Multitudes of widows, orphans and decrepit Masons will appeal to the helping hand of the Craft and although we are 7,000 miles away yet we shall have to be ready to answer the call when it came.[24]

Alongside the strains of war colonial Freemasonry felt other tensions of race and racial feeling. By this time the District Grand Lodge of Burma counted over a dozen member lodges. Some admitted brethren from diverse ethnic and racial backgrounds, while others remained exclusively white and English. By discouraging (and as a last resort actively excluding) non-white candidates, some lodges were determined to remain that way including Rangoon No. 1268 which, Ward later recalled, "consisted exclusively of white men, except our Tyler who was an elderly Eurasian, and the [Indian] Butler who arranged the dinners".[25] By contrast the Star of Burma Lodge No. 614 "consisted mainly of Jews, Parsees, and Eurasians, though there were a number of Englishmen among them", while the Victoria in Burma Lodge No. 832 was similarly diverse and reportedly had some difficulties of ritual given the diversity of languages spoken there. Such 'cosmopolitan' lodges could be regarded as living exemplars of the Masonic creed of universal fraternity. Although relations between these lodges and those that remained euphemistically 'English' were generally cordial, there were inevitably undercurrents and tensions. Ward noted, for example, that brethren in the mixed-race lodges were "pathetically diffident of exercising their undoubted right to visit the English Lodges. I invited them several times, and on the last occasion on which I visited them the W[orshipful] M[aster] promised that he would return my visit, but he never summoned up the courage to do so".[26]

Cosmopolitanism and the implications of multiracial lodge membership were among the pressing issues of colonial Freemasonry, especially in British India and the Burma of Ward's day. As a fraternal organisation, Freemasonry had its most obvious utility in binding together expatriate British across the globe as they soldiered, traded, and organised the territories and outposts of Empire. But Freemasonry itself, Jessica Harland-Jacobs argues, was transformed by this history. Its ideology of cosmopolitan fraternity opened up opportunities whereby subject peoples (indigenous Burmese, Indians, Parsees, men of diverse backgrounds and mixed racial heritage) might contest imperial authority, quite simply by applying to join the exclusive, all-white masculine enclave of the Masonic lodge and invoking the egalitarian notion of universal brotherhood in doing so.[27] At the peak of British imperial influence, from the early nineteenth century until after the First World War, it seems Freemasons imagined the Craft and its lodges as a globe-spanning family, united by kinship but with significant internal divisions. The rhetoric of a Masonic 'family' – its brotherly lodges comprising a unified whole but with distinct grades and echelons – was a response to these tensions of race and ethnicity. The United Grand Lodge in London repeatedly declared that admission policies which discriminated on the basis of skin colour or creed were contrary to Masonry's fraternal doctrine. Locally, of course, passions ran much stronger and often in the opposite direction. Racial prejudice was a reality of colonial life, and was a recurring problem for Masonic administration as debate raged over the admission of former slaves in North America and the West Indies, and Hindus and Eurasians in British India. In simple terms, some lodges preferred to remain exclusively white enclaves while others demonstrated the principles of universal brotherhood in practice. After the admission in 1872 of Prosonno Coomar Dutt, the first Hindu to obtain membership of an English lodge in Bengal, a new phase of Freemasonry opened in British India, "in which it was not unusual to see multiracial lodges and widespread admission of indigenous candidates, regardless of their religion". In keeping with the kinship metaphors of brotherhood and family, Harland-Jacobs argues, the Indians that followed Dutt into the Craft were often patronized as 'younger brothers', new to the ways and means of civilization on the European model, who might learn through lodge membership the habits and values of a civilized citizenry.[28]

When a deputation of the United Grand Lodge of England led by Lord Cornwallis visited the Indian dominions and Burma in 1927–28, some twelve years after Ward had returned to England, the members agreed that the extent of inter-racial fraternity they observed there was quite remarkable. The deputation reported that Masonic brotherhood was a living reality on the sub-continent, that the

> most impressive feature, par excellence . . . was the assembly in Lodge of Brethren of varying Nationalities, men of culture and distinction, working in amicable rivalry to render as perfectly as possible our beautiful Ritual. We have seen as many as five volumes of the Sacred Law in use at one & the same time, & Brethren of the following among other Races, taken at random – Europeans, Parsis, Chinese, Burmese, Hindus, Americans, Mohammedans, Sikhs, Armenians, Greeks, Bengalis, Jews, Arocanese, Ceylonese, Punjabis, Madrassis, etc., participating in the Ceremonies. The brotherhood of Man, under such circumstances, becomes a living reality.[29]

John Ward took a similarly progressive stance on native admissions and multiracial lodges. In fact at a basic level he claimed his own identity as a product of the cosmopolitan tendencies of Empire. "I can claim to be peculiarly fitted to marshal the arguments [about racial differences] on both sides as fairly as possible", he wrote, "for I was born of white parents in the West Indies, and drew my infant nurture from a 'coloured nurse'; subsequently I have lived in India, and actually took my Mark Degree in a lodge which included coloured Brothers".[30] With this background his views on the question of racial difference in Freemasonry were clear and consistent. He objected, for example, to the exclusion from European lodges of Indians, Chinese and Malays purely on the basis of colour, as, speaking for himself, their alternative cultural traditions provided one key to Freemasonry's complexity. "I freely acknowledge", he wrote in one of his early studies of Masonic tradition, "that Hindoo philosophy has helped me to unravel numerous difficult problems in Freemasonry, and I should be sorry to have to say that such men should be excluded simply because they are darker in colour than I am".[31] His endorsement of a common fraternity that transcended racial difference was strongly held, but on the other hand he respected the principle of Masonic fraternal solidarity enough not to impose such views on others or to pass judgment on their decisions when taken together as a lodge.

His wider views on race were more ambivalent. On one hand, he regarded overt racial prejudice with a vehement distaste. His account of one incident, albeit written thirty years later, makes this abundantly clear. In Ward's account, he had been approached by various Anglo-Indians in Rangoon during 1915 who were concerned about the stalemate that had arisen in the trenches of France and Flanders. Many were keen to contribute to the fighting forces by voluntary enlistment. At their prompting, Ward recalled, "I went to the military authorities and suggested we could raise a battalion at least among the Eurasians, who had come to me anxious to fight for the King-Emperor. The military were not very enthusiastic but agreed I might send a telegram to the War Office making the offer." The telegram was drawn up after further discussion with Ward's circle of patriotic colonials and dispatched.

> It said that the Anglo-Indian community (Eurasians) were most anxious to volunteer for service anywhere could arrangements be made for them to be recruited. I never got any direct reply although it was addressed to Kitchener, the Minister for War, but it was soon all over Rangoon that Kitchener had cabled, not even in code, to the Lieut. Governor: 'No half-breeds wanted.' As the Post Office was mainly staffed by Eurasians the insulting message was soon all over Rangoon and they were not unnaturally, very bitter.[32]

Ward was privately advised by the editor of a Rangoon newspaper to drop the idea entirely. He did so, but brooded on the incident for years after. Apart from the callous indifference of the official response, the crudely racist terms in which it was worded seemed arrogant and short-sighted in the Empire's hour of need.

But on the other hand, like many of his time Ward invoked racial categories in a way that is jarring to the modern ear. He candidly expressed views, for example, that drew upon the science of evolution to suggest that human diversity – cultural, social and ethnic, usually configured at this time through the notion of race and its labels – could be understood in basically hierarchical terms. "I don't believe all men are equal", he stated baldly, "and to pretend that a man whose grandparents were fetish worshippers in West Africa is the equal of the white man whose ancestors for thirty generations have been worshipping God under one of the most evolved conceptions we have of Him, is humbug".[33] His point of distinction was grounded in an evolutionary and comparative understanding of human civilizations. Far from the crude biology of populist Social Darwinism, Ward's sense of human difference tallied with his appreciation of the relative merits of the great civilizations, each of them borne on the great cyclical tide of human historical evolution. He numbered China, Japan and the civilizations of the Indian sub-continent among the "old Asiatic nations", that were "civilized peoples while we were still savages".[34] For this reason he had no objection to Masonic cosmopolitanism in British India and the Far East, because "among the higher types in Asia [there] are many worthy candidates, and though I consider more care should be exercised here than is necessary in England, yet I feel that we are justified in extending the hand of Brotherhood to suitable candidates, despite the fact that they may be, say, Chinese Buddhists". He nevertheless insisted —with a conviction that never wavered — that the conception of the Divine configured in the Christian revelation of western civilization was innately superior (because fuller and more sophisticated) to that of any preceding or rival civilization. In this respect, Freemasonry had an important role. Rather than excluding others outright, he suggested, "perhaps the right method is to prove to [them] that our civilization is the best, and that we can do so in Freemasonry".[35]

Thus the magnanimity of cosmopolitan Freemasonry had fixed limits in Ward's mind. Innate equality was a delusion, he insisted, because human cultures and civilizations could only be understood as a hierarchy that stretched up from the crude beliefs of primitive peoples to the sophisticated cosmologies of the great world civilizations. The benefit of mixed-race lodges was entirely due to their progressive character as Freemasonry sought to "humanise, civilise and fraternise mankind" (as the *Masonic Herald* in India put it in 1871) by the example set by its most advanced brethren.[36] Beyond this, there were limits that could only be explained in bluntly racial terms. The immediate descendents of 'primitive' African peoples should, Ward argued, be firmly excluded from Freemasonry: "Frankly, I fear that the indiscriminate admission of negroes would lower the standard of Masonry, and my object in life is to raise it, not lower it." His conclusion, then, was that although I dislike closing the doors of Freemasonry to any race, I do feel that there are certain races who are not yet sufficiently evolved intellectually, morally, and even spiritually to be suitable for admission: of these the Negro is the most obvious example.[37]

Despite his decision not to take up his primary membership in a cosmopolitan lodge, he found "much to interest me in them, and much worthy of praise".[38] But their sincere evocation of fellowship and fraternity was only one aspect of the cosmopolitan lodges that he felt worthy of acclaim. The regular gathering of men of so many faiths and creeds in the common working of Masonic ritual was, for Ward at least, a compelling and deeply significant spectacle. He found the multiracial Star of Burma Lodge, for example, where he took his Mark Master Degree, "most interesting, a Lodge in which practically every race in Burma was represented".

> The W[orshipful] Master was a Eurasian, the S[enior] Warden a Hindoo and a worshipper of Shiva, the Destroyer. The Junior Warden was a Hindoo and worshipper of Vishnu. The Secretary was a Mahomedan, the P[ast] M[aster] a Burmese, the Treasurer a Chinaman, the Senior Deacon an Armenian, the Junior Deacon an Eastern Jew, the Inner Guard a Parsee, and so on.[39]

Such a community of mixed belief was certainly a living testimony to the fraternal potential of Freemasonry. But for Ward it had a deeper significance. As his conviction grew that Freemasonry was a direct survival of an ancient belief system that underpinned all the major religions, he was encouraged in this view by the fact that followers of such diverse religious traditions could find common cause in the Craft, its symbolism and ritual. The assembly of diverse faiths – the adherents of so many differing deities, gospels, traditions and creeds – within the fraternal embrace of Freemasonry seemed a profound revelation to the young Masonic scholar.

✳ ✳ ✳

Ward savoured life in Rangoon. But amid this activity, with its rich texture of intellectual curiosity and spiritual exploration, he suffered persistently from debilitating and chronic diarhorrea, and no amount of medical opinion, dietary changes or cures were effective. Eventually he was diagnosed with sprue, "a kind of consumption of the bowels", he later described it, "in which the inner membrane gradually flakes off." This was later questioned by doctors, but not before Ward had regretfully handed his resignation to the diocese and prepared his family for a return to England. The Bishop agreed he "must leave Burma and go home before it got a firm grip on me",

Ward remembered thirty years later. On Christmas Day, 1915, he left the Diocesan Boys School for the last time. He sold his horse and gharry at a tidy profit, and packed his antiquities, books and souvenirs away for the passage. With some trepidation the Wards joined eight other passengers on a steamer loaded with a precious cargo of cotton for England, departing in early January. German submarines had wreaked havoc with Allied shipping, but the vessel safely re-traced their outward journey through the Suez Canal, across the Mediterranean and into a stormy Bay of Biscay. "We passed lots of wreckage", he recalled, "but saw no sign of an enemy."[40]

4

Gone West

Ward and his family disembarked at Liverpool in February 1916, and joined his parents in London at the St Mary's vicarage, Charing Cross Road. With the Great War approaching its destructive climax, hundreds of thousands of British civilians were signing up for military service and 'Kitchener's Army', the first mass civilian infantry in British history, was equipping for the carnage of the Western Front. Ward's brother Rex had volunteered, and was now a second lieutenant with the York and Lancaster Regiment in the trenches at Poperinge near Ypres. Sharing the mood of popular patriotism, Ward volunteered soon after arrival but was rejected as a recruit due to his poor physique and bad eyesight.

He returned to teaching, but the war was never far away. With Carrie and Blanche staying with friends in the country he accepted a position as private tutor to the son of a landed family near Falmouth in Devon. In his memoirs he tactfully omitted the family's full name and circumstances, recording only that 'The Colonel' was serving in France, and that his son John was a spoiled and difficult pupil. Doted on by his mother (identified only as 'Mrs G.'), young John was absent-minded and stubborn, and seemed careless about his admission prospects for the Royal Naval College. Ward could do little to enthuse him in his studies, but had more influence on his pupil's recreation time. "I found John had nothing to do outside lessons", he later recalled, "so I got him enthusiastic on building a 'Robinson Crusoe Hut'. This he thoroughly enjoyed although he somewhat spoilt the primitive atmosphere by insisting on installing electric light worked by batteries!"[1]

A spontaneous shopping trip to London with John and his mother in April 1916 gave Ward a chance to spend an evening with his parents. On the train down from Devon, he remarked to John's mother that he had dreamed vividly the night before he was standing on the deck of a ship that was burning furiously. An Irishwoman, 'Mrs G.' was well versed in dream lore and the symbolism of fire, and told him solemnly that he should be prepared for news of a death.

So perhaps it was with some foreboding that Ward approached his parents' house in Charing Cross Road. A charwoman opened the door, and told him his father had stepped out with the housekeeper. Ward climbed the stairs to wait in the drawing room on the second floor, and was surprised when after a moment the servant followed him. There was an awkward pause, until she broke the silence to say there was news of Rex.

> My heart almost stopped as I said, 'Is he wounded?' She replied, 'He's dead, sir.' (So my 'fire dream' was alas significant.)
>
> The shock completely unnerved me. I had never thought of the possibility of his being killed and I broke down completely. Later, my father came in. He had been for a long walk to try and pull himself together. He told me Rex had been killed on Good Friday April 7th 1916 when the German troops overran the trenches near Popperinge [sic] and the English troops had recaptured the trenches on Easter Day (April 9th) and recovered his body. How I got through the next few days I don't know.[2]

Rex's death was a crushing blow to the family. His mother, feeble and bedridden by the after-affects of several small strokes, was never told. She died that September unaware that her younger son had been killed five months earlier.

For her surviving son, however, Rex's death revealed "a new link with the 'Unseen World' which is all around us".[3] On April 29, Herbert Ward celebrated a requiem service for Rex in the chapel at St Mary's, placing his son's ceremonial sword on the altar behind the main crucifix. It was a moment of quiet grief and sombre reflection. That evening, as John Ward rested in the spare bedroom, he slipped into a state of trance. He later wrote down the intense vision he then experienced:

> Dark mists rolling by. Flashes of fire. In the distance a continuous roar as of the thunder of many guns. Hosts of spirits rushing to and fro. Chaos and gloom. Then I found Rex. He was seated on a bank by the roadside, clad in his uniform, but though I could see his face distinctly, yet his figure seemed rather indistinct.
>
> He was delighted to see me, and said, 'I have waited long for you.'
>
> 'How did you die?' I asked.
>
> 'I do not know,' he replied; 'everything seemed to be in a nightmarish state. There seemed to be a blank, and then I went on again, and it was not for some time that I realised that I was among unfamiliar surroundings. Even now I can't arrange things at all in any order, they seem jumbled up together.'[4]

❋   ❋   ❋

After nearly two years of ferocious trench warfare Britain was a nation of bereaved, a fact of demography that might alone explain the striking revival of popular spiritualism by 1917. Séances and spiritualist meetings swelled as "thousands of persons who had lost relations and friends . . . were attracted by the promise of a message from the departed".[5] The desire for spirit contact inflated the number of fraudulent mediums – one press exposé called them 'harpies of humanity' – and their cynical trade to exploit the grief of parents, wives and loved ones. In the longer term, the fact that newspapers and the courts rarely distinguished, as Nelson comments, "between the genuine and the fraudulent medium, between the 'spiritualist', who produced fake psychic phenomena solely for money and the Spiritualists, for whom phenomena were only an aspect of philosophy and religion",[6] served to confuse the evidence and encouraged the idea that all psychic manifestations were fakes or delusions. But despite a campaign waged in sermons and press opinion against the Spiritualist churches and fraudulent mediums alike, a wave of national grief carried the spiritualist message of survival and the possibility of communication with the 'Other Side' to willing and ever-larger audiences.

These developments were part of a powerful psychological and spiritual dislocation that, historians argue, was sharply manifested in European culture through the convulsions of the Great War. The daily horror of the Western Front, as young men were slaughtered in the mud like cattle, was a grotesque, deeply unsettling prospect. Rapid-fire machine guns, high explosive artillery, poisonous gas, barbed wire and armoured vehicles wrought a dreadful toll as industrial technology de-humanised the battlefield. The catastrophe shattered the complacency and confidence the generations of 1914 had inherited from the expansive, assertive nineteenth century. For historians like Modris Eksteins, 1914–1918 witnessed a clash of cultures as German militarism and the spirit of the modernist *avant-garde* marched arm in arm against the settled social, moral and aesthetic orderliness of the pre-war world. The way of life that had enshrined Victorian and Edwardian values was under assault, and all its naïve security – its faith in social and technological progress, free trade, Empire, institutionalised religion, bourgeois respectability and so on – seemed put to the sword.

The awful logic of the carnage in the trenches even shook confidence in the basic necessity of rational conduct. "Reality, a sense of proportion, and reason – these were the major casualties of the war", observes Eksteins.[7] Sir Arthur Conan Doyle, whose creation Sherlock Holmes had embodied such pre-war attributes, announced his conversion to spiritualism during the war after several decades of interest in the subject. His rationally-minded generation, he suggested, had felt a profound change of heart as the facts of modern warfare sank in; "when the War came it brought earnestness into all our souls and made us look more closely at our own beliefs and reassess their values", Conan Doyle later wrote. Men and women that previously had been blasé about reports of psychic phenomena were now seized by their profound significance.

In the presence of an agonized world, hearing every day the deaths of the flower of our race in the first promise of their unfulfilled youth, seeing around one the wives and mothers who had no clear conception whither their loved ones had gone to, I seemed suddenly to see that this subject [i.e. spiritualism] with which I had so long dallied was not merely a study of force outside the rules of science, but that it was something really tremendous, a breaking down of the walls between two worlds, a direct undeniable message from beyond, a call of hope and of guidance to the human race at the time of its deepest affliction.[8]

With the publication of his two books of spirit messages he had received clairvoyantly, John Ward's voice joined this "call of hope and guidance" amid the clamour of wartime distress and anxiety. Both appeared in print as popular demand in Britain for spiritualist revelations reached a new peak. The two books document how, as his trance visions and lucid dreams became a strangely commonplace part of his daily life and weekly routine, Ward came to accept his communications with these and other departed spirits as a natural consequence of the metaphysical reality of the afterlife. He became – like Conan Doyle and countless others – a convinced spiritualist. "And, after all," he asked his readers, "is the picture of life beyond the grave so unnatural? For my part I consider it absolutely rational and reasonable, and on its own account much more intrinsically probable than the misty and unconvincing stories of Heaven and Hell on which our early years were nurtured."[9]

The first, *Gone West: Three Narratives of After-Death Experiences*, appeared in autumn 1917; a reprint was issued by William Rider and Son a year later followed by another in the spring of 1920. Here Ward recounted the psychic dialogue he professed to have had with Henry Lanchester ('HJL' in Ward's text) and other departed spirits between January and September 1914. The testimony thus received explained the metaphysical arrangements of the afterlife and its various levels and planes in painstaking detail. HJL's life on the spirit plane, Ward explained to his readers, had commenced in the company of a 'set' of people who had been much like himself prior to their mortal deaths, with a similarly secular outlook and a general insouciance on religious matters. HJL equated it to the idea of Purgatory, except that "it's more a place of learning than of punishment", where the spirits of his 'set' gathered to learn from a higher being. These teachers were "somewhat like the angels of the parsons, but . . . don't look a bit like the silly pictures you usually see. This teacher instructs us in what we are lacking, and when that lack has been made good, we move on to the next set, which includes many more different people than our own".[10] As HJL learnt more of his surroundings, therefore, he relayed the information gained to his psychically receptive son-in-law. His knowledge was necessarily fragmentary and grew only gradually, because his teachers only explained problems that were within his comprehension. "If you were teaching a boy Euclid", he explained to Ward at one point, "and he suddenly asked you a question about some event in history, would you not tell him to wait until the history lesson came? Well, it's the same here. There is so much to learn that I must wait till I come to each thing in its proper place."[11] As his understanding and range of acquaintances grew, HJL augmented his testimony with accounts from other spirits willing to communicate their knowledge of aspects of the spirit plane that were unknown to him.

Ward's second spiritualist book elaborated further on all this. After the death of his brother in April 1916 he was able to establish a regular contact with 'RLW', as he identified Rex's spirit in his text. Their encounters focussed Ward's attention on RLW's situation in the disturbed conditions of the 'astral plane', the threshold region that lay between material reality and the higher spirit planes (such as HJL's purgatorial sphere) beyond. "Since the death of my brother in the trenches of Flanders", he explained, "I have devoted most of my attention to conditions on that Plane, and especially to the spirits of those who have died in battle. Their state is somewhat abnormal, and indeed, the whole Astral Plane is greatly disturbed."[12] *A Subaltern in Spirit Land*, described as a sequel to *Gone West*, was published in 1919, and reprinted the following year.

For all their idiosyncrasies, Ward's clairvoyant accounts should not be considered in isolation. The discussion that follows considers them as part of the popular revival and transformation of the spiritualist message that, as J.M. Winter observes, worked during the darkest days of the Great War to bridge the gulf between civilian normality and the mortal carnage of the trenches. Soldiers held strong superstitions and told ghost stories, and seemed comfortable with ideas of religious or supernatural agency that gave rise to stories like that of the Angel of Mons. "The reversion to pagan or prerational modes of thought under the appalling stress of combat should surprise no one", Winter comments. Likewise, on the home front stories of ghostly visitations, séance meetings with fallen soldiers, spirit photography and other psychic communications had powerful psychological traction. Interest in the afterlife deepened, Winter suggests, because it was "inevitably and inextricably tied up with the need expressed by many to communicate with the fallen."[13] Ward understood this implicitly. "Having myself suffered such a loss by the death within the same year of three close relations", he explained in his introduction to *A Subaltern in Spirit Land*, "I can realise how terribly many another has suffered during these last five years. I have had an advantage denied to most of my readers," he went on,

> that of being able to go out there and commune face to face with those who have passed over. Yet, despite this, I feel most bitterly their loss. How

much more, then, those who cannot do so! In giving this narrative to the general public, I have been actuated by the desire to bring comfort to others in a similar position of loss. I knew that the Dead die not, long before my brother died, but of the manner in which they live I knew only a little.[14]

Winter recognised a widespread and fervent desire to reach out to the fallen, to clasp the memory of the dead in a "spiritualist embrace" that might assuage crippling emotions of loss and grief. The literature of popular spiritualism, he suggests, was part of an invigorated language of transcendence "linking front and home front in a kind of spiritualist embrace".[15] Among other things, this embrace might provide a re-assurance that the war and the sacrifices it entailed were not ultimately meaningless. "We died that Justice, Truth, and Liberty might live", RLW stated emphatically in one communication. "We died, at least I died, that England might be free. For these things we died, and, having died, we live. This is our great reward, and nothing ye earth folk can do can take it from us."[16] Ward, a lifelong imperialist and British patriot, welcomed this kind of consolation. His brother had died, he wrote in dedicating *Gone West*, "for love of his native land in battle against a horde". Likewise, British soldiers of "every rank and creed" had given their all "in the cause of justice, honour and truth/Against the powers of evil that know nor pity nor ruth".[17] *A Subaltern in Spirit Land* was similarly dedicated:

> In the name of the dead, undying,
> Of the corpses silent lying
> Mid the thunderous battle's roar,
> In the name of the mother who bore me,
> And the brother who passed before me,
> I open the guarded door.

Confirmation that the war was being fought in a cause of high principle answered a basic psychological need among those left behind that the immense sacrifices involved were ultimately not in vain.

Historians like Winter interested in the social and cultural implications of the Great War examine such stories of clairvoyant contact with the dead as evidence of psychological distress. They register such experiences as a function of the inner, emotional life of people in a state of chronic anguish and examine them as a historically and culturally conditioned mechanism that served to obviate their pain. It is generally not their business to consider the deeper issue: whether these ineffable experiences were purely internal ones, or whether they were, in any sense, an irruption of some external agency. The difficulty for the biographer, of course, is that Ward firmly maintained his experiences were actually the result of deliberate actions of disembodied spirits of the dead. Thus this issue cannot very well be avoided in the present discussion, since the veracity or otherwise of his psychic experiences goes to the heart of John Ward's moral character. Was Ward simply a fraud, inventing these episodes for his own duplicitous reasons? More subtly, was he deluding himself in his desire to contact the deceased, and credulous enough to interpret normal dreams as something mystical and revelatory? Or was he responding to some anomalous and genuinely external stimulus, and doing his best to interpret and explain a highly unusual experience?

The evidence available to us simply does not shed light on these critical questions. Some were addressed obliquely in the introduction to *Gone West*, however, where Ward explained his conviction that the testimony he had received was genuine according to the principles of clairvoyance. He considered his visions to be external intrusions on his psychic being, rather than psychosomatic manifestations of his inner mental life, for several reasons. Firstly, the dream visions that had commenced so unexpectedly were remarkably lucid, coherent and persuasive. Unlike ordinary dreams, he wrote, "these visions were real through and through, coherent and logical in their development, and moreover, took up the narrative where it left off the week before". He was also struck by the fact that his visions "remained firmly impressed upon my mind until they were written down, which sometimes took a couple of days. Once they were written down they would tend to merge into the general body of remembrances which every mortal carries in his brain". Beyond that, Ward was convinced that he was not consciously (or, as far as he was aware, subconsciously) pre-disposed to irrational claims about the hidden dimensions of cosmic reality. He insisted that much of the information he gained by his involuntary dreams "was in violent opposition to my preconceived ideas on the subject, and it was some time before I would accept them, though I do so now entirely".[18] It all condensed into a conclusion that Ward, at least, found incontestable: external agents, that he identified as departed spirits known to him as members of his own family, had contacted him with the express purpose of communicating important spiritual knowledge. He dismissed the possibility that he had imagined or fantasised the communications based on subjective or subconscious desires. "With regard to the subconscious self", he concluded his self-defence,

> I would like to take this opportunity of protesting that while I am prepared to admit that such a thing does exist, I nevertheless hold that in most cases the word is a bogey set up by scientists to explain phenomena which they are unable to explain by the ordinary material laws, and which they are unwilling to ascribe to spirit influences. Yet, accepting the subconscious self at its highest valuation, it will not explain the presence of information

which was quite unknown to me, and which on its being investigated by others, proved to be correct.[19]

By the time he mounted a similar defence in *A Subaltern in Spirit Land*, Ward was prepared to address the sceptics of his day more directly. He had moved to a more evangelical posture as his spiritualist convictions grew ever stronger:

> Those of us who are endeavouring to spread the true knowledge of life beyond the grave, are doing so in the face of opposition alike from the ordinary man of the world and of the ministers of established religions. Sometimes we are laughed at, whilst at other times we are called necromancers. Some of our opponents even go so far as to hint that we are not quite sane, but this has always been the way in which new truths are received at first. Nevertheless, it may be of interest to my readers to know that I am a perfectly normal man – one who is earning his living in business, and who has every day to deal with complex mundane matters.[20]

The spirit encounters Ward described in his two books on the subject shared virtually all the themes that characterise the literature of wartime spiritualism. They agreed with the testimony, for example, of Sir Oliver Lodge's *Raymond, or Life and Death* (1916) and Conan Doyle's *The New Revelation* (1918) and *The Vital Message* (1919). Given the stature of their authors and their urgent, persuasive tone these particular books were highly influential presentations of the spiritualist case to the reading public during the Great War.

Lodge and Conan Doyle, just like Ward, presented in a very direct and personal way the basis for their conversion to the spiritualist view. Neither author, however, claimed to be mediumistic and had not personally received psychic messages as Ward believed he had. Both made contact with departed spirits under séance conditions, where messages were often fragmentary or inconclusive and, initially at least, not very convincing. Both had better success contacting departed spirits in repeated sessions with clairvoyant mediums. This involved a complicated series of exchanges, as the 'sitter' spoke with a medium in contact with a 'control', a disembodied spirit on the 'Other Side', who in turn transmitted personal messages to and from the spirit with whom the sitter was seeking contact. This arrangement was imagined as a psychic telegraph, with two operators (the medium and her control) in direct touch with each other 'down the line' and using that connection to relay messages between two other parties unable to establish a similar direct contact. Occasionally the departed spirit might communicate with the medium directly, but this led to confusion that might be minimised through the use of a control. Believers were convinced it worked, but few spiritualists claimed to understand fully the processes involved. "The question of mediumship", Conan Doyle commented, "what it is and how it acts, is one of the most mysterious in the whole range of science."

> It is a common objection to say that if our dead are there why should we only hear of them through people by no means remarkable for moral or mental gifts, who are often paid for their ministration. It is a plausible argument, and yet when we receive a telegram from a brother in Australia we do not say: 'It is strange that Tom should not communicate with me direct, but that the presence of that half-educated fellow in the telegraph office should be necessary.' The medium is in truth a mere passive machine, clerk and telegraph in one. Nothing comes from him. Every message is through him.[21]

Under these convoluted arrangements it is not surprising that sceptics often attempted many sittings and remained unconvinced. After an active interest in the spiritualist cause that dated back to the 1880s, Conan Doyle was only fully convinced of their claims around 1916, and could thus fairly claim "that I have not been hasty in forming my opinion".[22] At that time, he had been impressed by the psychic abilities of Lily Loder-Symonds, a close friend of his wife bedridden with a respiratory condition. Although many messages proved inaccurate, a significant number demanded attention, including striking messages from her brothers killed on the Western Front in 1915, produced by automatic writing. Later, Conan Doyle famously received communications from his deceased son Kingsley who had been injured on the Somme and subsequently died of pneumonia, and also believed he had contacted his brother Innes through a medium. Sir Oliver Lodge, on the other hand, was an eminent physicist, a pioneer of electro-magnetic theory, x-rays and radio-telegraphy. He was fascinated by evidence of telepathy, joined the Society for Psychical Research and, by the time he published *The Survival of Man* in 1909, was a convinced 'survivalist'. After the death of his son Raymond near Ypres in September 1915 Lodge used professional mediums and séances to seek out Raymond's departed spirit. Ever the empirical scientist, he carefully assembled records of the various attempts made and published them in November 1916, together with a touching personal memoir of Raymond's life. He concluded the volume with his own reflections on the significance of the evidence thus presented in two essays, 'Outlook on the Universe' and 'The Christian Idea of God.' *Raymond, or Life and Death* was a runaway success, reprinted a dozen times before the end of 1919 and re-issued in an abridged edition in 1922.[23]

Each of these famous men encapsulated an aspect of spiritualism's appeal to the wartime generations. Conan Doyle represented a romantic yearning for communion and belief, a 'new revelation', while Lodge – an eminent scientist, and president of over ten learned associations – exemplified an inquiring rationalism that was careful with the evidence and wary of extravagant claims.[24] But both accepted the evidence of survival and contact whole-heartedly, and, as we will see, shared Ward's view that the insights gained by clairvoyant contact should be used to grasp the metaphysics entailed by the survival of the human personality after death. In other words, all three characterised the effort of the wartime spiritualists to grasp the religious implications of spirit testimony. Conan Doyle was happy for fellow-researchers to treat psychical inquiry as a purely scientific exercise. "But the results of psychical research", he insisted, "the deductions which we may draw, and the lessons we may learn, teach us of the continued life of the soul, of the nature of that life, and of how it is influenced by our conduct here. If this is distinct from religion, I must confess that I do not understand the distinction. To me it *is* religion – the very essence of it."[25]

✴   ✴   ✴

Sir Oliver Lodge put the fundamental principle of Modern Spiritualism well: "I have made no secret of my conviction", he wrote in commencing the reflective section of *Raymond*, "not merely that personality persists, but that its continued existence is more entwined with the life of every day than has generally been imagined; that there is no real breach of continuity between the dead and the living; and that methods of intercommunion across what has seemed to be a gulf can be set going in response to the urgent demand of affection . . . ".[26] A comparison of other essential elements in the spiritualist outlook of this period helps draw out the common basis of this 'New Revelation', as Conan Doyle called it. Ward's testimony, it becomes clear, belongs firmly in its mainstream.

At a very fundamental level, the essential continuity of a human life was understood by spiritualists as exactly that. Conan Doyle, for example, described the disembodied spirit as "simply the person himself, containing all his strength and weakness, his wisdom and folly, exactly as he has retained his personal appearance".[27] At one sitting Lodge asked whether Raymond wanted to say anything about his body or circumstances. The answer was very direct: "Oh yes. He is bursting to tell you."

> He says, [said the 'control' Feda, speaking through the medium, Mrs Leonard] my body's very similar to the one I had before. I pinch myself sometimes to see if it's real, and it is, but it doesn't seem to hurt as much as when I pinched the flesh body. The internal organs don't seem constituted on the same lines as before. They can't be quite the same. But to all appearances, and outwardly, they are the same as before. I can move somewhat more freely, he says.[28]

Ward's first dream encounter with HJL occurred a week after his uncle's death, and four days after Ward had gazed upon his body in the coffin. "I dreamt I saw Uncle like, and yet unlike, he was before he died"; Ward recorded, "something between what he looked like before and what he looked like after death".[29] Similarly, his visions of Rex presented his brother clad in uniform: "I could see his face distinctly, yet his figure seemed rather indistinct."[30] Thereafter he treats each of his informants as a literal figure of the living person, conversing with them and moving about in a psychic landscape that corresponds visually and spatially to the familiar world of everyday experience.

Such continuity and correspondence arose, the spiritualists believed, because matter and spirit entwined with each other in ways that could only be dimly understood. The human personality, with all its moral and intellectual attributes, was conceived as an autonomous soul, temporarily vested in a bodily vehicle in order to function in the material sphere. "The physical basis of all psychic belief", Conan Doyle explained, "is that the soul is a complete duplicate of the body, resembling it in the smallest particular, although constructed in some far more tenuous material."[31] To this extent he, Ward and the rest of the modern spiritualists agreed with the essential dualism found in religious belief systems the world over. Conan Doyle pointed to evidence ranging from formal psychical research to anecdotal testimony "which vouches for the existence of this finer body containing the precious jewels of the mind and spirit, and leaving only gross confused animal functions in its heavier companion".[32] Sir Oliver Lodge, ever the cautious scientist, hypothesized a tentative theory of the 'ether', "the common factor of the material and spiritual worlds",[33] to speculate that "in order to become apparent to us, a psychical or vital entity must enter the material realm, and either clothe itself with, or temporarily assimilate, material particles".

> It may be that etherial bodies do not exist; the burden of proof rests upon those who conceive of their possible existence; but we are bound to admit that even if they did exist, they would make no impression on our senses. Hence if there are any intelligences in another order of existence interlocked with ours, and if they can in any sense be supposed to have bodies at all, those bodies must be made either of Ether or of something equally intangible to us in our present condition. [34]

This stance was appropriate for a prominent scientist committed to scrupulous reasoning on the basis of evidence. John Ward, on the other hand, was an obscure history teacher with no need to equivocate. He considered his experiences and the testimony he had received to be utterly compelling, and thus presented his conclusions in *Gone West* and its sequel without reservation. In his view, the inner spiritual being of the human individual had two parts: an ethereal, 'astral' form that itself held the true individual soul. Each human individual was like a three-part Russian *babushka* doll, their visible outer body containing an astral form which was itself a receptacle for the true, enduring soul. During bodily death, Ward maintained, the astral body (containing the inner soul, like a bird in a ghostly cage) leaves the physical body to continue its existence on the astral plane. In time, it endures a 'second death' as the pure, intrinsic soul sheds its ethereal form and passes beyond the astral plane to arrive at one of four 'levels' or 'realms' in the higher planes of pure disembodied spirit.

Under normal circumstances the first or bodily death was a natural and peaceful transition. Conan Doyle gave the general picture: "the departed all agree that passing is usually both easy and painless, and followed by an enormous reaction of peace and ease. The individual finds himself in a spirit body, which is the exact counterpart of his old one, save that all disease, weakness, or deformity has passed from it. This body is standing or floating beside the old body, and conscious both of it and of the surrounding people."[35] The account Ward received from his deceased uncle echoed this in its essential elements. After becoming unconscious, HJL reported to Ward that he then had the sensation of recovering and becoming aware of a heavy weight. "Gradually I realised that this weight was slipping away from me, or rather, I was sliding out from it, as if someone was drawing his hand out from a wet glove. Then I began to feel free at one end, so to speak, and then I began to see again." With a gathering elation HJL looked down on his material body:

> Then I was free! free! I saw myself lying stretched out on the bed, and from my mouth came, as it were, a cord of light. It vibrated for a moment, then snapped, and from my mouth came away. At that moment someone said 'I think he has gone'. Or if they did not say it, they thought it. Then I realised what I looked like for the first time. How different from what I had always seen in my looking-glass![36]

After experiencing pangs of intense cold, "an icy blast piercing me as no earthly wind ever did or can . . . I was a naked soul, no body, nothing to give me warmth", HJL's surroundings dissolved away and he gradually became aware of a new landscape of the afterlife.

A more jarring account was provided to Ward by the departed spirit of his brother Rex. RLW reported that his bodily death was a ghastly transition, wracked with violence, confusion and an awful psychic disturbance. At the moment of his death, under heavy attack in his trench, RLW felt a jolting blow, and then the sensation of falling. "I found myself in utter darkness, and my first thought was that the dug-out had been blown in and I was entombed alive." But after moving about, dazed and uncertain, he was alerted by the sound of approaching voices, until "the tide of battle rolled up and engulfed me . . . A Boche drove his bayonet into my chest, and I felt the pain for a moment, but still went on fighting, and forgot all about it."

> Amid this ceaseless strife I heard, far off, the words of the burial service, and the sound of spades digging, digging, digging. But it had no meaning for me. Only I knew I was dreadfully weary of the ceaseless struggle which seemed to lead nowhere, which appeared to have no result, and I longed to shake off the dazed sensation which made everything appear unreal.
>
> At last I cried to a Boche, 'Why the devil don't you die? I've shot you dead three times!' And he laughed, and though he spoke in German, I know, yet I understood his words as if they had been in English. 'You fool! How can I? Don't you realise that we are all dead here?' . . . He sprang towards me and drove his bayonet clean through my body. 'If you're alive, why don't you die now?' he asked, and I knew he spoke the truth.[37]

Another theme common to the spiritualist literature was that the departing spirit 'passed over' in the company of other disembodied spirits, and on entering the afterlife was quickly joined by kindred spirits of various kinds. Raymond described it as "like finding yourself in a strange place, like a strange city; with people you hadn't seen, or not seen for a long time, round you. Grandfather was with me straight away", he explained to his father, "and presently Robert. I got mixed up between two Roberts".[38] Observing his own funeral service, RLW became aware of other spirits around him. "I saw the service, you and father", he told Ward, "and the people in the church, and also a great crowd of spirit forms, many of them very beautiful, and as if made of light. Strangely enough, the idea that immediately struck me was that here I saw 'The Communion of Saints'. Anyway, the service did me more good than any other service I've ever attended. It soothed my troubled spirit and gave me hope."[39] Conan Doyle stated that the departing spirit, as his or her earthly life ebbs away in its last deathbed moments, "is presently aware that there are others in the room":

> and among these others, who seem to him as substantial as the living, there appear familiar faces, and he finds his hand grasped or kissed by those whom he had loved and lost. Then in their company, and with the help and guidance of some more radiant being who has stood by and waited for the newcomer, he drifts to his own surprise through all solid obstacles and out upon his new life.[40]

The account of his own passing that HJL provided to Ward dwells on the assistance he received from one such 'radiant being', that only later he came to know as his spirit guardian. He could not describe "this glorious being" adequately:

Even now he seems to change every moment. At one instant I seem to know him well, at another he changes and I can get no clear idea of his face and form. He shimmers and shines and flashes, and seems as if he were made of fire. Yet that word gives but a faint idea, nor would the word 'light' be any nearer. All colour, too, is there.[41]

The assistance of such a spirit guardian – a guide and teacher on the spiritual journey – was another recurring theme in the wartime spiritualist accounts. "Opinion is not absolutely uniform yonder", Conan Doyle acknowledged, "any more than it is here",

> but reading a number of messages upon this subject they amount to this. There are many higher spirits with our departed. They vary in degree. Call them 'angels,' and you are in touch with old religious thought. High above all these is the greatest spirit of whom they have cognisance – not God, since God is so infinite that He is not within their ken – but one who is nearer to God and to that extent represents God. This is the Christ spirit.[42]

Lodge was more circumspect, stating that he had removed the section from Raymond's testimony that dealt with the assistance of a 'higher being' because it was intrinsically mystical and unverifiable. "Until the case for survival is considered established", he asserted, "it is thought improper and unwise to relate an experience of a kind which may be imagined, in a book dealing for the most part with evidential matter". But a fragment of the testimony was presented to dispel any idea his son had no regard for these matters. "I felt exalted, purified, lifted up", Raymond explained to his family when describing the approach of a higher being.

> I was kneeling. I couldn't stand up, I wanted to kneel. Mother, I was thrilled from head to foot. He didn't come near me, and I didn't feel I wanted to go near him. Didn't feel I ought. The Voice was like a bell. I can't tell you what he was dressed or robed in. All seemed a mixture of shining colours.[43]

Again, John Ward had none of Lodge's reservations. Having seen HJL's guardian, a "great spirit form made of light", in a trance vision on 2 March 1914 he presented a fulsome account of his awe-inspiring presence in *Gone West*.

> His robes kept changing colour and seemed to run through all colours of the rainbow.
>
> He was far taller than HJL, and large in proportion, being perfectly made. He was at least three times as large as HJL, and his face was more

beautiful than any Greek sculpture – strong, noble, well-cut features –
there was nothing feminine about it. Yet it was a kind as well as a strong
face. It was a face that was neither old nor young. Nor did it seem to have
colour (e.g. brown hair) as we understand it, but rather to be a figure of
golden light. Yet there was both hair on the head and beard, majestic and
glowing.

No words can describe the majesty and beauty of this being.

I can quite understand whence the ancients drew their inspirations for
their gods. Then I thought, 'This is doubtless an angel,' and I looked
instinctively for his wings, but he had none.[44]

When RLW encountered his own spirit guardian for the first time it was
a moment of intense personal revelation. He had become aware of a vast
void, he explained to his earth-bound brother, and far away in it a distant
speck of light, approaching and growing brighter. It never assumed a form,
but RLW felt an ineffable communication, "like the note of a mighty organ
far, far away. It swelled and swelled as it grew nearer, and finally it burst like
a tempest upon me . . . The music was exquisite, yet the pain was intense,
it burst on me and over me. It overwhelmed me and shattered me. It beat
me to the dust." But at the same time he discerned a message of profound
comfort:

My son, you have started on the right path. You have broken down the
outer darkness which shuts me away from you. Go and prosper little by
little. I shall draw nearer, and remember, though you may drive me away
from you, yet will I never desert you. I cannot draw any nearer than this
lest I overwhelm you utterly. I see how this first vision of me has shattered and dazed you. Grow strong in good works, in loving acts, in
unselfish thoughts, and so, as you grow more able to bear the sight of the
Glory, it shall be revealed to you.[45]

Finally, the wartime spiritualist literature concurred in the somewhat
counter-intuitive view that the afterlife was experienced by the disembodied
spirit as a virtual landscape, a 'second life'. Raymond reported in an early
communication that, strangely, he lived in a brick house, "and there are trees
and flowers, and the ground is solid. And if you kneel down in the mud . . .
you get your clothes soiled".[46] Departed spirits maintained their earthly
personalities, sought out old friends, and continued to pursue their characteristic interests and hobbies. Ordinary human activities like reading, making
conversation and playing sport continued, although rarified and given new
significance in the spiritual realm. In occult studies this theme is known as
the doctrine of correspondence: things 'above' are much like they are here
'below'. Conan Doyle put it more idealistically:

The life has a close analogy to that of this world at its best. It is pre-eminently a life of the mind, as this is of the body. Preoccupations of food, money, lust, pain, etc., are of the body and are gone. Music, the Arts, intellectual and spiritual knowledge, and progress have increased. The people are clothed, as one would expect, since there is no reason why modesty should disappear with our new forms.[47]

Ward's testimony echoed this theme. "Life here seems to be very much like life on earth", he remarks to HJL after they have made a number of visits and journeys about the psychic landscape of the spirit plane. His uncle answers him very deliberately:

Like, yet different; very much like earth life at its noblest and best. But here there is no sickness or sin, neither evil nor pain enter here. These are left behind on the threshold of Hell [the lowest spirit realm]. There is still some sorrow and repentance for sins now past, but sin as on earth you understand the word can come to us no more. Lack of knowledge there is, and therefore complete satisfaction and rest are not to be found here, for one must progress. But deliberate opposition to the will of God is a thing of the past [for us]. Nothing that is ugly or evil, low or false, can survive here. Therefore, if any amusement is founded on evil, be it ever so intellectual, it is not found here.[48]

Another aspect of correspondence was that human sociability continued in the afterlife, so that individual spirits associate with each other according to tastes and interests. Conan Doyle's informants explained, for instance, that departed spirits "live in communities, as one would expect if like attracts like . . . Since connections still endure, and those in the same state of development keep abreast, one would expect that nations are still roughly divided from each other, though language is no longer a bar, since thought has become a medium of conversation."[49] Likewise, gender distinctions continued. Men and women "do not mix much in these realms", Ward was told by HJL. "It is desirable, as far as possible, to eliminate the old ideas of sex, ideas right and necessary on earth, but no longer needed here, other-wise spiritual progress would be rendered almost impossible by the old carnal feelings." But spiritual communion between the sexes is presented as a mark of growth and advancing spiritual capacity. In Conan Doyle's account, for instance, "the male spirit still finds his true mate though there is no sexuality in the grosser sense and no childbirth".[50] HJL developed a similar view: "as the last grains of earthly passion are eliminated", he informed Ward,

the male and female spirits begin to draw together again, for each is the complement of the other spiritually, just as they are on earth physically. The further we progress, the nearer together the two sexes draw, so that we understand ultimately there comes about a mystic union in spirit between one man and one woman. This is the real spiritual union, of which marriage on earth is a true symbol or sacrament. This consummation, this blending of two spirit entities, so that each becomes part of the other and yet retains its own individuality, cannot be understood by even us, much less by you. The earth marriage at its highest and best does give you some faint idea of what we really mean. This spiritual marriage, if I can so call it, takes place at a stage far above us . . . [51]

❋   ❋   ❋

To these convinced spiritualists, the endless investigation of psychic phenomena to assuage the scepticism of materialistic science seemed a barren exercise. Even if Sir Oliver Lodge was keen to pursue evidential testimony to further psychical research on a scientific basis, he was himself "as convinced of continuing existence, on the other side of death, as I am of existence here".[52] The weight of evidence for survival seemed to them irrefutable, and the task therefore was not to corroborate these facts with more of the same. The great challenge, rather, was to interpret what they *meant*. Conan Doyle put the imperative very clearly:

> For are we to satisfy ourselves by observing phenomena with no attention to what the phenomena mean, as a group of savages might stare at a wireless installation with no appreciation of the messages coming through it, or are we resolutely to set ourselves to define these subtle and elusive utterances from beyond, and to construct from them a religious scheme, which will be founded upon human reason on this side and upon spirit inspiration upon the other? These phenomena have passed through the stage of being a parlour game; they are now emerging from that of a debatable scientific novelty; and they are, or should be, taking shape as the foundations of a definite system of religious thought, in some ways confirmatory of ancient systems, in some ways entirely new.[53]

Lodge did not share Conan Doyle's evangelical zeal, but in concluding *Raymond* he reflected on the cosmological implications of the spiritualist message. "The Universe is a flux", he urged, "it is a becoming, it is a progress. Evolution is a reality."[54] His own research and experience, he stated plainly, strongly suggested that the effort to "assist souls striving on their upward path" was an essential animating principle in the cosmic order. What was more, inter-communication between the various states or grades of human existence on that 'upward path' "carries with it occasional, and sometimes unconscious, communion with lofty souls who have gone before. The truth of such continued influence corresponds with the highest of the Revelations vouchsafed to humanity."[55]

John Ward took up a similar challenge in *Gone West* and *A Subaltern in Spirit Land*. Like Conan Doyle and Lodge, he felt his clairvoyant communications had unveiled the transcendent reality of human existence. And like Conan Doyle's 'New Revelation', Ward was convinced his insights served a far larger purpose than simply solace for grief-stricken relatives of the fallen. One of his earliest spirit communications from HJL hinted at the religious implications of the testimony that was to come, and encouraged him to approach the task in an ecumenical spirit.

> It is not . . . so much that the original teaching of the Church was wrong, but that it has been misinterpreted by its teachers. At the best, however, they only show a part of the truth. Not even here do we know all the truth. Truth is like a diamond with many facets. Each facet contains part, but only part, of the truth. Some facets are larger than others; so all creeds exist because of the 'facet' of truth, however small, which they possess.[56]

We find a group of core beliefs and principles clearly expressed by Ward for the first time in *Gone West* and *A Subaltern in Spirit Land*. Some were nebulous, and gained fuller form as his insights developed, while others changed little throughout the remainder of his life. Certainly, these highly personalised revelations of the metaphysical realities of life and death provided the first threads of a religious synthesis that he wove in ever more elaborate patterns as the years passed. With his Dantesque vision of the psychic geography of the afterlife, in fact, Ward issued his first manifesto in a mystical calling that matured over the following decades into a full-blown and increasingly urgent spiritual mission. He was convinced the revelations he received clairvoyantly did in fact cohere into – in Conan Doyle's words – "a definite system of religious thought, in some ways confirmatory of ancient systems, in some ways entirely new". We will examine the key elements of that "definite system", at least as Ward first configured it in 1916–17, in the chapter that follows.

✸   ✸   ✸

If Ward's spiritual and esoteric interests were running at a high pitch in the years after his return to England, he was also obliged to secure an income to support his family. Teaching positions were difficult to find, and tutoring had limited advantages. In May 1916 he joined the War Department of HM Customs as a clerk. The repetitive clerical duties and modest salary were partly compensated by several factors. Foremost was the gratification of the sense of duty that clearly had motivated him during the darkest years of the war. After his brother's death he had tried again to enlist, but was again rejected by the Army, the Navy and even, this time, by the Royal Naval Volunteer Reserve. He recalled that one of the recruiting officials recognized his keen disappointment at these latest rebuffs, and suggested he apply to the Appointments Board for employment in one of the various government departments directing the war effort. This approach resulted in the Customs War Department position. Another small advantage was his accommodation: overlooking Customs House in Upper Thames Street, Ward's Department was accommodated in an elegant eighteenth-century board room. His view over the river was through a window dignified by a small stained glass panel of Charles II. "The salary was not very princely one of £200.0.0 a year," Ward recalled, "and I was warned that I should not be entitled to any holidays till I had been a year in the Department". Even then he would only be entitled to fourteen days per year. "There was however overtime pay which helped a little. After the generous holidays of my schoolmaster days, this short holiday outlook was a little disappointing but I was so glad to be on war work that I didn't mind."[57]

He was at Customs House when the first daylight raids on London by German warplanes occurred. Although nothing like the destructive Blitz of 1940–41, the raids gave homely clerks like Ward their first real taste of war:

> We always got a preliminary warning in the Customs and got the staff down to the ground floor passages just in time. I was on the last flight of stairs to the ground floor when through the big staircase window I saw the planes overhead. Then the whole building rocked and there was the sound of falling glass. We had been hit but no one was hurt. The bomb fell on Customs House wharf and riddled a temporary building which a few minutes before had been full of typists. The windows of our Pay Office were shattered and the framework charred black. Most of the windows in the Board Room were shattered and where I had been sitting when the alarm went, was covered with broken glass, yet strange to say the stained glass panel of King Charles II which hung in that window was unhurt. It was immediately removed to a place of safety.[58]

The threat of air attacks continued and civilian constables were enrolled locally to ensure that a black-out was maintained. Ward's patriotic zeal saw him volunteer as a Special Constable for the district of his family's home at Gidea Park near Romford in Essex. He was issued with an identifying armband and patrolled the district at night to ensure that all lights were extinguished or properly screened. In this way he contributed to civil order during the occasional moments of wartime emergency. After the raid on Customs Wharf, for instance, with fires and damage in the market buildings nearby,

Ward sprang into the breach. Once things had settled down in his office, he recalled, "I put on my Special Constables armlet and went out and helped the Metropolitan Specials to control the crowds which gathered near the bombed buildings in Fenchurch Street".[59]

The work of Customs administration that occupied Ward was dull and repetitive, but at least could be seen as a material contribution to the war effort. The enforcement of import-export restrictions and the maintenance of the naval blockade of Germany were by any measure crucial in the war of attrition being fought out in Western Europe. Much effort was therefore expended by Surveyors of Customs in the various ports searching cargoes for contraband items or goods in breach of British regulations. Ward's department also enforced the blockade on German importation (often through go-betweens in Holland) to prevent export of fuel, textiles, chemicals and other raw products to Germany.

But by the end of 1917 Ward was weary of repetitive clerical work and ready for new professional responsibilities. He took the advice of his supervisor and applied successfully for a position in the Intelligence Section at the Federation of British Industries. He moved with some relief across to the Federation's head office at 39 St James' Street, S.W.1, where he was principally engaged in the research and analysis of markets, trade conditions and economic trends for the benefit of the Federation membership. As he put it, "I specialised in the movements of Foreign Exchanges, in the sources of Raw Materials and so forth".[60] He responded well to the challenges of the position, and was quickly promoted to head the section with responsibility for a staff of around ten. It was a world far removed from the psychic and esoteric adventures that had occupied his spare time, but it was, at least, a living. It gave him an income and a professional standing, while his evenings and weekends remained his own.

5

Opening the Guarded Door

Ward's leisure time in 1916–17 was largely dedicated to the collation of the spirit testimony that was later published as *Gone West* and *A Subaltern in Spirit Land*. The first of these, baldly subtitled "Three Narratives of After-Death Experiences Communicated through the Mediumship of J. S. M. Ward," announced his firm belief in the doctrines of spiritualism and sought to educate readers on their metaphysical implications. His spirit informants, he explained to his readers, had determined to present him with a "description of the 'geography' of this region, if so it may be called".[1] To explain the psychic geography of the afterlife and give a sense of its structured arrangements was the first objective of Ward's spiritualist books. A second was to explain his sense of the great universal law of spiritual growth and progress that determined the destiny of each human soul in its passage beyond. In these two fundamental aspects, and in contrast to the more generic spiritualist literature of the Great War, Ward's account of 'Afterdeath' is extraordinarily lucid and precise.

Both are vividly present in the account HJL conveyed to Ward of his own arrival in the afterlife. His first visual sense of the spirit plane was of a gorgeous rural idyll. It was "the most exquisite scenery imaginable", HJL reported.

> Every lovely spot I had ever visited was there, and countless others which I had never seen – beautiful rolling hills, clothed with grass and trees; real trees, yes, and animals and even butterflies; flowers, too of every description, not only English wild and garden flowers, but all manner of foreign plants, orchids and so forth, the like of which I never saw on earth.

This was "the land of Afterdeath", HJL was informed by his spirit guide, containing "every thought which you have ever thought . . . here come also the spiritual forms of all that ever lived. Thus is our Spirit World built up and thus it constantly increases." By its very nature the psychic landscape around him was unstable, altering with the mental rhythm of HJL's inner turmoil. The rural idyll gave way to nightmarish visions and fantasies that "seem[ed] to press me round". These were the memories of his past misdeeds, thoughtless actions and selfish conduct. "I saw them not with my mortal eyes," he told Ward, "I perceived them with my whole being. I call them visions, but they were in real bodily form, like tableaux, moving and acting again before me all my past." So began the moral reckoning as his life and deeds were brought to account:

My past deeds crowded before me, not in order, but like a dream, all at once. Oh! the anguish as once more rose up deeds long since forgotten. Little or great, nothing was now forgotten. At last, after what seemed countless ages, an inspiration seemed to seize me, and I prayed. I had not done so for years and years, but now I prayed, 'O God, help me,' and as I prayed, really prayed, slowly the wild chaos began as it were to sort itself out. It, as it were, took a kind of chronological order, and the scenes took the form, as it were of a street which stretched far away, far beyond my ken; and they will go on increasing as I progress until they reach to the judgment seat of God.

The psychic landscape that unfolded in HJL's account was thus a setting for the moral drama of spiritual progression. It brimmed with multitudes of living souls, each busily engaged in the business of spiritual growth or 'soul study', as HJL called it, in their evolution towards final communion with the Absolute. Progress might be measured in many ways, beginning most essentially with emancipation from the base demands of the material world. A developing comprehension of the great cosmic principles of growth, compassion, faith and tolerance was also important, as were good works in the service of others. The one universal certainty was that each departed soul occupied a position in a spiritual hierarchy, and would continue to be challenged as it made its way onward into ever-higher states of being. "[W]e catch dim glimpses", Conan Doyle wrote in a passage that echoed Ward's sense of the spiritual hierarchy of the afterlife, "of endless circles below, descending into gloom, and endless circles above, ascending into glory, all improving, all purposeful, all intensely alive".[2]

All religions and faiths had comprehended aspects of this metaphysical truth, HJL explained, but none could supply a complete account. Yet "the larger the amount of truth, the stronger that faith will as a rule grow. Thus the Roman Catholics are a numerous body, but neither they, nor any sect, possess all the truth."[3] But in order to explain clearly the arrangement of the afterlife he had to resort to the conventional classifications of Christian orthodoxy. As "it is easier for you to comprehend the new facts with which I am about to deal, if you can attach them to some theory with which you are acquainted," he explained, "I shall adopt the general Plan of Heaven, Purgatory and Hell". These were misleading terms, he warned, "but if accepted as a convenient and rough classification, they will be helpful. One fact, however, you must clearly grasp. So far as I can discover there is no evidence of the *eternity* of Hell. Drop that idea, and the rest will be easy to understand."[4]

To help his explanation he presented Ward with an illustration, unveiled on a huge grey sheet engraved with 'characters of fire', demonstrating in a single elaborate diagram the arrangement of the various divisions of the spirit plane. Although it seemed rigid and formalised, HJL advised that it was a highly simplified figure; it ignored many "fluctuations and cross-currents" and should be treated as an indicative scheme only. "Now do not turn my diagrams into a cast-iron system", HJL cautioned. "Remember there is far more flux here than on earth."[5] For one thing, all activity was mental and constantly changing; time and space had no controlling influence, and all forms were essentially creations of thought. Moreover, "souls fluctuate within their plane", and move between the various divisions, sometimes fitfully but more generally as they graduated from one level to the next.

Thus Ward's 'Plan of the Spirit Plane' and the accompanying account of life on these metaphysical planes did not lack lucidity or conviction. It presented a spiritual hierarchy of 'realms', marked into divisions equating to the spiritual condition and the degree of advancement of the spirits that dwelt there. The initial destination of each soul – which division and 'set' it joined, in HJL's terminology – was decided by its earthly conduct and thereafter by its continuing spiritual development. Broadly speaking, the hierarchy was based on the passage from the absence of any kind of faith and an indulgence in carnal sins of various kinds (which confined spirits to the hellish chaos of the 'Realm of Unbelief') to the three higher 'Purgatorial' realms: those of 'Half Belief', 'Belief lacking in Works' and finally 'Belief shown forth in Works'. An advanced soul progressed directly from the astral plane to the latter, the highest of the spirit realms, and there continued his or her spiritual education and progression in the company of similar highly-evolved spirits; but others such as agnostics or well-meaning religious sceptics might have more work to do in the 'Realm of Half Belief' or 'of Belief Lacking Works' to which their earthly habits and preferences had consigned them. Finally, recalcitrant types that had made little spiritual progress at all during their earthly lives through their selfishness, sin and wickedness would suffer for a time the dark and anguished depths of the 'Realm of Unbelief'.

Ward's transcendent hierarchy and the scheme of moral progression thus echoed Eastern notions of karma, spiritual evolution and an ultimate mystical communion with the Absolute in a state of *nirvana* or cosmic enlightenment and pure being. But it was not incompatible with the essential revelations of doctrinal Christianity. Notions of sin, judgment, penance and redemption were pervasive, and moral categories of conduct ranging from sinfulness to saintliness equated with states of being in the afterlife (hell, purgatory, heaven). The spiritual presence and agency of angels or 'advanced souls', guides and helpers, had much in common with Christian scripture understood literally, as did the presence of an omnipresent Redeemer, a being of radiant goodness that shared the essential nature of God. In fact it was only when it came to the doctrines of original sin and eternal damnation that Ward departed from the vital tenets of Christianity. Neither, he insisted firmly, had any place in the accounts he had received of Afterdeath and the distinct realms of its cosmic geography.

* * *

Certainly, John Ward was not the first Christian to find his faith renewed and transformed in the light cast by Modern Spiritualism. Although much of the formal Spiritualist movement was hostile to traditional Church teachings and the dogmatic authority of an earthly ministry on the Christian pattern,[6] the potential for common ground between the two had been apparent since séances first captured public attention in Britain in the early 1850s. The London-based spiritualist group centred on William Howitt and the *Spiritual Magazine* between the late 1850s and 1875 was among the first to address the religious implications of the new movement directly, followed by the eloquent medium William Stainton Moses and his celebrated *Spirit Teachings*, the so-called 'spiritualist bible'. Such men regarded the latest spirit testimony "as supplementing rather than supplanting Christianity", and many turned to the doctrines of the Swedish seer and savant Emmanuel Swedenborg to mediate "between the old revelation and the new, and to unite them in one apocalyptic whole", as the psychic researcher, historian and sceptic Frank Podmore commented in 1902.[7] One might easily arrive at the view that the revelations of life after death contained in spiritualism provided, according to Conan Doyle, "the great unifying force, the one provable thing connected with every religion, Christian or non-Christian, forming the common solid basis upon which each raises, if it must needs raise, that separate system which appeals to the varied types of mind."[8] One of Howitt's characteristically extended passages captures the bright hopes of these first Christian spiritualists:

> Spiritualism has taught what the soul is; what becomes of it after death; that there are purgatorial or intermediate states; where these lie; that there is progression in them; that the dead seek for our prayers and sympathies; that the Communion of Saints is real, and far more extensive and precious than was ever before conceived of; that there is no cessation of miracles or prophecy . . . it has taught us not to fear death, which is but a momentary passage to life; that God is disciplining the human race for an eventual and universal restoration; that He is beginning to teach laws of matter hitherto unnoticed by the acutest men of gases and crucibles; and that, above all, Spiritualism teaches us the authenticity of the Scriptures now

so violently attacked, and their great law of the love of God and of the neighbour; that no Christianity but the primitive Christianity is worth a straw; and that the dry bones of the present death-in-life churches must receive His fresh breath of life if they are ever to live again. Finally, it teaches us to live in all purity of thought and deed, knowing that not only the ever-open eye of God is constantly upon us, but those of an innumerable company of angels and devils, to whom we are as well and as openly known as to our own consciences.[9]

Such observations raised the possibility of conciliation between Spiritualism and the fundamental tenets of revelatory Christianity in a kind of spiritual ecumenism embracing faiths, churches and sects of all kinds. But the emphasis on *primitive* Christianity, the miraculous faith celebrated by believers immediately after the "fresh breath" of Christ's earthly incarnation, is also noteworthy, not least because it was a striking feature of Ward's own religious mission after 1929.

Whatever the sceptic might think of their ultimate source, the cosmic revelations Ward felt he had received cohered for him in a way that clarified the essential mysteries of life and human destiny in a vast and fathomless universe. Indeed the spiritual awakening he experienced between 1914 and 1916 anchored his personal faith and philosophy for the rest of his life. It was his own intensely personal version of Conan Doyle's 'New Revelation', providing Ward with the compass points and bearings for the spiritual journey to which he thereafter dedicated himself.

✻　　✻　　✻

If we are to understand that journey we need to grasp the central principles Ward drew from this rich spiritual panorama and how those principles transformed his outlook on life and its meaning. It seems that a group of inter-related themes crystallised for him at this time, and from then onwards directly shaped all his subsequent endeavours. Three elements were foremost among them, the first being a universal principle of mental and spiritual progress, that necessitated the reality of divine or cosmic judgment. A second was the ontological reality of Platonic 'thought-forms' in this psychic landscape, and a third was the active guiding agency of departed spirits, guardian beings and angels. These three insights invested his youthful preoccupations with a new significance, as his enthusiasm for history, historic antiquities and esoteric heritage (especially Freemasonry) matured and deepened. Each of these core interests became infused with a new sense of their cosmic significance. Ward's philosophy of history, such as it was, enlarged to embrace hidden or esoteric dimensions of supernatural agency and cyclical patterns of evolution and regression. Historical relics and artworks assumed a new significance because he now understood them as the material counterparts of higher, eternal 'thought-forms' that embodied metaphysical truths or exalted achievement. The wisdom encapsulated in archaic traditions and rituals might defy ordinary comprehension, but could now be understood as fragments of profound transcendent insight. These principles came together to sustain Ward's own religious calling as he plunged into the mysterious, bracing waters of occult Christianity.

The first theme we have noted occurs so frequently in Ward's spirit narratives as to be their one great and constant refrain. On the spirit plane, as in their earth-bound lives, each living human being had an absolute responsibility to self-educate and self-improve in order to progress to higher states of being. They did this with the assistance of the guardian spirits and teachers that descended from higher, empyrean spheres to assist others on their protracted upward journey. As Conan Doyle commented, "the lower cannot [easily] ascend, but the higher can descend at will".[10] Whether known as angels, masters, guardians or spirit guides, such higher beings were charged with a duty to assist their charges in the difficult progress towards spiritual fulfilment. But they could not do the work for them, and the challenges they offered were intrinsic to the process of growth. As HJL prepared to accompany his spirit guide to visit the forbidding 'Realm of Unbelief', for instance, he became afraid of the uncertainty and risks the journey would involve. His guide stated the matter clearly: "Here there is no standing still. You must progress either upwards or downwards, and this journey must be taken."[11] He came to learn the great unifying principles of existence: life is a state of flux, a continuum in which only spiritual growth or regression is possible.

But if they received help from others, the disembodied spirits of Afterdeath were actively working to improve those around them. They were learning, but they were also themselves teachers and helpers, spiritual attributes that echoed the earthly qualities of the philosopher and the philanthropist in a combination praised by the Christian spiritualist Stainton Moses as the marker of the truly 'advanced soul'. "The union of these two – the philanthropist and the philosopher – makes the perfect man," he testified, "[and] those who unite the two, progress further than spirits who progress alone."[12] HJL had his own 'soul-study' to grasp the new realities around him, but was also contacting Ward primarily to assist the latter's spiritual enlightenment in the same way that he had guided Rex's spirit through the astral plane. This lower sphere was busy with spirit philanthropy, as many lingered there assisting the recently deceased during the difficult confusion of their bodily death. They oriented the new arrivals to their surroundings, eased their psychic wounds, helped them shake off their earthly habits and warned them of debased spirits who would tempt them to 'obsess' on the material matters and pleasures they had now properly left behind.

In Ward's scheme the business of spiritual growth in Afterdeath was fostered in a series of idealised institutions that paralleled those of everyday life in the material sphere. Higher spirits taught in centres that could be imagined as the schools and universities of the spirit realms, or engaged in missionary work on the fringes of the Realm of Unbelief. Others worked in great psychic hospitals to aid restless souls in states of distress, or to ease the mental torment of the recently deceased. Their afflictions derived from earthly experiences, which manifested as unhealthy obsessions, debilitating feelings of sorrow, grief and guilt, or insanity and chronic mental instbility. In all cases the spirit mentors offered advice and guidance – the classroom sessions HJL described to Ward, for example, took the form of Socratic discourse, with his teacher "asking cleverly arranged questions, and the answer to each led on to the next question" – but the ultimate responsibility for spiritual progress rested with the individual soul. It all rested on the principles of free will and moral responsibility: "Each soul must strive to answer his own questions", HJL was told at one point, "and if he really strives, he will succeed."[13]

Spirits might also progress by applying themselves to creative work that developed their own capacities and interests. HJL was continuing to enlarge his interest in architecture by building wondrous and immaterial structures as 'idea-creations', in company with like-minded spirits. Other spirit artists continue the work of creative expression; painters and sculptors, for example, created works "out of our own 'mind stuff'", as HJL explained to Ward, "which takes the form of marble or bronze, according as we conceive it. We may be said to build them up like a man does a clay model, but the clay is our own 'mind stuff'. I can give you no better word."[14] The keynote of spiritual activity and progress rang out most clearly as HJL tried to encapsulate his circumstances in a single, thorough statement. "Consider me", he asked Ward,

> as a man still much like yourself, but freed at last of the trammels of a body; no longer subject to pain, no longer needing material food or sleep, and therefore as one freed from the drudgery of life, dwelling among pleasant surroundings, with boundless opportunities, not for idle sloth and endless psalm-singing, but to study all subjects in which I am interested and the means to pursue those studies far further than any man can do on earth. Consider me able and anxious to help others, and by doing so preparing myself to climb higher and higher from division to division, making new friends and learning new truths day by day as time seems to you.
>
> Consider me happy and contented in a measure, glad to have escaped from the material world, but do not think of me as absolutely happy yet.
>
> Perfect happiness is a long way off still, and can only be attained by steady effort concentrated by a set and determined will after many ages,

during all of which the spirit is undergoing fresh experiences, and learning new truths.

Think of me thus, at all times, busy alike with work and recreation. The work is that which will help me to climb upward step by step, the recreation that which on earth I considered as work.[15]

Good company, mental effort, creativity, assistance to others and, above all, spiritual progress: these distinguished the life that beckoned in Ward's testimony from beyond the grave.

But it remained beholden to a solemn and universal moral responsibility. Human actions on earth were answerable to a higher judgment; their metaphysical consequences were determined within a strict moral framework of good (i.e. that which tended to spiritual and ethical progress) and evil (that which tended to regression). But judgment, while a cosmic certainty, was not an eternal condemnation and was not imposed by the vengeful Jehovah-figure found in the Old Testament. Rather, the individual soul stood 'self-condemned' in the light of all their previous thoughts and actions. Indeed, "the word 'judged' is misused", HJL explained. "It implies that someone outside ourselves judges us. This is not so; we stand self-condemned. Our spirit cannot rise to higher realms than those for which it has fitted itself. There is no necessity to enforce any law, for the law is self-acting."[16] But in line with the notion of eternal progress, the opportunity for redemption and self-improvement is ever-present. Conan Doyle agreed that the afterlife did not offer an equivalent state to a permanent 'Hell', but "the idea of punishment, of purifying chastisement, in fact of Purgatory, is justified by the reports from the other side . . . ". Punishment, he continued,

is very certain and very serious, though in its less severe forms it only consists in the fact that the grosser souls are in the lower spheres with a knowledge that their own deeds have placed them there, but also with the hope that expiation and the help of those above them will educate them and bring them level with the others. In this saving process the higher spirits find part of their employment.[17]

✳   ✳   ✳

The reader of Ward's spiritualist testimony is struck by a second theme: the perhaps disconcerting tangibility of the psychic landscapes Ward encountered in his trance visions. He observed spirits moving around and conversing with each other, pursuing their hobbies and interests, attending schools and colleges to learn, being confined in hospitals when they are sick or distraught. Although there is no controlling structure of time and space, such activities occur in a setting of forms and elements that corresponded directly to the natural and human environments of the earth plane. From flowers, trees and buildings to rivers, mountains, monuments and whole townscapes, the metaphysical spheres of the afterlife – the astral plane and the higher realms – directly paralleled the visible arrangements of material reality.

On the astral plane, the ghostly threshold of the higher spheres, the psychic landscape related closely to the earthly setting and was populated by partly-materialised astral beings and the astral forms of all the accoutrements of everyday life. Ward saw flowers waving in the breeze, roads filled with traffic, buildings perpetuated in various states of repair and astral shops displaying the ethereal forms of worldly goods. He is naturally drawn to one stuffed with curios and antiques run by a wizened old man, a spirit who had formerly been an antique dealer in Ypres. "Truly, he had a marvellous collection of all sorts of stuff", Ward reported. "Furniture of every period and country, weapons, armour, china, old glass, Roman gods and Indian idols; there seemed no end to the things he had. When I told him I had recently returned from the East, and told him of the things I had obtained there, he was greatly interested."[18]

The higher planes, in contrast, are explained in essentially Platonic terms as spheres of pure thought-form, a state of being that applies to the discarnate spirits themselves. "Compare us to a thought", HJL suggested during one of their early contacts. "We are more than a thought, for we continue to think; but compare us to a thought; you may then get some idea of what I mean." But the principle of 'thought-forms', pure and eternal, applied to all the visible elements that Ward encountered in his trance visions of the higher realms. HJL shows Ward great libraries, art galleries and sculpture gardens filled with the creative achievements of spirits in their own endeavours. In Afterdeath, he is told, abstract 'thought-forms' were the pure and ideal correspondences of their material equivalents on the earth planes. "If you have picture galleries, I presume you have museums?" Ward asked at one point. "We have them, but not so many as you would expect," HJL answered.

> You see, so far as is possible, we put ancient art objects to their original use in their original homes – Egyptian chairs in an Egyptian palace, and Egyptian jewels on their original owners or makers for example. New objects of art, created over here, usually remain attached to their creator. But some spirits invent them for the purpose of being put on exhibition to delight others. For these there are museums.[19]

Ward's avid antiquarianism needed little encouragement, but this was manna from heaven: the clearest possible endorsement of its higher meaning and significance.

A final theme emphasised in Ward's 'New Revelation' was the historical reality of supernatural agency in human affairs. He became convinced that disembodied personalities – whether interfering spirits 'obsessing' over gross material pleasures, or angelic guardians and spirit teachers helping the spiritual progress of others – used the psychic telegraphy that he himself had experienced to intervene in everyday life. Mischievous interference was regarded as commonplace by convinced spiritualists, and many mediums reported the presence of disruptive or misleading spirits. Poltergeist activity and forms of 'diabolic' possession could likewise be understood in these terms. Ward came to endorse the view that, in certain cases, psychological processes and visible behaviour might be subject to occult forces beyond ordinary human comprehension. He extended that view to recognise that the broader patterns of human history were likewise shaped by cosmic and supernatural forces of which most people had very little understanding, and even then only dimly.

Ward also learnt enough through his visions and spirit testimony to convince him that the time-honoured notion of a 'guardian angel' was, in fact, a representation of a great cosmic reality. Each soul, on passing over, met with its guardian spirit, an advanced being from the higher planes of existence beyond the 'wall of fire' who returned to the four lower realms to assist others as a guide and mentor. He was sure that throughout human history spirits and higher beings had communicated with 'sensitive' individuals, often in a state of visionary trance but also by physical manifestation, by clairaudience (the hearing of voices) and more recently by automatic writing, raps and messages obtained in séance. Spirit beings, moreover, were busy providing telepathic inspiration to ordinary men and women engaged in the whole range of human activity. "Let me tell you", HJL informed him bluntly, "that all inspiration comes from this side. The works of genius are really the inspirations of spirits acting through that man who is really mediumistic." He elaborated on this theme at some length:

Art, literature, music, even mechanical inventions, are almost always inspired from this side. Slight improvements and adjustments to enable the great idea to fit the conditions of earth life are the kind of advances which men make on earth. I hesitate to say that no great idea was ever invented on the earth, but I know of none, and am sure that they are few and far between. This explains in part why it is that progress is so slow in the early centuries of life on this planet and of late has proceeded at such a rate. Men come over to us with some knowledge and a keen interest in various subjects, and in these more advanced surroundings they discover new laws, and in the light of this new knowledge inspire those who are following in their footsteps.

All the same, men are often very stupid. We send out a brilliant idea, and the best parts are often misunderstood by, or fail to penetrate, the denser minds of those still on earth. Again and again we see our finest ideas reduced to a miserable travesty of their real selves.[20]

To make the point HJL took Ward through a splendid Renaissance piazza, pausing outside the magnificent edifice of a church that was, as HJL explained, "far finer than anything they've got on earth". He felt sure nothing like it could now be built in the mortal sphere. "It's such a materialistic age that we simply cannot get our ideas through", he lamented. "That is why the earlier periods, for example, the Middle Ages, were so much finer – they were less materialistic, and so responded more to our inspirations." Ward asked whether this meant that human beings contributed nothing, and deserved no credit for their artistic and mental achievements. Was it all due to "the mighty dead"? "On the contrary", he was reassured,

> they deserve all the credit they can get, for it means that they have preserved and developed their higher and spiritual faculties, at any rate on the artistic or engineering side. This at any rate is something. Even a blackguardly immoral man, who seems materialistic on most matters, must have developed his spiritual faculties to some extent if he is able to receive and carry out fine inspirations sent from this side. [21]

Such insights infused Ward's worldly interests with a new and vivid significance. His historical curiosity and antiquarianism, in particular, took on a new consequence. Not only were museums, art galleries, historic architecture and cultural monuments all perpetuated on the higher planes of disembodied being, but the great achievements of human culture were now understood as direct products of 'divine inspiration' – due quite literally to higher souls working on the receptive faculties of talented human beings. Furthermore the deeper patterns of human history could be traced, he now came to understand, according to the progress or regression of the human spirit. The heightened spiritual consciousness of particular epochs – the Greece of Pericles, Rome in the days of the Republic, the Christian Middle Ages, to take the prime examples that occurred to Ward immediately – were manifested in the glory of their artistic and intellectual achievements, while periods of regression, materialism and moral decay could be measured likewise. When it came to Freemasonry, too, the principles of fraternity, good conduct and self-improvement that drew him to the Craft were similarly endorsed specifically in these spirit revelations. After being informed that HJL's 'college' in the Realm of Half-Belief was arranged into three divisions according to the spiritual status of its members, presided over by a 'Master', a deputy and a presiding committee, Ward recognised the correspondence immediately:

> JW: Like a Freemasons' lodge – a master, senior and junior warden.
>
> HJL: I don't know much about Freemasons, but that's rather the idea. The members of the college consist of three divisions, and we are promoted from first to the second, and from the second to the third, according as we learn the great spiritual truths. From the third or highest division the committee are elected. The various officers are chosen by the head of the college from this committee.
>
> JW: Its really rather like a Freemasons' lodge with its three degrees, and so on.
>
> HJL: Very likely. Probably the idea was inspired from this side. Still, it's a very natural arrangement and somewhat similar to college on earth with its first, second, and third-year men and its fellows.[22]

Perhaps most importantly, the insights Ward gained by spirit testimony confirmed for him the essential compatibility of the great world religions. Each was a distinct version of a single, unitary cosmic truth, necessarily partial and coloured by the historical era and social setting in which it had emerged but with an essential commonality that transcended social and cultural boundaries. Modern Spiritualism was merely the latest instalment, it seemed to Ward, of a vast and unfolding revelation that cascaded through the ages and across all human cultures and creeds. Again it was Conan Doyle who expressed this ecumenical theme, the basic keynote of this 'New Revelation', most lucidly. "All are agreed", he stated in concluding his survey of spirit testimony, "that no religion upon earth has any advantage over another, but that character and refinement are everything. At the same time, all are also in agreement that all religions which inculcate prayer, and an upward glance rather than eyes for ever on the level, is good."[23] Conan Doyle took up the task of evangelising this new 'psychic religion' to the world at large, convinced that it expressed the universal principles that underpinned all systems of faith. "To me the religious aspect of this question [of spiritualism] is everything", he told a luncheon at the Holborn Restaurant in London prior to departing to evangelise Australia and New Zealand in mid-1920. "What the dead tell us is a description of the universe which is accurate and logical. They give us something to hope for, and make us realise it is indeed not only an all powerful, but an all-loving God. This is the real revelation which casts a search-light from heaven down upon the darkened earth."[24]

This 'search-light' might also be a beacon for religious tolerance and mutual respect. In an age when religious and sectarian prejudices were deeply ingrained and often bolstered aggressive imperialism, ethnic hatred and other malignant impulses, thoughtful spiritualists like Ward and Conan Doyle followed the Theosophists to imagine the possibility of a universal synthesis of world religions. They might still regard Christianity as the keystone, but readily found a place for the spiritual tenets of Buddhism, Islam, Hinduism, Confucianism and other traditions in a composite edifice of universal faith. "The science of Comparative Religions", Ward later wrote in *The Psychic Powers of Christ*,

> is a subject which must be studied, and a man must be prepared to face the possibility that other races may have received Divine Revelation, even though they be not Christian, and he must be prepared to explain how this is possible, despite the fact that he himself believes that the Christian Faith is the highest revelation as yet given to man. If our faith is so weak that we cannot bear to look into the Faiths which guide millions of other human beings, for fear that these should shake our own, then obviously our own is not well founded and has no strength in it. It is a mere formula, with neither driving force nor vitality.[25]

For Ward, the Christian revelation offered the fullest and most complete of those that had been implanted by higher forces into the mortal affairs of human history. But he was an amiable and tolerant fellow traveller alongside those of complementary faith traditions. "A Buddhist once said to me", he remembered, "'If you do not see that the Buddhist faith is the true faith, it merely shows that you have not reached that stage of spiritual evolution in which you can perceive the perfection of its beauty.' To him, I replied: 'To me, my brother, it seems as if I might reverse your remark. One day you will have evolved sufficiently far to see that Christianity excels even Buddhism. Until then, go on in the Light which guides you!'"[26]

Ward's appreciation of the cosmic and spiritual values inherent in all the major religions had other implications. It helped sustain his deep convictions on the importance of revealed doctrine, enduring institutions, systematic worship and time-honoured ritual in human faith and spirituality. The heritage of religious practice and ritual seemed a source of wisdom and a path to enlightenment in an era of mortal spiritual crisis. He revered the Christian heritage of ritual and liturgy in particular, even if the spiritual teaching contained in these ritual forms had been distorted or lost over time. As he later wrote in theological vein:

> for my part I hold strongly that one should not discard lightly a teaching [such as original sin absolved by baptism] which has been held by the vast bulk of Christians from as early a date as we can trace any definite records of their beliefs. I hold that many of the doctrines of the Christian Church have in the course of years ceased to be intelligible to thinking men,

because those who should expound them have themselves lost their inner meaning and are therefore unable to make them intelligible. It does not, however, follow that such doctrines are wrong, and it may be that hidden in them lies a key which will unlock many of the mysteries of life, but the tragedy is that those who hold the keys often seem to have mislaid them.[27]

In the decades that followed these convictions synchronised in Ward's mind with an urgent sense of the crisis in Britain's spiritual life. He later wrote that as "quite a young man", he came to the realization that "the National Church of the country was approaching a serious crisis; perhaps more serious than that which took place at the so-called Reformation . . . it was not only the Established Church that was affected but the same processes were at work in all the Nonconformist bodies."[28] The general tone of secularization and materialism, the challenges of a "hard, mechanical age, filled with scientific ideas of efficiency",[29] lay at the heart of the crisis. But denominational bigotry and the widespread neglect of basic spiritual truths, he came to realise, were also root causes. He took up this latter theme when he considered the evidence for psychical powers in the miracles of Christian scripture. "My plea", he concluded, "is addressed to all men of sincere faith to re-examine the fundamental teachings of the early Church, to agree on what is essential, and to unite in defending these essentials against the agnostic and un-believer".[30] The true enemy was the casual, ignorant atheism of a materialistic age.

Ward came to believe that he was an agent of the higher intervention that would resolve the crisis of complacency, selfishness and materialism visible all around. As he later came to see it, the psychic communications he received in his trance visions during the Great War were a preparation for a religious calling, which was only revealed to him during further visions in the late 1920s. His first excursions to the spirit and astral planes concluded in April 1919, however, in a moment of high spiritual drama that forecast the prophetic revelations Ward was to receive a decade later. As he reported in the final chapter of *A Subaltern in Spirit Land*, bidding farewell to his spiritual mentors in a vision on the night of 20 April he was blessed with a personal vision of his own "guardian angel", a "celestial presence" with a face more radiant than the sun and a voice "like the notes of a splendid organ". The words spoken rang in Ward's consciousness like pealing bells:

'Your work on this plane is, for the time, finished. Give forth the message and the knowledge to the world. For the world is in travail, and much sorrow lies before her, as well as behind, ere she enters the haven of peace. For a new age is being born, and a new order arises. Old faiths perish, and only He the Unknown remaineth immutable. But out of sorrow cometh forth joy, and out of war ultimate peace.

For all things are of set design, and though the souls of men are ever moving onward, there is no stagnation or decay, but out of corruption arises incorruption, and out of death life.

Though darkness encompass the earth, yet the dawn is at hand, and the new day shall be better than the old, for even the high powers tremble at the might and glory of the Supreme.'

He ceased, and I fell amid the clash of warring worlds and the tumult of elemental chaos.[31]

Armed with his psychic insights, Ward's response to the spiritual crisis and creeping materialism of his day could thus be disarmingly simple. He urged a recognition of the essentials of spiritual doctrine inherent to the various creeds and communities of faith that constituted the great religious traditions of East and West. No single religious tradition could claim to contain the entire and exclusive revelation of spiritual truth. But true insight was possible, because messengers in the form of higher souls and angelic beings were cosmic agents that could manifest on the material plane to impart crucial teaching and guide souls on their path to enlightenment.

Ten years later his work on the spirit plane re-commenced as John Ward felt himself to be charged by another angelic messenger with a solemn and sacred duty. He was instructed to prepare for the return of Christ, the supreme 'higher being' presiding in the uppermost reaches of the spiritual realm. From 1929, as he published a range of pentecostal and increasingly apocalyptic statements of this prophetic mission, the first insights he had gained through spirit communication did indeed take shape (as in Conan Doyle's words) as a "definite system of religious thought, in some ways confirmatory of ancient messages and in some ways entirely new".

6

Explorations in the Craft

There was an orderly daily routine amid all this mysticism and spiritual inquiry. Ward was employed as an economic analyst at the Federation of British Industries throughout the 1920s, working from an office in prestigious St James as he undertook research and analysis of markets, trade conditions and economic trends for Federation members. As he put it prosaically, "I specialised in the movements of Foreign Exchanges, in the sources of Raw Materials and so forth".[1] Responding well to the challenges of the position, he was quickly promoted to head the Intelligence Department with responsibility for a staff of around ten. These were arranged in two groups, a Research Section dealing with matters requiring detailed analysis and an Enquiry Section to handle more immediate requests for information. The Intelligence Department maintained its own reference library and indexes, but as one internal report noted during Ward's tenure, "we try as far as possible not to pile up and classify information here but to be in touch with as many outside sources of information as possible".[2] Ward's duties thus involved maintaining contact with libraries and analysts throughout Britain and overseas, and co-ordinating the internal flow of statistics and reports to other Federation departments. Now a Fellow of the Royal Economic Society, he developed considerable expertise on a range of industrial and economic matters. An article on the British dyeing industry for the *Encyclopædia Britannica*, for example, focused on the impact of the Great War on production and the rise of protectionism.[3] Other short articles for the encyclopaedia looked at fibre technology and recent developments in silk manufacture and consumption; in 1924 he contributed a book on *Textile Fibres and Yarns* to Ernest Benn's 'Resources of the Empire' series.[4]

Ward also prepared annual reports on the prevailing financial conditions for British and global business. These official booklets outlined fluctuations in exchange rates and commodity prices, shifts in the prices of precious metals, economic statistics and so on. At one level they contained merely routine economic analysis, but in summarising the broad international outlook Ward – a committed free trader – drew some spirited conclusions. Post-war Europe had many economic difficulties and dislocations, he observed in 1919, which would continue until all economic barriers were dismantled. The nations and peoples of Europe "must be prepared to sink their differences, and to work together to a common purpose – and . . . unless they do this they must realise that their industrial life will surely die". "These are hard words", he concluded, "but they are written in the face of hard facts. The lesson of them is obvious, namely, a need for economy, a need for hard work, and a need for less thought for the individual or the nation, and more thought for humanity and the world."[5] This seems an oddly moralistic tone in which to review economic circumstances, but faced with wild fluctuations in inflation and exchange rates in 1919–1920 Ward took a similar view a year later:

> The outlook is dark enough, though gleams of light are showing here and there. But the storm is now upon us, and there is bound to be much suffering and unemployment before we can hope to emerge from it. It must be recognised that this storm is largely of our own creation, and was born from widespread extravagance, and the hatreds and suspicions left behind by the war. If our industrial system is to survive we must cease violating the fundamental economic laws. Each country must live within her means, and realise that the only way to recover is by economy and hard work. Wranglings and suspicions must cease, and all, both individually and nations, must work in union. If men can learn to pull together, then and only then can they hope for recovery.[6]

Ward wanted his dire prophecies to reach a wider audience than the members of the Federation. "As none of our leaders appear to see where we are drifting", he announced melodramatically at the start of his 1921 pamphlet, *Can Our Industrial System Survive?*, "or, if they see it, dare not speak out, I have felt it my duty to try to arouse the nation from its apathy." The pamphlet repeated the conclusions of his F.B.I. report in far more urgent terms, and sought to demonstrate that European economies were overstretched even before the war and now, in its aftermath, were staggering towards complete collapse. Britain might still be saved, he urged, but "Russia has already gone, Poland is going, and practically all the Continent is threatened with a like fate. Yet all the while leaders continue to hinder her recovery by continuing to violate the very economic laws by which she lives."[7]

Much of the pamphlet was shrewd and commonsensical economic analysis on topics such as wartime disruptions, the terms of the Peace Treaties and problems of exchange rates and inflation. But a very different tone dominated the chapter entitled 'Can The Industrial System Be Saved?', in which Ward marshalled the evidence that pointed to the likelihood that it could not. Civil war raged in Eastern Europe, currencies were ruined, liberal democracies had collapsed and much of the European economy had fallen into the hands of Bolsheviks and advocates of proletarian revolution. A kind of economic madness was taking hold. In Italy, for instance, Ward lamented that the Communists were "requisitioning money and houses at their own sweet will, while the recent outbreak, when the workers seized the factories, was only partially crushed". Government and civil order seemed everywhere to be descending into chaos and lawlessness, while rural depopulation and mass emigration were indexes of misery and despair on a vast scale.

The end of civilization itself was in view, Ward was convinced, because these grim developments were accompanied by striking evidence of morbid decline. In the time-honoured prophetic manner he listed these 'signs of the times': decadence in art, as in cubist abstraction and exaggerated expression-ism, was a clear marker of a decline in aesthetic taste and sensibility. Immorality was on the rise, along with "the extravagance, fast living and aimless search after empty, if not vicious, pleasures, which we see every-where at a time when nearly half our fellow-men are suffering bitterly". A "spirit of selfish lawlessness" was abroad, evidenced by the terrorist violence in Ireland that suggested "the rising generation are utterly devoid of disci-pline, obedience, or self-restraint." Blasé apathy seemed to have taken root among the young and frivolous, so that "nothing seems to rouse them; they drift on from day to day, and nothing really matters". The failing authority of the formal churches signalled that established conceptions of the sacred had lost their hold, leaving anxiety and uncertainty in their wake:

> Men no longer follow the faith of their fathers; but it would be wrong to think that those who turn from orthodox religion are necessarily blatant materialists. Indeed, in many cases they have heard the call for a new conception of the divine and are groping their way towards it. They dream of a new salvator and turn their faces to the East; but the old gods are dead, and to them they look no more.[8]

Taken as individual portents, he concluded, such signs might indicate only a temporary malaise. But taken together, "they become a formidable warning; but when coupled with the terrible economic situation their meaning becomes tragically plain". The questions, at least, were terribly plain to him: "Can our civilisation be saved? Can we yet save Europe? Or will our pleadings fall on deaf ears, and the apathy we have alluded to result in our readers throwing this book aside with a contemptuous shrug of the shoulders? Frankly, we are not very hopeful."[9] "No doubt I shall be called a Jeremiah", he acknowledged with a certain relish, "but, after all, Jeremiah was right."

> His warning fell on deaf ears – had it been heeded his people might have been saved. So to-day there is still time to save Great Britain. It may even

yet be possible to save Europe; but if we continue to behave as we have done, during the last two years, for another three, nothing can save Europe, and its civilisation, like its industrial system, will follow the same path as that taken by Russia; for an economic blockade is closing round the Continent, through which nothing will be able to pass to the relief of its starving millions.[10]

In some ways, this dystopic vision of Europe's industrial prosperity strangled in the vice of Bolshevik centralised planning is merely a curious relic of the economic insecurity that followed the end of the Great War. But we also find in it a hint of the prophetic role that Ward took up with even greater relish and conviction when, in the even darker and more troubled years of the early 1930s, he turned his ample energies to an apocalyptic Christianity.

❋   ❋   ❋

The Federation position was important work and well paid, but also somewhat dull. Perhaps not surprisingly, then, these years coincided with a new enthusiasm for Freemasonry. Ward's appetite for Masonic learning and practice was insatiable throughout the 1920s, from the moment he drew on his Burmese experience to found the British Industries Lodge No. 4100 in May 1920, based upon his circle of connections at the Federation.[11] He willingly shouldered the duties of founding Secretary as he rekindled his deep and abiding passion for the Craft and its esoteric heritage. "While at the FBI my interest in Freemasonry revived . . . [and] I proceeded to take a whole series of fresh Degrees", he recorded thirty years later. If one workaday week followed another in predictable office routine, his evenings and spare time were spent in Masonic and esoteric reading, attendance at lodges and installations, and correspondence with men of similar interests. He studied the arcane 'higher degrees' associated with Freemasonry, hermetic and chivalric traditions such as "the Rose Croix, [Knights] Templar, the Allied Degrees, the Cryptic Degrees, the Secret Monitor, Royal Order of Scotland, the Rosicrucians and so on".[12] He was the driving force in the formation of the Masonic Study Society in 1921, and served as its Secretary, Librarian and later Vice-President. As his circle of associates and connections grew, and with them his profile and status in the Masonic world, Bro. Ward was recognised as one of the leading esoteric scholars of the day. A crowning moment came when his updated and expanded entry on Freemasonry was published in the thirteenth edition of the *Encyclopædia Britannica* in 1926.[13] Another was his election as Worshipful Master of the British Industries Lodge in May 1923. The *Masonic Record* commented: "The new W.M., Bro. John S.M. Ward (many will be surprised to know) had been a Mason for 17 years, but had not hitherto attained the Chair of any Lodge." At the dinner following his election, "the new W.M. proved himself efficient in quickly getting through an extra long toast list", followed by songs and "really humorous stories by members of the Lodge".[14]

A sociable dinner was far from being the primary benefit of Freemasonry for an inquisitive mind such as Ward's. His developing comprehension of the esoteric significance of the rituals, symbols and traditions that punctuated lodge life promised a much deeper and more profound dividend. His wide reading in comparative ethnography, heightened by his personal experiences in the Far East, had convinced him that Freemasonry, like the great religions of the world, was indeed 'The Heir of the Ancient Mysteries'. As he explained in his *An Outline History of Freemasonry*, "despite the apparent changes wrought by differences of time and place, in the great fundamentals, which really matter, [Freemasonry] is still the same as she was when in Egypt the Mysteries were young, and in India the Gods were without a name".[15] Even earlier than that, he went on, the Craft had originated "in the primitive initiatory rites of prehistoric man, and from those rites have been built up all the ancient mysteries, and thence all the modern religious systems".[16] A tenuous but unbroken line of evolutionary development could

3 Ward in Masonic regalia with statuette of Buddha 'touching the earth', 1921. *Masonic Record 1,7 (1921): 290; AMAA 3 WB 1/1.*

be traced, he insisted, from the primitive cults and proto-religions of the ancient world directly to modern Freemasonry. In his view, the Craft had evolved from prehistoric origins alongside the great modern religious traditions, rather than as a latter-day derivative of them.

Bro. Ward's esoteric studies resulted in a flood of Masonic writings during the early 1920s as he developed and promoted these bold views. Articles, essays and books exploring the origins and meaning of Freemasonry and its practices appeared under Ward's name throughout the decade. Some were little more than esoteric journalism, but he was justifiably proud of longer studies such as *Freemasonry and the Ancient Gods* (his first Masonic book, published in mid-1921), *An Interpretation of our Masonic Symbols* (1924), *Who Was Hiram Abiff?* (1926) and the two volumes of *The Sign Language of the Mysteries* (1928). He also pioneered research and interpretation of the Chinese triads and secret societies in a three-volume work *The Hung Society* (1925) with fellow-Mason W. G. Stirling, a colonial official in Singapore. By the end of the decade he was one of the best-known Masonic scholars in the English-speaking world, and had helped lead a new anthropological school of Masonic historians into controversial new territory.

His views provoked some fierce criticism. As we will see, to his detractors Ward was an avid promoter of pseudo-scientific theories that fired the imagination but lacked concrete evidence and critical objectivity. His approach was dismissed as speculative and poorly grounded in verifiable evidence. Certainly, his approach and reasoning had its flaws and his command of examples was not always foolproof, but on the strength of these publications and many shorter articles Ward was generally regarded by Freemasons of his day as a learned authority on symbolism and esoteric tradition. His innate curiosity led him to the study of Eastern mysticism and theology, primitive mystery cults, the Chinese triads, the Knights Templar and other occult traditions; obscure topics with their own mystique and fascination that he brought to bear on Freemasonry in interesting and challenging ways. "Bro. Ward has established a reputation as an earnest and efficient investigator", wrote one reviewer of his first book. "He appears as a welcome visitor and an interesting personality at many Masonic gatherings. His addresses on the antiquity and universality of Masonic Symbolism are invariably listened to with rapt attention."[17]

Reaching a wide audience was clearly important to him, and in 1923 Ward commenced his own publishing imprint, the Warrington Press, to promote his scholarship and preoccupations to a wider readership. This venture began as an important collaboration with a new companion, a woman he had met during 1918–1919 at a lodge of the Co-Masonic Order run under the auspices of the Theosophical Society. 'Co-Masonry' was an attempt to welcome women into the Craft without offending the all-masculine character of the traditional lodge. Its meetings provided a forum for men and women to pursue shared interests in occult and esoteric studies. Jessie Page was a schoolmistress and Theosophist who shared Ward's deepest interests and quickly became his confidante. But as his notion that Masonry had originated in male initiation rites strengthened, Ward "came to the conclusion that visiting the Co-Masonic Order was not consistent with my Masonic obligations", and ceased to attend its gatherings.[18] The friendship with Jessie Page continued to gain strength to the extent that they began the Warrington Press together as vehicle for Ward's Masonic research. It published the first three volumes of his Masonic Handbook Series that year, subtitled 'Studies in the meaning of our ritual'. These were handbooks to the three degrees studied by all Freemasons: the 'Entered Apprentice' or E. A., the 'Fellowship of the Craft' or F. C., and finally the M. M. or 'Master Mason' degree. Ward's handbooks explained the rituals and symbolism – as Ward understood them, at least – that marked the three stages of every Mason's initiation.

The title chosen for their enterprise proved unfortunate, as it was already registered to a firm of Garrick Street printers to produce papers for Grand Lodge. Warrington & Co. commenced a successful action in the High Court Chancery Division, and secured costs of £80 and an order preventing their continued use of the name. The matter seems innocuous enough, but was clearly embarrassing for Ward. A notice in the *Masonic Record* in early 1924 would have compounded his discomfort; it reproduced the order made by Mr Justice Astbury,

> whereby the said Jessie Page undertook not at any time hereafter to carry on the business of a Publisher or Printer of any Masonic works or other Masonic publications under the style of 'The Warrington Publishing Company' or under any other style of which the name 'Warrington' formed part, and forthwith to call in all Masonic books or other Masonic publications already issued or published by her still remaining under her control, so that she should block out the name 'Warrington' appearing in or upon such books or publications, and the said J. S. M. Ward undertook not to permit the Defendant, Jessie Page, to issue or publish any Masonic book or other Masonic publication of which he is the author under the style of 'The Warrington Publishing Company' or under any other style of which the name 'Warrington' forms part.[19]

The awkward incident did not constrain Ward's publishing activities. He and Jessie promptly re-named their firm the Baskerville Press, and continued to issue Ward's titles from a rented office in New Bond Street. The Masonic Handbook Series sold quite strongly, providing him with a modest income, and twenty years later the imprint was sold to A. Lewis & Co., another

Masonic publisher. But it seems certain that, in the short term, the Warrington fiasco tarnished Bro. Ward's lustre in Masonic circles, and may have helped marginalise him and his views to a certain extent. His prolific contributions to the *Masonic Record*, for example, suddenly came to an end. Since the journal commenced in December 1920, Ward had been one of its most regular contributors with some two dozen articles over three years. With the Warrington dispute, his name disappeared abruptly from the lists of contributors.

Probably more significant, though, was the intrinsic character of Ward's Masonic research itself. His idiosyncratic approach – at once speculative and provocative, as we will see – clearly riled other scholars of Masonic history. Viewing Freemasonry as essentially a religion, a survival of ancient rites or 'mysteries', Ward aimed to study it in comparative terms as an anthropologist might study primitive belief amongst tribal peoples. His analysis of symbols and iconography embraced gestures, rituals and myths, stories, legends, fragments of history and symbolism, and so his books and articles brimmed with vivid incidents and examples, gathered together as fascinating relics of a submerged but continuous tradition.

At a basic level this approach arose from Ward's personal experience. His curiosity had been excited by the essential similarities he found in the diverse cultures and faiths that confronted him in British India, where Buddhism, Hinduism, Islamic and Confucian beliefs mingled with a host of local cults and exotic forms of indigenous Christianity such as those of India's Malabar coast. He delighted in his discovery that signs and symbols that were essentially Masonic flourished in these complex cultural and religious environments. He remembered, for example, seeing two Pathans – Muslims from Northern India – greet each other in a secluded alley in Colombo. Their gestures had convinced him immediately they were Masonic brethren. "Sign by sign they went through *all* the signs of the three degrees", he reported in the *Masonic Record*. "What words they used I could not hear, and while I believe that the grips were the same, with the exception of the last, I could not swear to them." The final grip and handshake, however, "was one permitting no possibility of mistake." But when he approached the two men Ward was quickly disabused of his assumption. Both were devout Muslims, and took offence at the suggestion that they were connected to a Masonic lodge. "Naturally somewhat abashed", Ward continued, "I withdrew hastily, but the incident proved to me conclusively what I had heard from numerous stories current in India but had hesitated to believe, namely, that the Mahomedans had an indigenous system similar to craft masonry."[20]

The basic flavour of his Masonic research also derived from his reverence for the great antiquity of Masonic tradition. His delight at the great antiquity of Masonic symbols and gestures, and his sense of a brotherhood that had conquered the ravages of time as it threaded through all the cultures of the globe, was expressed poetically in three simple stanzas he entitled 'From Time Immemorial' and published in 1926:

> From Yucatan to Java's strand
> We have followed thy trail o'er sea and land.
> When Pharoah lived he knew this sign,
> Brother of mine, Brother of mine.
>
> Where Vishnu sits enthroned on high
> I noted Hunuman passing by,
> And as he passed he made this sign,
> Brother of mine, Brother of mine.
>
> In the ocean of peace I came to a land
> Where silence broods on an empty strand,
> Where ancient Gods of carven stone
> Gaze o'er waters, still and lone,
> And, search as I might, I could but find
> Fragments of wood, which bring to mind
> Ancient writings of bygone days . . .
> Whilst on the hieroglyphs I gaze
> I find that they also knew the sign,
> Brothers now dead, yet Brothers of mine![21]

This living heritage had an antique sense of mystery that had attracted men throughout the ages in the same way that it had first seduced him as a young mason at Cambridge. It answered his romantic historical instincts; and as his curiosity and delight in the past and its relics remained a defining feature of his outlook throughout his adult life, so too did his love of Freemasonry continue beyond his active Masonic career. If Freemasonry provided a unique panorama of a universal human heritage, Ward was eager to number himself among its loyal and dedicated custodians. "It should be remembered", he wrote in *Freemasonry, its aims and ideals*,

> that there are large numbers of men who love things just because they are old, old castles, old churches, old furniture appeal to them, – not only because they are usually artistic, but because they glimpse some of the romance and history of the past. Such men have sufficient imagination to be able to envisage the life of the past, and it interests them. Naturally, a living organism, such as Freemasonry, which avowedly traces its roots back into the distant past and claims to be working ceremonies which have come down through at least two centuries, and possibly longer,

arouses their enthusiasm. Moreover, such men form a much-needed brake on those who are forever desiring to revise and alter our old ceremonies, or to introduce innovations . . .[22]

Allowing these impulses free reign, Ward thus took a very lively and imaginative approach to Masonic lore and tradition. If his motives were innocent enough, however, the provocative claim that his anthropological mode of inquiry gave his insights the authority of scientific conclusions was bound to provoke sharp disagreement.

The inevitable disputes arose because most Masonic historians of Ward's day, by contrast, were devout worshippers in the temple of critical objectivity. They sought to establish their research as a legitimate branch of mainstream historical scholarship through the careful sifting of records and official documents, separating myth from fact and so developing sound empirical conclusions. Calling themselves the 'Authentic School' of Masonic research, these historians concentrated exclusively on administrative developments since the foundation of Grand Lodge in 1717, favouring topics such as the spread of affiliated lodges overseas, biographies of leading Masons, the eighteenth-century split between 'Ancients' and 'Moderns', the administration of degrees and so forth. They published their findings in dedicated journals such as *Ars Quatuor Coronatorum* (*AQC*), the journal of the Quatuor Coronati Lodge (QCL) No. 2076, then as now the premier research lodge of Masonic history. Established by nine Masonic scholars in 1884, QCL institutionalised the scholarly practices of R. F. Gould, the pre-eminent nineteenth-century Masonic historian whose definitive *History of Freemasonry* had prised loose much of the specious mythology that encrusted Freemasonry like barnacles to a whale. Gould's scholarly approach exemplified the historical method: careful documentary research in archives and official documents, a diligent criticism of these sources to reveal verified facts, and the testing of reasonable hypotheses purely in the light of these 'authentic' facts and the documents that gave rise to them. Ward's provocative attempt to establish a rival 'Anthropological School' ruffled the feathers of Gould's heirs and allies, the self-proclaimed Authentic historians of modern Freemasonry.

Ward's point of departure was the severely limited scope of the Authentic School's interest. As a secret society of uncertain origin and mysterious ritual, he pointed out, how could the inner history and ultimate meaning of Freemasonry ever be deduced from formal documents alone? He was not persuaded (as members of the Authentic School were) that a modern paraphernalia of esoteric ritual had been grafted artificially onto older craft traditions by Freemasons in the decades around 1717. With his characteristic zest for submerged truths and obscure deeper meanings, Ward suggested that an alternative approach to the history of the Craft might cast a light into the shadows of Masonic tradition. "Let the Authentic School still concentrate on documents", he proclaimed in a generously fraternal spirit,

[as] there is still enough work to be done to occupy it fully for many years – but let others follow the anthropological line of research, and the sum total of our knowledge will be vastly increased. Above all, it is along this line of research that we may hope to discover the true esoteric meaning of our symbols and ritual.[23]

Like secular historians who turned to the insights of anthropologists to illuminate the social customs of prehistoric humanity, he suggested, Masonic historians should be prepared to get adventurous and enlarge their interests. Mainstream pre-historians, Ward pointed out, had no documents or texts to develop their knowledge of Palaeolithic life; to explain the living societies suggested by archaeological discoveries of skeletons and flint tools they had therefore turned to comparative anthropology. "[O]ur real comprehension of our prehistoric ancestors", he pointed out, "is due to the researches of scientific anthropologists. By studying the customs of primitive man today we are able to reconstruct the life of primitive man, and so it will be with Freemasonry."[24]

Masonic History must similarly push back its horizon nearer to its original source. Nothing is created de novo, it grows out of what has gone before, changing during the process in many details, yet containing within it innumerable traces of its far distant origin. Just as the man is externally different to the boy, and yet is but that same boy grown to man's estate, so it is with our own beloved Order.[25]

If a close and informed study of the secretive ritual and symbolism of modern Masonry uncovered clear parallels with the rites and symbols studied by ethnographers and classical scholars, why shun the clear and obvious implication of this discovery? What right-minded and inquisitive Freemason could afford to ignore these new keys that offered to unlock the ancient mysteries of their Craft?

This provocative message threaded through all Ward's Masonic writings of the early 1920s. His short articles for the *Masonic Record*, booklets like *An Outline History of Freemasonry* (1924) and longer works such as *Freemasonry and the Ancient Gods* stoutly maintained that the claim to great antiquity made in Masonic rituals was factual rather than merely metaphorical. Even though every Worshipful Master was bound to inform new initiates to his lodge that the Craft had existed since time immemorial, "probably most of them acquiesce in the view", Ward observed, "that this is a white lie, and few have ventured to maintain that they really believe it".[26] He, on the other hand, was certainly prepared to believe it, and to argue for it with a stubborn persistence. He used the evidence of rituals, signs, symbols and gestures in lodge practice and Masonic iconography to trace a direct line from the workings of a modern Masonic lodge back to the trade secrets of the medieval craft guilds. From there Ward projected a further line of inheritance, back via the religious practices of the classical world to the ancient religions administered by priests and clerics initiated into esoteric knowledge. These 'mysteries' were in turn derived from even earlier traditions back to their ultimate source, namely the "primitive initiatory rites of our savage ancestors".[27]

Ward's grand vista of Freemasonry's tangled history thus deliberately eschewed the schisms and disputes, "the small details and somewhat undignified controversies of 18th century Masonic History",[28] that took centre stage in most histories of the Craft. His ambition was at once simpler and much broader; to push the history of Freemasonry "back [over] its horizon nearer to its original source." Despite the tangled thicket of evidence and example, it all rested, in fact, on a bald premise: given that certain signs and symbols used in modern Masonic practices were visible among tribal initiation rites in Nyasaland, on Easter Island, in ancient Mexico, in the art of Classical India, and so on, only one conclusion was possible:

> How then comes it that the Primitive Savage and the Pagan Gods make our S[ig]ns? The only rational explanation is that these S[ig]ns were part of the original initiatory rites of a boy into manhood, and were originally used to convey certain spiritual meanings, which were difficult for men to put into words, since their vocabularies were very limited . . . These initiatory rites (which still survive among the savage races) were originally magical in their object. From them have developed the Ancient Mysteries, and later the Modern Religious Systems of the world. These S[ig]ns, being already holy things, (mantras or spells in fact) naturally became associated with certain Gods as men's conception of the spiritual evolved.[29]

This entire historical scheme rested heavily on the elusive evidence of cultural symbolism (as construed, moreover, by Ward himself) and little else. Historians then as now have an inbuilt hostility to this kind of extrapolation from the evidence, especially when used to support conclusions in the absence of more conventional historical sources. Anticipating some resistance to his line of thinking, Ward affected a kind of modesty that those in disagreement with his dogmatic conclusions would have regarded as disingenuous. He urged his readers to bear in mind "when studying the meaning and origin of all customs, ritual practices, and symbols . . . that, as time passes, men are apt to forget the true origin and meaning and invent new and ingenious explanations. They weave new legends round old customs, or import them from another school of belief."[30] Even if Freemasonry was particularly fertile ground for this 'invention of tradition', as recent historical scholarship puts it, [31] Ward insisted that anthropological conclusions like his were not merely "the weaving of petty fancies drawn from our own fertile imaginations". He insisted there were "laws of symbolism like those of any other science, and, though some freedom is permitted the interpreter, yet he is bounded and limited in his interpretation by the fundamental meaning of the symbols he is explaining".[32] Ward's reasoning on such occasions could be somewhat circular. But to his credit he was not so doctrinaire as to disallow other, perhaps contradictory, interpretations of the same 'survivals'. As he wrote in *An Interpretation of our Masonic Symbols*,

> more than one meaning lies hidden in our silent emblems, and the ostensible explanation given in the ceremony is usually neither the original nor the most profound meaning attached to it. My object . . . is to arouse in others the desire to probe into their inner meaning and to study it for themselves. I have not attempted to be exhaustive, but have aimed at leading others to embark on the same fascinating task. I assure them that there is room for others, and that, though my interpretations be correct, there is no reason why other interpretations should not be equally valid, and of equal assistance to others in the task of learning to understand what our mysteries strive to teach.[33]

Ward thus offered to his readers an esoteric history of ritual that explained how certain basic spiritual truths had been sequestered in secret rites and teachings, and so endured through successive historical civilizations. He followed the comparative anthropologists of his day in assembling examples that supported his case from all sorts of cultural, historical and religious contexts, and argued that the correlation of gestures, narrative motifs, symbolic elements of sacred rites and architecture between those contexts were expressive of their shared origins deep in human prehistory. A favoured example was the hand sign depicting distress or 'S.O.S.', and the closely related gesture of the open hand depicting 'preservation' or 'P.' Ward discussed examples of both of these in circumcision rites in East Africa; in archaological sites from ancient Assyria, Egypt, Mexico and Peru; in Indian carvings of Shiva and Javanese images of the Buddha; being used as a sign of identification by Dervishes; in frescoes at Pompeii; in Byzantine sculptures of Daniel in the lion's den and in twelfth-century Italian mosaics depicting Jonah emerging from the whale.[34] Chinese illustrations of the Buddha depicted hand gestures that were "practically the same [as] taught in certain higher degrees" in the Masonic tradition. A *bas-relief* in Java "shows the

Buddha making the p.s. of a degree." A native dancing belt presented to a tribal initiate in New Guinea featured "the Scotch s. of G. and D.". His lists of examples went on and on, and Ward was willing to draw certain definite conclusions from them:

> Ancient Assyria reveals our signs and symbols, the Thibetans use a sign of the R[oyal] A[rch], and others, and Asia is but typical of all the Continents. Australasia, Africa, Ancient America, and Ancient Europe, all bear witness to the same truth that these ancient landmarks have indeed subsisted since time immemorial; but why India appears to me to hold the master key is because there the Ancient Wisdom is still a living force, and the secret doctrine has been carried down to the present day from a time to which the memory of man runneth not.[35]

All in all, when he laid out his theory in clear terms to the readers of the *Masonic Record*, it all amounted to a breath-takingly ambitious claim:

> I suggest that Freemasonry has, as we claim, subsisted from time immemorial and dates its origin from the first simple initiatory rites of the savages. That these rites became in time the basis out of which the Mysteries, and with them all modern religious systems, developed. That the priests who organised these mysteries, appropriated to their Gods the early signs used by man to denote certain ideas which could not at that early date be conveniently put into words.[36]

✳ ✳ ✳

Thus Ward's Masonic scholarship had two interlinked objectives. Firstly he sought to demonstrate an essential continuity for the esoteric practices of the Craft; a continuous heritage that was vividly embodied, he argued, in the secret Masonic traditions revealed to its initiates. His was an adventurous, speculative history of Freemasonry that seemed calculated to offend the empirically-minded sensibilities of mainstream Masonic historians. We are not surprised that the earnest empiricists of the Quatuor Coronati Lodge regarded such arguments for the historical continuity of Masonic practice to be far-fetched. At best it was poorly grounded in evidence, but at worst it was naïve and credulous; and certainly Ward's habit of using anthropological evidence to support historical conclusions about Freemasonry's institutional continuity is disconcerting. But if this methodological hybrid was vulnerable to accusations of selective evidence and special pleading, it was essential to Ward's second objective: the clarification of the intrinsic meaning of the symbols and rituals that were now, to his eyes, embodied in modern

Freemasonry. Anthropological interpretations could pinpoint the precise inner or esoteric truth that ultimately was the reason for the continued utility and survival of these precious traditions. In pursuing this latter objective, Ward turned to the fashionable anthropology of his day to secure scientific credibility for his sense of Freemasonry's profound esoteric significance.

Other Masonic researchers had been tending in the same direction under the influence of modern anthropology, particularly Dr Albert Churchward, whose *Origin and Antiquity of Freemasonry* (1898), *Signs and Symbols of Primordial Man* (1910) and *The Arcana of Freemasonry* (1915) had taken a similar line of interpretation with a focus on Freemasonry's debt to Egyptian mystery cults. Ward claimed him "as the pioneer of the new school of masonic research which I hope that my work will call into existence, for which I suggest the name of the Anthropological School in contradistinction to the present Authentic School". He was confident that he was not alone in following Churchward's lead:

> I have little doubt that scattered over the world there are other brothers who, like myself, have been studying Masonry from the anthropological point of view. At present they are inarticulate, or known at most to a few. My greatest desire is to bring them into the open; let them come forward to confirm or contradict my facts and conclusions, and one of my objects will be achieved.[37]

This plea to bring an anthropological approach to Masonic study "into the open" helped inspire the foundation of a study circle later in 1921. The Masonic Study Society (MSS) was dedicated to the study of the symbolism of all the degrees in Freemasonry, including the obscure higher degrees so beloved to Ward. The Society held its first meeting at Mark Mason's Hall in June 1921, with Ward as its founding Secretary and co-editor of its journal. He was later credited by one MSS president as "the father and only begetter of this Society,"[38] and by another as its founder.[39] The Society's formal objectives as published in the first volume of its *Transactions* embodied Ward's approach utterly:

> To study the Symbolism of Freemasonry in its various degrees and to investigate its origin and meaning on Anthropological lines. The Society aims at avoiding those aspects of Masonic Research which are already dealt with by existing Research Societies, and will endeavour to study the Craft, in the light of similar systems past and present and on the lines of comparative Religions, Anthropology and Folklore. In short, the Society will study Masonry as a living organism, as well as on the basis of documents.[40]

Special attention to the "symbolic and mystical meaning of the various degrees" was promised. After the inaugural meeting had heard a paper from Sir John Cockburn on 'The Meaning of Some of the Craft Symbols' that dwelt on the significance of the Square, its relationship to the Christian cross, and the influence of mason's marks on the alphabet, brethren conducted an avid discussion of their new Society's role and objectives. A. E. Waite, the celebrated mystical scholar and author of *Studies in Mysticism*, proposed the vote of thanks, and observed that their new Society was "badly needed at the present time . . . [as it would] endeavour to teach Masons what their ancient ritual meant, and the more brethren got together and put forward suggestions, the more interest they would find in the Masonic ritual and the greater the advantage to their own intellectual well being". Several other members present (including, we might assume, Bro. Ward) spoke in agreement, "and there was unanimous agreement that the new Society in no way infringed on the existing Masonic research societies, but rather that it filled a gap".

> The Anthropological, Symbolical and Mystical side of Freemasonry had, during recent years, tended to be neglected in favour of Archaeological research, but although there was still plenty of work to be done on the Archaeological side, it was full time that attention was directed to the other aspects in which a most attractive field of study awaited the keen student.[41]

The terms are slightly different, but the basic factional division between 'documentary' and 'anthropological' research into the Masonic past was clear.

Thereafter the Society met regularly to hear papers from leading Masonic scholars on topics dear to Bro. Ward's heart. The MSS meetings provided satisfying intellectual companionship – perhaps the most rewarding Ward ever knew – and he continued to attend them long after he had severed his other links to Freemasonry. Over the next fifteen years he delivered over a dozen papers to the Society, including studies on 'The Meaning of Some Parts of our Ritual', 'The Universality of our Signs and Symbols', the history and significance of the Knights Templar and the Chinese Triad society, Masonic emblems of mortality and an analysis of cryptic ornamentation in Peterborough Cathedral. He listened avidly as others broached topics as diverse as initiation rites among tribal peoples, numerology and esoteric mathematics, fertility cults and other correlations between Masonic practice and folklore or mythology. His close friend W. A. Wigram spoke on the mysteries of Eleusis, Mithraism, Orphism, 'Isis and her Mysteries', 'The Kabeiroi and Their Mysteries', and 'Mystery Rites among Primitive Peoples' at MSS meetings between 1922 and 1937. On each occasion Bro. Ward attended in person and joined the ensuing discussion with great enthusiasm.[42]

The Masonic Study Society went beyond academic anthropology to encourage discussions of Freemasonry as a vehicle for mystical and occult enlightenment. This was of course another favourite theme for Bro. Ward. When A. E. Waite explained 'The Mystical Search in Freemasonry' to the fifth meeting of the group in October 1921, it was "listened to with rapt attention by a very large gathering of Brethren, and it was remarked by everyone that the high spiritual tone adopted by the lecturer met with a ready response from those who were present".[43] In June 1925, in a similar paper entitled 'The Fundamental Philosophic Secrets within Masonry', W. L. Wilmshurst argued that, at its heart, Masonic initiation taught "the solemn fact that God and the human soul are in essence a unity, not a duality, and the sole intention of our Initiatory-system is, by instruction and discipline, to bring about in each of us the conscious realisation of that unity". Ward rose and applauded the paper heartily, suggesting the group "had never had a more important paper with such absolutely clear definitions of the secrets of Masonry". "Mysticism might be defined", he went on,

> as the search of the soul after union with the Supreme. It lay behind every important faith, and was found among Hindoos, Muslims, Buddhists and Christians. The Roman Catholic Church had her mystical school. Bunyan was a mystic, and it was the key which unlocked the mysteries of Freemasonry.[44]

✴ ✴ ✴

Ward and others like him in the Masonic Study Society were giving new life to a view of Masonry's origins and universality that was, in fact, already deeply entrenched: one commentator at the turn of the century listed no fewer than nine separate theories claiming to explain its deep origins prior to 1717.[45] Among them was the view Ward promoted in *An Outline History of Freemasonry* that a direct succession could be traced from the 'ancient mysteries' (and more specifically, the builders of Solomon's Temple) via the Roman Colleges of Artificers to the medieval operative masons. While other lines of succession had been traced by Masonic antiquarians to Noah, Enoch and even Adam, and ancient sects such as the Essenes and the Culdees, these were understood in legendary or metaphorical terms rather than as a literal point of commencement and with a direct line of historical continuity, as Ward maintained in his account. Among the more historically-minded Masonic scholars were various explanations, just as exotic as Ward's, that suggested that Masonic ritual was sustained by returning Crusaders, by refugee Templars after the suppression of their order in 1312, by errant Rosicrucians and Jacobite subversives.

So even if Ward saw himself at the forefront of a new, scientific approach to Masonic tradition, in effect he was reinforcing quite commonplace views of Freemasonry's great antiquity. Rudyard Kipling, himself an influential and dedicated Freemason fascinated like Ward by India and its multitude of faiths, had popularised this sense of Masonry as a universal and quasi-religious heritage of rite and symbol. His short story 'The Man Who Would Be King', first published in 1888, worked this theme as its central motif. Kipling's heroes, two freewheeling Masons and rugged soldier-adventurers Daniel Dravot and 'Peachy' Carnehan, carve out an imperial fiefdom in Kafiristan north-west of India assisted by the secret rituals of the Craft that, unexpectedly, prove identical to the rites practiced by local priests. After being proclaimed by the priests as the heirs of Alexander the Great, the two adventurers opportunistically establish a homespun Lodge to ensure their grip on power. With this arrangement the business of control and government became, in Dravot's railway analogy, "as easy as a four-wheeled bogie on a down grade". When the 'Grand-Master's chair', a great square stone in the local temple, is over-turned in the middle of their mock-Masonic ritual, the visual revelation of Kipling's theme is unveiled:

'The priest begins rubbing the bottom end of it to clear away the black dirt, and presently he shows all the other priests the Master's Mark, same as was on Dravot's apron, cut into the stone. Not even the priests of the temple of Imbra knew it was there. The old chap falls flat on his face at Dravot's feet and kisses 'em.'[46]

In effect, Ward's anthropological approach to the interpretation of Masonic ritual dignified this vague but potent sense of the Craft's great antiquity and geographic spread by re-casting it as a scientific hypothesis. But while he was keen to stress the scientific credentials of his self-taught anthropology, it seems clear that Ward's antiquarian romanticism, his instinctive delight in a heritage descended from cultural forms lost in the mists of antiquity, shaped his approach in a much more fundamental way. Noel Gist, an American scholar of esoteric fraternities writing in 1940, shrewdly grasped the deeper psychological drivers of this kind of esoteric enquiry:

the realities attendant upon the prosaic beginning of Masonry in fairly recent times are probably less convincing to many than the romantic accounts of a supposed antiquity of origin. There is reason to believe that these legends, which give the organization the stamp of antiquity, afford an element of prestige to those who accept them. It is also reasonable to assume that the legendary accounts represent a form of wish-fulfilment and a type of fantasy-thinking.[47]

No doubt many of his contemporaries – outside the keen symbologists of the MSS, at least – shared this diagnosis. "The attempts on the part of Masonic enthusiasts to trace the origin of Freemasonry to the ancient Mysteries", Gist concluded, "have been rewarded with the discovery of a number of similarities between the modern and early societies but no conclusive evidence of any rectilinear evolutionary development." This neatly captured Ward's dilemma.

> The ancient Egyptian Mysteries, the Eleusinian Mysteries of Greece, the Mithraic Mysteries of Persia, the Adonaic Mysteries of Syria, the Cabiric Mysteries of the island of Samothrace, the Druidic Mysteries of primordial Britain, and the Gnostics of the early Christian era have possessed a number of traits, if rather fragmentary evidences are to be accepted, that are likewise characteristic of modern Masonry. These traits have constituted the basis for origin theories of the most extravagant kinds.[48]

We get a clearer understanding of the basis for Ward's own extravagant conclusions if we grasp his debt to J. G. Frazer's masterpiece of comparative religion, *The Golden Bough*, one of the most influential books of the early twentieth century. Frazer's twelve-volume opus, published in three editions between 1890 and 1915, accumulated a multitude of examples from myth, folklore, primitive magic and religious rites; from classical literature to the reports of missionaries and explorers on the imperial frontier. The evidence thus assembled evoked the universal prevalence of earth and sun worship, the harvest and fertility festivals and animistic deities of forest, lake and stream in primitive humanity. The rhythm of the seasons and the eternal cycles of birth, growth, decay, death and rebirth offered in nature were echoed in male and female initiation rites, but they also shaped the archetypal beliefs and ritual practices of early humanity. They gave rise to the folkloric motif of the dying and resurrected God, along with other potent and enduring themes in humanity's myths and rituals. For Frazer, religion (like magic) embodied through the ages humanity's effort to formally recognize and appease the forces that "control and direct the course of nature and of human life".[49]

The Golden Bough's frank declaration of the functionally comparable roles of magic and religion in human social life was sophisticated and modern. At the same time, however, it was very much a work of the nineteenth century, with its insistence on universal patterns of evolution. Like other early works of modern anthropology, it interpreted folk customs as "cultural fossils, left over from the earlier stages of civilised societies, [so that] a comparative study of them could provide a general theory of religious development for the human race",[50] an approach formally discredited in the 1920s. By this time the book had popularised Frazer's comparative method and his apparent success in drawing out the inner coherence and intrinsic meaning of surviving fragments of myth, folklore, ritual, superstition and primitive religion found across the globe and through time. His approach was thus enormously influential upon early twentieth-century studies of primitive cultures and mythology. Margaret Murray's *The Witch-Cult in Western Europe* published in 1921, for example, took a Frazerian line in explaining witch-craft as the survival of the ancient Diana myth and earth worship into the Christian era.

Ward took a similarly Frazerian approach to his Masonic studies. His compilation of masses of fragmentary and diverse evidence, assembled to discover correlations and deeper patterns, matched the patient accumulation characteristic of Frazer's scholarly method. Like Frazer, too, he revelled in the dramatic potential of his material and favoured striking, vivid imagery that appealed to the general reader. He followed Frazer in positing a close association between the rites and symbols that embodied certain quasi-religious traditions and the myths that were composed over time to convey those traditions in narrative form. Ward's conclusions, moreover, were essentially those of *The Golden Bough* applied to modern esoteric tradition, in that a comparison between Freemasonry and other systems of belief and practice seemed to reveal their common ancestry in the proto-religious outlook of prehistoric humanity.

Yet his anthropology shaded into an explicit mysticism as Ward insisted that the mystery cults and ancient belief systems that underpinned Freemasonry taught a universal message that remained essentially valid and intact. While they "varied considerably in detail", he insisted, "they seem always to have had the same great aim. They taught of the soul of man, whence he came and whither he was going. Above all they taught of a mystic quest, of the desire of the soul for reunion with God, whence it had come."[51] This conviction, simple as it was but deeply felt, added an occult dimension to Ward's Frazerian perspective on the history and heritage of Freemasonry, and owed much to Ward's Spiritualist conviction that material existence was merely a veil across a deeper spiritual reality. To those capable of deciphering them, the ancient mysteries revealed a mystical teaching with universal human significance.

> And what did these mysteries teach? The lower degrees taught of Birth, both physical and spiritual. How the child came to be born and whence the spirit came which animated the body – of Life and its trials and dangers and the moral code of the community – of Death, before whose dread sceptre monarch and beggar alike must bow, and that death does not end all.[52]

Mystery cults such as that of Osiris in ancient Egypt and the famed Eleusinian rites of the Greek world contained deep spiritual truths, Ward insisted, through which the "spiritually minded and educated 'Pagans'" of the pre-Christian era "taught their higher conceptions of God":

> While they paid an outward reverence to the Gods, and to the official religion of their own country, in the Mysteries they taught the deeper truths of religion, which it would not have been safe to reveal to the ignorant and ill-educated world outside. These truths usually included the belief in the unity of God and in the Resurrection, and in many cases also taught the initiate what life was like in the realm beyond the grave.[53]

Here Ward was not simply betraying his sense of Christianity as the supreme revelation of spiritual truth, a truth that was implicit in primitive religions but concealed as esoteric higher knowledge. He was also speaking with the certainty of the convinced Spiritualist because, in short, he found in the rituals of the ancient mystery cults a confirmation of what his deceased brother, his father-in-law and other mentors in the spirit world had imparted to him of the Afterlife. The ancient mystery cults, he stated emphatically,

> went on to talk of what befell the soul after death. How it passed through the under World and crossed the dread bridge between the astral and the spirit planes. How thence it climbed the ladder which led to the Mansions of the Blest, and entered into the Kingdom of the Gods. Yet still upward, the high grades led men on, teaching in allegory and symbol that at long last the purified soul became one with God, the Infinite, and so obtained Union and Peace.[54]

He found the same esoteric message in the animistic cults of primitive peoples, and in all the major faiths and religious traditions of humanity. Freemasonry – the 'heir of the ancient mysteries' – was thus a relic of the most ancient insights into metaphysics and transcendent reality to be found anywhere. "How many realize that the Ancient Mysteries are not dead", he asked the readers of the *Occult Review,* "but exist among us in the twentieth century as strong and virile as ever they were in the days of Ancient Rome? They have changed their name, but they are with us nevertheless, and find their most notable expression in Freemasonry."[55]

Thus Ward's Masonic scholarship through this period repeatedly emphasized the richness and coherence of Masonic teachings and traditions as a tool for metaphysical enlightenment. Themes he explored in his shorter papers for the *Masonic Record* and the *Occult Review* were developed in his major writings on Masonic heritage, ritual and symbolism. In *An Interpretation of our Masonic Symbols* published in 1924, for example, his sense of the holistic unity and harmony visible in Masonic rites provided a foundation for his whole study. "The longer one studies the Masonic system of symbols", he wrote, "the more impressed we become with the wonderful symmetry of the whole system, and the manner in which each symbol plays its appropriate part in our Mysteries."[56] He wanted "to give a scientific explanation of the meaning of these symbols, based on the recognized laws of symbology and on the age-old interpretation of them that has come down from the long distant past".[57] Similarly, his later two-volume work *The Sign Language of the Mysteries* expanded on this interpretive scheme and presented scores of examples of non-Masonic semiotic "survivals" in medieval frescoes, stained glass, illuminations and sculpture. His stated intention, however, was the same: to demonstrate that "everything that takes place in the Masonic ceremonies has a definite inner meaning and is not arbitrary or accidental".[58]

Ward accordingly took the idea of Masonic induction and growth in knowledge very seriously. A seven-part series of articles for the *Masonic Record* in 1921–1922 entitled 'All the Degrees in Freemasonry' gave him a chance to expand on the subject. He argued that the three basic degrees (the E. A., the F. C. and thirdly the M. M., which had been mandated as the compulsory 'Craft Degrees' for all Freemasons by Grand Lodge in 1813) corresponded with the mysteries of birth, life and death in both the physical and the spiritual senses. While this much was commonly observed in the ordinary business of most lodges, his articles sought to make their inner meanings explicit. He explained that the first degree, taken by the 'Entered Apprentice', used symbolism to teach the cosmic truths of "birth and of our entry into this world". When the initiate is symbolically bound and blind-folded, for example, his bondage evoked "the hampering bonds of the flesh, which weigh down the Soul on its entry into mortal life from the free realms of the spirit from which it comes". Other rituals and symbols taught the new Freemason that "the Spirit inspires us to advance towards the light, but the Soul alone can invest us with the emblem of our advancement . . . in other words, the Soul which is the link between the Divine Spirit and the mortal body is the only means we have on earth by which we can progress".[59] For Ward, in other words, the initiation ceremonies undertaken by all Freemasons corroborated the metaphysical truths that had been revealed to him clairvoyantly by spirit contact.

Similarly, the second or 'Fellow Craftsman' degree elaborated on themes of spiritual and moral development in the individual's lifespan. Ward felt that moral education was a central theme in the degree's esoteric meaning, symbolised by its veiled references to the seven liberal arts and sciences. The degree also taught, he suggested, that the individual's growth could also be measured by conformity to the laws established by divine agency (by the G.A.O.T.U., in Masonic code) and the accumulation of worldly goods and spiritual insight as the reward for the individual's labour and dedication. The third or Master Mason's degree "teaches us of the inevitable end, but it also hints that death does not end all". More importantly, the M.M. degree warned the Freemason that material success was a hindrance to true spiritual advancement. "Lest, therefore, we should be prevented by the weight of worldly possessions from entering [the Kingdom of Heaven]", Ward inferred, "we are [symbolically] cut off before our spiritual nature has become clogged and ruined by our possessions." He went on in veiled terms to interpret the rituals themselves:

> But a word was lost and the Brethren, despite the promise of assistance from the W[orshipful] M[aster] [of the Lodge] fail to find it. They have to be content with a substitution. What is that which was lost? We are told that we hope to find it at the centre. Now the geometrical figure here described in India stands for Paramatma, the All Pervading, i.e. God. Whence we have all come and to whom, as the Hindoos and others teach, we shall all ultimately return. Therefore, what is lost is our comprehension of the Nature of God . . . Man, being finite, cannot comprehend the Infinite, yet, because of the Divine Spark within him he is always sensible of a feeling of separation and loss, and to repair that loss he starts on the Quest.[60]

With this preparation the mystical journey of Masonic learning might continue beyond these degrees, as "through a series of little understood high degrees the earnest candidate pursues the search for the lost word". Ward encouraged all Masons, once qualified in the Craft Degrees, to continue their quest for spiritual enlightenment through the arcane rituals of the Mark and Royal Arch degrees, and from there to esoteric degrees administered by the likes of the Knights Templar and various Rosicrucian orders. "Freemasonry is like a Gothic cathedral", he wrote characteristically, "and if the foundations and crypt are the craft [embodied in the teachings of the first three degrees], then the higher degrees represent the nave and isles, the side chapels and fretted roof whose spires point up to the Heavens."[61] Ward's enthusiasm for this arcane heritage reached a crescendo in another highly characteristic passage:

> [The candidate] obtains one answer in the Royal Arch [degree] – an explanation non-Christian, and in many ways similar to that given to the Hindu mystic. In other grades he learns that the lost word is the Logos, to us Christians, Christ. Our candidate journeys through Hell, crosses the dread Bridge, he passes through veil after veil, which mark stages of spiritual evolution till in symbolism he learns of the Beatific Vision, of the mystic rose of Dante – in short of the true end of the quest. And in and out runs the shuttle of the life of the mystic set forth with astonishing clearness in the degrees of Knights Templar, Knights of Malta, Knights of the Holy Sepulchre, pageant on pageant, mystery on mystery, full to the

brim of ancient symbolism and old world wisdom, now but little understood by the bulk of those who pass through them, yet having such magic that even the most materialistic are caught by the splendour of the hidden glory and love these ancient rites – though they know not why.[62]

In this progress the graduating Freemason – penetrating ever-deeper into the veiled truths of ancient wisdom – followed the archetypal mystical quest, overcoming doubts, difficulties and challenges so that he might ultimately reach the "Beatific Vision of the Splendour of God . . . a real experience, as real as any that are physical. The Soul becomes able to comprehend God with all its being, He becomes one with God, and the final peace is won."[63]

In this way Ward ultimately imagined Freemasonry as a powerful, enduring project for the spiritual evolution of humanity. He placed the Craft alongside the great world faiths, each with their own traditions of mysticism and enlightenment, all of them keepers of the sacred flame of spiritual truth that fostered the spiritual education of humankind. In the heritage and traditions of Freemasonry, in other words, he felt he could unlock the profound narrative of humanity's cosmic journey and its ultimate destiny. Each individual lodge had a part to play, because in bringing together seekers for spiritual insight each was "part of the great Temple which the G.A.O.T.U. has planned for the benefit of humanity". The transcendent 'Temple' Ward had in mind was universal, non-sectarian and non-theological, with "many chambers, halls, and passages, great courts and secret sanctuaries".

> It is built for the whole universe, and consists of the living and the dead. The stones thereof are men and women. Its courts and halls, [are] those men and women banded together in Lodge, Church, or Chapel. No mortal man can see its whole dimensions. Sufficient for them if they concentrate their whole endeavour on making the Lodge of which they are members as perfect as possible, and fit to be included in such a vast and glorious edifice.[64]

But if the stones of the Temple proved unworthy, Ward went on, the 'Great Architect' would "assume His character of the Destroyer, and raze that Lodge to its very foundations, in order that one more worthy may be built upon the site". Not for the last time, Ward presented an eschatological view of human history and plotted its course according to the spiritual enlightenment of succeeding civilizations:

> The cold pages of history bear silent testimony to this great truth. Nothing which is not perfect will be passed by the Great Architect. Among the ruins of Babylon, of Athens, and of Thebes we find traces of great religious systems which failed to complete the work upon which they were

engaged, and were therefore rejected, and their superstructures razed to the ground to make room for others more in consonance with the Divine plans. Freemasons should ever bear in mind this salutary warning, for assuredly only the best work will be accepted, and if our Lodges do not produce this work, in due time they also will pass into oblivion . . . In the great temple of humanity there is no room for any system of moral or religious instruction which becomes hide-bound and stereotyped, and, failing to develop with the spiritual evolution of the human race, becomes a mere relic of the past.[65]

And the message for Masons of Ward's own day? Looking around he saw great and forbidding portents; much as he did when confronted with the economic chaos of post-war Europe. Once again Ward felt he understood the terrible signs of the times:

The world in which we are living today shows all the signs of a changing epoch. Old religious conceptions and political institutions are crumbling. The very fabric of society is now in a state of flux. These are signs of a new and fundamental change in the spiritual outlook of humanity, and if Freemasonry is to serve a useful purpose, she must be among the first to recognize this fact, and be prepared to co-operate with the great spiritual forces which are at work. In days of old the majority of the ancient mysteries failed to recognize the profound change caused by the advent of Christianity and the collapse of the old classical civilization, and there-fore they perished. Today similar changes are upon us. Will the modern representative of the ancient mysteries, Freemasonry, take to heart that old-time lesson? That is the question which the men of this generation must answer. If they answer aright Freemasonry will grow and expand, and become an even greater power for good than heretofore, but if they fail, then will arise a new and mightier force, whilst she will decline and perish, for it will sweep her aside even as Christianity gradually obliter-ated the Mysteries.[66]

✹   ✹   ✹

Ward's bold views on Freemasonry's ancient origins, its esoteric significance and its message for the present age were not, of course, immune to criticism. Even kindred spirits in the Masonic Study Society found it difficult to support him unequivocally. Reviewing one of his publications, 'A Masonic Student' wrote that Bro. Ward was "a widely read author who expresses himself in a very readable and interesting way", but it was important to realise that Masonic scholars were "not altogether in agreement with all his conclu-sions." Such differences of opinion, he concluded piously, "should only serve to whet the appetite of the serious student and lead him to sift the evidence for himself and form his own conclusions".[67] With the appearance of *Freemasonry and the Ancient Gods*, however, Ward's intellectual adversaries within Masonic research circles mounted a determined effort to rubbish his anthropological approach and conclusions altogether.

Among the leading Authentic historians of Freemasonry active in the early 1920s were Bro. Lionel Vibert and Bro. J. Walter Hobbs. These and other luminaries were *habitués* of the Quatuor Coronati Lodge, where members of the lodge and their visitors gathered to discuss and absorb research papers on various aspects of Masonic history. Ward dearly craved membership and acceptance in this influential Masonic forum. During the early 1920s, however, the learned brethren of the QCL circle were starting at the shadows thrown by his modish anthropological school and were in no mood to compromise.[68] Ward's *Freemasonry and the Ancient Gods* played on popular conceptions of Freemasonry's occult character with the suggestion that it perpetuated threads of ancient mysticism, and so provided a flashpoint for the wider methodological tensions within Masonic scholarship.

Closer examination of one highly-charged occasion, when Ward ventured into the inner sanctum of the Authentic School, throws their dispute into sharp relief. As a member of QCL's Correspondence Circle, Ward attended a meeting of the lodge at Freemasons Hall on the evening of 5 May 1922 to hear Bro. Hobbs read a short paper on "The Antiquity of Freemasonry". The paper cut to the heart of the dispute between the rival schools, and in it Ward's controversial views were mercilessly flayed. The discussion that followed was robust and protracted, with Ward himself entering the fray to defend his corner.

Hobbs, a lawyer with a masterful knowledge of the great Masonic documents, focussed in his paper on two themes: the meaning of the term 'time immemorial' that was used in Masonic ceremonial (which, treating it as a legal term, he convincingly suggested was of comparatively recent origin) and the character of Freemasonry itself as it emerged in 1717, a fraternal edifice erected on the re-invented traditions of the medieval craft fraternities. He dismissed suggestions that English Freemasonry could have been derived from ancient mystery cults by pointing to the difficulties of any direct transmission through the upheavals of history.[69] He similarly dismissed the idea that the craftsmen engaged in the construction of King Solomon's Temple might be in some sense 'Freemasons' by pointing out that they were levied labourers "who could not be considered as 'free' men".[70] On neither front did he directly confront Ward's contention that the master masons (rather than the entire labour force) of the Ancient Near East were initiates of a mystery cult, and that the Comacine order had sustained the remnants of this cult and preserved its esoteric teachings as the basis for modern

Freemasonry. He did, however, address one comment squarely at Ward's recent book.

> Then those claims to an origin with, or from Ancient Gods, and aboriginal rites, and so forth, seem to be attempts to find something which is already before your eyes, but entirely different. There is nothing of the essentials of Freemasonry to be found therein. The great danger of all this class of material, apart from the fact that it is not history, or credible history, is that it is open to the suggestion that the authors 'arrive at conclusions first and marshal their arguments afterwards.'[71]

"Anthropomorphism, and all its adjuncts", he declared in dismissing Ward's book and indeed the whole basis of his scholarly effort, "seem to me entirely unnecessary to real Freemasonry, and to be a kind of excrescence or fungus growing on the wall of 'our hallowed Institution', but which never formed a part of it."[72] At this point, Ward's cheeks were probably burning with indignation.

Hobbs' substantive conclusion as he drew to a close was that the term 'free' was the crucial defining element in Freemasonry. Given that the ideal of individual freedom was gathering strength in England between the tenth and fourteenth centuries as parts of the population emerged from serfdom to be 'freemen' of towns, cities, guilds and companies, Hobbs suggested, it was to there that Freemasonry's origins could most accurately be traced. "I doubt not", he concluded in another swipe at the upstart new school, "that those who place the origin of Freemasonry within, or as rising out of, the Craft Guilds, or some body akin thereto, are more nearly right than all the strivings after the vain shadows pursued by many who have held themselves up as guides to historical accuracy." After Hobbs had finished, a written statement was read from the other titan of the Authentic School, who had read the paper but had left the gathering by this time to catch a train. Bro. Lionel Vibert largely endorsed Hobbs' views, and agreed that modesty and caution on the topic were appropriate: Masonic scholarship was too immature and fragmentary to posit definitive answers to such weighty questions. "My own inclination", Vibert wrote, "is to see in the Craft a Trade Gild [sic] with an unusual stock of traditional history. This may have come into existence in different ways of which actual transmission is only one."

For most in the lodge that evening the topic was invested with considerable significance, and consequently the discussion brought the conflicting views of the two schools into sharp relief. For Authentics such as Bro. Gordon Hills, Hobbs' paper provided "good service in endeavouring to bring the study [of Freemasonry's origins] back from the clouds to actualities". Bro. W. B. Hextall was like-minded, and took the opportunity to attack Ward's idea that symbols could be used as evidence for institutional transmission. He finished with another plea for evidence-based historical analysis. "I would emphasize", he declared,

> the benefit to the Craft at large of having questions of Masonic history dealt with by historical methods; thus keeping, as far as may be, on grounds affording firm and sure foothold, not being easily tempted aside by theories having little beyond imagination in support, and avoiding paths of dalliance leading to morasses of unsatisfying perplexity and doubt.[73]

Standing against these voices were Hobbs' chief adversaries, Bro. W. A. Wigram and Bro. Ward himself, who, as Tony Baker writes, was probably "fidgeting in his seat, itching to rise and respond".[74] Wigram spoke first, and confessed he was frankly astonished by Hobbs' view that Freemasonry had no connection with the mystical. Defining mysticism as "the attempt to penetrate through the appearance of things to the spiritual reality that the appearance veils", Wigram entreated his fellow masons to remain mindful that, by their own assertions, their membership in the Craft carried a deep and profound significance. After all, the basic quest declared by Freemasons in stating their creed echoed the great mystical traditions the world over.

> We go from the East to the West to seek for that which was lost; now this peculiar 'quest' is one that appears in every mystic system; no matter how varied its symbolism otherwise. It is the central feature of the 'Ishtar-myth' of ancient Babylon; of the 'Hymn of the Soul' of Bar-Daisan in the year 120 A.D.; of the 'Grail Legend' of King Arthur. In like fashion, the central feature of every one of the old Mysteries, those of Isis, Eleusis, the Orphic, and the Mithraic, was just this. The Initiate was ceremonially identified with the hero of the cult in question, died as he died, and was raised from death as he was raised.[75]

As a leading advocate for Freemasonry's mystical significance, Wigram's interjection was no doubt fully expected by the Authentics present. However his comments moved on to provide support for the views of his friend J. S. M. Ward. He raised Ward's argument about the possible role of the Comacine masons as Freemasonry's missing link; as evidence emerged that the Roman *collegia* had "a ritual dealing with the mystery of death [and resurrection], possibility becomes probability". On the deepening rift between the schools, Wigram approached the heart of the situation in his closing comments.

> In conclusion, let me hope that the two Schools of Masonic Research, namely, the authentic and what we may call the anthropological school,

may be able to work in harmony, side by side. Each needs the other, and there is ample room for both. To quote Archbishop Benson's words to two contending factions of clergy: 'Except these abide in the ship, ye cannot be saved.'[76]

Ward rose to speak next, evidently in a pugnacious mood. He certainly appears to have relished the tenor of robust debate peculiar to QCL meetings. He was nominated for membership of the lodge that year, but was not endorsed by QCL's selection committee. After considering seventeen nominations, "including that of J. S. M. Ward, whose Masonic writings were not considered in line with the objects of the lodge", the committee endorsed five candidates for consideration by the lodge as a whole, a list that did not include Bro. Ward's name.[77] Thereafter, Ward withdrew from the QC Correspondence Circle and thus his attendance at lodge meetings as a visitor was curtailed. His attendance as a visitor during 1920–2, then, was his only opportunity to participate in the scholarly atmosphere of Freemasonry's premier lodge dedicated to historical research. He therefore seized his moment that evening to deliver a detailed and lengthy response to Hobbs' paper. It was also typically feisty: at one point, perhaps seeking to lighten the mood, he poked fun at Hobbs' torturously legalistic prose. Quoting one convoluted passage, Ward commented: "I don't know if all the brethren understand what he means, but certainly I would suggest that the lawyer can be quite as cryptic as the mystic!" *AQC* does not record whether this garnered any laughter from the assembly; it may be that the joke fell embarrassingly flat. Most of those present, after all, shared the dour, pedantic outlook of the earnest Bro. Hobbs.

At heart the dispute was a question of approach. Ward dismissed the 'head in the sand' conservatism of his adversaries given recent advances in social science. "I protest against the attitude of the older type of Masonic student", he declared,

who pins his faith to a few musty minute books and entirely ignores the vast field which modern research has opened to him, namely, in the science of Anthropology, of Folklore, and of Comparative Religions. Considering that Freemasonry clearly forbids the writing of any part of its secrets it should be obvious that its study must be followed more on anthropological than on strictly documentary lines. If historians had adopted the non-possumus attitude of some Masonic students of to-day the world would still know nothing of palaeolithic man or of half the ancient civilisations of the world and our horizons would remain bounded by the Bible and the writings of a few Roman and Greek historians.[78]

Much of his response was a restatement of Ward's own theory of Freemasonry's line of transmission in rebutting Hobbs' more conventional sense of the movement's pedigree. If medieval Freemasonry was as far as Hobbs' analysis was prepared to go, Ward vigorously re-stated his view that it went back to the Roman *collegia*, which were contemporaneous with the surviving mystery cults of the classical world. In characteristic fashion Ward cited archaeological evidence in frescoes and mosaics at Pompeii that preserved Masonic signs and symbols. Perhaps sensing he was piling example on example with little effect, he paused to reassure listeners that "there are many other details given in my own book, which can be studied by all who are interested". His tone became more personal as he answered Hobbs directly on the subject of Freemasonry's debt to 'aboriginal rites'. This reflected the fact that Hobbs' paper and the apparently impersonal comments of earlier speakers were in fact direct attacks on his scholarship.

> Bro. Hobbs says that there is nothing of the essentials of Freemasonry to be found in aboriginal rites, etc., to which my answer is I consider there is abundant evidence there is. I have not restricted myself to my own experiences, though I have seen things which support my arguments. I have submitted photographs of ceremonies showing our signs being used. I have shown illustrations, alike of gods, and of candidates being initiated, in almost every part of the world, and I have ruthlessly rejected anything which I could possibly think might be accidental . . . [79]

This evidence, he charged, Hobbs and other documentary historians like him chose simply to ignore. In finishing up with a congenial vote of thanks to his adversary, Ward, unlike Wigram, offered no pious statement of mutual tolerance and reconciliation. Rather he quite mischievously characterised their opposing views by invoking the historical schism between 'Ancients' and 'Moderns' that had split English Freemasonry between 1752 and 1813.

> In conclusion, I feel sure that everyone will agree that Bro. Hobbs is entitled to a hearty vote of thanks for his paper because of his courage in tackling this thorny subject and thus giving us an opportunity of showing the definite cleavage which exists between those who, like himself, claim to belong to the School of 'Modern Masons' and those of use who regard ourselves as the spiritual descendents of the Ancient Freemasons of the eighteenth century.[80]

Ward seemed invigorated by the atmosphere of factional hostility, perhaps because at the very least the frank debate had flattered his anthropological approach and lent it a degree of legitimacy in this exalted scholarly setting. Hobbs, for one, was unconvinced. His written response to the discussion concluded with another direct injunction to Ward, Wigram and their fellow travellers in the Masonic Study Society. "I urge every Brother", Hobbs wrote,

> who investigates the history of the Craft, or endeavours to elucidate its ritual and principles by reference to Anthropology or Mysticism, or to ascertain from them, or clothe them with, any symbolic meaning, to take care that there is at least some real historical or reasonable justification in fact for their statements.[81]

Some "reasonable justification in *fact*": the cautious empiricism of the Authentics was once again raised like a shield against the speculative adventurism of Ward's Anthropological School.

7

Kingdom of the Wise

Ward's career in esoteric scholarship blossomed against a private backdrop that was increasingly difficult. Relations with his wife had deteriorated since their return to England in 1916. Carrie was some years older than him, and their marriage was strained by their parental responsibilities as Blanche grew up. "Relations with my wife had grown steadily worse", wrote Ward in his recollections of the period around 1917, "the child being a constant bone of contention."

> However naughty she might be, her mother would never allow her to be corrected and if I attempted even the mildest reprimand took her side using the most unbridled language. The child . . . was quick to take advantage of the fact. Therefore home conditions were not happy. We did consider separating but decided to try again.[1]

On Ward's modest salary it was not feasible to rent or purchase a home in any proximity to central London where he worked. Instead they took a house at Gidea Park near Romford, Essex, in the developing commuter belt. Lengthy train trips to and from Liverpool Street, early departures and late returns to the family home, reinforced the sense of separate lives. He and Carrie formally separated in 1923, and she took Blanche with her to Leamington Spa as her health began to fail noticeably.

The separation was at least partly induced by the close friendship Ward had established with Jessie Page that grew stronger with their collaboration on the Baskerville Press. We have no clue as to Carrie's outlook or state of mind as her marriage deteriorated, but it is fair to say that she and John had never been emotionally close and she had little interest in his esoteric and historical studies. In Jessie Page, by contrast, Ward felt he had a soul companion. She made quite a striking figure: a childhood fall through a greenhouse roof had left a long scar from her left eyebrow down to the mouth; her pale but refined features, slight form and marked curvature of the spine gave her a look of dignified affliction.[2] Like Ward she was a teacher, the principal at a primary school in Finchley; she also shared his deep interests in spiritualism, esoteric religion and the mystical tradition. Her initial attraction to clairvoyance and Theosophy resulted in her initiation into the Order of the Eastern Star, an esoteric fraternity that introduced women to Masonic ritual through five degrees based on feminine virtues.

Together they founded a new group in 1920 dedicated to Eastern mysticism and spiritual inquiry known as the Order of Indian Wisdom. This obscure fraternity, about which little is known either of its membership or activities, gathered regularly until around 1929. Ward described it as "a Mystical Society with an elaborate ritual derived from South India which expounded Hindoo philosophy".[3] Its meetings helped focus Ward's fascination with the East and doctrines such as reincarnation and karma, and attracted like-minded students of occult and religious traditions. A. E. Waite, a Masonic associate of Ward's also interested in Freemasonry as a mystical tradition, was invited to join in late 1921. He regarded Ward's group as "a kind of Yogi order" and attended regularly the following year before quitting his membership in December 1922, deciding that the meetings had become "rather frivolous".[4]

Ward persisted in his attendance, not least because in Jessie Page he had found a catalyst for his own psychic and spiritual development. She shared his conviction that the ordinary dream state provided psychic access to higher realms of transcendental reality; a faculty that might be trained as a path to metaphysical insight through 'astral travelling'. "One and all of us", as Ward later explained in a public lecture, "have a second life and a second set of experiences which come to us when we sleep . . . [as we enter] the world of spirit which lies around us, that world in which we must function when this earthly life is ended."[5] As John and Jessie met each week and talked over the dreams each had experienced in the meantime, they began to realise they seemed to offer a strange interlocking narrative, a coherence that pointed to a higher meaning and purpose.

> This started with Jessie reaching a door, but no more. The same night, Ward in his dream had reached the same door too, and he had seen beyond it. Other dreams followed, and they continued in an extraordinarily interlocking format which surprised them both. Each dream only made sense when it was set side by side with the other's dream, and the elements then combined to give a complete picture. They were able to compare dreams at weekends.[6]

Carrie Ward died in September 1926, shortly after her estranged husband and Jessie Page returned from a trip to the Continent, North Africa and Palestine. Blanche was taken in by the Lanchesters, an arrangement Ward does not appear to have contested. He was left a widower and the somewhat awkward status of his relationship with Jessie Page was resolved. Within seven months the couple were married, in a service at St John's Church,

Leytonstone in April 1927 officiated by Ward's father who had also re-married by this time.

John and Jessie Ward established their marital home with Jessie's mother at 29 Ashbourne Avenue, Golders Green. This ordinary late-Victorian terrace was the setting for increasingly elaborate lucid dreams and visions that, to begin with, were quite baffling. As Peter Strong, an early member of Ward's Confraternity, puts it: "Because the dreams were thus interwoven they could not deny their validity, but they wondered where it was all heading".[7] In time the dream visions became more coherent and explicit. As in the psychic projection Ward had earlier experienced as a spirit medium, in these later visions he and Jessie were able to explore a strangely tangible psychic landscape that corresponded to the ordinary conditions of daily life. There they encountered the presence of a great angelic being – that they afterwards called their 'Angelic Guardian', or the 'Master of the Work' – and were told they were being prepared for a special task.

That task became clearer in due course. One set of long and complex dreams transported them both to a kind of monastery, where men and women dedicated themselves to a life of prayer, worship and spiritual labours. In the dream state they remained for a full day in this 'Astral Abbey' observing its ceremonies and routine. The names and faces of the brethren, their clothing and meals, the furniture and domestic arrangements and the rituals of prayer and worship they practised all seemed revealed with incredible lucidity. "John Ward was able to remember perfectly all the words of the ceremonies that had taken place", Strong recalled, "but they seemed to make little sense until added to Jessie's dream, which was about all the rubrics and ceremonial details. Then the ceremonies came alive . . . stressing old and new Christian teachings in a dramatic fashion."[8] The joint dreams continued regularly in the months that followed, and culminated in a supremely awe-inspiring joint vision on 13 May 1929, when they both were taken by the Angelic Guardian into the presence of Christ Himself, crowned in majesty as a celestial king.

During this divine audience, which they later regarded as a mystical initi-ation, the Wards were "solemnly consecrated for the task and given the requisite authority to organise the work and to found the Abbey . . . At the same time the promise was made to them that Christ would ever guide them in their Mission."[9] They were warned "that the end of this Age was approaching, that the Civilisation of the West was doomed, and that before its final collapse Christ would come in judgment, not to destroy the physical world, but to end the Age and give a new Revelation which would serve as the spiritual foundation of the Age and Civilisation to follow."[10] They were charged, in other words, to begin a community of the faithful – a 'Kingdom of the Wise' – to prepare for the sacred advent in the return of Christ the King.

The Wards were profoundly moved by these extraordinary revelations. Henceforth their life together was dedicated absolutely to the daily labours of 'the work', as they called their adventist mission. Ward resigned his position at the Federation, and withdrew from his Masonic lodges and active participation in the Masonic Study Society. "They were to begin this work", Peter Strong explains, "by gathering a nucleus of chosen souls, but they did not know who these were." The Order of Indian Wisdom was inactive by this time, and in any event its members may not have been responsive to a more explicitly Christian and millenarian religious teaching. But in time (as we will see below) a small group of followers came to share the Wards' convictions, and joined together with them as a Confraternity to pursue 'the work'. Ward wrote lectures and pamphlets explaining their mission and its philosophy, developed religious services and a liturgy to re-interpret Christian theology and worship according to the revelations he and Jessie had received, composed hundreds of hymns and prayers to guide the devotions of the faithful, and set about the practical business of establishing the earthly counterpart of the abbey they had witnessed in their visions.

Five years later, on Whitsunday in 1934, Ward's Confraternity of the Kingdom of Christ issued the most urgent statement of their religious calling. It declared:

> Our Civilisation is based on Christianity, and although Christianity needs re-stating to fit it for the New Age, there is only ONE WHO can truly and accurately re-state it, and He is the FOUNDER of CHRISTIANITY HIMSELF.
>
> Certain premonitions and advance information can be given through those who are Preparing the Way for the Coming of Christ to Earth, so that the new re-statement shall not appear too startling, but the final and complete work can only be done by the Founder, CHRIST THE KING.
>
> We must face the fact that when Christ comes He comes to Judgment; to condemn both individuals and Nations, and even Social Systems, and that He will inevitably come to that Nation which is least unworthy of his condemnation and therefore the most suitable for the relaunching of His new revelation. For which reason we must make England, so far as we can, a fit country for Him to come to and DWELL IN and one where He can TEACH the New Revelation most effectively.
>
> THE CONFRATERNITY OF THE KINGDOM OF CHRIST has been called into existence to do this work, and its task includes the preservation of such material relics of the past as will serve as a nucleus for the Civilisation to come.[11]

The choice of Whitsunday – the English feast day of the Pentecost – for the publication of this urgent religious entreaty is significant. John Ward was proclaiming a renewal of the Christian message that had first been delivered by the Holy Spirit to the Apostles gathered at Jerusalem as described in Acts ii, 2–4: "Suddenly there came from heaven a sound like the rushing of a violent wind, and it filled the whole house where they were sitting. And there appeared to them tongues like flames of fire, divided among them and resting on each one. And they were all filled with the Holy Spirit." Just as the announcement in Jerusalem had been followed by the baptism of thousands and the formation of the first Christian community, so too was Ward's pentecostal declaration intended to initiate a wholesale re-organisation of spiritual life both in the individual and the nation at large. No longer merely a spirit medium, John Ward had assumed the mantle of a religious prophet.

✳   ✳   ✳

By any measure this was a wayward redirection of Ward's public career, even given his esoteric and psychic preoccupations. At first sight it seems bizarre and baffling. Was he suffering some mental breakdown, or delusions of self-importance that bordered on the pathological? It is important to clarify that, contrary to general opinion, the kind of anomalous visionary experiences that Ward and his wife reported are not necessarily indicators of schizophrenia, psychosis or related forms of mental illness. Indeed, Ward's everyday behaviour at the time of his trance visions – as during his earlier periods of clairvoyance – exhibit the classic markers that distinguish the normal person from the schizophrenic or mentally ill. His anomalous visions were short-term and transient, and did not interfere with his "ongoing orderly development" and "retention of social attachments", while Ward continued to recognise the "demands of logic and collective knowledge".[12] In all these ways, Ward was and remained a supremely normal man.

Did he and Jessie simply invent their visions to boost their self-importance? If this was the case, it seems an irrational calculation. The Wards gained very little in the eyes of the world by claiming a direct and personal communication with angelic beings that had announced the sacred advent and entrusted it into their own particular care. Indeed the scholarly legitimacy that John Ward had worked so hard to develop in the esoteric field, and clearly continued to crave during the 1930s with his Abbey Folk Park, was quite fatally undermined by this stance. Few paid him much attention, preferring to regard him (as the Anglican establishment did, as we will see) as a crank and misfit.

His urgent sense of a personal divine revelation is more intelligible if we recall Ward's life experiences, his earlier psychic episodes and esoteric interests. His accounts of his own mediumship, if taken at face value, suggest a psychic sensibility that was 'receptive' and prone to anomalous experiences.

His emergence as a mystic and prophet in the late 1920s can thus be regarded as the maturation of the proto-mystical tendencies of his early adulthood. But it was also shaped by the particular interests – spiritualism, Freemasonry, Eastern mysticism, antiquarianism – that, as we have seen, shaped those tendencies into something distinctive. As his clairvoyance deepened into an active mysticism, so too did Ward's intellectual interests cohere into a systematic religious scheme.

Ward's mysticism is also less baffling if we recognise that it came on the heels of a revival of interest in mystical phenomena among theologians and philosophers of religion. The philosopher William James was one influential voice at this time, whose inquiries helped characterise the mystic state as a heightened psychological experience. His Gifford lectures at the turn of the century, published as the classic text *The Varieties of Religious Experience*, presented the psychology of mysticism as the extreme limits of an everyday phenomenon; a view that Ward shared. Most of us, James suggested, have moments of sharp but elusive and ineffable insight, often when caught up in inspirational music or some other sublime influence that releases our emotional inhibitions. The lucidity of these moments, and their sense of "vague vistas of a life continuous with our own, beckoning and inviting, yet ever eluding our pursuit", was for James the most commonplace form of mystical experience. Another was the perplexing sense of *déjà vu*, also a relatively common experience when our perception seems mysteriously to enlarge and grasp at the "metaphysical duality of things".[13] Both were stages on the way to more profound mystical experiences that typically, as they did with Ward, took the form of trance-like dream states. Narcotic and anaesthetic stimulus could prompt transcendental awareness and metaphysical insight; so too could the contemplation of natural majesty of mountains, stars and the ocean. But it was also a state of mind that could burst upon an individual quite unexpectedly. James cited the testimony of J. A. Symonds, the writer and critic, who had often experienced ineffable moments of trance as he "followed the last thread of being to the verge of the abyss" in moments of relaxation or contemplation. Symonds tried to put the experience into words:

> a gradual but swiftly progressive obliteration of space, time, sensation, and the multitudinous factors of experience which seem to qualify what we are please to call our Self. In proportion as these conditions of ordinary consciousness were subtracted, the sense of an underlying or essential consciousness acquired intensity. At last nothing remained but a pure, absolute, abstract Self. The universe became without form and void of content. But Self persisted, formidable in its vivid keenness, feeling the most poignant doubt about reality, ready, as it seemed, to find existence break as breaks a bubble round about it.[14]

Although Symonds reported on his experiences with a slightly vexed air, for William James they encapsulated those moments of pure immersion in the spiritual life that distinguished the true religious mystics. Saints and seers, he suggested, had moved beyond Symonds' involuntary and occasional experiences of a transcendental reality to a methodical cultivation of such experiences in their spiritual life. They also arrived at an understanding of this dissolution of the familiar Self into the Absolute as an encounter with the presence of God.

This theme was amplified for British readers in the work of figures like Dean W. R. Inge and Evelyn Underhill. The latter was particularly persuasive: her books *Mysticism* and *The Mystic Way* (published 1911 and 1913 respectively) were "romantic and engaged rather than dispassionate and objective",[15] and so popularised more scholarly work in making sense of Christian mysticism for Ward's generation. Describing the human consciousness as trapped in the "prison of the sense-world", Underhill explored the powers of contemplation and insight that enabled its escape. Perhaps "the self was mistaken in supposing herself to be entirely shut off from the true external universe", she mused.

> She has, it seems certain tentacles which, once she learns to uncurl them, will stretch sensitive fingers far beyond that limiting envelope in which her normal consciousness is contained, and give her news of a higher reality than that which can be deduced from the reports of the senses. The fully developed and completely conscious human soul can open as an anemone does, and know the ocean in which she is bathed. This act, this condition of consciousness, in which barriers are obliterated, the Absolute flows in on us, and we, rushing out to its embrace, 'find and feel the Infinite above all reason and above all knowledge,' is the true 'mystical state.'[16]

The modern notion of the psychological unconscious, the subliminal dimension of the human personality resting below the threshold of everyday awareness, was for Underhill the latest of many notions and symbols to express "the point of contact between man's life and the divine life in which it is immersed and sustained".[17] The ability to transcend the ordinary and limited world of our conscious selves and so to relate to a world of ultimate, metaphysical reality depended, Underhill explained, on our ability to bring this internal 'spark' of the Infinite into our everyday consciousness. The fact that human beings possessed an innate sense that communion with 'the Absolute' - paradoxically located within 'the Self' - was possible meant that their cults, religions and cultures were decisively shaped by the implications of this central fact.

The existence of such a 'sense', such an integral part or function of the complete human being, has been affirmed and dwelt upon not only by the mystics, but by seers and teachers of all times and creeds: by Egypt, Greece and India, the poets, the fakirs, the philosophers, and the saints. A belief in its actuality is the pivot of the Christian position; indeed of every religion worthy of the name. It is the justification of mysticism, asceticism, the whole machinery of the self-renouncing life. That there is an extreme point at which man's nature touches the Absolute: that his ground, or substance, his true being is penetrated by the Divine Life which constitutes the underlying reality of things; this is the basis on which the whole mystic claim of possible union with God must rest.[18]

Psychology today calls this the 'transliminal' state, but in religious contexts this faculty and the experiences it generates have always been understood as a vehicle for spiritual wisdom.

As we have seen, Ward regarded this connection between 'man's nature' and 'the Absolute', the "search of the soul after union with the supreme",[19] as the core mystical doctrine taught by Freemasonry. Further, his own receptivity as a spiritualist medium had taught him both of the experiential reality of transliminal insight and the profound knowledge to be gained thereby. Thus with the onset of his specifically mystical visions in 1928, Ward felt he had moved beyond the passive receptivity of the clairvoyant, and was now a participant in something far larger and more profound, with a clear directing purpose. Utterly convinced by the psychic irruptions they regarded as visions of divine revelation, John and Jessie Ward joined the ranks of the Christian mystics.

❋　❋　❋

The public face of 'the work' began in early 1929 when Ward announced a series of six weekly lectures on 'Life and Its Problems', to be held upstairs at the Lindora restaurant, 184 Regent Street on Sunday evenings through January and February. His leaflet advised that "all who are anxious to solve the problems of life are welcome", and a small audience of friends, acquaintances and curious strangers gathered to listen. The lectures were later published as *Life's Problems*: 'Whence Came We at Birth?' and 'The Law of Retribution' introduced Ward's views on reincarnation and karmic justice, followed by talks on sin, suffering, the meaning of death and the transcendent reality of the Afterlife.

His talks were simple and direct, free of religious jargon or abstractions and with effective use of examples and illustrative stories, and those of his audience who remained for the whole series received a thorough explanation of Ward's spiritual outlook. They were told of the realms of the Afterlife he had encountered as a spirit medium, and the reality of the continuation of the human soul on its great path of progress and evolutionary development. To this extent the lectures followed closely the spiritualist principles Ward had expounded in *Gone West* and its sequel ten years before: at bodily death the 'silver cord' breaks and the astral body progresses to a disembodied plane, where it is met by spirits of the departed and so begins its labours anew in the higher realms of the spirit. What was new, however, were themes that had dominated his and Jessie's contemplative rituals in the Order of Indian Wisdom: the animating principles of progressive evolution, reincarnation and karma that were now used to explain a universal cycle of incarnation and self-development. The lectures on *Life's Problems*, in other words, fused Modern Spiritualism with the doctrines of reincarnation and karmic retribution found in Hindu and Buddhist teachings.

With little fuss or distraction Ward's opening lecture on the evening of 20 January took his listeners to an eternal problem: "whence comes the Divine Spark within us, the immortal ego, that which makes you, 'you', and seems to differentiate you from every human being?" Neither secular materialism nor conventional Christianity provided the answer, Ward suggested. The first denied the possibility of an immortal soul at all, and was thus contrary to humanity's deepest convictions. Conventional Christian theology might recognise the reality of a metaphysical human soul, but the paradoxical notion taught by the church that each child was born in a state of original sin, but nevertheless with a unique soul created specially by God, was for Ward a striking example of how the Christian revelation had become confused and contradictory over the centuries. "I hold that many of the doctrines of the Christian Church have in the course of years ceased to be intelligible to thinking men", he declared, "because those who should expound on them have themselves lost their inner meaning and are therefore unable to make them intelligible."[20] Ward therefore urged his audience to consider a third alternative: the doctrine of reincarnation, and the cosmic realities that made a cycle of birth and rebirth possible. The rest of the discussion that night, and the remainder of the Lindora lectures, amplified these principles in detail. They are familiar enough today in a world of global communications and multiculturalism that has made commonplace the idea of a 'spiritual journey'. But to his audience, many of whom were wrestling with problems of spiritual purpose and religious identity, Ward's scheme seemed timeless and universal, a bold and refreshing synthesis of the great traditions of human faith and spirituality. It also offered a personal future in a life of contemplation, fellowship and spiritual growth in pursuing 'the work'.

His first lecture announced the great religious principle at the heart of Ward's theology; namely, that the nature of God was a universal immanence. "God is One and all things that exist are part of Him, being created by His

Will, out of His own substance", he declared, "and what we call spirit and matter are both alike emanations from Him. He is all in all; all things are part of Him and outside Him nothing can, or does, exist. He is the life force of the Universe and from Him descends a Spark, the Divine Spark within us." Each individual human, by virtue of the soul they carried within them as their true and eternal being, was thus "truly a Son of God, begotten of His essence, and therefore Divine, immortal and everlasting." Ward deliberately commenced his address that night by greeting his "Brothers and Sisters": "we are the sons and daughters of God", he explained, " . . . [and] it is but the literal truth to say that all men and women are brothers and sisters".[21]

Ward followed Buddhist and Hindu teachings in seeing an eternal rhythm of cosmic life underpinning and animating the material universe. He described how the descending 'Spark' of the Divine Absolute "clothes itself with a series of envelopes" until it enters matter "in the lowest form of life, [and] thence by death and birth and rebirth it evolves upwards", moving from one plane of existence to the next until "passing from the animal kingdom, it is born in the lowest type of man". Humanity occupies its place on the 'Ladder of Evolution' – the cycle of incarnation and reincarnation – that enables the long, slow return to the 'Source of All':

> Therein for many ages [the spark] passed through birth and life and death and fresh rebirth, gaining from each life experience, and developing each hidden talent which lies innate within it. Not ever upwards was this journey; sometimes it fell aback, but even in its fall it learnt. Nothing in all these lives was ever lost. And so the soul evolved.
>
> But still beyond it stretches up the ladder, far out of human sight, and the vast immensity stretches through planes of Spirit Beings, many of whom are as much, or more, evolved above us as we are raised above the humblest creature on God's earth. In this vast chain each soul performs its task, a vital link. It comes from God; it journeys back to God; and in its journey still remains a part of Him.[22]

The prayers and hymns Ward began to compose at this time expressed these themes in poetic form. One hymn explained how God, "the Source of Life and the Lord of All", had "fashioned the world in wondrous guise, With the flame of His burning breath". Another spoke of how "the Fire of Love Divine, Passes down the endless chain, Bringing life and joy unending, From that high Celestial Plane".[23] Ward informed his audience in the first Lindora lecture that all cultures and epochs during the slow progress of human evolution had perceived fragments of this great essential truth of the cosmos. Although considered Eastern in origin, like "every great religion which still lives to-day" and most closely associated with Hindu and Buddhist thought, "we find the same idea underlying the beliefs even of primitive savages, while on the other hand that great writer Virgil set it forth in unequivocal terms in the Sixth Book of the *Aeneid*".[24] A striking parallel is evident with Ward's conception of Freemasonry as a historical vehicle for the occluded knowledge he felt had been sequestered in its rites and symbols, and thus preserved through time.

The "Perfecting of our Humanity" through self-development, earthly conduct and 'soul study' in the afterlife was the great animating principle of creation. Ward was thus able to explain to his listeners the essential meaning of our existence on earth: to learn moral lessons in exercising free will, to embrace the good and shun evil, to control our passions and educate our faculties, to learn the great principles of love and justice as we come to understand that hardship and sorrow are necessary to our spiritual, moral and intellectual education. "The purpose of life", he urged, "is to develop a rounded and perfectly developed being, not a lop-sided creature."[25]Above all Ward emphasised that we learn by worldly experiences that our actions have consequences. He presented the over-arching principle of retribution, "known in the East as the Law of Karma", as a universal law of justice that demanded that "every act, good or evil, inevitably brings its own retribution. This repayment comes sooner or later to every soul, and until every debt has been settled, the soul cannot shake itself free from its ceaseless round of earthly lives."[26] Only then would it be released from the cycle of reincarnation and so proceed beyond the 'Wall of Fire' to the higher realms of the spirit. Ward's lectures thus replaced the Christian notion of direct personal salvation or damnation with an endless chain of being:

> We are part of an endless chain, stretching back through the animal creation, through un-individualised spirit planes, back to the Source of All. Above us, beyond the material plane, the chain continues, link by link, through realms of spirit entities far vaster and greater in intelligence and in spiritual power than we are, until ultimately it once more joins the Source of All.[27]

Amid all this mysticism Ward also appealed directly to his listeners' commonsense and rationality. A cosmos arranged like this, he argued, would not contradict the findings of modern biology and psychology. The enduring soul equated to the individual human personality, and was the basis for the Freudian notion of the subconscious. Its progress paralleled the pattern of biological evolution, because "just as there has been a physical evolution of the material envelope we call our body, through the animal to the semi-ape, and from the semi-ape to the semi-man, so have the souls of men evolved [to higher forms]".[28] His scheme also offered explanation for familiar conundrums of *déjà vu*, or the instinctual sense of attraction or recognition we often get when meeting strangers: if past life experiences accrued at the subconscious level, they might occasionally intrude into our objective awareness. These cosmic arrangements also explained moral dilemmas such as why love, charity, forgiveness and compassion were intrinsically good and necessary. If there was a great law of God and of the evolutionary process He had set in motion, Ward concluded, it was that "all advance upward is achieved by helping those below".

Thus Ward bluntly rejected the conventional Christian doctrines of original sin, of eternal damnation and the idea that each human soul was created uniquely and directly by God at the moment of conception. "We did not come straight from the Source of All Good", he stated emphatically, "but came bringing with us the experience gained in previous lives and the guilt of sins we had committed therein, and hence our different stations, alike physical, mental and spiritual."[29] Yet from this perspective, the deeper significance of baptism, among other Christian practices, became apparent. Far from the dogmatic and illogical notion of original sin, Ward considered the sacrament of baptism as an address "to the sub-conscious self, wherein lie hidden memories of past lives, including memories of offences against the law". In performing the sacrament, then, the priest conveyed a message, even if unwittingly: "Peace, troubled heart. You have turned over a new page in the book of life; God is merciful, and by this sacrament I proclaim His forgiveness of your previous sins. Go forth to the new life in Peace, and strive to keep the new page clean from sin."[30]

Other elements of Christian doctrine were likewise re-interpreted in Ward's scheme. The higher beings of Christian theology, those "spiritual beings, whom in the West we call Angels, Archangels, and the like," for instance, were in truth supremely advanced souls no longer in need of physical existence. Yet even they could only progress by helping "those lower than they on the spiritual ladder".[31] Likewise the saints, mystics and great spiritual teachers of history were advanced souls in their last earth-lives that had returned to the worldly plane for the purpose of aiding fellow-travellers on their return to the 'Source of All'. Ward tactfully left the issue of Christ's divinity to one side in the Lindora lectures, but later presented his understanding of the New Testament miracles in his book *The Psychic Powers of Christ*. In the meantime, he quoted scripture to argue that Christ did not explicitly repudiate the doctrine of reincarnation even when given the opportunity, just as the Christian Church, he maintained, had never specifically condemned reincarnation as heretical.

But all this needed an explanation as to why Christian teachings had denied the fundamental truths of spiritual evolution, rebirth and karma and why the Church had promoted contrary notions of special creation, eternal damnation and original sin. To this end Ward mustered essentially the same quasi-historical argument he had used to insist that Freemasonry was a survival of an ancient belief system, buffeted by the storms of historical accident but enduring through lodge ritual as a submerged tradition of esoteric knowledge. In short, he suggested that the doctrine of reincarnation was known to the early Church but had been deliberately suppressed by its elite. He pointed to the historical origins of organised Christianity during the fall of the Roman Empire; a celebrated event, he insisted, that was not the result of political or social decline but rather the inevitable consequence of a mass exodus of advanced souls from the mortal sphere. He therefore understood the collapse of Rome in occult terms:

> What actually was taking place was that vast numbers of souls were reaching the end of their series of journeys through earth-life, having evolved sufficiently highly on this plane. When they died these departed to higher spheres of work, leaving their places to be filled by cruder, younger, and more savage souls . . . represented in the historical accounts by the barbarian hordes who finally overwhelmed the old civilisation and who were largely incapable of functioning under the complex conditions that that civilisation involved.[32]

In these circumstances, Ward suggested, Church leaders "developed a simple, crude, exoteric faith suitable for the young souls who were coming into the Empire, while they gradually hid away most of the more recondite teachings which such souls would have misunderstood." While the mysteries of recurring life and an evolutionary cosmos were secreted into the monasteries and into esoteric texts, the outward task of converting barbarous Goths, Anglo-Saxons, Franks and the like to the subtleties of Christian theology required its brazen simplification. The moral improvement of these semi-civilised northern tribesmen would have been impossible if individuals were guaranteed another life in which to reform their brutish ways. "But if these half-savage, half-childish people were allowed to think that they had only one life in which to save themselves from Hell", Ward explained, "it was probable they would make a serious effort to control their lower natures and try to gain the alluring prize of Heaven, and thus make the maximum amount of progress which it is possible for them to make in one incarnation." If conventional Christian teachings were historically conditioned and thus distorted of their true meaning, they yet retained a kernel of divine wisdom.

Ward's lectures thus expressed a philosophy of history that was fundamentally occultist. It was not just that spirits and higher beings were an active presence in human affairs, who might intercede to help or hinder the evolution of incarnate souls. It was also that the broad pattern of human affairs over time – of human history itself – could not but reflect the cosmic drama of evolution and regression as countless millions of these incarnated sparks of the Divine essence struggled their way through the material realm and its challenges. This cosmic revelation, that infused Ward's sense of the great panoramas of human history, also found a poetic expression in the hymns he had begun to compose. In one, Hymn 7: 'Hail to the King', he evoked the enormous vistas of history punctuated by cycles of incarnation and re-incarnation as "Souls pass on in endless pageant, Tribes and nations rise and wane".

The Lindora lectures explained the implications of this occult history in a direct and vivid way, presenting spiritual progress in the individual and in his or her wider civilization as the hidden mechanism of historical change and continuity. Empires might rise and fall, human ingenuity might advance or recede, moral enlightenment might accelerate or dwindle depending on their degree of advancement or regression. 'Lower' forms of human society reflected the primitive, immature character of the human souls that peopled them; 'higher' civilizations, meanwhile, might fall victim to overweening intellectualism and sensuality. Ward spoke at length of the 'Spiritual Evolution of Man' in the second lecture of the series:

> Each soul when it becomes incarnate has within it all the characteristics of its Divine Father, but at first only the crudest ones can function in the material surroundings in which it is placed. The lower the type of society into which the soul is born, the less opportunity there exists for the development of those finer characteristics which are set forth in the Sermon on the Mount. Yet even in the most primitive society the ex-perience of coming into conflict with other souls is bound by degrees to affect the character.[33]

Conflict and fear were thus the predominating characteristics of primi-tive societies. In time they consequently taught the limits of violence and selfishness and that co-operation was essential. Each caveman might be cruel and ruthless in order to survive, but "a hundred hunters working together may boldly face the mammoth, slay it and feed on its carcass, whereas a single man would be the helpless victim of that great brute. Hence he learns to co-operate with others and to subordinate his individual will to some leader who has acquired more skill than most of the other members of the tribe."[34] From such discipline and self-denial, Ward suggested, arose the first inklings of intelligence and mutual dependence. As the tribal leader divided the spoils of the hunt and issued to each hunter his rightful share, so was kindled a sense of justice and right conduct. In time the bonds of affection develop to draw together the brotherhood in their common cause. "This then is the begin-ning of the evolution of the higher side of man, and we see the process continued right throughout history, while the bonds of love and fellowship are being continually extended."

But in any given age, the intermingling of advanced souls with younger, cruder human beings ("souls born into the same social state but obviously in different stages of evolution") was a powerful catalyst for moral progress. Thus older souls among the enlightened Romans passed on their wisdom to the brutish tribesmen sweeping in from the northern forests, even if they needed to simplify their spiritual doctrines in the process. So too in the present day, Ward explained, it could be seen

> that there are many classes of souls incarnate at the same time among us. Some of the crude, primitive souls are but little evolved above our primitive ancestors, the reason being that they are comparatively young, and from them we find an ascending order of souls, until here and there we meet with one wise in spiritual knowledge, who seems to be approaching the end of his earthly journeys. Such souls can teach the younger brethren much if they will condescend to learn.[35]

His invitation, then, was for his listeners to join him in the Kingdom of the Wise to learn and prepare for the imminent cosmic upheaval of which he had been warned.

✳   ✳   ✳

As the weeks passed the numbers at the Lindora meetings dwindled to fewer than ten. From this group the original membership of the Confraternity of the Kingdom of Christ – the Founders, as they were later known – was drawn. Meetings for services, prayer and meditation continued throughout 1929 at the Wards' home at Golders Green where an altar was set up in one of the spare rooms. Although most remained employed elsewhere – five of the original seven members were schoolteachers – they met constantly for daily religious devotions in ceremonies and mediative prayers "to cement their contact with the Angel Master", as a later member of Ward's community put it.[36] Some moved to Ashbourne Avenue permanently, including a pair of well-to-do newlyweds, Colin and Elizabeth Chamberlain, who donated a great stock of furniture from their previous homes to the Confraternity. They were joined by the sisters Rose and Laura Hall, and another young woman, a Miss Mott. Little is known of the latter as she left the group in early 1931 and "went back to the world she had renounced", as Ward wrote, but the others remained with the Wards and dedicated to the Confraternity's cause for the rest of their lives.[37]

Even at this early stage, with Ward's community in its infancy, the performance of sacramental worship and sacred ritual was taken very seriously by its members. Despite not being ordained by ecclesiastical authority, Ward adopted the title 'Reverend Father' and celebrated communion for the group in the traditional Christian manner using bread and wine. Feast days were celebrated in honour of saints according to the traditional Anglican calendar, with a special place for the festival of Christ the King on the Sunday before Advent. Tapestries and altar cloths were embroidered by the women to adorn their impromptu chapel, and religious relics and artworks from Ward's collection were put to use as needed. A painting of a feminine figure of the Holy Spirit was commissioned from a commercial artist, Anson Dyer, for the ornamental screen behind the altar; the artist later undertook representations of God the Father, and Christ as an enthroned king for the Confraternity, modern icons that were venerated as the visual statement of their pentecostal mission. They adopted an emblem, known in the community as the 'Ensign of the King': the red cross of St George and England on a white ground surmounted by a golden crown, embroidered into their vestments, made up as a banner and worn as a small brooch or lapel pin.

Within a few months Ward had also compiled a hymnal of several hundred short lyrics and poetic pieces, inspired by the angelic guidance that was now understood to be present in all their daily labours. But he had no ear for music at all, and it fell to Jessie to compose the accompanying music according to melodies she could hear while in a state of trance but was unable to write down as she had never learnt musical notation. Again it seemed to the Wards and their followers that a higher purpose was directing proceedings: Ward was 'channelling' the words from the 'Master of the Work', while Jessie received musical inspiration from the same source. After some study she was able to transcribe music for the hymns adequately. Given that few other traces of the early rituals and ceremonies are available to us, the themes expressed in Ward's hymnal are of particular significance. They gave vivid poetic expression to the Confraternity's mission and its fusion of Eastern mystical doctrines with the Anglo-Catholic sacramental tradition; the 'old and the new teachings of the Church', as Ward and his followers put it.

Many were devotional or intercessional prayers, sung in celebration of particular feast days and festivals, and that would not have been obviously misplaced in an ordinary Anglican service. One hymn addressed the 'Master of the Work' directly: "Gracious Angel, send thy teaching, Unto those who hear thy voice; Leading us from out the darkness, Till thou canst thyself rejoice." (9) Another devotional hymn was composed for morning prayer as Father Ward and his followers gathered together at daybreak and raised their voices in song: "The roseate hues of dawning day, Awaken us to work and pray, And worship Thee, O Christ our King, Whose praise the Angels ever sing." (180) Likewise in the evening, devotional prayers offered thanks for the blessings of the day, promised continued humility and penitence, and asked again for God's blessing "Upon the work from which we turn". (185) Others were developed for sacraments or for ritual processions, alongside more general hymns of supplication or praise that appealed to God, the saints and the heavenly hierarchy of angels and departed souls. Some served as clarion calls for Ward's pentecostal mission. "Souls who are sleeping through life", began one, "Rise from your slumber and wake, Hark to the voice of the King, Bidding ye work for His sake." (43) A devotional hymn, Number 128: 'We kneel in supplication', declared: "We pray for strength and wisdom, O mighty Lord Most High, To warn the heedless world below, That Thou art drawing nigh." Others more subtly embodied Ward's idiosyncrasies of theology and scriptural interpretation as they dealt with the Holy Trinity; the mysteries of Incarnation, the Ascension, Resurrection; and the significance of Pentecost, the Holy Week, Easter and other points of the Christian calendar. As a whole, then, the hymnal documents the elaborate piety and devotion that permeated the religious labours of Ward and his community.

Themes of visionary insight and mystical enlightenment were a recurring refrain in the hymnal. Hymn 58 asked: "Who hath desired the Light, Glory unbounded? Who hath envisaged the Lord, seraph surrounded? Who hath but gathered a glimpse, of Light beyond measure? His is a rapture Supreme, priceless his treasure." Likewise Hymn 35, 'Life of Life from Heaven', asked for divine guidance so that humanity might realise "that through service only, They can climb the stairs of light, [and] Pass at length into Thy presence". The "upward way" was a "Pathway which the Saints have trod, For 'tis by love and sacrifice, That man doth journey back to God". ('To Thee, O Lord of Splendour', 126) A recessional hymn expressed the role of angels and higher beings in "this wonderful school" of divine creation:

Angels and Archangels, mighty with glory,
Dwell in Thy Sanctuary, help us to pray;
Training and aiding us, leading us onwards,
Changing our characters, slowly each day.

Throughout the Universe, Father Almighty,
Runs Thy most wonderful, unchanging plan,
Angels by sacrifice, worship and service,
Aid their own inner growth, likewise do man.
('Lord God, Omnipotent', 33)

Astral projection and the experience of spiritual communion that had so transformed Ward's outlook also featured. "As the darkness gathers", the Confraternity sang together in one evening hymn, "Our souls prepare to wend, Towards another country, Where dead and living blend; There we shall find our lost ones, And while our bodies rest, Our souls shall find communion, With those we loved the best." (192) Ideas of reincarnation and progressive evolution were also regularly invoked. 'Soldiers of Christ, be watchful', for instance, promised that "when He at length descendeth, His power and throne to take, For those who have served him truly, The wheel of rebirth will break". (12) A later hymn composed by Ward in the early years of the Second World War expressed the theme even more explicitly. Appealing to 'the Father, Eternal, Omnipotent' it presented free will as the motor of spiritual evolution:

through sorrow and labour and joy and pain,
Each evolving atom He guides;
Till it passes from Life on this mortal plane
And with Angels and Saints resides.

And He leaveth each free to reject His help,
And follow its wayward will,
Till it feeleth its need of a Heavenly Guide
Who will wisdom and strength instil.

So through many a physical life we pass,
With its labour and joy and pain,
But our friendships, cemented by bonds of love,
Through eternity are the same. (164)

Even if generalised religious sentiments camouflage the idiosyncratic theology of Ward's hymns, they do not conceal it entirely. In their essence the hymns captured the ecstatic revelation of a Primitive Christianity that had been re-interpreted and thereby renewed, even as the essential mysteries of the Christian faith had been transformed. In reflecting on the Holy Trinity, a "mystery stupendous" that might "sustain us amid darkness" ('O Trinity in Unity', 85), one group of hymns taught that a feminised Holy Spirit was the active agent of the Divine in everyday worldly affairs. Hymn 13, 'Sing the praise of God Eternal', described 'God the Spirit' as 'She, Who as the Holy Mother, Comprehends our grief and shame'. Other hymns praised the Holy Mother and asked for her intercession and guidance through prayer. "Wisdom from the Holy Spirit, Comes to guide us on the way", explained Hymn 47, "Backward as to God we journey, If from Her we learn to pray." "The splendour of the Godhead exceeds all human thought", Hymn 83 began, but proceeded to outline the Confraternity's feminised conception of the trinitarian God:

The glory of the Father embraces all mankind,
His words they are that loosen, and His the thoughts that bind,
From Him comes all Creation, of bird or man or beast,
All things we see come from Him, the greatest and the least.

The glory of the Spirit exceeds our fondest dream,
In every loving action we catch a tiny gleam,

With wisdom and with knowledge she girdles all the earth,
And guards each trembling mortal twixt life and death and birth.

The glory of the Saviour was proved in years gone by,
When God became a mortal and came on earth to die,
In glory more stupendous He comes again as King,
And then shall every nation with loud Hosannas ring. (83)

If the mystery of the Trinity in unity surpassed all human conception, the hymn concluded, "Love has solved the problem and given to us the key, To comprehend the Godhead and make His children free."

The spiritual labours demanded of Ward and his followers provided another recurring theme in the hymns they sang daily. "Give us the self control which springs, From careful work and discipline', ran one typically devotional hymn, "Help us turn from earthly things often, To contemplate the self within." ('O Jesus, Son of God Most High', 130) Hymn 219 was sung during the Holy Eucharist, and made plain the Confraternity's awareness of the spiritual heritage it represented:

In the early days of Christian teaching,
When Thy servants, Lord, were sorely tried,
Through this Sacrament Thou hadst provided
Thou didst strengthen all who to Thee cried.

We, O Christ, have likewise been entrusted
With a great and sacred task by Thee;
Overshadow, sanctify and strengthen
All who would Thy faithful servants be.

Finally, a group of forthright processional hymns used martial imagery to invoke the time-honoured Christian theme of 'raising the cross', the adventist symbol of Christ's promised return. They sang: "Lift up the Cross, marching on to war, With the hosts of mammon, lo the strife is sore; Fast before the ensign darkness fades away, Lift up the Cross, onward to the fray." (2) This fervid millennialism found perhaps its fullest expression in Hymn 11: 'The Song of the Sons of Michael', Hymn 12: 'Soldiers of Christ, be watchful' and Hymn 3: 'March, for the dawn is breaking':

Hail to the hour of glory,
Hail to the hour of doom,
Faintly the human story
Flickers amid the gloom.
March, for the world is reeling,

Tottering systems fall;
Numbed by the shock, is feeling,
Hark how the trumpets call.

Men of Faith awaken,
Read ye the signs aright;
Earth hath the Lord forsaken,
Turned from the Source of Light.
Now is the dawn wind singing,
Christ to the Judgment comes,
Unto His standard clinging,
Hark to the echoing drums.

✸ ✸ ✸

In January 1930 Ward resigned from his position at the Federation of British Industries to dedicate himself entirely to his religious calling. After twelve years' service, he secured a separation bonus of some £750, the equivalent of a year's salary, that was immediately used to commence the Confraternity.[38] Its seven members pledged oaths of poverty and obedience, pooling their assets and devoutly committing to a common life of prayer and service. Together they were, as Father Ward explained, "a Society of men and women who believe that this Age is drawing to its conclusion; that the Second Coming of Christ is not an idle myth, but a solemn promise, which will before very long be fulfilled . . . " It was, moreover, "in a very real sense a 'Brotherhood', with its common form of worship, its special activities, and above all a mission which it is striving to fulfil".[39] Male members were known as 'canons regular' in the order, and the women as deaconesses or sisters. John and Jessie Ward were elected as Father and Mother Superior and like the others surrendered their joint wealth to the Confraternity as a whole. Ward later recalled that apart from he and his wife, "only one other person [of the original community] had any money, a woman who had something under £90 . . . [we] all took life vows to live and work together, to share everything in common, and to work to prepare for the coming of Christ the King, the second advent".[40] They also each took up a new name to signify their new life in 'the work'. The Chamberlains were known as Fr Filius Domini and Sr Filia Regina, and the Hall sisters took the names Sr Immanibus Dei ('towards God') and Sr Via Crucis ('by the way of the cross'). John Ward adapted a title 'Custos Custodiens' based on the Ward family motto ('let the Wards keep guard'), while his wife's new name, 'Altius Tendo', embodied the idea of reaching higher towards spiritual enlightenment. In practice these names were rarely used, and they were known more simply as Reverend Father and Reverend Mother.

By their very nature millenarian prophets and proclaimers of an imminent sacred advent are easy targets for derision and mockery. Peter Anson, for one, assumed in his *Bishops at Large* that the Wards imagined they would conceive the Christ child themselves, and that "out of all the millions of the world's inhabitants they had been chosen as the twentieth century Holy Family".[41] In fact there is no such suggestion in any of the Confraternity's published statements; surviving members of the original Abbey recall that Ward expected Christ to be incarnated into a royal family such as the House of Windsor.[42]

The Confraternity purchased Hadley Hall at New Barnet on London's northern outskirts and took up residence there on June 24, 1930. This large late-Victorian mansion at 89 Park Road had been erected by J. Webster Kirkham and his brother George in the mid-1880s. Built across two allotments, Hadley Hall was designed as two homes under one roof, with separate entrances and internal arrangements to suit the brothers' separate lives.[43] The portion of the house bought by the Confraternity as their new Abbey of Christ the King was ideal for their neo-monastic lifestyle and its strict daily routine. Set in three acres of open gardens fringed by a gently sloping meadow and fruit orchard, it had private bedrooms, a library and study for the Reverend Father, a shared dining room and enclosed conservatory at the

4 Ward's collection displayed in the basement at Hadley Hall, *c.* early 1930s; later used as bomb shelter. *AMAA 1 WD 2/6.*

rear. A basement room housed Ward's cherished collection of antiquities, artworks and collectibles. Broad tables were laid out with artefacts and rare books, shelves cluttered with objects and the walls adorned with tapestries and prints.[44] Another room nearby was hung with Italianate paintings, furnished with an organ and used as a temporary chapel.

The Abbey's daily routine followed an austere pattern of piety, labour and frugality. No servants were kept, and the housework, cleaning, shopping and cooking was shared between the members. Rising from their dormitories at 5.15 am, all began the day with private meditation and prayer. Household duties followed for the sisters, who made the beds, organised laundry and swept out the bedrooms and dormitories. The menfolk, we assume, continued with their study and devotions. Between 6.45 am and breakfast at 7.30, Father Ward administered communion to each member of his Abbey. Meals were taken in the communal refectory, with men and women sitting at different tables as one read aloud from a religious text.

Name	Name in religion	Date joined CKC	Other information
Founding members			
John Ward	Custos Custodiens; or Reverend Father	1929-1930	Formerly a schoolmaster and economic analyst, d. 1949.
Jessie Ward	Altius Tendo; or Reverend Mother	1929-1930	Formerly a schoolmistress, d. 1965.
Colin Chamberlain	Fr Filius Domini	1929-1930	South African, formerly an engineer and an advocate of arts and crafts. Elected Archbishop on Ward's death, d. 1964.
Elizabeth Chamberlain	Sr Filia Regina	1929-1930	A schoolteacher, d. 1985.
Rose Hall	Sr Immanibus Dei	1929-1930	Left New Barnet in September 1940 to found the 'Daughter House' in Bournemouth, d. prior to 1946.
Laura Hall	Sr Via Crucis	1929-1930	Left New Barnet in September 1940 to found the 'Daughter House' in Bournemouth, d. prior to 1946.
Miss Mott	Unknown	1929-1930	Left seven months after foundation of CKC, c. 1930.
Later members			
Monica Hopping	Sr Gabrielle	August 1938	d. 1999.
Winifred Southern	Sr Martha	May 1942	d. Caboolture.
Joan Mary Cursons	Sr Mary	October 1938	Later married Fr Peter, and elected Reverend Mother in 1965.
Dorothy Lough	Sr Terese (after 1946, Sr Nina or Lillian)	August 1943	Subject of 1945 'enticement case', d. Brisbane 1963.
Peter Strong	Fr Peter	c. 1941	Later married Sr Mary, and elected Archbishop on Chamberlain's death.
Doris May Ball	Sr Ursula	May 1940	Married Maurice Cuffe, but later divorced; d. Caboolture 2010.
Brenda Ball	Sr Bridget	September 1940	d. Cyprus c. 1951.
Donald John Ball	Fr Francis	c. late 1950s	Younger brother of Sr Ursula; served in military police, Suez Crisis 1956; joined CKC after that time, elected Archbishop after Fr Peter departed the community; d. 2000
Beatrice Olive Cuffe (née Bridges)	Sr Bertha	April 1940	A popular singer known as 'Olive Bridges', a member of the Third Order of CKC; joined Abbey August 3 1940 with two children; d. Cyprus 1951.
Maurice Cuffe	Fr Ignatius	April 1940	Son of Sr Bertha; married Doris Ball (Sr Ursula), and later Monica Hopping (Sr Gabrielle); d. 1999.
Lorna Marie Cuffe	Sr Helena	April 1940	Daughter of Sr Bertha.

5 Early members of the Confraternity of the Kingdom of Christ.

'Morning office' – a form of service in the chapel – was completed by 10 am, followed by time for gardening, manual labour or needlework. Another religious service and lunch occurred from noon, followed by classes for novices, further working time and afternoon tea at 4 pm. Private meditation and prayer ran to 6 pm, followed by further classes, 'evening office' and private study before evening dinner was taken in the refectory at nine o'clock. 'Compline', the last religious service of the day, started at 9.30, followed by more private meditation and bed at ten o'clock.[45]

Despite the strict demands of these daily devotions community members were not necessarily reclusive; all went shopping in Barnet, attended local events and welcomed visitors. The Confraternity's Austin motorcar was constantly used for trips into the countryside and to coastal towns. They made an eye-catching group, especially the two heads of the order. Father Ward favoured a flamboyant scarlet cassock and biretta in the Italian manner, partnered by the Reverend Mother's immaculate white starched habit adorned with an Ensign of the King brooch and a large crucifix on a chain. She was, one follower recalled, "spotless white from head to foot – a white nun indeed".[46] By contrast, her husband paid little attention to his personal grooming, and the fabric of his garments was often grubby and creased by his daily activities. One visitor to the Abbey in 1934 described him as "a very courteous gentleman, wearing a cassock and biretta of bright crimson, but a collar of secular cut".[47] When Peter Strong, an impressionable young man in search of his own calling, met Ward for the first time in his study at the Abbey in the early 1940s he was struck, he later recalled, "by the penetrating intensity and clearness of his bright blue eyes . . . [which] seemed to sum up my soul in one passing glance". Like other members of the Confraternity, Strong responded to Father Ward's blend of intellect and austerity, his other-worldliness and disregard for personal appearances:

> [Ward] wore a stained old red cassock loosely girdled, and a badge with a red cross on a white background and a gold crown on top of it was pinned crookedly to his left breast. His freckled neck was enclosed by a clerical collar and he wore a large pectoral crucifix. His face and hands were freckled, too, and red-brown from the sun . . . I concluded, very correctly, that he never thought about his appearance – his life was in his mind, and he could discuss any subject with clarity and ease, as I discovered later.[48]

A small private school, St Michael's College, was established in one of the spare rooms at Hadley Hall and from September 1930 was taking pupils. It generated a modest income, but closed in mid-1934 as the members concentrated their energies on the Abbey's ambitious new museum. In 1936 the Abbey's educational work resumed with the commencement of a

Sunday School for local children. At least two of the Sunday School pupils were entranced by the atmosphere of piety and frugal application they encountered at the Abbey. Mary Cursons, later elected the Reverend Mother's successor, attended the school at the age of thirteen and found the Abbey satisfied a deep spiritual yearning. She asked almost immediately what was required in order to become a sister there, and subsequently joined when she was sixteen in 1938. The desire of another young pupil, Dorothy Lough, to join Ward's Confraternity in 1943 ended in legal proceedings that, as we will see, proved catastrophic for the Abbey and its Reverend Father.

One difficulty with these arrangements, of course, was that neither Ward nor any of his followers were ordained clergy. None had taken holy orders in any denomination, and Father Ward had no recognised authority to celebrate communion and other holy sacraments. All had sworn vows as members of the Confraternity, but the Confraternity itself had no formal ecclesiastical standing.

Consequently in mid-1930 Ward met the Bishop of St Albans, Michael Furse, to explain his new community and to seek his endorsement for an affiliation with the Church of England. Canon W. A. Wigram, a fellow Freemason and close confidant of Ward's, had vouched for him personally and "assured me that they were all right", as Furse later put it. Wigram also explained the Wards' "experiment in forming a community consisting of married persons and unmarried" in a long letter to the Bishop, who then corresponded with and met Ward personally.[49] Apparently satisfied as to Ward's sincerity, despite private misgivings about his claims to mystical enlightenment, Furse asked Wigram if he would be prepared to supervise them as an officiating chaplain, a request that is likely to have originated with Ward. Wigram was happy to oblige, but felt "that he was away so much that he thought [Furse] should [be] safe in licensing the Vicar of the parish as Chaplain that he might celebrate [for them] at least once a week". In August that year Rev. R. S. Phillips, vicar of St James', New Barnet, was duly licensed "to perform the office of Chaplain to St Michael's College Hadley Hall, Barnet" according to the Bishop's pleasure.[50] Thereafter, the Rev. Mr Phillips celebrated weekly services for the Abbey of Christ the King and its school. There is no evidence, meanwhile, that Father Ward was licensed to act as a lay public preacher as occurred in numerous other instances throughout the diocese. Bishop Furse personally dedicated the Abbey's new chapel in February 1931, "on the distinct understanding", he later wrote, "that it should be used only by members of the Community. The vicar of the parish celebrated there from time to time, and did what he could for them."[51]

This arrangement continued amicably for three and a half years. Local parish relations were cordial, especially as the fine needlework and embroidery undertaken by the women of the Confraternity was put to good use within a few months of their foundation. As well as donating work to church decorations and parish fund-raising, the community set up a stall at the regular parish fetes.[52] The Annual Parochial Church Council meeting held in January 1931 was told of the vicar's warm regard for their efforts:

> The residents at St Michael's College, Hadley Hall were trying to help us. The vicar mentioned that he was acting as chaplain there & stated that as a community the members were taking a share in the Free Will Offering Scheme. They were working a banner for the Church and would be conducting a stall at the Summer Sale.[53]

The Confraternity's sisters also embroidered hangings donated by one parishioner, a Mrs Bull, for the new sanctuary and children's play area in the chancel at St James'. The 1931 Annual Report thus recorded the Council's "appreciation of Mrs Bull's kindness in presenting Hangings for the Sanctuary & of the Hadley Hall Community's kindness in embroidering them",[54] and the Rev. Mr Phillips reported to the annual parish meeting early the following year:

> We have added beauty to the Chancel by the hangings so kindly provided by Mrs Bull, and worked by the Hadley Hall Community, and by the carpets furnished by Mrs Tyler Sen and Miss Clover . . . The Vicar was also grateful to those who had helped in decorating the Church but he hoped that more people would be able to assist in this work in future.[55]

Accordingly, the Council's secretary was instructed in January 1932 to write letters of appreciation to Ward's Confraternity for their gifts to the Church.[56] In mid-1934, too, Ward sent a cheque for £5 as a donation to St James' latest appeal, although a letter to the local newspaper was necessary to clarify that the donation was from the Confraternity as a whole. It was not a personal gift from Ward, "who, of course, as a member of the Order, possesses no money".[57]

Through such small but whole-hearted efforts the Confraternity of the Kingdom of Christ contributed to the general well-being of their neighbourhood. Tensions developed – perhaps inevitably – in their relationship with the Anglican establishment, but it is clear they did not originate at the parish level. For their part, the Confraternity and its Reverend Father appear to have been very contented in the Anglican fold. When promoting the museum he had commenced in the grounds of the Abbey in 1934, for example, Ward was keen to point out that his order enjoyed an affiliation with the Church of England.[58]

✳   ✳   ✳

The joint visions experienced by Reverend Father and Reverend Mother, meanwhile, continued to provide guidance for 'the work' of the Abbey. The regular instructions they received while in states of trance were a feature of everyday life in the Confraternity that, Peter Strong recalls, "everyone took for granted".[59] One vision directed them to visit Birchington-on-Sea, near Margate in Kent, where they were told they would find a building to use as a chapel. The resulting expedition encountered an impressive late-medieval tithe barn, scheduled for demolition to make way for building development. The barn was estimated to date to the fifteenth century; one account linked it to the Augustinian house of Salmerston near Margate and dated it to 1450–1475.[60] It was immediately purchased, and a local builder dismantled it in the summer of 1930. This was a major undertaking, Father Ward recorded, "as all the timbers were pegged together including even the rafters and the braces of the rafters. Each peg had to be knocked out by means of iron rods, approximately the same width as the peg. If the rods were too narrow the workmen found that they could drive the rod through the peg", which caused a problem as it held the timbers fast and prevented them being dismantled at all.[61]

Over fifty tons of carefully numbered oak timbers were brought by lorry to New Barnet. The rubble foundations were found to be badly perished and so were left at the original site, but other than that Ward insisted the tithe barn be re-built with scrupulous attention to historical and architectural authenticity. Dozens of photographs were taken to carefully record each stage of its re-construction as the Abbey Church in the grounds at Hadley Hall.[62] "As far as possible the timbers were put back in their original positions and so excellent was the work of the old medieval craftsmen", Ward wrote, "that when the great west pillars . . . were dropped back into the sockets of their hammer plates they fitted as closely and exactly as when they had been originally made. New pegs were made out of pieces of timber which had come from portions of the hipped roof and the whole of the timbers including the studding is original. So far as the structure itself is concerned no new timber was required."[63] The relocation and renewal of the Abbey Church, in fact, was suffused with the same religious spirit that spurred all their labours at the Abbey. The medieval timbers, newly established as the chapel's walls and roof, symbolised their effort to revive the ancient fabric of the Christian communion and mesh the new with the old in a seamless whole. The Confraternity's dedication to historic authenticity in erecting their new Abbey Church was thus truly devout: metaphorically, it declared their zealous commitment to a re-interpreted Christian revelation, a medieval intensity of faith renewed for the twentieth century.

The timbers rose from their new foundations during September, and by the end of the month the bare skeleton of the roof was framed against the sky and the brick walls were being re-established. Up to six or seven brick-layers, carpenters and a blacksmith worked daily at the site, and made rapid progress through October. By then the steep-raked gabled roof was clad in shingles and the half-timbered walls at either end were completed. The sturdy engineering of the old walls obviously delighted Ward: his guide for visitors to the completed church pointed out "the clever way in which the great braces stretch high up from the pillars down to the hammer plates [at the eastern end]. As they are pegged into both and also into heavy cross pieces they act both as a tie and a buttress without throwing any strain on the wall".[64]

Equivalent care and attention were lavished on the Abbey Church's ornate interior, where Ward's collection of Christian religious artefacts was displayed publicly for the first time. Once again, the gorgeous decoration and sacred imagery claimed a spiritual heritage for Ward's Confraternity, as through the physical fabric of their Abbey Church they proclaimed the glory of God, His revelation in Christ and the great mystical traditions that had preceded their own pentecostal mission. The result was a profusion of religious symbolism and iconography: stained glass and painted windows, statuary in timber and gilt, carved screens with cherubim and stylised foliage, medieval choir stalls, furnished with lanterns, chalices, candlesticks and other fixtures all illuminating the spiritual heritage claimed by the Kingdom of the Wise. The impression produced on visitors could be quite overwhelming. One journalist visiting the Abbey in 1934 described it as "truly a remarkable and memorable fane [temple] . . . adorned with accessories brought from all over Europe: old glass, old pews, old panels, paintings, sculpture, and stonework, including an exquisite Romanesque font."[65]

This remarkable treasury of religious relics and artworks reminds us how relatively undervalued such antiquities were in the first half of the twentieth century. As British society modernized and many historic properties fell into decay, countless mansions, townhouses, country estates, churches and chapels across the landscape were stripped of their contents and often demolished. Architectural historians, art curators and antiquarians decried the loss of the nation's heritage, but collectors like Ward were the immediate beneficiaries. Meanwhile an international trade in antiquities and collectables had opened up during the 1920s in the wake of the awful destruction of 1914–1918. Several religious statuettes on display in the Abbey Church, for example, had come onto the market in England from the "devastated area in France", as Ward put it in reference to the many hundreds of churches and religious houses that had been damaged or destroyed along the Western Front. A superb figurine of the Virgin Mary installed in the chapel's sanctuary showed "numerous marks of gun fire and several bullet holes can be

6 Unnamed builder working on the construction of the Abbey Church, New Barnet, September 1930. *AMAA 10 WA 1/8.*

seen. It is fortunate that the face, which has an almost Grecian purity of line, has escaped damage."[66]

The completed interior was visually stunning. When the transformed barn was consecrated as the Confraternity's chapel by the Bishop of St Albans in February 1931, we understand why he hoped "it would become, so to say, 'a lighthouse in the spiritual life of the district'".[67] Daylight streamed in through rare medieval stained-glass and painted windows rich in Christian iconography, catching on the gilt-framed portraits of saints and paintings of scenes in the life of Christ and the Virgin. A six foot-tall gilt crucifix with Baroque sunburst details stood at the high altar at the end of the aisle. Roman and medieval tiles were inlaid on the floor, presenting geometric and heraldic patterns. Decorative screens and panelling with *bas reliefs* of the saints, Byzantine and Russian icons, and alabaster statuettes caught the visitor's eye, as did the mystical symbols on the altar cloths embroidered by the Abbey sisters. The Bishop's ornate vestments and tall mitre were not out of place, even if his elaborate headgear nearly collided with the medieval sanctuary lamps as he moved about in front of the altar.[68]

The Abbey Church and its astonishing interior encapsulated the essence of the Confraternity's philosophy and mission. Its veneration in symbols and iconography of the saints and angels paid homage to the thread of mysticism running through the Christian tradition. The main aisle and altar was flanked on either side by two smaller chapels, one dedicated to the Holy Spirit and its counterpart on the right to Christ the King. As we have seen, both had a talismanic place in the Confraternity's theology. The four holy angelic

7 Interior of Abbey Church, *c.* early 1930s, with choir stalls illuminated. *AMAA 10 WA 3/17.*

8 East end of the Abbey Church, with altar and stained glass windows, November 1935. *AMAA 10 WA 3/4.*

beings – revered in the Kingdom of the Wise as uniquely advanced souls charged with the care of humanity and able to intervene in human affairs – were also displayed for veneration. The great archangels or seraphs of Hebraic tradition, Gabriel, Raphael, Azrael and Michael, were depicted in works commissioned from Anson Dyer and hung behind the main altar. Each presented an archangel bearing the emblems of their appointed role: Gabriel's lily symbolized birth, and Raphael bore a pilgrim's staff and gourd because he was, Father Ward explained, "the Angel of Life who conducts men through the pitfalls of this our mortal existence". Azrael, the Angel of Death, carried a reaping hook while Dyer depicted Michael, the Angel of Judgment, holding a set of scales to weigh human souls in judgment. Under his feet was a struggling dragon, symbolising "the war between the hosts of heaven and evil which is ever raging".[69]

An image above the altar in the Abbey Church sanctuary, meanwhile, depicted the Holy Spirit in female form, "at Whose Knees stand two children representing the human race. The little boy stretches out his hands to

9 Father Ward in south aisle of Abbey Church, c. mid-1930s. *AMAA 10 WA 4/5.*

grasp the world but the little girl seems less certain that she desires it." In the Chapel of Christ the King nearby the Saviour was depicted (again by Dyer) as He would appear at His return: in a state of majesty, crowned, enthroned and holding the orb and sceptre of royal office. Another image of Christ as the Heavenly King appeared in a stained glass window above the main altar, surmounting three stained glass windows depicting the Black Prince, St Helena (mother of Constantine) and Edward the Confessor. These had been chosen, Ward stated, to represent all the Christian rulers that would bow down before the enthroned Christ upon His promised return. A decade after the church was completed, an arresting, life-size timber statue of Christ the King was commissioned to complete the Abbey's statuary, carved by a London church furnisher using Dyer's paintings as a model. The crowned figure holding sceptre and orb took its place at the centre of Ward's Abbey Church, seated on a throne finished in gold leaf and painted with a flowing gown of rich scarlet.[70]

❋   ❋   ❋

Here in this extraordinary setting, dazzling to the senses and rich in mystic symbolism, John and Jessie Ward directed the devotions and daily routine of the Confraternity of the Kingdom of Christ and their Abbey of Christ the King. They taught of the 'Law of Spiritual Evolution', grounded in the principles of reincarnation and a cosmic order assembled by divine providence that had purpose and meaning. This might have been bound up in the spiritual progress of the human individual, but it was a law with fundamentally historical implications:

> The Confraternity teaches that at the end of an AGE there is a special Judgment of individual souls. At such a time large numbers of souls have reached the point in their spiritual evolution when they have passed through many lives and in them have learnt many lessons and paid many debts. They are therefore in a position in which, if they make a special effort, they can end for ever their need for return to earth [after death and reincarnation]. They can, in short, pass to the Plane of the Saints, from which there is NO RETURN, and thereby make the greatest advance they have made since they passed from the animal to the human plane.[71]

While Englishmen and women could serve the cause of a returning Christ the King, and thus spiritual promotion to the ranks of the saints and angels, the Confraternity also spelt out its message to the nation at large. Here, in contrast to the promise of personal salvation, Ward presented a blunt warning "that the present Civilisation has almost run its course and like the

152

previous Civilisation of Rome is doomed to disintegration". Echoing the German historical philosopher and pessimist Oswald Spengler, Ward saw an impending 'decline of the west' that might still carry the seeds of a subsequent revival. "History shows", he wrote with all the certainty of his schoolteaching days,

> that when a great Civilisation collapses, there is always somewhere a district which survives the general collapse and preserves for the future Civilisation some remnants of the knowledge of the past. Thus when Rome fell Byzantium fulfilled this purpose, and like the Ark of Noah . . . preserved some remnant of the Classical Civilisation amid the flood of barbarism which submerged the rest of Europe.[72]

And here was England's destiny. "It is the intention of God to use England as the 'Ark'", Ward announced in characteristic tones, "which will preserve all that it is possible to save from the dying civilisation."[73] The private collection of antiquities, curiosities and 'bygones' he had begun as a boy thus took on a profound significance in the overall scheme of his pentecostal mission. As the *Message to the Nation and to the Individual* announced, the Confraternity took as part of its task "the preservation of such material relics of the past as will serve as a nucleus for the Civilisation to come".[74]

'The work' may have been a new calling, grounded in the intense mysticism of his and Jessie's trance visions, but it bore the unmistakeable imprint of the scholarly passions that had driven Ward's career since childhood. A close study of history lay at the heart of it, tethered to his deep appreciation of tradition and heritage. Like his interest in Freemasonry – which as we have seen was centred on the idea that cosmic truths could be gleaned from historical 'survivals' – Ward saw the relics of history as precious documents bearing witness to the venerable wisdom of the ages. 'Tradition', he stated in *Life's Problems*,

> is not lightly to be cast aside, for it is often only another name for the stored up wisdom of many generations of men who have pondered deeply: the knowledge and experience passed down to us by great thinkers of the past. We may be incapable of understanding rightly what they tried to teach us, but before we lightly cast aside what they have handed on as a priceless heritage we should endeavour to understand the kernel of truth underlying their teaching.[75]

Much like his earlier delight in the elaborate pageantry of Masonic regalia and ritual, his fascination for historical relics and the vast patterns of world history provided a touchstone in Ward's pentecostal mission, that was visibly manifested in the extraordinary interior of the Abbey Church. As he looked back over his youth and early adulthood, his early interests and passions seemed to be, in a sense, pre-destined. His studies in academic history, in antiquities, spiritualism, Eastern religions, comparative ethnography and Freemasonry could all be regarded as crucial preparations for 'the work' that now became the governing purpose of Ward's life. When he established an equally extraordinary heritage museum in the grounds of his Abbey in the early summer of 1934, that work – insofar as its historical dimensions were concerned – reached its climax.

8

An Ark for England

Despite his mystical preoccupations Ward never lost his love of antiquities, nor the magpie instincts of his boyhood. His early taste for medieval relics ripened into a voracious appetite for curiosities and 'bygones', artworks and historic furniture, ornaments, weaponry and handicrafts. He cultivated friendships with antique dealers, poked around construction sites for archaeological finds, and looked out for curios at market stalls and auction rooms around London. From a March 1933 receipt issued by Fenton and Sons of New Oxford Street, where he had gone for antiques since he was a schoolboy, for instance, we learn that for £27 Ward bought a suit of seventeenth-century steel armour, around seventy armour fragments from the same period, a Peruvian pottery vase, three swords, two spear heads, a vase handle and necklace in bronze, a wooden crucifix and a Japanese lacquer hat. Two replica items (a lead figure and bronze dagger) were included in this typically eclectic bundle of artefacts.[1] By the early 1930s, then, Ward had shelves and boxes full of Neolithic flints, Roman and medieval pottery, ancient glassware, old clocks and sundials, primitive masks, helmets and armour, Chinese ceramics, Egyptian grave goods, coins, bowls and figurines. His fascination with esoteric lore and religious symbolism attracted him to exotica like shamanic totems, Tibetan prayer wheels, primitive masks and ritual material from the Chinese secret societies. As we have seen, the Abbey Church became the repository for the stained glass and religious artworks he had collected by 1930; illuminated manuscripts and all manner of ecclesiastical paraphernalia featured in his larger collection.[2] We are not surprised, then, that this compulsive hobby was swept along in the wake of Ward's religious mission at the Abbey of Christ the King.

He threw his remarkable collection open to the public on a Thursday afternoon in the summer of 1934. The initial plan was for a three-day exhibition entitled 'Everyday Life in Britain Through the Ages', centred on a group of replica prehistoric huts Ward and the members of his Abbey had built in one corner of the grounds. Nestled among the fruit trees and artfully arranged either side of a linking path, the seven huts demonstrated the primitive home life of prehistoric and Roman Britain. Newspaper reporters were advised the work had been completed under "expert guidance",[3] although the precise nature of this guidance was not specified. Together with other displays at the Abbey, the Prehistoric Village showed "the evolution of social life in Great Britain from prehistoric times down to the nineteenth century", the local newspaper reported.[4] Local dignitaries gathered in the grassy quadrangle behind the Abbey Church to hear Barnet MP Sir Francis Fremantle declare the exhibition open. He saw many reasons to praise the Confraternity's display, some of them doubtless prompted by the beaming figure of the Father Superior standing beside him. He found it, he said, "a most interesting exhibition in that it showed how prehistoric men lived in Great Britain, and how the Church and State had co-operated in the spiritual and material development of mankind". Its story of primitivism and its evolution to the sublime was particularly relevant, Fremantle went on:

> The inspiration which had guided the growth of the Church was very evident in the half-timbered chapel, which clearly showed that, despite the terrible conditions in which many people lived in the dark ages, they still retained their love of worship and art. It was the duty of the present-day generation . . . to realise the strength of that splendid spirit which had brought mankind through the dark ages, and to determine to improve still further on the sound foundations which had been laid, not by wild-cat schemes of revolution, not by Fascism nor Socialism, but by that steady development and evolution which the Church had taught mankind in the past.[5]

10 Fr Filius Domini (Colin Chamberlain) and Mr Simmonds, lay guide, demonstrate tools and weapons in front of the Neolithic Lake Dwelling, Abbey Folk Park, *c. 1937. AMAA 23 WE 1/19.*

If the Abbey Church and the Prehistoric Village dominated the display, more conventional museum galleries in the Abbey's former schoolroom displayed examples of tools, ceramics and handicrafts "exhibited in cases, for they are too rare and valuable to be left lying about in the huts".[6] Visitors could also take in replicas of a Roman kitchen, a bedroom from the Tudor period and a Stuart-era dining room. But the Prehistoric Village offered the greatest novelty. "Here is no series of cases containing dull-looking objects of the past", concluded the *Barnet Press*, "but a highly successful attempt to reproduce, in a vivid manner, the homes and manners of life of prehistoric inhabitants of the British Isles."[7]

Ward claimed to have no definite plans to make his exhibition permanent, stating "whether it remains permanently or is only opened occasionally for special exhibitions depends entirely on the support which is promptly forthcoming".[8] The first signs were encouraging: after 1,650 people visited the exhibition on the first three days and were reported to be "amazed at the unique collection of relics on view", the exhibition was extended for the rest of the summer. School groups made the trip to New Barnet from as far abroad as Cambridge and Reigate especially to visit the displays.[9]

When the national press responded to the Abbey's museum as enthusiastically as the local newspapers, it became clear that the Confraternity's labours were likely to generate lasting results. *The Times* was thoroughly impressed by the "tools, weapons, pottery, ornaments, furniture &c., showing the social history and evolution of man from the Paleolithic Age, on through the Neolithic and Bronze Ages, the Roman Empire, the Middle Ages, and the Tudor and Stuart Periods, down to the eighteenth and nineteenth centuries".[10] The *Daily Telegraph* hailed Ward's exhibition as "an open-air Folk Museum, the first of its kind in Great Britain". This became a mantra that worked very much to Ward's advantage. "The early cultures are linked up with the Continental influences to emphasise the continuity of European civilization", the *Telegraph* continued, "and the Confraternity provides guide-lecturers to explain the exhibits." Descriptions of this 'unique', 'wonderful', and 'striking' museum littered the press reports, while the *Illustrated London News* featured the Prehistoric Village in a photographic essay that highlighted its striking visual interest.[11] A delegation from the District Council visited the exhibition a fortnight after its opening, and five councillors and their wives, council clerks and the district surveyor spent a pleasant few hours among the prehistoric huts and examining the relics in the Abbey Church. During afternoon tea on the lawn, the Chairman moved a vote of thanks to Ward and his community, and "congratulated the Confraternity on having undertaken and carried through such an important and interesting educational development". Each of them, he said, "was amazed and delighted at what they had seen, and he hoped that ere long the Folk Park at New Barnet would be well known throughout the length and breadth of the country".[12] He promised Council assistance into the future.

With this level of interest, Ward decided to retain his prehistoric display as the nucleus of a permanent open-air museum and by the end of July he was outlining ambitious plans for its growth. "Having completed the pre-historic section", he wrote in a press notice,

> we are at the moment busily engaged in developing other sides of the work. Thus the preservation of old vehicles will constitute another section, and we are also busy collecting the fittings for a blacksmith's shop, a trade which is rapidly passing away. The need for a folk park is urgent because with the spread of the mechanical age, old buildings and old trades are rapidly vanishing and if anything is to be preserved for the instruction of future generations, it must be done during the next few years.[13]

The Abbey Folk Park, as the new museum was christened, flourished to become arguably John Ward's greatest achievement and perhaps the most extraordinary small museum of its time.[14] The bold aspirations of 1934 inspired frenetic building work, new acquisitions and donations. Ward and his followers dedicated themselves single-mindedly to the 'work in the orchard', as they called it, and at its peak several years later the Abbey Folk Park contained some 43,000 objects displayed in over forty buildings, five period rooms and eleven galleries. The tithe barn had been joined by galleries, free-standing huts and cottages, work sheds and a smithy. Some were reproductions, but most were authentic historical buildings that, like the Abbey Church, had been dismantled at their original site and carefully re-assembled at Hadley Hall. Formal gardens in historical styles, a wishing well, maypole and village stocks provided additional interest.

In this beguiling setting, Ward's collection came to life and grew famous. It featured in press reports, magazine articles and newsreel films, and thousands of visitors marvelled at its eclectic attractions: school students, families, tourists, bicycle clubs, day-trippers and ramblers, amateur photographers, hobby groups and adult education classes. For six years until it closed with the onset of the London Blitz in 1940, the Abbey Folk Park was a brief but spectacular success; generating sufficient revenue to meet the household expenses of the Abbey itself. And at the centre of the whirlwind of activity, bubbling with enthusiasm and dedication, was the energetic, enigmatic Father Ward.

✳ ✳ ✳

By any measure Ward's Abbey Folk Park was an extraordinary venture that deserves close attention. A private collection run by enthusiastic amateurs without systematic funding, it was inevitably quirky and idiosyncratic. What is more remarkable, however, is its genuinely innovative character. The Folk Park offered a kind of immersive realism that at that time was almost unprecedented in formal museum practice, anticipating the 'theme park' experience of the latter twentieth century even as it harked back to the shows and exhibitions of the Victorian era.[15] Other collections had been presented in the 'period room' style, certainly, but as we read the testimony of visitors it is clear that Ward's museum took this interpretive technique to a new level of sophistication and charm. In this way the Abbey Folk Park answered the public taste for more vivid and engaging displays far better than did more prominent museums of the time. It seemed a curious anomaly, a dynamic museum set paradoxically in the grounds of a pentecostal abbey that evoked the religious spirit of the Middle Ages, and accordingly visitors found its charms hard to resist. "Strange medieval things can happen still," wrote one journalist for the *Sunday Times* the year the Folk Park opened,

> even in this mechanical age, with its intense modernity and unrest, but I never expected to be led through the grounds of a new abbey, half an hour from London, by the Father Superior wearing a crimson cassock and a crimson biretta . . . But so it is. The Abbey of Christ the King at New Barnet divides its enthusiasm, so to speak, between archangels and archaeology, and you may there visit a museum, partly under cover and partly in the open air, where 'the history of every-day life in Britain through the ages' can be followed step by step.[16]

Certain factors were clearly important as the Abbey Folk Park took shape. We have seen earlier how powerfully influenced Ward was by the Indian City at the Earls Court exhibitions of the mid-1890s, and we can readily imagine that he yearned to recreate through his own collection that captivating sense of immersion in the exotic. Perhaps a pure nostalgia for the dizzy escapism he had experienced as a boy at Earls Court was the ultimate inspiration for his vivid, enthralling Folk Park. In more intellectual terms, on the other hand, Ward cited the influence of a Royal Commission of 1929 and other proponents of the folk museum model. More broadly still, he evidently shared a desire with conservation groups such as the National Trust and the Council for the Preservation of Rural England to preserve the country's heritage of buildings, monuments, objects and ways of life that were held to be fast disappearing amid suburban expansion. In this context small museums of social history were becoming a feature of British county towns and centres, and some, such as the Geffrye Museum at Shoreditch, had also experimented with the kind of period reconstructions that Ward favoured at New Barnet.[17]

But the intrinsic *raison d'être* for the Abbey Folk Park ran deeper than merely showing off Ward's collection and salvaging a handful of historic buildings. An enterprising museum nestled in a secluded suburban abbey seemed a strange anomaly, but the Folk Park was nevertheless integral to the work of Ward's Confraternity. It shared the essential character and purposes of Ward's pentecostal mission in announcing the 'Kingdom of the Wise'. He conceived his Abbey's museum in esoteric and grandiose terms: utterly convinced of the imminent return of Christ the King, for him the Folk Park was nothing less than an ark for the ages, a vessel to carry the surviving fragments of English civilization into an uncertain and cataclysmic future. He darkly hinted as much during the opening ceremonies of June 1934. "We believe that our civilisation is crumbling," he told the *Barnet Press* reporter. "It is becoming top-heavy, and man the slave of the machine age which he created. As in olden days, the monastic church served as the storehouse of the artistic treasures of Roman civilisation, so we, at this Abbey are building up a reservoir of knowledge and information which may be retained when our civilisation collapses."[18]

Few visitors to the Folk Park's opening day are likely to have grasped this deeper purpose. But all would have understood the ethos of historic preservation that it embodied so effectively. Its engaging, lifelike displays of ordinary life in historical times became typical of a new model of popular museum – the social history or folk museum, where everyday items and artefacts were assembled in lively and informative reconstructions. Ward's museum, however, did not tell the intimate stories of everyday life for their own sake. Rather it aimed to tell the grand history of human effort and progress 'from the bottom up'. "The history of a nation and of a Civilisation," began one guide to his collections, "is reflected in the every-day things which go to make up its Social Life; the commonplace household possessions of the people are the true historical records."[19] This principle governed the approach to the display of everyday objects that filled the buildings of Ward's Folk Park. "This museum is interesting", the *Children's Newspaper* reported, "because it makes a point of showing us the evolution of things, of Man's tools and implements, of shoes, of chairs, of fashions, even of inkpots, and gives us a thousand helpful insights into the problems our ancestors faced."[20]

Dr Cyril Fox, president of the Museums Association, explained the vogue concept of open-air museums in a conference address the same week, coincidentally, that Ward's displays opened to the public. His speech called for a new approach to museum interpretation at a time when the dusty displays of the nation's cheerless public museums were increasingly lamented. Fox recommended a closer attention to the familiar everyday items of domestic life as a means to capture a modern audience's interest, much as Ward was doing at New Barnet. "The deep-seated love in homely people like ourselves of looking into other people's houses", said Fox to the chuckles of delegates, "has never been properly exploited educationally in this country."[21] The label 'folk museum' came into currency to express this new thinking. Five years earlier, a Royal Commission into Britain's museums and galleries had recommended a more systematic approach to the preservation of the country's endangered heritage. Folk museums were seen in this context as a way to ensure some preservation of rural traditions, and a means to present that heritage to audiences as a form of public education. In its aftermath, a committee reporting to the Board of Education was established to consider whether a national folk museum should be established in London and its likely cost; a concept that was quietly shelved in the depressed economic climate of the 1930s.[22] Earlier still, calls for a 'National Folk Museum' for the British Isles had been voiced in the Anthropological Institute at the turn of the century, while a later proposal of 1912 for the Crystal Palace at Sydenham to display evidence of the "culture-history, and the modes of life in times past of the English peoples" had also come to naught.[23]

Thus the folk museum cause had not immediately prospered despite fairly widespread professional and public interest, and by the early 1930s it was an idea considered long overdue for realisation. At this time the National Museum of Wales' Department of Folk Culture and Industries had built a strong collection, and was mooted as the basis for an open-air folk museum. One supporter of a proposal raised in 1937 for a site near Cardiff suggested that such a museum could host "educational conferences, summer schools, crafts instructions, folk-dancing, [and] youth *eisteddfodau* . . . a permanent centre for the inspiration of Welsh national schools of art and architecture".[24] These proposals culminated in 1946 with the establishment at St Fagan's of

11 Visiting group of folklorists with maypole in the Abbey Folk Park quadrangle, June 1937. Father Ward seated in front row, centre left. *AMAA 11 WB 1/1.*

the National Museum of Wales, which became perhaps the best institutional example of the folk museum model in Britain. By the time the Corporation of Leicester was planning to establish a folk museum 1955, then, the term had crystallized into a clear and recognized meaning. A government report expressed it neatly: "It is understood that by the expression "folk museum" . . . is intended an area of land on which would be erected copies of old buildings, or perhaps original old buildings, in which would be displayed articles of an appropriate kind for the purpose of representing conditions of living in previous times."[25]

Ward's Abbey Folk Park was among the first to implement this model as it coalesced in the early 1930s. He told a group of visitors in July 1934 that "[his] Confraternity [had] decided four years ago that their social and educational work should be to found a folk park, and thereby fill the gap which the Royal Commission on Museums and Galleries admitted still existed in our higher educational system".[26] If the great national and private collections of Britain had ignored the Commission's lead, Ward stood almost alone in claiming some practical implementation of its vision. "For thirty years", he wrote to *Country Life* in December 1934, "people have been advocating the establishment of a folk park similar to those which already exist on the Continent, and the idea has even been endorsed by a Royal Commission, namely, in September 1929; but it has been left to us, a Church of England community, to bring the ideal into existence."[27] He was also keen to demonstrate that their approach followed current professional opinion. "We began the exhibition as a temporary affair", Ward told a reporter from the *Daily Telegraph*, "rather on the lines suggested by Dr Cyril Fox in his address to the Museums Association, though it was entirely our own idea."[28]

Although at least two dozen village folk museums appeared throughout Britain in the interwar period, heralding a new era of homely local history and rural conservation,[29] Ward's museum pioneered the idea of historical reconstructions (now called 'experimental archaeology', when done systematically) to create a realistic, evocative environment for the displayed objects. Its only contemporary rival in England, it seems, was Dr John Kirk's collection of 'Yorkshire Bygones' installed as a permanent display in the old Female Prison in York Castle from December 1934. A replica street known as Kirkgate was built there for the collection by 1938, with fifteen shops and half-timbered houses of various periods displaying old wares and household items.[30] Other museums on this innovative pattern could be found overseas, most notably in the displays of Scandinavian life and folk tradition presented at the Skansen folk village near Stockholm in Sweden. One Barnet councillor had personally visited Skansen, and told a gathering at the Folk Park in July 1934 that "to find Father Ward setting out to do for this country what Arthur Hazelius had done for Stockholm gave him great pleasure . . . He looked forward to the day when New Barnet would be as famous not only in England, but throughout the whole world, as was Skansen in Sweden."[31] In the British Isles, however, the Abbey Folk Park was almost peerless; visitors to New Barnet were told there was nothing similar anywhere in the country. This claim became Ward's repeated refrain, picked up by the press, visitors and commentators alike. "I was surprised to read in the *New Statesman*", wrote one London visitor to Ward's Folk Park to that newspaper in mid-1936, "that there are no Open-air Museums or Folk Parks in England. What about the Abbey Folk Park, at New Barnet? It is well worth a visit and deserves to be better known."[32]

✳ ✳ ✳

The Abbey Folk Park's displays presented historical objects in reconstructed settings that told a story and evoked a mood in a way that isolated artefacts could not; a simple and effective approach that readily made sense to visitors. As one wrote in 1936, the Folk Park aimed at "increasing public interest in Social History by placing relics of the past in their natural setting".[33] Replica Neolithic tools leaned in the doorway of a prehistoric hut, swords, pikes and halberds were piled in racks in an Elizabethan armourer's shop, and a fire glowed dark-red in the hearth of a historic smithy where volunteers demonstrated the forge, anvil and bellows at work. Father Ward showed how potions were mixed up and spells cast in a half-timbered witch's cottage decorated with talismans and implements, its walls daubed with arcane symbols, and demonstrated cooking techniques on a first-century oven assembled from bricks excavated at a Roman villa. He stated his museum's philosophy in characteristically vivid terms:

> The success of a Museum depends on its ability to enable those who visit it to forget the things of the present and for a brief space live the life of long ago.
>
> A Roman Stylus by itself appears to be merely a small piece of old bronze, but place it with the wooden tablets which, when covered with wax, served the Roman Schoolboy as a slate on which to write his homework, put beside them the little lamp by the light of which he had to see to work, and a glass such as he used to refresh himself when he found his home studies somewhat dry work, and perchance also the oil flask from which he refilled the little lamp when the light began to burn low, and the Museum becomes alive and the small boy, who might otherwise have deemed it a dull, dry place thrills with excitement.[34]

It all encouraged a sense of playful make-believe, with atmosphere and touches of drama and suspense, and so broadened the frame of the traditional museum to involve the senses and the imagination.[35] One visitor suggested that parents with children like her own daughter, "who know their more obvious historical London", would discover that the Folk Park was "somewhere romantic and yet instructive, stimulating to young imaginations".[36] It offered a kind of sensory time travel that made palpable the disjunction between past and present. Returning home to Kings Cross that night after a day's visit to the Folk Park, she continued, one felt a "wave of emotional gratitude for electric light and a vacuum cleaner". Her daughter was suitably impressed by the experience: "'Thank you so much for taking me to see how all those poor things lived,' she said after supper. 'What I *can't* see is, how on earth they ever managed!' and she meant it."[37] Ward's attempt to bring history alive in the imagination was likewise applauded by *Rover World*:

> Perhaps you have wondered what the dwelling place of a Stone Age man was like, or how the Iron Age man lived. Here in this Folk Park you are not expected to enthuse over cases of flints and bones without first having been into a life-size replica of the seven different types of prehistoric dwellings that form the 'Village.' Then, when you have been through the primitive mound scooped out of the ground, seen the living roof trees, watched the growth and evolution of sleeping quarters, and graduated up to thatched, moated and windowed huts, your 'interest' in flint arrowheads is revived and kindled afresh.[38]

The displays were intended to captivate the young and the young at heart, hopes that shone through in a comic short story Ward wrote about a fictional working-class family, the Tilies. They visit his museum after Mrs Tilie reads about the Abbey Folk Park in a Sunday newspaper. She asks, "Wot's a Folk Park?", and is quickly answered by her daughter Sally: "Teacher was telling us all about it larst Thursday. She saws as 'ow there's only one Folk Park in Hengland and it's a most wunerful place. She showed us some postcards, and told us we ought to ask our Mas to tike us there on Easter Monday." The conversation that Ward imagined ensuing after this exchange encapsulated one of his main hopes for the new Folk Park – that children's thrill of discovery would carry their elders along with them.

> Sally . . . warmed to her subject. 'A Folk Park is a sort ov hopen air Museum', she said, 'where they preserves old buildings wots going ter be destroyed . . . they furnishes 'em with old furniture and shows people over 'em.'
> 'Wot's the good of furnishing 'em', asked Tilie, 'if no one ain't going ter live in 'em?'
> 'Ter show people 'ow folks used ter live 'undreds of years ago', said Sally.[39]

This was fiction, but it imitated the facts of the matter. The prolific children's author, editor of the *Children's Encyclopaedia* and local historian Arthur Mee, a visitor in the late 1930s, tried to express the charm of this "Wonderful Outdoor Museum . . . packed with treasure". Suggesting it was "difficult to exaggerate the appeal that this captivating place makes to a traveller", Mee found the essence of this appeal in its vivid diversity of objects, and the range of responses they inspired. "It has crude things and splendid things", he wrote, "historic things and curious things, terrifying things and beautiful things, and a walk round it is . . . probably worth a month of schooling to any boy or girl."[40] In time dozens of school parties followed this recommendation and kept the Folk Park's volunteers busy with visits and excursions.

But the Folk Park collections were not simply a substitute for time in the classroom. "[I]t is not only for the benefit of school children that this Collection has been made", Ward's catalogue explained. "Here adults may study the evolution of the everyday things of life – of lamps, of weapons, of writing materials, of pottery, of the manufacture of glass and of the use of coins and the story they have to tell . . . "[41] The last point was the most important. For Ward, the objects themselves had a story. They could be associated with thrilling episodes and incidents of familiar history. They could evoke great ambitions, shameful secrets, curious habits, mysterious rituals. They embodied habits, manners and tastes, the very life of a past epoch. A museum's objects could put a magnifying glass over small details of life in the past and enlarge them for scrutiny. But individual objects lost something when isolated and placed in a display cabinet with a label. With characteristic emphasis Ward explained in his first *Brief Guide* to the Folk Park that conventional museum displays of objects in glass cases seemed "dull and uninteresting, because [visitors] . . . are unable to envisage the LIFE and SURROUNDINGS of the PEOPLE who MADE THEM." He wanted to avoid this trap, firstly by placing the artefacts, the precious 'relics of the past', carefully "in their appropriate settings, in short, in the huts, houses and other buildings – either original or reproduced – of the men and women who made them".[42] History was personalised by the vivid immediacy of an object placed in its human context. A second strategy saw all visitors conducted around the displays by guides, who explained the history and significance of the buildings and items and so elaborated the story they told. Father Ward often lectured to visitors, and his encyclopaedic knowledge and brimming enthusiasm were frequent cause for comment. A *Daily Telegraph* reporter joined Ward to inspect stained glass windows newly received at the Folk Park in mid-1935, "and by the time I had wondered at the miniature-like workmanship in the faces, I was as keen as he. The spell of his enthusiasm is irresistible."[43]

All members of Ward's Abbey performed this task – they were described in some reports as 'Brethren Guides' – and one 'lay guide', a Mr Simmonds, was engaged for busy times and school vacations. All the guides approached the task energetically: "it is advisable", one reporter wrote, "not to ask questions, but to allow the flow of the lecturer to go on without breaking the thread of information."[44] But Father Ward, especially, relished this role and was often described as the Folk Park's star attraction. One visitor confessed herself charmed by "the glimpse of colourful personal pageantry afforded by the Father Superior, in cherry-coloured habit and biretta walking slowly past a little garden brilliant with blue flowers of every shade".[45] His boundless energy and enthusiasm was evident to a group from the St Pancras Antiquarian Society visiting the Folk Park a month after it opened. Explaining that "his community held the view that a religious body should have a definite social work", Ward proceeded to lecture them animatedly for several hours on his displays, their quirks and significance. It was all very memorable: he explained that the deep moat of the pit dwelling in the Prehistoric Village was needed to keep wolves at bay; that water was heated in the stone circle hut by casting hot stones into the 'cooking-hole'. He held up a Roman helmet to show its owner's name, 'Marcus', scratched into the metal, and suggested the unglazed pottery of the Middle Ages "was the cause of many plagues . . . [the pots] could not be cleaned properly with consequent foulness". After a short pause for afternoon tea served on the lawn, the group was shown the new smithy being erected in the far corner of the grounds, and rooms displaying the domestic furniture of the seventeenth and eighteenth centuries. As the afternoon wound up, Ward showed the group through the Abbey Church and explained its internal arrangements, artworks, carved stalls and statuary. "This Chapel is a museum in itself", wrote one of the party, "with pictures by many of the old masters, a beautiful Italian font and a series of stained glass windows illustrating the development of the stained glass art from earliest times to the present year".[46] Perhaps even Ward's energies flagged at this point, as one of the Confraternity's sisters stepped in to elaborate upon the illuminated manuscripts, old bibles and prayer-books displayed in a nearby room. The day ended with the St Pancras antiquarians in agreement "that in Fr Ward they had met a man of vast knowledge and that a noteworthy place had been seen".[47]

Clearly the Abbey Folk Park was earnestly committed to public education, rather than mere entertainment. The guides relied on carefully crafted scripts they had committed to memory, and some of the tiny handwritten notes on thin strips of paper they used as basic memory prompts survive.[48] Although now fragmentary and difficult to decipher, these cards sketched the basic content of the guides' talks, the stories and anecdotes that were characteristic of Ward's speculative approach to anthropological and historical evidence. At the Prehistoric Village, for example, the guide

12 Father Ward demonstrates the Roman stove, Abbey Folk Park, October 1937. *AMAA 22 WA 1/8.*

explained that the phrase 'under my roof tree' derived from the basic elements of the Neolithic 'roof-tree' hut, and that the nursery story of the Three Pigs and the Wolf also derived from this pattern of dwelling. The cooking vents of the Stone Age huts were lined with clay; a method, visitors were told, that was also used by the "backwoodsmen of N.Z. and America". Fragments of scholarly interpretation were sometimes offered off the cuff, especially by Father Ward and Father Filius Domini, another avid antiquarian and devotee of folk crafts. But most guides stuck to the script that was carefully threaded through with this kind of interpretive detail and colourful speculation. We get the flavour of this commentary from visitor accounts: "A chance remark from the guide", commented one, "sketched a vivid mental picture of the Neolithic lake dwellers, marooned on their last stronghold, fighting the Bronze Age men against very extinction: then of their final defeat when the thatch overhead was set alight by arrows carrying blazing flax. How much more interesting to learn history this way!"[49] This imagery, in fact, was no chance remark; rather, it was typical of the vivid historical interpretation that Ward favoured, and was carefully woven into many press reports and the printed souvenir guides as well as the scripts for his lecturers.

The new folk museums offered other benefits alongside public education. Concern at the destruction of Britain's heritage mounted during the 1930s, in the face of continued industrial development (especially in England's south-east, where economic fortunes contrasted with the depressed north), the decline of agriculture and country life, the expansion of road networks and suburban sprawl. The efforts of the Council for the Preservation of Rural

England, founded 1926, and books such as Clough Williams-Ellis' *England and the Octopus* expressed the depth of this anxiety in some quarters.[50] In this context, the salvage of threatened buildings was intrinsic to the appeal of the folk park model, and consequently featured prominently in Ward's promotion of his new museum. Alongside the educational objectives of the new folk museums, Ward suggested, was the fact that

> a FOLK PARK renders it possible to save from destruction numerous interesting old buildings which, owing to the change in economic and social conditions, have to make way for modern improvements. Such buildings, instead of being destroyed, can often be taken down and rebuilt in the FOLK PARK, where they form interesting exhibits in themselves, while serving to house the smaller objects which are thereby placed in their appropriate settings.[51]

Ward was able to offer his Folk Park as a pragmatic solution to the dilemmas of historic conservation. "It is becoming increasingly impossible to preserve old buildings on their original site", he wrote to *The Times* with characteristic opportunism during the furore that accompanied the demolition of Sir Joshua Reynolds' stately townhouse on Leicester Square in 1937, "but now that the Abbey Folk Park is in existence, it is quite possible to remove such a building and rebuild it here."[52] The proposal underlined Ward's confidence in his new role, his ambitions for the continued growth of his museum, and the diverse objectives and efforts that might come together in an enterprise like the Folk Park.

✳ ✳ ✳

But Ward's museum had an underlying purpose that often passed unremarked amid its public work of education and historic conservation. "The Folk Park was meant to preserve many valuable antiques", Peter Strong later recalled. "There was, however, an ulterior motive for the display of all this history – to encourage people to discuss spiritual matters like life and death, for the old civilisation was about to pass away, the Second Coming of Christ was drawing near, and so it was a time of special opportunity for many."[53]

What did the Folk Park teach in this time of 'special opportunity'? In the first place it taught that history mattered, and that 'survivals' of the past continued to have relevance to contemporary life. The great enduring themes of the human condition – basic daily needs like shelter, clothing, sustenance and communication; the deeper challenges of life, faith, creativity and the mastery of nature – might be always with us and therefore often dismissed, but they were also keynotes in the great symphony of human history. Everyday matters helped make sense of grander patterns; Father

Ward wanted visitors to understand that the difficulties they wrestled with in the present echoed those of their distant ancestors. More specifically, his displays illuminated the evolutionary pattern that could be distinguished in this vast tapestry of human endeavour through time. He wanted his collection to tell a grand story of the restless, questing human spirit, manifested in the immediate practical difficulties of everyday life as much as in the rise and fall of civilizations, empires and nation-states. Whether great or small, grand or homely, in each of these stories the Folk Park demonstrated that moral and material progress were entwined.

But the Folk Park had an even more essential place in Ward's religious mission than this. Ward believed that his work in the museum was directly guided by the Confraternity's 'Angelic Messenger', and that the Folk Park had a central part in the mystical scheme he and his wife had laid out for the Kingdom of the Wise. The same higher intelligence that spoke to them when they slipped into trance, that had initiated them into 'the work' and escorted them into the presence of Christ the King, also delivered specific instructions to guide the operations of the Abbey's museum. Through Ward's visions the 'Guardian of the Work' presented him with direct instructions on a host of matters, describing the arrangement of displays, requesting specific purchases (showing where they would be found, and the right price to be paid) or explaining the importance of particular themes in the overall scheme of the museum. Sometimes these instructions were plain to the point of banality; other times they were cryptic. But in all cases Ward and his followers detected the guiding hand of their 'Angelic Messenger' at work. Peter Strong remembered how the visions punctuated daily life in the community:

> Nearly every week the Superiors [i.e. John and Jessie Ward] would go out in their car, saying 'We are being sent by the Master to buy an article for the Church' (or 'for the Museum'). Detailed information was given them as to which shops to visit and where in them to find the required objects of art, for often they were not immediately visible, second-hand shops not being renowned for their tidiness. This had been going on since before they entered the Abbey house . . . and the whole thing was regarded as quite commonplace. John Ward would go into a trance . . . and would contact the Angel (the Master) who gave him instructions which were written down or typed by Jessie Ward. This contact for instructions continued almost to the day of his death.[54]

While there is no substantial record of these instructions, some of the notepaper fragments that Strong describes survive today in the archives of the Confraternity of the Kingdom of Christ. They are slender evidence, but capture the tone and character of the directions that Ward and his community worked under. One instruction contained in a note dated 8 March

1934 was later re-typed by Jessie Ward for clarity. Describing the presence
of the "Angelic Messenger, the Master of the work", it records the vision
that explained to Father Ward how the Folk Park's Prehistoric Village was
to be arranged. The 'Messenger' announced his intentions:

> I have not come to show thee the high heavens or the depths of hell, nor
> things which are to come to pass years hence, but rather something im-
> mediate, and near at hand, for I would show ye the work in the Orchard
> as it should be, and therefore shall be, so that what shall be, shall be what
> should be.

The 'work in the Orchard' was the budding idea of the Folk Park itself.
The vision described spring in the Abbey's orchard, with the daffodils flow-
ering and the fruit trees in blossom, just as it was that month as Ward began
to build his Prehistoric Village. But it also outlined eminently practical
matters. The level of detail presented in this instruction was treated as a blue-
print for the building work that lay ahead. Putting the experience into words,
Ward recorded that every detail of carpentry and joinery had been revealed
to him:

> And the stockade was made of stakes whose points had been sharpened
> in a fire and interwoven between the stakes was wattle work. And I
> studied the stockage [sic] carefully so that I might know how to make it,
> and in front of the stockade was a shallow moat or ditch, which was dry.
> And he said, 'See how savage man protected the entering in'.
>
> Now the entrance was not wide; some six feet and no more, and it bent
> back slightly. And inside there were massive upright posts, and a move-
> able piece of palisade which they slid between the upright posts. And they
> had on the inside stout pegs, two in either post, which went through the
> inner post, through the moveable panel and into the other post. And these
> themselves were crossed pegged through on the inner post. Thus the door
> could not be slid back neither could the . . . [typescript damaged]cked
> inward from the outside.[55]

Another fragment, scribbled on Federation of British Industries notepaper
that has been well creased in the decades since, records another and similarly
detailed instruction received by Ward in a state of trance. It is an example of
the highly specific directions he and Jessie received from time to time,
identifying precisely the items they should obtain for the Abbey collection,
their location and cost. For the members of Ward's community this
continued the pattern of divine inspiration they believed had commenced
with the vision directing them to Birchington and the discovery of their tithe
barn; a concrete demonstration for them that Christ and His angelic assist-

ants were actively guiding their work. The vision described in this surviving fragment was urgent and direct:

> Go at once to the usual place & there purchase a Russian icon depicting Our Lord & two Saints. It is a beautiful piece of work [. . .] a gold background & a heavy frame [de]corated with bunches of grapes. It shall cost you [corrected to 'thee'] not more than 35/- & thou shalt give it unto our [illegible] Christ the King who because of her [great?] affection for Him would thus signify His love for her & also for thee. Go swiftly.[56]

Such scribbled fragments and notes cannot, of course, provide absolute proof of Ward's claims, and nobody could ever be absolutely certain – even perhaps John and Jessie Ward themselves – of the ultimate veracity of their visions. They might be dismissed as evidence of an extravagant wish fulfilment, a desire perhaps even deeper than Ward's conscious motivation to convince his followers to embrace the Folk Park scheme, and to legitimise new purchases for his collection from the Confraternity's funds. But they make sense in biographical terms: as we have seen, Ward was prone to anomalous psychic experiences, which he found persuasive to the extent that they came to direct his life's work. For Ward himself, it seemed that his life-long passion for antiquities and the human history they revealed could now be regarded as a prefiguration of his destined role. A prophet of Christ's return as an enthroned earthly King, he was inspired to conduct his museum, not just to the glory of God in an abstract sense but specifically to prepare the way for the sacred advent. He had been instructed, he believed, to gather together items and artefacts that would explain the very process of history, to make its underlying rhythm and significance plain to human comprehension. Ultimately the treasury of artworks and artefacts held at his modern abbey – a monastery for the troubled twentieth century – would survive the rising tide of barbarism that marked the collapse of Western civilization. As an 'ark for England', Ward was convinced, his Folk Park would endure as a record of past achievements to inspire a revival of learning in the New Age.

As the Folk Park prospered, detailed statements of its visionary origins and prophetic mission became rare. But an American journalist visiting in early 1936 found the Wards to be quite candid on the millenarian aspects of their museum work. His feature article, published in the US in March that year, was headlined 'The Founders of Abbey Park, London, Believing This Age Is Nearing Its End, Show How Our Ancestors Made Their Way Up From Savagery, as They Say Humanity May Again Have to Do When the Collapse Comes'. Its coverage was as exhaustive as the title, but included an unusually concise statement of the Wards' work.

The Confraternity of the Kingdom of Christ founded by the Rev. S. M. Ward [sic] M. A., Cambridge University, and his wife, teaches that the present age is rapidly drawing to a close, pictures the ultimate ruin of all western civilization and holds that on the smashup of our present world order the Christ will establish a new kingdom which will be erected gradually by his faithful followers in the same manner that civilization was rebuilt after the destruction of the Roman Empire, and by those who have been trained for the work. They have established an Abbey for the members of the order and as part of their preparation for the coming advent they have established The Abbey Folk Park and Museum.[57]

Despite the American slang and the Reverend Father's incomplete initials, this accurately encapsulated the millenarian fervour that fired the Confraternity's 'work in the Orchard'. As the *American Weekly* reported, the Abbey's museum was commenced in obedience to mystical visions that "told them where to go to find the necessary materials, buildings, etc." The result was a singular museum indeed:

Now there are many folk parks scattered all over the globe, but most of them are purely recreative places or enclosures for sports, or have been constructed, like museum models of bygone cities, for the enjoyment of the modeler and the archaeologist. This new folk park is for a quite different end. In it the members of the Confraternity are expected to learn how to do things for themselves so that when civilization as now understood has been destroyed, they will be equipped to go ahead on the new basis . . . Part of their training is based on the historic fact that when Rome fell some fragments of its civilization, learning and art were saved from the wreckage by the religious communities that then existed in the old Roman Empire. The directors of the new Confraternity, seeking to do likewise, have set themselves to work to preserve as far as possible a record and reconstruction of the past with a view to their being used in the rehabilitation of society under the new order.[58]

9

A Walk in the Folk Park

Just a fortnight after the Abbey Folk Park opened, the *Daily Telegraph* received a letter from Father Ward announcing that his new museum had salvaged the timbers and roof of a seventeenth-century smithy recently pulled down in Barnet. The village smithy was "an institution rapidly becoming extinct", Ward reminded readers, and the picturesque example they had secured was sure to make an attractive exhibit. They had also secured a set of bellows, an anvil and a set of "old-time tongs . . . many of them of most fantastic shape" from the same site, but a hammer and water trough were still needed for the reconstruction. "If any of your readers happen to possess these or other tools of the old-time blacksmith, and would care to present them", he continued,

> we should greatly appreciate their gifts. Almost daily the old smithies are being replaced by petrol-filling stations. Even when the buildings them-selves are left standing, their fittings are apt to be sold off for old iron. I was only just in time to save the old set of tongs to which I have referred.[1]

This was among the first of Ward's many appeals for donations to his museum, and his characteristically deft touch is very much in evidence: a written appeal that piqued his readers' curiosity, eulogised a disappearing way of life, and captured the vaguely heroic flavour of their salvage work all in a few short sentences. Soon after he wrote in a similar vein to *The Field*, a popular magazine covering country life and leisure topics, introducing his Folk Park as the first in the country and asking for "small objects connected with the horse, with sporting life, or with agriculture".[2] Among countless other letters, one was sent to *Tobacco* seeking donations of pipes, snuff boxes and tobacco pouches for a 'smoker's corner', and another to the *Children's Newspaper* seeking gifts of historical toys. Such efforts ensured constant press attention and a stream of donations that soon appeared as new exhibits at New Barnet.

In these endeavours Ward was the very model of the modern museum manager, with promotional talents that propelled the Folk Park to quite remarkable contemporary fame. Photographs and leaflets were regularly sent out to the press, and short articles and public appeals for donations kept his museum in the local eye. A Gaumont newsreel film featuring Ward's museum helped raise its profile even further. When the film played in picture theatres across the country in November 1934 it led to calls for imitators to follow the example he had set. In Northamptonshire "the pictures of [Father Ward's] open-air museum shown recently in some of the Northampton Cinemas inspire the hope that Northamptonshire may be encouraged by his example and provide a reproduction of rural life which could become one of the show places of the county and attract hosts of visitors". Already the energetic secretary of the Northamptonshire Record Society, evidently inspired by Ward's example, had arranged "exhibitions of past ages with objects borrowed from mansions, farmsteads and cottages illustrating old rural techniques, costumes, etc.".[3] A Southampton newspaper echoed the call: "What a splendid thing it would be, from an educational point of view, if part of the Southampton Civic Sports Centre could be devoted to the purposes of a Folk Park . . . [it] gives a wonderful 'bird's-eye view' of social evolution from the prehistoric village to Victorian domestic 'décor'. There must be plenty of material in Hampshire for such a scheme."[4] When East Barnet councillor Geoffrey Marchand opened a new section of the Abbey Folk Park in June 1936, he remarked that "all Barnet . . . had cause to be proud of the Folk Park, which was making New Barnet famous throughout the world. To visit the Folk Park, people came not only from every county in England, but as far afield as America, South Africa, New Zealand, and Australia". He felt it a privilege to help with the work: "The progress made was amazing, and the members of the Abbey deserved the warmest congratulations on the result of their labours".[5]

Their efforts saw nearly thirty buildings and features established or re-erected in the Abbey Folk Park's first year, followed by others as Father Ward relentlessly pursued his vision of a comprehensive 'pageant of the ages'. By re-tracing their steps during a typical visit in the late 1930s we might gain a sense, firstly, of the Folk Park's physical layout and also of visitors' responses to its various attractions as expressed in the many newspaper reports of that time.

Immediately upon entry, as they moved up the leafy drive towards the impressive bulk of the Abbey Church, visitors encountered a small timbered cottage nestled in the garden by the driveway. Known as the Apothecary's Shop and lined with old bottles, bunches of herbs and ointment jars, this quaint half-timbered lodge had been brought in pieces from a farm on London's outskirts. It was re-established at the Park during 1934 and served as a porter's lodge for collecting 'entrance pennies'.[6] Entrance fees were set at modest levels; "sensible charges", one report in 1936 explained, based on a 1s. 3d. all-inclusive ticket, a "passport to at least three hours of constant interest".[7] Individual sections could be visited at a fraction of this figure. The

13 Site plan of
Abbey Folk Park,
Park Road, New
Barnet, *c*.1937.

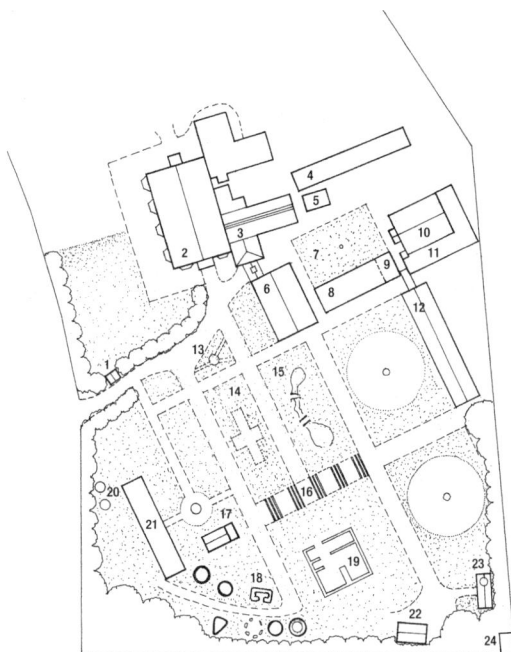

1	Apothecary's Shop	13	Wishing Well
2	Hadley Hall	14	Tudor Garden
3	Conservatory	15	Japanese Garden
4	Greenhouse	16	Pergola
5	Workshop	17	Smithy & Wheelwright's Shop
6	Abbey Church	18	Prehistoric Village
7	Quadrangle	19	Roman Villa (foundations)
8	Prehistoric, Roman & Medieval Gallery	20	African Village & Bazaar
9	Chinese Temple of Initiation	21	Carriage Shed
10	The Cottage	22	Oratory of the Angels
11	Arcade of Old-Time Shops	23	Witch's Cottage
12	Ethnographical Gallery	24	Forge

Apothecary's Shop had a door "with a sliding panel and a wicket made so that the apothecary could ascertain whether the caller who arrived after dark was really a sick person or a footpad", as Ward's description explained with characteristic colour.[8] Inside, one visitor reported, "it has some beautiful old electuary jars and bottles of sixteenth-century Italian ware, such as were used for the peppermint, squills, friar's balsam and other medical remedies of antiquity".[9] Several blackened jars, one lined with charred ointment and said to date from the Great London Fire of 1666, were pointed out as items of particular interest.[10]

Organised visitor groups were met outside the Apothecary's Shop by their guide, and from there were shepherded around the site as the guide explained the exhibits and their significance. The first stop was the Prehistoric Village,

175

14 The view from the front entrance, Abbey of Christ the King and Abbey Folk Park. Rev. Mother Jessie Ward and another member of the Confraternity and the Abbey Church, *c.*1934. *AMAA 10 WA 2/14.*

a group of six huts beginning with a turf-covered hunting shelter of around 20,000 BC, and concluding at an Iron Age hut of the early Roman period. "To go through the stockade into the Prehistoric Village is a thrilling experience," the *Children's Newspaper* reported. "We pass the village corn patch, turn to our right and drop back through 22 thousand years . . . [arriving] at the hut of Stone Age Man."[11] Visitors were encouraged to walk through the village in historical sequence, pausing to examine items of interest or listen to a guide explaining the flints, baskets, rough tools and furniture displayed in each hut. They could not fail to appreciate the clear pattern of progressive social evolution it depicted. "The various types of dwelling", the *Barnet Press* surmised helpfully, "clearly show how mankind first had to camaflouge [*sic*] and burrow his dwellings in his endeavour to combat the raids of wild beasts, and how, later, when he had fashioned weapons of attack and defence, he became more self-reliant, and was able to emerge into the open and erect more substantial and comfortable dwellings."[12] Thus if the prehistoric village presented "the gropings of primitive man towards homeliness and craftsmanship",[13] it also suggested the slow but steady unfolding of human social evolution. "The slowness of development through this long stretch of years is very marked", one reporter commented, "but it is impossible not to admire man's ingenuity when he used the shoulder-blade of an animal as a shovel."[14]

The rough, grass-covered form of a rudimentary hunting shelter appeared first to visitors making their way down from the Folk Park's entrance. This was the summer residence, as Ward put it, of Northern Europe's cave-dwellers twenty centuries before Christ.[15] "Crude though this hut seems", he wrote in one guide for visitors, "when we realise that its owner possessed neither axe nor saw, but had to cut off the boughs of which it was constructed with small flint flakes, we cannot fail to be struck by his ingenuity . . . at a short distance it resembled a green hill, and might easily escape the notice of his enemies."[16] The pit-dwelling nearby also appeared to be a mound of earth, its gaping entrance plunging six feet underground and fringed by thick grass. Reflecting a structure of the period 5,000 BC, it showed improvements on the rude hunting shelter the visitor had just left behind: inside, a rough timber framework was visible beneath a thatched roof, covered with turf and supporting the roots of a tree. Flagstones and primitive furniture completed the picture. "Here . . . is to be seen the forerunner of the four-poster bed", observed the *Barnet Press,* "consisting of wattle-work fastened to four upright wooden posts, looking like a cradle, and lined with a mattress of straw, hay, and bracken."[17] A third structure represented a permanent dwelling of the period *c.*3,000–2,000 BC, described as a Neolithic Earth Circle hut. "Here we notice great improvements", Ward informed visitors, "for the floor of the hut is only a foot below earth level . . . , and although a living tree is still used for the roof tree, instead of a mound of earth we have a bell-shaped roof, neatly thatched, and quite a presentable porch."[18] Daylight trickled in under the eaves, illuminating a homely scene with crude shelves made from tree branches, a primitive loom and wickerwork beds. Ox-blade shovels, wicker baskets and flint tools were scattered artfully about to hint at the daily labour of Neolithic existence.

At the end of the pathway, the Neolithic Lake Dwelling hut of *c.*1,800 BC was a complete wattle-and-daub cottage, with small eyelet windows and a heavy thatched roof. It was the Prehistoric Village's most elaborate and impressive structure, described in one pictorial as 'The First House in England',[19] standing upright behind a surrounding moat formed by a low stockade, its mud walls caked and dry in the summer hear of 1934. Inside visitors picked their way around a central hearth surrounded by a portable loom, flint-tipped spears and tools and another wickerwork bed. "Here Neolithic man made his last stand against the advancing men of the Bronze Age", wrote Ward melodramatically. "Alas, his reed thatch enabled his enemies to burn him out."[20] The adjacent Bronze Age Stone Circle hut of the period *c.*1,500–600 BC was a set of low, circular dry-stone foundations without walls or roof and modelled on the archaeological sites of Dartmoor. It remained uncompleted throughout the life of the Folk Park despite the Confraternity's best efforts. "Rather than show us something that might be inaccurate", the *Children's Newspaper* explained, "Father Ward has laid down the ground plan alone."[21]

Returning to the bottom of the main path, two matching wattle-and-daub Iron Age huts, dated to *c.*100 BC and *c.*43 AD respectively, completed Ward's survey of prehistoric domesticity. The first was set up as a potter's hut; its low mud-caked walls and thatched roof surmounted by a bull's skull dramatically mounted on the central pole. This indicated, Ward explained in notes to a slide show of his village, "that its owner has sacrificed an ox to the god of cattle, in the hope that in return for his sacrifice his herds will be increased."[22] A potter's wheel and simple pole lathe were placed close to the door, and were used by various guides and members of the Confraternity to demonstrate primitive craft techniques. A second Iron Age replica stood nearby: a weaver's hut typical of the era of the Roman conquest of Britain in 50 BC, with thatched roof and wicker shutters over the window apertures. "Queen Boadicea lived in just such a dwelling", explained the printed caption on one of the Folk Park's postcards.[23] Taken by a friend of the Abbey, professional photographer Michael Scott, this image appeared in dozens of magazines and newspapers and became the single most reproduced image of the Abbey Folk Park. A telling caption accompanied it in the *American Weekly*, March 1936: "Fifty or More Years Before the Dawn of the Christian Era, Britons Made Their Homes in Huts Constructed of Twigs Held Together With Clay. Visitors to the Park Wonder If They Will Have to Adopt This Sort of Dwelling in the Indefinite Future."[24]

After following the path through the Prehistoric Village, visitors continued along it to arrive at the African Village, opened to the public in May 1935 as the centrepiece of a new 'Ethnographical Section' for the Folk Park. The two villages were complementary attractions, following the anthropology of the day in telling parallel stories of primitive home life at the dawn of human social progress. A huddle of square and cone-shaped dwellings, echoing its prehistoric counterpart in form and arrangement, the African Village displays made an unambiguous statement in popular primitivism. "How akin [the prehistoric hut-dweller] was to the present-day African is evident", wrote one reporter, "when we pass through another palisade into the African Village", where a Sudanese 'Dinka' hut built around a tree trunk stood alongside "pigmy huts of the little people who fight with bow, knife and poisoned arrow; diminutive ghost-house to propitiate spirits; a witch-doctor's hut, with the human bones he wears; the chief's hut with royal stool, always the tallest in the village."[25] An open bazaar "with its strange assortment of native wares and the Fetish house with its fantastic images", as the *Finchley Press* described them, completed the lesson in popular anthropology.[26] From the exotic warfare of tribesmen to primitive superstition and the despotic pretensions of African chieftains, the African Village encouraged visitors to reflect on the instructive contrasts offered. "[W]hile enabling interesting comparisons to be made between the primitive types of dwellings once used in this country, which can be seen in the 'prehistoric' village, and those in use among the more backward races in the world," *The Times* reporter responded thoughtfully, "it will also be a reminder that Great Britain is the centre of an Empire embracing numerous races and tongues."[27]

✻ ✻ ✻

Leaving the lessons of the Prehistoric and African Villages behind, visitors moved up a gravel path and under the gatehouse that linked Hadley Hall to the Abbey Church. Further up the gentle slope they arrived at the Folk Park's two major gallery buildings. One, a long timbered building originally used as the Confraternity's schoolroom, ran at right angles to the rear of the Abbey Church and held the Prehistoric Galleries, the Roman Collection and several medieval displays. When the Folk Park first opened cabinets in this building displayed "relics of every century, from the Palaeolithic Age down to the Nineteenth Century; but they all show the evolution of the everyday things of life", Ward explained.[28] Thereafter it housed temporary exhibitions from Ward's collection: Egyptian tomb relics, Japanese prints, historic furniture, glassware, Persian pottery and Arabic brassware showcasing recent acquisitions or particularly precious items. A display of historical footwear "with specimens ranging all the way from the nailed sandals of a Roman soldier to a dainty brocade shoe which once adorned the foot of tragic Mary Queen of Scots" was a special highlight, at least for the *Footwear Organiser*'s correspondent.[29] When a Persian exhibition opened in August 1934, blue glazed earthenware vessels of the fourth, eighth, and ninth centuries were on view, and a superb milk-white Zoroastrian jug of the thirteenth century. Lustrous late-medieval Turkish bowls, a green-glazed fourteenth-century lamp, vases, religious icons and decorative tiles lined the walls and tables. Ward's magpie instinct, his loose eclecticism and his talent for vivid interpretation were all manifest:

> There are many other interesting things in the exhibition, including examples of Persian rugs, and a strange battle axe, no doubt medieval Arab in date, with a double blade, and, affixed to the end, a sword breaker, namely, two flanges of steel, between which the sword of an enemy was caught and snapped by a sharp twist of the wrist. Old though it is, this axe was used as recently as the Battle of Omdaman [*sic*] [in the Sudan, 1898], for it was captured by an English Tommy from the foe.[30]

Behind the long gallery was a two-story building known as The Cottage. This was half-timbered, with an archaic clock tower rearing up over the

15 Ward in the library on upper floor of 'The Cottage', Abbey of Christ the King, 1931. *AMAA 12 WP 5/1.*

green quadrangle, and also housed permanent indoor displays. Its corridors were lined with framed prints and elegant glass-fronted bookshelves for the Abbey's library. Several period rooms were established upstairs: a massive carved four-poster bed from Yorkshire, inlaid with holly and ebony, dominated the Elizabethan bedroom, while its neighbour represented the years around 1820 with a late-Georgian bed, washstand, china and bath. Outside in the hallway a fully-outfitted Cromwellian trooper stood guard; further along a Victorian parlour exhibited the cluttered kitsch of the late nineteenth century. "Shades of our grandparents!", chortled one description, " . . . with aspidistra, stuffed birds, wax fruit and other Victorian atrocities arranged on the old harpsichord."[31] Looking through the heavy curtains down to the quadrangle a visitor could see groups taking tea and scones on the grassy lawn while children frolicked around the replica village stocks and maypole.

An Egyptian Mummy Room was established on the ground floor of the Cottage during 1937. Its windows were screened with fabrics, and in the gloom visitors made out the elements of an Egyptian tomb arranged around the mummy and mask of a priest of Amun–Re dated to *c.*580 BC. The exhibit shot to national attention in May 1937 when a crow was observed to return repeatedly to tap at the window into the room every morning for several hours. Sensing a promotional opportunity Father Ward wondered aloud in a letter to the *Star* newspaper whether the crow might be the spirit of the departed priest returning according to Egyptian belief. "Mystery of a Mummy – Big Black Crow's Nightly Visits – Legend Revived – Barnet Watchers Puzzled" ran the headlines in the *Star* alongside a photograph of the crow in its curious routine. The story predictably re-appeared in newspapers across the country: "Its Tappings Bring Thoughts of Nile's Dark Gods" offered the *Daily Sketch*, while under the heading 'Crow's Homage to Mummy at Dawn' the *Daily Mirror* was convinced its movements were eerily regular: "First it bows three times to the north, then three times to the south, turns, and with its beak, gives three distinct raps on the window. Ancient Egyptians believed that the souls of the dead returned as birds."[32] The *Daily Express* consulted a specialist at the London Zoo. "The crow has discovered that when he looks at a window of a darkened room he can see a bird like himself", they were told. "He thinks it is another crow, a stranger thereabouts, and wants to fight him."[33]

In the first months of 1936, part of the ground floor and adjacent passageway of The Cottage was re-configured to house another ambitious reconstruction, as the L-shaped Arcade of Old-Time Shops was built along one side of the building and around the back. With its heavy-timbered facades and narrow doorways, dimly lit and hung with iron-work signs, the Arcade was particularly atmospheric. Visitors could step into one of ten shops opening onto the corridor, from "a sixteenth-century armourer's in

16 Fr Filius Domini (Colin Chamberlain) and the Armourer's Shop in the Arcade of Old-Time Shops, Abbey Folk Park, *c*.1936. *AMAA 13 WA 10/1.*

herringbone brick and timber [and] seventeenth-century pottery shop, half-timber and plaster", the group ran through to an "eighteenth-century weaver's and china shop, late eighteenth and early nineteenth-century costumier's, and a series of the nineteenth-century shops devoted to jewellery and fancy goods, knick-knacks, curiosities, china and glass".[34] Although motley to the eye, when understood chronologically the Arcade demonstrated a history of increasing sophistication in retail and consumption. In the Hanoverian-era china shop, for example, and in contrast to the gloomy and rudimentary spaces of the earlier shops, "we notice that the window has at last come into its own . . . in the eighteenth century practically the whole front became a window. The small leaded panes gave way to square panes, about a foot across set in wooden sash-bars."[35]

A major new attraction that embodied the ever-wider horizons of Ward's Folk Park, the Arcade opened to the public on a rainy day in mid-June 1936. Following suitable words by Councillor Marchand, visitors and invited guests crowded through the arcade, peering through the glass fronts and taking in the new exhibits. From the heavy timbers of the armourer's shop, for example, where a picturesque assortment of Tudor helmets, breastplates, swords, pikes and halberds glinted in the lantern-light, visitors progressed along past china shops and weavers' premises to the crinolines and bustles of

17 John and Jessie Ward in the Victorian Toyshop, Arcade of Old-Time Shops, Abbey Folk Park, June 1937. *AMAA 13 WA 2/4.*

the Victorian-era costumiers at the end of the arcade. The progressive evolution of taste, technique and artisanal finesse was tangible: crossing over from the Stuart-era stoneware of one shop to the Derby and Worcester china of its eighteenth-century neighbour, for instance, visitors saw a clear progression. "No two shops", commented the *Finchley Press,* "more clearly bring out the remarkable change which took place in the social life of Britain in the short time which divides the two." This latest addition to the Folk Park was truly appropriate for a 'Nation of Shopkeepers', the *Star* proclaimed.

> Charles Lamb would have loved it. So, we imagine, will thousands of visitors old and young. We are proud to be a nation of shopkeepers, and this display will show that there is no reason why we should not be. Through the years, our shops have grown brighter and better and more generously stocked with an infinite variety of good things. We want to see the process go on with increasing capacity, among all classes, to buy the brighter and better things which the shops of to-day and to-morrow will stock.[36]

Ward's wider horizons were also evident in the confident public appeals he made to outfit the new shops. An appeal seeking Victorian costumes resulted in nearly two hundred items, ranging from complete crinoline dresses to hats, fans and shoes, all donated within a month by the public. Members of the Abbey posed with Jessie Ward's mother for promotional photographs in complete Victorian costumes, and a new Gaumont newsreel was filmed of the group milling about in the Victorian shop.[37] Victorian 'knick-knacks' were called for in February 1936, resulting in another flood of donations including items gifted personally by Queen Mary after reading the appeal in the *Daily Telegraph.*[38] A mahogany tea-caddy, papier-mâché inkstand, stationery box and blotter trinket tray inlaid in mother-of-pearl, an embroidered needle-book, writing tablet and two samplers made their way from the royal household to New Barnet for display. Another appeal of September 1936 called for children's toys of the nineteenth century to cater to the many school parties that visited the Folk Park. Over five hundred donations had streamed in by the end of that month, including an intricate 1880s miniature of a wedding party, with bustle-skirted ladies and gentlemen in minute Scottish kilts, that was remarkable for its detail and realism.[39]

✴ ✴ ✴

By mid-1935, the grounds of Hadley Hall had been landscaped in an eclectic mix of historical periods and national styles. Moving eastwards down the main path from the front door, visitors encountered a picturesque Japanese garden with a rocky lake and drooping willows on one side; on the other a paved Tudor garden suggested the arborial tastes of the sixteenth century. A rose garden, pergolas, shaded walkways, manicured lawns, hedges and remnants of the original fruit orchard all contributed to the charm. Away from the well-trodden paths about the main attractions, visitors came upon secluded parts of the Folk Park with a sense of surprise and discovery.

A Chinese Temple of Initiation was built at the far end of the Prehistoric Gallery, and opened in early July 1935 to mark the Folk Park's first anniversary. Father Ward wanted it to "appeal particularly to Freemasons and those interested in the Ancient Mysteries", [40] and here his extensive collection of Hung Society and Triad ceremonial material was displayed. It was set out with all the paraphernalia of the secret society's six-hour long initiation ceremony. "On entering it", Ward wrote for the *Children's Newspaper*, "the visitor finds himself in a strange and unfamiliar world – a world which in some ways has more in common with the days of the Roman Empire than with our world of planes and cars." [41] The new attraction confirmed his long-standing interest in the allegories and symbolism of secret ritual. "The Ceremony itself is extremely interesting and dramatically represents the journey of the soul through the underworld to the City of the Gods", he told readers of the magazine *Educational Handwork*.

> It has curious analogies with the Egypt Book of the Dead, for the soul of the candidate is symbolically weighed and the Solar Barque, here called the HUNG BOAT, plays a prominent part in the Ceremony. Among the relics are copies of the rituals, banners, the Magic Censer, the scales with which the soul is weighed and the china cups from which the Oath of Blood Brotherhood is drunk . . . All these features are shown, and the room itself, with its red hangings and strange Chinese paintings, is both interesting and impressive. [42]

Close to the Folk Park's boundary, at the eastern end of the main avenue, a small chapel offered visitors a haven of quiet that evoked the devout reverence of the Confraternity's religious work. For all its elaborate title, the Oratory of the Angels was a simple re-built cottage lined with statues of saints and angels, reliquaries and gilded crucifixes. Ward had been an avid collector of stained glass panels and fragments for decades, as the glorious interior of the Abbey Church demonstrated. In September and October 1934, the Abbey purchased another ten panels of stained glass in fragments, four of which were identified as late fifteenth century work, probably by the glazier William Neave and originally set in the east window of the Lady Chapel in Winchester Cathedral. The panels depicted themes from the Nativity, a Jesse Tree symbolising the genealogy of Christ and elements from the Book of Revelation featuring, Ward wrote to the local newspaper, "some delightful little angels and a somewhat fearsome-looking beast, which is, nevertheless, adorned with a golden halo". [43] The glass had been damaged during the

English Civil War, and then removed entirely in 1898 to make way for a new window commemorating Victoria's Diamond Jubilee. Four other panels were considered to be French and Flemish work of the sixteenth century, and another two contained English fragments of the thirteenth century.[44]

The Oratory of the Angels was erected in late 1934 to house the magnificent glass to best effect.[45] Visitors reported themselves enthralled by its charmed atmosphere. "It must be like a jewelled cavern in the early morning when the sun shines through the panels of thirteenth, fifteenth, and sixteenth century glass", wrote one. "There were two little antique wooden angels with the expression of children left at Grannie's for tea, and stoically determined to behave beautifully at *all* costs, that I coveted."[46] The Oratory was a place of solace and contemplation, its oak pews providing seats to admire the altar piece, tall candlesticks, saints' relics and statuary flooded in the glorious light of the coloured glass. By January 1935 a further twelve panels of glass had been purchased and installed, depicting various winged cherubim dated to around 1460, decorative foliage and canopies and a Dove of the Holy Spirit.[47] Another ten panels of the Winchester stained glass were acquired that year. Students of aesthetics might visit his museum solely to

18 Ward inspects the thatched roof of the Witch's Cottage, Abbey Folk Park, *c. 1936. AMAA 19 WA 1/3.*

study the Oratory of the Angels, Ward wrote in April 1935, with its "complete windows of thirteenth century glass; very rare and choice this, and one of them tells a story, the story of a Crusading King whose wife saved his life by sucking the poison from the wound caused by the dagger of the assassin, for this window contains the shield of Eleanor of Castile, and in the next light, on a red field, gleam the three golden roses of Edward I".[48] Once again we see Ward's instinct for historical colour given full rein. Amid the panoply of medieval iconography, meanwhile, the attentive visitor might make out the Dove of the Holy Spirit, a French glass depicting a standing figure of God the Father, various angels, saints, cherubim and symbols of St Luke and St Mark. With this reverential imagery washing over them in a golden blaze, perhaps the visitor might leave the "jewelled cavern" of the Oratory a little more attuned to the tenor of the Abbey's devotions than when they had entered.

Visitors encountered another isolated cottage at the end of the avenue that provided a slightly unnerving contrast to the ornate piety of the nearby Oratory. Ward's reconstruction of a sixteenth-century Witch's Cottage was another half-timbered dwelling with small leadlight windows and a thatched gabled roof. But the mood darkened as visitors ducked their head to enter the low doorway. Some basic furniture, a spinning wheel, candlesticks and a broomstick could be made out in the gloomy interior. The brushed flagstones were neat and well-kept, but Ward had laid on a series of disconcerting touches with relish: talismans dangled on threads from the rafters, pentangles and other esoteric emblems scratched vividly into the plastered walls, and a skull leered from one corner. "It is an uncanny experience, standing in this den of witchcraft and imagining oneself a credulous client of long ago for the old hag's sooth", wrote one reporter.

> All the paraphernalia of the old dame's magic are included. Over the central hearth is the cauldron for brewing potions, supported by [an] iron crane. Crocodile, sea parrot and sea porcupine hang suspended from the roof, ready to take her on nocturnal rides; in the corner is the inevitable birch broom. A grinning skull, her 'familiar,' magic circle, staff, and blasting rods of hazel with cryptic inscriptions complete the sinister equipment.[49]

For all these stimulating effects and experiences, a visit to the Abbey Folk Park did not climax until people stepped into the Abbey Church situated at its very heart. As we have seen, the interior was simply stunning, with stained-glass and painted windows, carved timber panels, ornate screens and choir stalls, Eastern icons and paintings of saints and scenes from the life of Christ. In all it contained "over two hundred examples of Ecclesiastical treasures", Ward wrote, "showing the evolution of Christian Ecclesiastical Art

. . . a magnificent Renaissance screen, and wonderful carved plaques show the skill of the wood carver, and there are numerous other statues in wood, sculptures in stone, encaustic tiles and Mediaeval metal work, constituting this an epitome of the history of Mediaeval Art".[50] From this point of view Ward's Abbey Church seemed less a pentecostal chapel of pious devotion, and more a treasure house of art history. "I have called the chapel 'remarkable', and so it is", wrote one visitor.

> [I]t has been furnished, within a few months, with genuine treasures brought from every part of Europe: sacred pictures by old masters, arranged not haphazard, but in perfect sequence; an exquisite old French font of grey-green stone; marvellous Spanish carved plaques, in deep relief; lovely fragments of ancient glass in almost every window; antique stalls and a screen of surpassing beauty; paintings, sculpture, and stonework of the very best periods of ecclesiastical art. This imperfect summary gives only a faint idea of the really priceless contents of this unique sanctuary which, if it proves nothing else, at least shows the presiding genius of this establishment to be an absolutely born collector, and also a most competent cicerone.[51]

Ward's museum also documented more recent themes in English social history. Immediately after the Folk Park opened to the public in June 1934, an appeal called for donations of nineteenth-century horse-drawn vehicles. "Probably still stored away in London and the suburbs", Ward wrote to *The Times* in July 1934, "are specimens of the hansom cab, the victoria, the landau, the brougham, and other vehicles, which with the coming of the motor car will never ply the streets again. Before they are broken up for old metal or firewood, we who are in charge of the Folk Park would be glad to give house-room for a characteristic example of such vehicles so that they may be preserved for future generations."[52] Within two weeks over a dozen vehicles had been offered by the public, and many were soon making their way to New Barnet to be housed in a carriage shed built near the Prehistoric Village. The first, a pony cart, was donated by a reader of the *Hertfordshire Mercury* "in memory of many happy pony cart drives with a much loved one now on the Other Side".[53]

Four more substantial carriages were donated by a Mrs Wharrie of Warnham Lodge in Horsham, Sussex. Resplendent in their original harness and upholstery, the coaches were railed to New Barnet station and paraded in convoy through town *en route* to the Folk Park. The press coverage gives a sense of the Abbey Folk Park's growing local importance only two months after it had opened, and of how squarely Ward's innovative heritage museum had captured the prevailing mood of popular nostalgia welling up amid the turmoil and change of the twentieth century. "A most unusual sight was witnessed last week in the streets of New Barnet", observed the *Finchley Herald*,

> where a veritable procession of Victorian carriages went down the Station Approach and wound its way round the War Memorial on the final stage of its journey to the Abbey Folk Park. It is difficult for the middle aged to realise how completely obsolete such vehicles have become, for hidden away in some corner of their memory are recollections of having seen them in the streets in child-hood days, even perchance of having ridden in them, but when one looked at the faces of the children and heard their remarks one realised that they are already antiquities, as strange to the rising generation as would seem the chariot of Boadicea . . . It is only in a place such as a Folk Park that it is possible to find room for the preservation of these interesting old vehicles . . . Yes, the triumph of the motor car is complete, and this passing of the old time horse vehicles through the streets of New Barnet reminds us that with the triumph of speed, much of the slow but gracious life of Victorian days has passed into the limbo of forgotten things![54]

Two sheds from related trades were re-assembled at the Folk Park during 1936. The dilapidated East Barnet smithy, which had ceased trading in June 1936, was donated to the Park by the owner, a Mr E. Leak, to permit new development at the site. Believed to date to the late seventeenth century, it had two brick forges and an old smith's bench; and "with its moss-covered pantiles and its old weather-boarding . . . was a most picturesque building, and will be a real acquisition to the Folk Park".[55] "Various members of the Abbey descended on the old smithy" in mid-September, reported the *Barnet Press*, "took it down piece by piece, and transported it to Park-road, where in due course it will be re-built".[56] It was soon re-established in the Park complete with its original bellows, anvil and tongs. Similarly, the old wheelwright shop on the East Barnet Road had ceased trading in August, and its owner was happy to transfer most of its contents directly to Father Ward's museum. A huge circular iron plate measuring over six feet across, weighing three-quarters of a ton and used to fix iron-work to the rim of cart wheels, accompanied the elements of the dismantled building to Park Road. "In short", reported the local newspaper approvingly, "although Mr Harmer's wheelwright's shop has officially ceased to exist, it will rise again ere long in the Folk Park, and constitute one of its most interesting exhibits."[57]

✳ ✳ ✳

For the attentive visitor, certainly, an air of wondrous historical mystery shrouded the Abbey Folk Park. The intriguing structures gathered in its didactic landscape, its carefully orchestrated displays and the animated lectures of its guides all taught that the social history of ordinary life could be vivid and engaging, riddled with compelling stories and manifested in fascinating objects with a life and a story of their own. It traced the age-long struggle of the human spirit for comfort and dignity, spiritual insight and self-expression, and documented very plainly a pattern of slow but progressive evolution in all these endeavours.

These at least were the themes that captivated Ward's antiquarian imag-ination, and he did his utmost to kindle a similar enthusiasm in his audience. "From Neolithic stone axes to a Regency four-poster", wrote one reporter in 1935, "from a 17th century Venetian mosaic of fastidious delicacy to a clumsy, prehistoric potter's-wheel – all the wonders and oddments [Father Ward] has collected at Abbey Folk Park fill him with delight."[58] To this the museum guides added commentary on spiritual matters whenever possible as they took groups around the displays: the story of the crow visiting the mummy in The Cottage helped introduce the subject of reincarnation, while another anecdote (the sad tale of their kitten that had fallen in the Folk Park's wishing well, but could still be heard miaowing) encouraged children to wonder whether animals had souls.[59] Inspired by Ward's visions and guided by angelic intervention, the Abbey Folk Park had a directly religious purpose that may have been lost on casual visitors, but which nevertheless rested at the heart of Father Ward's pentecostal mission. The *American Weekly*'s corre-spondent concluded his highly revealing piece on Ward's Folk Park with a pithy 'mass observation' on this theme:

> While some of the visitors to the Abbey Folk Park are impressed with the religious thought on which it is founded, by far the larger proportion is unmindful of it. They do not see in the wide range of exhibits, from the prehistoric huts to the hoopskirts and brandy bottles, anything to give them pause or to awaken them to a feeling that any great and unsettling change is in sight.
>
> Whether a knowledge of the construction of the many exhibits will be of service in a coming age, few seem to care. Some actually laugh at the prophecy of the end. . . .
>
> 'Where', observed one woman with a titter to her husband, 'could we put the reading-lamp?'
>
> 'Or the radio?' added the man.
>
> 'Or the day-couch?' continued the woman.
>
> And not more than a rifle-shot away from the warning exhibits stands the palace of the King, the stately mansions of Mayfair, and all the other show places of the British capital. London doesn't seem to be frightened.[60]

10

Anglican Outcasts and Orthodox Catholicism

At one and the same time, the Abbey Folk Park was both an ambitious experiment in popular education and an artful vehicle for Ward's pentecostal mission. It illustrated the material and spiritual progress of humankind, teaching of the age-long struggles of the human spirit to master the material circumstances of life. It gave a sense of the rise and fall of civilizations, and the importance of material heritage and cultural artefacts to mark that progress. But the eschatological principle underlying Ward's mission – that the onward march of history would shortly reach its consummation in the return of Christ the King – could only be suggested indirectly, such as through the luscious iconography of the Abbey Church. The guide-lecturers might mention religious matters in passing, but a full and explicit statement of the Confraternity's adventist creed was inimical to its success as a popular attraction. The curious visitor needed to pay close attention to the daily life of prayer, worship, preaching and discussion that swirled around the more prosaic activities of the Abbey's museum to gain that particular insight.

Challenges were rising to confront Ward's Confraternity despite the success of the Abbey Folk Park. Relations with the Anglican establishment had never been especially close, but they deteriorated rapidly during 1934. This was a pivotal year for the Confraternity on at least three fronts: after the opening of the Abbey Folk Park and the publication of their pentecostal manifesto "Message to the Nation and to the Individual", which as we have seen announced 'the work' in strident and unambiguous terms, that year saw another development that brought their adventist mission more clearly into the public eye. In the spring and early summer Father Ward used a programme of fortnightly public lectures in the Abbey schoolroom to make a much more direct statement of his prophetic mission than was possible in the Folk Park. The series was titled 'The Decline and Fall of Christendom: The Writing on the Wall.' Hymns were sung at each lecture with solos performed by Olive Bridges, a professional singer who joined the Confraternity as Sister Bertha, to provide a soothing counterpoint to the Reverend Father's urgent preaching.[1] On 12 May he spoke of "The Death Throes of the Christian Faith", followed by "The Disintegration of the Political Fabric and the Advance of Asia". The impending economic collapse of the western system was treated next, as was "The Decay of the British Nation". The series climaxed in early July with an address on "The Man of Destiny: Christ or Antichrist". We do not know the exact content of these virtual sermons, but their titles suggest their general tone clearly enough.

Public statements such as these damaged Ward's relationship with the Church of England, both locally and with its higher authorities, and it quickly deteriorated beyond repair. As his millenarian outlook became widely known, it was probably inevitable that tensions developed between Father Ward and the Lord Bishop of St Albans, Michael Furse. Initially supportive, if not entirely enamoured, of the Hadley Hall community, Furse had decided by December 1934 that his support would continue no longer. In tracing the collapse of that relationship we contrast the tone and character of Ward's idiosyncratic mysticism against the pragmatism of clergymen such as Furse with whom he dealt. Nothing is surprising in this, of course; as Dean W. R. Inge observed, mysticism and established Christian institutions are fated to conflict and are at best uneasy bedfellows.[2] What is more intriguing is Ward's choice of ecclesiastical affiliation thereafter. The following pages explain why, after his institutional affinity with the Church of England became untenable, Ward took up new status as a 'bishop at large' and found a natural home for his Confraternity in the hybrid modern tradition of Orthodox Catholicism.[3]

✳   ✳   ✳

The deterioration of this relationship and the Confraternity's subsequent severing of all ties with the Anglican Church took on an enormous significance in the affairs and outlook of Ward's small and marginal community. It was the precise moment, Ward became convinced, when England and her spiritual guardians in the Established Church first demonstrated their determined opposition to his message 'to the Nation and to the Individual'. The affair was thus mythologised by he and his followers, especially in the difficult years that followed their departure from New Barnet; distorted in their memory and encrusted with hearsay, the split with St Albans took on an ominous and exaggerated significance.

Documents detailing the deterioration of the relationship are retained in several places, including the relevant parish and diocesan records at the Hertfordshire Local Studies Library and the present-day archives of the Confraternity. Unfortunately neither Ward's nor the Lord Bishop's personal correspondence, which would provide full evidence of the affair, appear to survive. However the Lambeth Palace papers of Cosmo Gordon Lang, Archbishop of Canterbury between 1928 and 1942, contain an exchange of letters that shed substantial light on Furse's position. The Archbishop wrote to Furse in December 1934 indicating that he had been informed about Ward's museum and community, and asked for further information about Ward's connection to Furse's diocese. The Bishop's long and exasperated reply detailed the gradual dissolution of his relationship with the Confraternity. "If you saw my file on this matter", he began, "you would realise that I may not know much about it, but I have spent a good deal of time on the subject!"

The central charge Furse levelled against Ward and the Confraternity was that they had misled him by not revealing the basic character of their religious mission and their determination to preach that mission in their new Church. He owned that Ward had told him of "certain mystical experiences" at their first meeting, but only in a general sense. His measured report to his Archbishop certainly suggests an innate resistance:

> According to what he told me, in October 1928 he and his wife began to have a series of mystical experiences. In the next month he received a definite summons to found a Confraternity to prepare the world for the end of the age that was approaching and for the coming of Christ and Judgment, not to destroy the physical world but to end the age and give a new revelation. Though at my first interview with him he told me of certain mystical experiences, he did not tell me these details.[4]

As noted earlier Furse licensed a local Anglican vicar, Mr Phillips, to perform religious services for the Confraternity in their Abbey Church. "I made it clear in my letters to Mr. Ward", Furse later stated, "that the Chapel was [solely] for the Community and for a School that they were running."

The first alteration to this arrangement came in March 1931 when Furse advised Ward's group "that if they wished to have an official connection with the Church of England it would be advisable for them to have a Visitor and draw up a proper Constitution: this they agreed to, and proceeded to draw up a Constitution. It seemed to me in many respects very unsatisfactory". No further details are provided, but it seems that after taking further advice from the Bishop of Truro on the matter, Furse suggested amendments to the proposed constitution to Ward, "especially with regard to married persons and the care of the children (if any) of the members of the Community". Despite further misgivings about the Confraternity's inadequate rules and regulations, he decided to let the matter rest as a new advisory body on Christian communities was being formed among the Anglican episcopate. He was sure he had made his reservations clear during an interview with John and Jessie Ward.

Meanwhile, Ward had raised the subject of ordination, suggesting to Furse that he might be an appropriate candidate for Holy Orders in order to preach, administer the sacraments and thus 'minister the Word' directly. Although written in hindsight, Furse's account neatly encapsulates his uncertainty and reluctance on this score:

> I again saw Wigram about this and was not at all happy about it, though Wigram thought it would be rather a good thing to do. I then had a long letter from Mr. Ward with regard to the history of mixed Communities, and also with regard to certain amendments that were suggested to meet my difficulties about their Constitution and also with regard to his Ordination: that was last year (1933), and as the Bishops had not then appointed the Advisory Committee I let things rest as they were for the time being.

Matters came to a head late the following year. Ward wrote to the bishop in November regarding a successor to Mr Phillips, who had resigned his living at St James' to undertake missionary work in the north. This communication coincided with a rash of letters from various people drawing Furse's attention to the Confraternity's publications and its use of the Abbey Church for public services. According to Furse, this was clear evidence of duplicity on Ward's part. "I was entirely unaware until then", he wrote, "that the public were being admitted to the Chapel, and that Mr. Ward and his friends were using it as a centre from which to preach their message." Ward remembered it a little differently: "The new vicar, named Canham Russell, complained to the Bishop of our having our church open to outsiders although it had been open to them ever since its dedication . . . with the full approval of his predecessor Phillips."[5] The relationship deteriorated sharply as Furse informed Ward

> that I now gathered that the general public were being admitted to the Chapel, this had never been my intention, and I had made it clear in my letters that the Chapel was only to be used for the Community and the School. I then got rather an angry letter from Mr. Ward suggesting that I had known this all along, and that I had raised no objection to it and frankly saying that he was called by Christ the King for this work and that he must obey that call.

After consulting legal and ecclesiastical opinion, Furse replied to the effect that Ward "had no authority from me to minister the Word". He concluded his letter (as he reported later that month to the Archbishop of Canterbury) with an explicit statement:

and then I added these words 'If, as it appears from your letter, you wish to continue to do this (that is to say, minister the word to the general public) you will, of course, be at liberty to do so. But in that case I cannot see my way to license one of my clergy to be Chaplain. For if I do so I shall be allowing the public to infer that the message which you give has my approval and authority. And therefore it seems that the only course open to me is to refuse to license a clergyman as Chaplain for your Community Chapel, and in that case I shall have to ask you to make it clear to the public generally that no one has my authority for ministering the Word or Sacraments in your Chapel.'

This was a line in the sand. Ward's indignant response ran to "twenty-three closely typewritten quarto sheets", which unfortunately have not been retained in the diocesan archives to provide the Confraternity's side of events. It is patently clear, even relying on Furse's account alone, that the relationship had deteriorated dramatically: "at the present moment he is in extremely bad temper with me and thinks I have treated him abominably;

19 A gathering of the Confraternity and guests to mark John Ward's ordination, September 1935. Mar Kwamin of the Autonomous African Universal Church is to the left of Jessie Ward; the bearded priest beside John Ward is unidentified. *AMAA 3 WC 3/1.*

amongst other things he is particularly annoyed because I addressed him as 'Mr.' Ward . . . " Of course Ward's discontent ran deeper than this. Furse was essentially withdrawing the only shred of recognition the Confraternity enjoyed as a formal religious organization. It appears from the circumstantial evidence that Ward felt that both the nature of his calling and his intention to hold public services in the Abbey Church were perfectly plain to Furse from the outset and thus had his tacit blessing. But the Bishop was resolute. As he advised the Archbishop, "so long as Mr. Ward takes the line that he can and will minister the word in his Chapel and admit, indeed, invite, the general public to go there, without any authority from me as Bishop of the Diocese, I cannot see how I can recognise the Community". He ruefully summarised his position:

> I always felt that Mr. Ward was a bit of a crank, and perhaps I ought to have adopted the easier course from the beginning of refusing to have anything to do with him, but it did seem a bit difficult to do that after what Wigram told me about him and his ideas generally.

The split was perhaps inevitable; but it certainly was not something Ward had actively pursued. As the relationship with St Albans deteriorated and the veneer of Anglican recognition peeled away, the Confraternity of the Kingdom of Christ found itself adrift without institutional affiliation. For their Father Superior, it seems, official recognition within a established religious hierarchy conferred legitimacy and a degree of *gravitas* upon his Confraternity that he valued highly. He began an urgent search for a new ecclesiastical connection.

His first attempt to secure an institutional affiliation outside the Anglican fold ended in frustration. In September 1935, soon after the break with St Albans, Ward was ordained deacon and priest in the Autonomous African Universal Church by its Primate, Mar Kwamin.[6] Kwamin was a black West African, sometimes known as Ebenezer Johnson Anderson and a former trader based in Accra on the Gold Coast, then living at Hornsey in North London. He had been a Methodist minister for some years before adopting the tribal name Kwamin Nsetse Bresi-Ando in keeping with his pan-African convictions. His journey into the Autonomous African Universal Church, which claimed to unify various Orthodox church sects in West Africa and the United States, is somewhat obscure, but he was delighted to ordain Ward according to the authority vested in him as its prelate. On 12 September Mar Kwamin travelled to New Barnet to consecrate Ward as a bishop in his church: photographs taken to document the event show a happy and relaxed group, splendid in their vestments, gathered on the steps of the conservatory at Hadley Hall. By the end of the month Ward had loftily informed St Albans "that he and his Confraternity had severed all relations with the Established

Church".[7] When doubt was cast over the legitimacy of Mar Kwamin's investiture and authority to conduct his office in England, however, a disconcerted Father Ward cast about for advice. He travelled to West Chelsea to meet another autonomous bishop, the elderly Archbishop Sibley of the Orthodox Catholic Church in England, to clarify the validity of Kwamin's consecration. When he met with Sibley, Ward "took to him at once", as he later wrote. Their immediate friendship provided a bond on which a deeper alliance was forged.

The charming and eccentric John Churchill Sibley, with his close-trimmed beard, bushy military moustache, snappy black suit and spats, was an even more colourful and complex figure than Mar Kwamin. A dedicated musician with a taste for ecclesiastical pomp, he was chancellor of the Inter-collegiate University, an uncredited college offering degrees in theology, arts, music and business. Sibley was also an eclectic scholar in Ward's own style, with keen spiritual interests. In a ceremony at St Edythe's Chapel, London in 1924 Sibley had been ordained a priest in the American Catholic Church (Western Orthodox), a schismatic Old Catholic church founded nine years earlier. The ordination was performed by the lapsed Anglican priest and former missionary Frederick Lloyd, an American resident and Archbishop of the fledgling church. In 1929 he consecrated Sibley in Chicago as a bishop and authorised him as 'Metropolitan of the American Catholic Church for the British Empire'. Sibley returned to England to establish a branch of Lloyd's church as the Orthodox Catholic Church in England. Peter Anson's research convinced him Sibley was a "religious confidence trickster"[8] on a par with Joseph René Vilatte (of whom more shortly); Ward, on the other hand, remembered him as "one of the most saintly men I ever knew".[9]

Their first meeting resulted in an offer. To remove any doubt of valid consecration, Ward would be re-ordained priest and re-consecrated bishop by Sibley according to the rites of his church. Simultaneously the Abbey of Christ the King would be registered as part of the Orthodox Catholic Church in England. Both men would be advantaged: Ward and his followers would gain the institutional affiliation they so ardently desired, and Sibley would substantially increase his Church, "which until then", Anson comments sardonically, "had got little further than its Metropolitan's writing paper, and had made no visible advance within the British Empire".[10] Accordingly, the decision was made to align Father Ward's Confraternity with Archbishop Sibley's tiny Orthodox Catholic Church in England. The move reflected Ward's innate desire for clerical authority – for the sanction of an established church to preach, 'minister the Word' and practice the sacraments in its name. It also offered institutional recognition, and thus a measure of legitimacy, for his Confraternity and its pentecostal work preaching the fall of western civilization and the imminent return of Christ the King.

In early October 1935, then, just a month after Mar Kwamin's ultimately fruitless visit, Sibley arrived at Park Road in full regalia and was similarly welcomed by the simple hospitality of the Abbey. Over the two days that followed Ward and his brethren were ritually inducted into Sibley's Orthodox Catholic Church in England. On the first day, 5 October, after Sibley re-dedicated the Abbey Church and celebrated the Holy Eucharist, Ward was baptised and re-confirmed, ordained deacon and, finally, "solemnly admitted to the Sacred Office of the Priesthood" by the authority of Archbishop Sibley's hand and seal. In further ceremonies the following day, Ward was "solemnly consecrated as a Bishop in the Church of God" and commissioned as its Chancellor of the Province (England). "The ceremony was performed before many witnesses", Ward later wrote, "and the Roman Rite was used in this and in all previous ceremonies [of the Church], because it is well known in the West and acknowledged by all authorities to be valid both in its Intention and in its Form".[11] He was also issued with a Doctor of Divinity from Sibley's Intercollegiate University for good measure, while Jessie Ward was ordained a deacon in her own right.

Ward later explained his conversion to Orthodox Catholicism, after his Abbey had "for five years . . . struggled to remain in communion with the Anglican Church", in his brief history of the Orthodox Catholic Church published in 1944. His account encapsulated his personal antipathy to the Bishop of St Albans, his frustration at the latter's refusal to renew the chaplain's license, and his forceful denial of the legitimacy of the Established Church itself. The accusation that he had no authority to 'minister the Word' clearly rankled, because it led him

> to study carefully the whole question of the validity of Anglican Orders and therefore the right of an Anglican Bishop to make such a claim, and the result of his investigation was to convince him that the attitude of the Western and Eastern Churches was right, and that in the ecclesiastical sense the Anglican Church has no valid orders, and therefore no Priests and no Bishops, and that the gentleman who calls himself a Bishop is only a layman given the name of Bishop by Act of Parliament, and appointed by the State like any other State Official.[12]

There was a good deal of retrospective self-justification in this. In truth, Ward would have preferred to remain in the Anglican Communion, and by tethering his cause to Archbishop Sibley he made what proved a fateful commitment. By embracing Orthodox Catholicism he joined Sibley, Mar Kwamin and scores of others in the ranks of the modern *episcopi vagantes*, the 'bishops at large' of an extraordinary ecclesiastical underworld of idealists, eccentrics and schismatics that, as we will see, had proliferated on the fringe of organised religion since the mid-nineteenth century. If this affiliation was of doubtful benefit in the long run, Ward seized its direct advantages in the shorter term. Through Orthodox Catholicism and his claimed status as a consecrated bishop in a line of episcopal succession that arguably stretched back to antiquity, Ward was able to claim for his community a religious heritage far beyond the Protestant Reformation – and thus far more ancient and substantial than that embodied in the Anglican Church. If the move was initially opportunistic and compelled by the collapse of his relationship with St Albans, Ward found the mystical doctrine and rites of worship incorporated in Orthodox Catholicism deeply satisfying at a number of levels.

Archbishop Sibley died, aged eighty, on 15 December 1938 after being confined to St Luke's Hospital, Chelsea. His body was brought to New Barnet, where for four days it lay in state at the Abbey's Oratory of the Angels while a requiem mass was prepared and celebrated. He was buried in the frozen earth of Southgate Cemetery during a snowstorm, and Ward was immediately elected his successor by the Holy Synod of the Orthodox Catholic Church in England (in effect, the members of Ward's Confraternity) meeting at the Abbey on the same day. The certificate of election was witnessed by the Synod Secretary, Colin Chamberlain, Jessie Ward, and another Orthodox Catholic priest, Fr William Martin Andrew. It announced Father Ward's new title: Archbishop Metropolitan of the Orthodox Catholic Church in the British Empire. To grasp properly this blossoming of Ward's episcopal status, from priest to bishop to archbishop, we need to consider in some detail the exotic underworld of the modern *episcopi vagantes*.

✳ ✳ ✳

Irregular bishops without established sees or ordinary diocesan responsibilities – free, in effect, to 'wander at large' among the faithful - have long been a feature of Western ecclesiastical life. In the first centuries after Christ, such figures were simply bishops "dispossessed of jurisdiction, though not of orders, on account of heresy or schism, or moral offences".[13] Others might have been consecrated to an appointment for various reasons before the position itself was properly vacant. Like the wandering Irish bishops, those driven out by persecution or invasion in places like Spain and Prussia, and titular bishops appointed to sees in the Holy Land under Saracen control during the crusading period, such *episcopi vagantes* were a commonplace anomaly of ecclesiastical administration. Their modern counterparts, on the other hand, likewise have no fixed jurisdiction but their story is "one of the strangest and most fantastic religious movements to be found in the . . . erratic 'goings on' of the ecclesiastical underworld".[14] This controversial and colourful breed proliferated in the United States and to a lesser extent elsewhere from the 1860s, giving rise to what is now termed the independent sacramental movement.[15]

Driven by a religious calling or more worldly motives, modern *episcopi vagantes* – many of them lapsed Catholics or, like Ward, disgruntled and headstrong Anglicans – have secured their ordinations and consecrations within certain obscure lines of episcopal succession. Without exception these lines of succession are disputed – indeed, rejected – by conventional church authorities in the major denominations. Undeterred, the bishops in question claim rightful legitimacy as bishops simply because they possess valid orders, having been formally consecrated according to legitimate rites and ceremonies that (they claim) stretch back in a line of succession to Apostolic authority, often culminating in St Peter at Antioch prior to his removal to Rome. Critics see a common pattern:

> In almost every case the leaders of these multiple movements have been at pains to obtain episcopal consecration, from sources often remote and seldom wholly unquestionable, which they hoped would be indisputable. Having obtained episcopal character they proceeded to found a 'Church' based upon it, and their own particular version of what true Catholic orthodoxy is. In this way, so the visionary hope takes shape in the minds of these dreamers, their Church will become the centre and foundation upon which the unity of Christ's Church could be re-built.[16]

Of the several hundred such bishops active in Britain and the United States between the 1860s and the 1950s, most had only tiny numbers of followers, practiced their rites in rented churches, were constantly at odds with each other, and were either ignored or ridiculed by the mainstream churches. But they took themselves very seriously. At the heart of their ministry often lay a desire – one that could be quite sincere and deeply felt – to administer holy offices in the name of catholic universality, yet independently of organisational or doctrinal control. The various primates, patriarchs, archbishops, bishops and monsignors of this religious fringe have thus been an irritant to the recognised churches of the religious mainstream. They are usually dismissed as deluded and self-important eccentrics, with few followers or worldly assets beyond their rich vestments and fragrant rituals. A memorandum prepared for the Archbishop of Canterbury during the 1930s (when their presence was beginning to trouble many Anglicans) encapsulates the mainstream view:

> A man is included in this group when he has been, or claims to have been, consecrated as a bishop in some irregular or clandestine manner; or, even if he has been regularly consecrated, when, because he has been excommunicated by the church which consecrated him, or for some other reason, he is not in communion with any well-known see; or when the total number of those in communion with him is very small, so that

the church appears to exist for the sake of the bishop rather than the bishop for the sake of the church. These are not exact definitions . . . [but] it can be maintained that the 'episcopi vagantes' . . . have no real excuse for their position; that though some of them are, or have been, quite sincere, they have for the most part been in some way mentally abnormal; and that the movements which they represent are of no value to the Christian cause, while in some cases they are extremely injurious to it.[17]

Rejoicing in a bewildering variety of titles and offices, the British autonomous bishops of this period claimed their episcopal status through one or more of several lines of consecration and succession. The major lines were summarised by the Rev. Henry Brandreth, author of *Episcopi Vagantes and the Anglican Church*, in his report to Lambeth Conference in 1948. The oldest was the 'Ferrete Succession' descending from Julius Ferrete, a French Dominican priest who had abandoned Catholicism in the course of a chequered missionary career in the Middle East. He appeared in England in 1866, "claiming to have been consecrated 'Bishop of Iona' by the Jacobite Bishop of Homs . . . [but] produced no evidence of this consecration beyond a printed certificate".[18] He consecrated a Welsh Anglican, Richard William Morgan, as the first Patriarch of the restored Ancient British Church, from whom proceeded further ordinations and consecrations, the most prominent being that of Hugh George de Willmott Newman. A London-born bicycle salesman and secretary of the National Association of Cycle Traders and Repairers, Newman had been ordained a priest by James McFall of the Old Catholic Church in Ireland in 1938. After he was consecrated a bishop in the Ferrete line of succession in 1943 he commenced an extraordinary effort – as we will see in the following chapter – to unite all the lines of succession in Britain under a single governing body based in Glastonbury (the 'Occidental Jerusalem', as he called it).

A second and more recent line, that had flourished in the United States and to a lesser extent in Britain, was the 'Aftimios Succession' based on the claimed consecration of Aftimios Ofiesh, Archbishop of Brooklyn, according to the rites of the Russian Orthodox Church in around 1927. The most widespread, however, was the 'Mathew Succession', derived from Arnold Harris Mathew, consecrated in 1908 by Archbishop Gul of Utrecht. Brandreth reported that by 1948 the Church of Utrecht maintained "that the consecration was obtained by the production of false evidence for which Mathew himself was responsible, and that therefore the consecration was null and void".[19] This did not prevent the various bishops (numbering upwards of sixty, according to Brandreth's count, some thirteen of whom were resident in Britain) consecrated by Mathew to claim legitimate succession through the Utrecht connection. Finally, and most significantly in Father Ward's case, Brandreth pointed to the 'Vilatte Succession' descended from the French-born American resident and lapsed Catholic Joseph René Vilatte.

A detailed analysis of these various lines of succession is beyond our purposes here. But it is fair to say that few historians or commentators have taken their claims and posturing seriously. Mainstream churches are actively hostile to their claims, while the tone of wry mockery Peter Anson adopted in his study does little to illuminate their sense of self-identity and purpose. His attention to external details – the bishops' frequent disputes, their splintered church organisations, their love of high-sounding titles and ecclesiastical finery – discourages any consideration of their private motivations. But since (as Anson admits) many of the modern *episcopi vagantes* were not malicious frauds, but were instead driven by an inner calling that might be mystical, esoteric or otherwise unusual, we should at least attempt to make sense of that calling as we consider Father Ward's ministry as one of their number.

Another reason to consider their stance a little more carefully is that their legacy is by no means exhausted. Many of their successors remain active today, and like Lewis Keizer, not a few see themselves as 'Apostles of a New Spirituality'. Among his episcopal predecessors, in Keizer's view, were men and women "as diverse and talented as the original Apostles of Jesus. They searched for the Divine Mysteries of the Master that had long ago been lost to gentile Christianity. They delved deeply into the Western Mystery Tradition that had been driven underground by the Church, and they made pilgrimage to other religions and traditions of the East and Near East".[20] In the autumn of 1935, following his split with St Albans and his decisive liaison with Archbishop Sibley, John Ward became the latest of them, but by no means the last.

✻ ✻ ✻

If one feature is common through the bewildering diversity of the modern *episcopi vagantes*, it is that every one of them has solemnly insisted on the legitimacy of his episcopal consecration. Each one insists that his consecration (or at least, his *latest* consecration, as many were ordained and consecrated many times over) is valid by virtue of its adherence to the proper forms and rites, and by the fact that it was administered by another bishop whose 'valid orders' were likewise above dispute. The notion of valid orders, therefore, is the essence of his sense of ecclesiastical authority and religious identity. Ward was drawn into the Orthodox Catholic Church in England, for instance, by the opportunity to gain valid orders at Archbishop Sibley's hand. Likewise the study of the Orthodox Catholic Church in England he wrote and published in 1944 was subtitled "Showing Its History and the Validity of its Orders".

Some background is necessary to clarify this theme. Henry Brandreth, the Anglican Church's expert on the subject in the 1940s, identified two main theories of validity: one derived from St Augustine, the other dominant in the Orthodox Church. The Augustinian tradition held that a Bishop, once validly consecrated, retained his orders even when excommunicated or cut off from the Church, and retained the power to consecrate others in a similarly valid fashion (according to the traditional formula of matter, form, minister and intention). But even if valid, these consecrations might also be held by Church authorities to be irregular and at odds with church law. The Augustinian view thus differentiated between "the power conferred in ordination and consecration, and the legitimate exercise of that power".[21] "Heretics have the power to pass it on", according to one canonical authority cited by Brandreth, "but they do not possess and cannot pass on its legitimate exercise."[22] The Orthodox Church's view on the other hand was more mystical than legalistic, and did not distinguish between valid form and valid authority. Stressing the single and indivisible Holy Communion of the Apostolic Church (from which all other churches were schismatic), Orthodoxy simply required that the "bishops who performed the consecration, or the bishop who performed the ordination, had authority to perform it" within that Communion.[23] The validity or otherwise of a consecration, in other words, was subsumed into the broader exercise of authority by fidelity to Orthodox tradition. This more elusive notion of validity seems to have attracted many of the modern autonomous bishops, in that they often claimed episcopal succession from branches of Orthodox or Near-Eastern Christianity, but utilising an essentially Augustinian and legalistic argument of valid consecration according to appropriate rituals in a continuous line of succession. The idea of an unbroken 'line of succession' was just as essential as the notion of valid orders in their claims for legitimacy.

Thus as the modern *episcopi vagantes* proliferated in the decades after the 1860s, most can be traced through a half-dozen major lines of succession, often centred on individuals "connected with movements of a 'Catholic' type mainly deriving from dissatisfied and unstable elements in Catholicism or Anglo-Catholicism".[24] Anson's book, a massive scholarly compendium of the wandering bishops in Britain based on Brandreth's research, concentrates on Jules Ferette, Joseph René Vilatte, Vernon Herford, and Arnold Harris Mathew and those that followed in each one's line of succession. He describes a tidal wave of colourful cranks and religious misfits, animated by spiritual aspirations in some cases and worldly ambition in others, united only by their desire for episcopal status, elaborate titles and the ecclesiastical pomp that went with them. Joseph René Vilatte is a prime example: a Frenchman, a lapsed Catholic, who spent time in French Canada and then as a lay missionary among Belgian immigrants on the shores of Lake Michigan. In 1885 he was ordained a priest for this work by an Old Catholic bishop in

Switzerland, and then in 1892 was raised to the episcopate by Bishop Alvarez of a breakaway Catholic sect in Goa, India and Ceylon that separated from Rome in 1888. Alvarez and Vilatte both claimed their consecrations were performed under the legitimate authority of the Syrian Orthodox (or 'Jacobite') Patriarch, Ignatius Peter III of Antioch. They were therefore endorsed, they claimed, by the autocephalous church that had been founded in Antioch by St Peter himself in 34 AD according to Church tradition, and which had broken with the other Patriarchates in the fifth century. The consecration of Vilatte in an 1892 ceremony at Colombo as Archbishop for the West, they maintained, had occurred under the explicit instructions of a Patriarchal Bull of Ignatius Peter III issued from his palace at the monastery of Mardin and dated 29 December 1891 (a claim dismissed by Ignatius Peter's successors). Vilatte returned to the United States to establish the American Catholic Church (Western Orthodox) incorporated in Illinois, and subsequently consecrated a number of other bishops in the so-called 'Vilatte succession' or 'Syrian-Malabar line'.[25]

One of them was Archbishop Lloyd, who (as we saw above) in turn consecrated Archbishop Sibley as his representative in the United Kingdom. Sibley's consecration of John Ward as a bishop in his church, then, gave Ward episcopal authority by virtue of the Vilatte succession. After over two decades of effort in America, meanwhile, Vilatte resigned as Archbishop of the American Catholic Church and returned to France where he was received into the Roman Catholic Church in 1925, four years before his death by heart failure. To successors such as Father Ward, Vilatte's late conversion seemed a heroic sacrifice rather than a renunciation of the Orthodox Catholic cause. By delaying his return to Catholicism and receiving from Rome its recognition, Ward wrote vehemently, Vilatte "did his duty to the Church he founded and only when that was done sought his own peace, and in so doing established the validity not merely of his own Episcopacy but of that of the Church he had founded, for he was not received as a Priest or a layman, but acknowledged as an Archbishop who had returned to the fold and was treated as such". Rome's reception of Vilatte was a dignified gesture that, to Ward at least, contrasted with the hostility of the Church of England. "[Vilatte's] Anglican foes may throw what mud they like and tell what untruths they like", he continued,

> But they cannot get away from the fact that Rome who has completely rejected the validity of their orders and declared them Null and Void, by this gracious act and generous treatment of an old enemy established the validity of his Church, the Orthodox Catholic Church of the West, and of its Orders. Moreover, by this action Rome established once again before the whole world her respect for TRUTH, even if it were a bitter truth to her, in striking contradiction to the Anglican Church.[26]

Such was the extent of Ward's bitterness towards the Church of England. Sibley's church, tiny and of debateable authority as it was, by contrast offered something very precious: the authority, even if contentious, to celebrate a version of Christianity that answered Ward's mysticism, his ritualism and his antiquarianism. It answered his need for doctrinal autonomy, free of canonical oversight, so that his preaching and the forms of worship practiced in his Abbey of Christ the King might tally with the revelations he and Jessie had received personally rather than the requirements of a mainstream church. He embraced Orthodox Catholicism, that is to say, because it matched the creative needs of his pentecostal mission, and not simply for the superficial, 'titular' advantages on offer. We will consider the terms of that embrace in more detail shortly. At a more general level, however, the heritage of Eastern Orthodoxy evoked by Sibley's church utterly seduced Ward's vivid historical imagination. Such was the enchantment he discovered in one of the epic narratives of world civilization that Father Ward fell, as if in a swoon, in surrender to its charms.

Eastern Orthodoxy traces its origins to the first generation after Christ and the apostolic teaching of the disciples and early missionaries in the eastern, Greek-speaking part of the Roman Empire. Bishoprics were established in the cities of Constantinople, Antioch, Jerusalem and Alexandria as well as at Rome. In an age of poor communications and regional difference each developed its own localised character and traditions of theology and worship. The great Church Councils, beginning with the Council of Nicea in 325, met to resolve disputes and deliberate on matters of church doctrine and so permitted dialogue between these epicentres of early Christianity. The councils decided on matters of heresy, resulting in the condemnation of ideas like Nestorianism and Monophysitism (their precise character is outside our present concern) at meetings in the fifth century. Such condemnations resulted in schismatic separations from the universal church. The Syrian Orthodox Church, formerly of Antioch, for example – important to us because it generated the so-called 'Syrian-Malabar' line of succession claimed to culminate in Sibley and Ward's church in the 1930s – separated after the Council of Chalcedon in 451 over the thorny issue of Christ's intrinsic nature. It held to the Monophysite creed outlawed at Chalcedon – that Christ was not separately divine and human but rather "one nature out of two natures" – and is thus numbered among the 'Separated' or 'Oriental Orthodox' churches that recognise neither the Pope nor the Oecumenical Patriarch. In time these included the Coptic Orthodox Patriarchate of Alexandria, the Church of Armenia (Armenian Apostolic) and churches in Ethiopia, Eritrea and Malankara, India.

The erosion of the broader relationship between Greek and Latin Christianity climaxed in the Great Schism, effected by a flurry of mutual excommunication in 1054, and thereafter the Orthodox tradition developed independently of Rome and its popes. This was especially so because the issue of Rome's authority had been a principal point of difference leading up to the Great Schism. From the Eastern viewpoint after 1054, in which all churches were regarded as autonomous but a symbolic primacy only was given to the Patriarch at Constantinople (the 'New Rome'), Roman Catholicism was a schismatic splintering from the true and universal Church of Christ. Eastern Orthodoxy in its traditions and fidelity to the apostolic faith carried the true seed of Christ's ministry, and to it alone belonged the authority of apostolic succession and the guiding presence of the Holy Spirit.

The Orthodox communion had expanded with missionary activity into the Slavic territories, Kiev and Muscovite Russia in the ninth and tenth centuries so that with the fall of Constantinople to the Ottoman Turks in 1453, Russian Orthodoxy proposed Moscow as its legitimate successor and the centre of Christ's true and universal earthly church. Sequestered within the Ottoman state, meanwhile, were the autocephalous Orthodox churches aligned with Constantinople, Antioch, Alexandria and Jerusalem and most of the so-called 'Separated' churches. The nineteenth-century struggles for Greek independence confirmed the patriotic credentials of the Orthodox clergy; beyond this, however, little was known of them or their liturgical traditions in the west until the collapse of Ottoman authority during World War One.[27]

To Ward's generation in the 1930s, then, Eastern Orthodoxy was a beguiling creature of this expansive, drama-filled history. It consisted of some twenty-two autocephalous churches, which varied in size from the vastness of the Russian Orthodox Church to the single monastery clinging to the slopes of Mount Sinai that proudly retained its ancient status.[28] A robust tradition of local autonomy had proved essential to their survival in the face of persecution. From the Latin Crusaders' sacking of Constantinople in 1204 to Turkish atrocities and the Stalinist executions of Russian clergy, the faithful had remained true to the creed preached by the Church Fathers in the first generations after Christ. By its very nature Orthodoxy was fiercely conservative: traditions of faith and worship were upheld according to the doctrines decided by the seven ecumenical councils between the fourth and eighth centuries. Innovations held to be inconsistent with the statements issued by those earliest councils were anathematised. In its supreme, all-conquering conviction Eastern Orthodoxy simply ignored the tumults of Latin-speaking Catholicism and the revolts of the various Protestant churches, and held firmly to its own, unbroken apostolic heritage of mysticism, faith and worship.

By any measure the Great Schism was a momentous development in the history of the Christian faith. Despite several ecumenical councils and occasional diplomacy, the two halves of Christ's church remained sundered through medieval times and into modernity as their theological and cultural differences grew wider. Perhaps inevitably the idea that the two great traditions of Christianity might be reconciled – even to create, in effect, a new synthesis of Orthodox Catholicism – arose to inspire some western Christians blessed with powerful historical imaginations. High Church Anglicans had commenced tentative efforts at *rapprochement*, founding the Association for the Promotion of the Unity of Christendom (from 1857) and the Anglican and Eastern Churches Association (dating to 1864) to explore the possibility of mutual recognition. Prophetic visionaries like John Ward, however, had no such modest ambitions. A late convert to the effort in the 1930s, he believed a historic reconciliation had in fact been achieved in the Orthodox Catholic Church of Vilatte, Lloyd and Sibley. It had, Ward wrote,

> two distinct lines of Consecration and Ordination; one, from the Western Church, and so back via Rome to St. Peter, and the other, from the Eastern Church, via the Patriarch of Antioch, and also back to St. Peter, who founded the Church at Antioch in the year 38. Thus this Church united in itself the essential elements of both the Eastern and the Western Churches, and to-day, to signify that fact, is known as the ORTHODOX CATHOLIC CHURCH, the former word denoting its Eastern connection and the latter, its Western.[29]

He was certainly not the first to be dazzled by this prospect. Similar grandiose aspirations had inspired a series of like-minded efforts in the so-called 'Western Rite' movement since the 1860s, a reaction within Catholic circles against various authoritarian doctrines such as that of papal infallibility. The rich sacramental tradition and apostolic authority embodied in Eastern Orthodoxy had been just as seductive to the German-born scholar and priest Dr J. J. Overbeck who single-handedly led the Orthodox Catholic movement in Britain through the last decades of the nineteenth century. Although his efforts had come to little by his death in 1905, Overbeck's trenchant views and preoccupations anticipated key elements in Ward's outlook three decades later.

An ordained Catholic priest and pastor in Westphalia, Overbeck studied the early Eastern Church through the Theological Faculty of the University of Bonn in the mid-1850s. His studies drew him away from Roman Catholicism, and he married and practiced as a Lutheran before emigrating to England in the early 1860s where he taught German at the Royal Military Academy, Woolwich. Historical and theological studies, meanwhile, had convinced him of the superior claims of Eastern Orthodoxy to be the true Catholic and Apostolic Church of the Christian creed.[30] His book *Light from the East* examined Roman Catholicism and Protestantism from the Orthodox point of view; quite intemperate in its hostility to both, it proved immensely popular when translated into Russian. Rather than arguing that like-minded Christians should convert to Russian or Greek patterns of

Orthodox observance, however, Overbeck argued for the re-establishment of Western rites and customs within this 'Catholic and Apostolic' tradition. He sought to rescue a lost heritage of western liturgy as practiced by early figures such as Sts. Cyprian, Ambrose, Augustine, Jerome, Leo and Gregory the Great, and rejuvenate that heritage in communion with the one true and continuous Christian inheritance that he now saw in Eastern Orthodoxy. He insisted that Orthodoxy had to be resuscitated in the West, "but it was 'suicidal' to think that the West could be Orientalized, *i.e.*, that Western people could become Eastern in their customs, traditions, and rites, in the process of returning to the ancient Catholic faith and doctrine".[31] Overbeck's proposed 'Western Orthodox Catholic Church' took shape as he re-worked the Latin mass and other rites to conform to Orthodox practices to the satisfaction of both the Holy Synod of Moscow and the Greek Patriarch. Their approval (in 1870 and 1882 respectively) established Overbeck's Western Rite as the basis for an Orthodox community of faith in Western Europe and the United States.

This interest in the Orthodox tradition can also be regarded as a reaction against liberal trends in Christian observance to accommodate an increasingly secular and materialistic age. Anglicanism, with its mild and undemanding theology and Broad Church habits of tolerance and inclusion, seemed a particularly grievous offender. Dr Overbeck rejected such tendencies, and offered instead an unreconstructed 'Primitive' Christianity of apostolic teaching and Orthodox tradition, "though the present age may think it clumsy, uncouth, superstitious and uncharitable". "Let us not have," he continued,

> that highly clarified decoction of 'fashionable nineteenth century Christianity', so refined and tender-hearted, so charitable and comprehensive, that it not only includes all Christian sects, but embraces Reform-Jews, Mohammedans, Parsees, and Brahmos. Anglican Bishops boast of the comprehensiveness of their Church, and ignore the ill-assorted elements in the same, commending religious indifference, and, though unconsciously, colluding with growing infidelity. Truth is essentially exclusive, i.e. intolerant of error. Truth cannot overlook or make light of error for peace's sake.[32]

This 'truth' was guaranteed by the historical continuities of Orthodoxy, and by the authority of the church that remained their faithful guardian. As Overbeck put it, "Christ's Church was not a 'Scripture Club' or 'Theological Debating Society', but an institution vested with *authority*, doctrinal, sacramental, and disciplinary authority. This authority was exercised by the Apostles and their lawful successors, the Bishops. This we learn from the Bible and Tradition."[33]

On these terms, then, the evocative rites and devotions associated with the primitive Church could be powerfully alluring, especially for those blessed with vivid historical imaginations and a love of antiquarian rites and mystical tradition. Perhaps for many the appeal of Orthodox Catholicism was not specious, but lay ultimately in its promise of an ancient, pre-schismatic heritage of church liturgy, preserved for centuries in the Orthodox tradition but now once more available in a re-unified and truly universal Church.

❋   ❋   ❋

Certainly John Ward was enthralled by this tantalising, quixotic idea of Christian unity through Orthodox Catholicism, and embraced it whole-heartedly for the remainder of his life. Foremost among its attractions for him was, firstly, access to a Christianity that was understood as a kind of deep spiritual heritage, that cherished its traditions above all else. This aspect appealed to Ward's historical romanticism and his intense fascination with cultural 'survivals'. Secondly, Orthodox Catholicism gave him a route to the rich traditions of Christian mysticism and eschatology preserved in the practices of Eastern Orthodoxy. Thirdly, participation in a living heritage of liturgy (forms of worship, the sacraments, rituals and procedures) also became possible, that satisfied the practical, daily needs arising in his pentecostal mission in the Abbey of Christ the King. Fourthly, Eastern Orthodoxy favoured a tradition of episcopal autonomy that also answered his needs in New Barnet. We will consider these in turn.

The essential changelessness of Eastern Orthodoxy, its avowed "determination to remain loyal to the past, its sense of *living continuity* with the Church of ancient times",[34] appealed strongly to Ward's taste for historical antiquity. Orthodoxy's historical claim that it alone represented the true heritage of Christian doctrine and practice amid the schisms and dissensions of European history, that it was truly 'the one, holy, Catholic, and Apostolic Church', was deeply attractive. He was not alone in this regard, as virtually every advocate of Orthodox Catholicism was enthralled by the claims of historical and apostolic continuity that were touchstones of Eastern Orthodoxy and its certainty of faith. One 'bishop at large' and Orthodox Catholic primate, Mar Georgius I of the Patriarchate of the West centred at Glastonbury, for instance, carefully explained the implications of their sense of history in his newsletter *Hieratika* in 1949:

We stand for a form of Catholicism unaffected by the political traditions of the Roman or Byzantine Empires, or for those of Tudor England, faith-fully handed down to us from the Syrian homeland of the Church of the Apostolic Age. This we call ORTHODOX APOSTOLIC CATHOLI-

CISM, for it is Orthodox, and it is Catholicism of the Holy Apostles and Fathers, which was found both in the East and in the West in the days of the Undivided Church, before either Rome or Byzantium exercised any influence upon the Church of Christ, and before Protestantism or Anglicanism were even dreamed of.[35]

Apostolic tradition, in this view, was vested in the early church as it deliberated issues of theology and scriptural interpretation at the first Church Councils. It remained with the Eastern half of Christianity (including Separated churches such as the Syrian Orthodox) as a result of the Great Schism; a seismic event, the Orthodox Catholics insisted, resulting from Rome's heretical deviations from an apostolic purity of faith that was thereby preserved only in Eastern Orthodoxy. The consequences of both the sin of schism and the fidelity of the Eastern tradition to the truth of Christ's ministry, they argued, were clearly in evidence in the patterns of Christian history ever since. Overbeck, again, warmed to this theme:

The East exercised always a wholesome check on Western arbitrariness and greed of power. Now, since the bond in 1054 was severed, the Western passions went rapidly down-hill. The bitter fruits of Schism soon showed themselves. And the finger of God is not less visible in preserving the Eastern Church in its pure ancient Orthodoxy than it is in allowing the West to follow its own vain conceits.[36]

Thus Orthodox Catholics hotly proclaimed that a basic historical continuity was intrinsic to the Christian truth practised in Eastern Orthodoxy. Orthodoxy's witness to Christ's message was guaranteed not by scripture alone, but also by the unshakeable apostolic succession that ensured its correct interpretation, and the continuous celebration of those teachings in a community of the faithful (*i.e.* one of the Orthodox Churches) guided by the Holy Spirit. Christian truth, for the Orthodox, thus rested on *both* scriptural authority and the interpretive authority of the apostolic Church exercised through time. An individualized faith was not possible; given that "only ignorance or self-conceit" could assert that a full comprehension of Christian doctrine was possible.[37] Not surprisingly Overbeck and others among the Orthodox Catholics argued that such a conceit lay at the heart of Protestantism: "if the Bible is man's sole authority, man – who is the sole interpreter of the Bible – is *his own authority*. Certainly nothing is more pleasing and acceptable to fallen mankind. Hence the enormous success of Protestantism."[38] Hence the idea of *sole fide* ("by faith alone") that had helped inspire the Protestant revolt was simply contemptible vanity. "Thus the Bible in possession of the Church", explained Overbeck, is the fountain of life, and does not give currency to doctrinal errors or adulterate the meaning of the words of the Apostles, because it was just the oral teaching of the Apostles which constitutes the doctrine of the Church, and has constituted it before a single word of the New Testament was written down. Whatever improvements critical scholars will introduce into the text of the Bible, we thankfully accept them, since we know that any sound critical improvement can only be in accordance with the Church's doctrine; for the Holy Ghost, both guiding the Church and inspiring the authors of the Holy Scriptures, cannot contradict Himself.[39]

In Overbeck's words, where the "Bible-Christian is startled and despondently shakes his head when he sees the pruning-knife of sound criticism cutting away favourite props and evidences of his belief . . . , the Orthodox is perfectly quiet and unshaken, for his belief does not depend on a passage of the Bible, but on the teachings of the Church".[40]

As we would expect, Ward responded avidly to this notion that a continuous ecclesiastical heritage served as a vehicle for the pure and undiluted doctrine of the early Church. He was certain his Orthodox Catholic Church in England, for all its meagre resources and latter-day character, followed in the line of the Church Fathers and the grand edifice of Eastern Orthodoxy by its fidelity to apostolic truth. After all, it too possessed by necessity a purity of doctrine as it, too, was divinely guided by the Holy Spirit working through the angelic 'Guardian of the Work'.

Orthodox Catholicism gave him, moreover, a vantage point to attack his adversaries in the Church of England. He was sure that Anglican antagonism to the claims of the Orthodox Catholics was deeply rooted in fear and jealousy. He detected, in the words of Mar Georgius, "a concerted plot in certain quarters of Anglican officialdom to persecute and harry out of existence the Bishops of all Orthodox Catholic and Old Catholic bodies, and organizations of a kindred type, who are not in communion with the Parliamentary Church". A basic motive was suggested for their hostility:

Such movements from the official Anglican standpoint are a menace, for possessing indisputably valid orders and sacraments, even in the eyes of Rome, there is always the possibility that at some time or another one of such bodies may secure the interest of a wealthy supporter, garner in a large membership from among the churchless millions, become possessed of many beautiful cathedrals and church edifices, and become a serious rival to the Anglo-Catholic section of the Establishment, which at the moment fancies itself as the centre of non-Papal Catholicism. Indeed one might well prophesy that this is bound to happen eventually.[41]

Ward entirely agreed with these sentiments, suggesting that "the history of the Orthodox Catholic Church in the West is marred and disfigured by the way in which its leaders and Bishops have been subjected to systematic persecution and vilification by the Anglican clergy, and it is quite time that someone sets forth the facts so that the average Englishman who does honestly dislike religious bigotry in any form should know the treatment meted out to this deserving body of Christians".[42] Ward had clearly taken the rebuff by St Albans to heart, and now regarded it as a *leit-motif* of Orthodox Catholic history considered broadly.

✳ ✳ ✳

A second attractive feature of Orthodox Catholicism for Ward was the access it provided to a rich tradition of Christian mysticism and eschatology embodied in the Primitive Christianity of Eastern Orthodoxy. While it is not possible to consider Orthodoxy's broad range of mystical doctrines here, a brief survey of some of their primary elements will demonstrate their close sympathy with Ward's spiritual and cosmic outlook. We can usefully concentrate on the Incarnation of God, episodes in Christ's earthly life such as the Transfiguration and Ascension, the central unifying revelation of the Resurrection itself, the continued agency of the Holy Spirit, ideas such as the Communion of Saints and the notion of Deification or *theosis*. Orthodox Christianity also taught a profound and literal belief in Christ's ultimate return, the General Resurrection and the transfiguration of all creation in the Kingdom of God. In each of these aspects John Ward found powerful echoes of the occult cosmology he had first discovered as a spirit medium and the religious instructions he believed he had personally received from the angelic 'Guardian of the Work'.

Canon W. A. Wigram, a close friend of Ward's and an expert on the Syrian churches, elaborated on the appeal of Orthodoxy in the Nikaean Lecture delivered to King's College in 1930. Emphasizing that the "general heritage of Christianity" was emphasized in Orthodoxy in a way that differed to practices in Western Europe, Wigram highlighted a basic distinction: the Eastern Church had an "oriental outlook on all problems 'mystic', that is, that the visible was only a veil of spiritual reality".[43] At the risk of over-simplification, we might say that Orthodox theology distinguishes between the 'essence' of God, which is absolutely transcendent and unknowable, and the 'energies' of God that are immanent in all creation. Humanity experiences the latter as deifying grace and divine light, thus resolving the paradox that "God is a God who hides Himself, yet He is also a God who acts – the God of history, intervening directly in concrete situations".[44] This was a cosmic mystery, in other words, that might be known in certain moments of mystical insight (like those Ward was convinced he had experienced) and that could be traced in the visible patterns of human history (in the way he so delighted to do).

He found further corroboration of his spiritual outlook in other more abstruse elements of Eastern theology. Orthodoxy's insistence that God the Father was the unique source of Godhead, "born from none and proceeding from none", for instance, meant that He was also the ultimate and only source of the Holy Spirit (unlike Roman Catholicism that holds that the Holy Spirit proceeds from *both* the Father and the Son – this difference being the primary theological rift underpinning the Great Schism). This view, again, was warmly endorsed by Ward because of its close fit with the religious metaphysics he presented in the Lindora lectures and *Life's Problems*. When it came to his religious vocation, likewise, Ward found that that the Orthodox communion was intrinsically pentecostal: like the creed he presented in the work of his Confraternity, Orthodoxy taught that God's love and the Holy Spirit was freely endowed on all the faithful, and that it was specially embodied in the 'Body of Christ', that is, the Church of Christ considered in its mystical state. Wigram explained this in the Nikean lecture:

> The Church [to the Orthodox] . . . is 'the Body of Christ' knit together by Love . . . the embodiment of the life of God in the Mind of man. All spirits, whether those once on earth, those now on earth, or those never on earth belong to it and work with it. This is expressed by the 'Communion of Saints' with us, but whereas that idea sinks to back of the western mind, it colours all oriental thought.[45]

The mystical presence of departed spirits, saints and angelic beings in the one true Church was thus a centrepiece of Orthodox mysticism. Wigram's observations are echoed by Orthodox theologians such as A. S. Khomiakov, who felt the unity of the Church was "in reality, true and absolute", and encompassed the spiritual, material, divine and human: "Those who are alive on earth, those who have finished their earthly course, those who, like the angels, were not created for a life on earth, those in future generations who have not yet begun their earthly course, are all united together in one Church, in one and the same grace of God."[46]

As the 'Body of Christ', the Orthodox Church was thus an extension of the miracle of the Incarnation itself, projected into human history by the actions of the faithful.[47] United in love and fidelity through the Church and its sacraments to Christ's true message, the faithful might, through the agency of the Holy Spirit acting through the Church, rise to knowledge and love of Christ and God. In Orthodox theology this principle is known as 'Deification' (*theosis*), as each human individual acquired the Holy Spirit and thus became (as St Peter put it in his second epistle, i, 4) "partakers of the divine nature". Deification was essentially a process of sanctification "whereby the human person responds to the divine initiative and moves ever closer to the living God, through a life that reflects and imitates the divine love . . . Through this relationship, the human person not only grows closer to God, the source of life and holiness, but also becomes more fully human."[48] Ward shared this conviction whole-heartedly; as we have seen, his cosmology echoed the Christian observation that 'the Kingdom of God is within you", as Luke taught (Luke xvii, 21). Orthodoxy had taken this theme literally: St Isaac the Syrian, an Orthodox theologian of the late seventh century, wrote: "If you are pure, heaven is within you; within yourself you will see the angels and the Lord of the angels."[49] As a cosmic principle, this conception corresponded precisely to the conception of God Ward had outlined in his first lecture at the Lindora restaurant in January 1929: "God is One and all things that exist are part of Him, being created by His will, out of His own substance, and what we call spirit and matter are both alike emanations from Him . . . He is the life force of the universe and from Him descends a Spark, the Divine Spark within us."[50]

Orthodoxy taught, moreover, that the physical as well as the spiritual is redeemed by God's love and the action of the Holy Spirit, what scholars of Orthodoxy call 'cosmic redemption'.[51] Deification of the human soul was paralleled by a similar transfiguration of all creation that would be manifest on the Last Day, the General Resurrection. This theme was explored by Nicholas Arseniev, a Russian scholar of Orthodoxy lodged in Germany after the Bolshevik revolution, whose essay on mysticism in the Eastern Church was welcomed by English scholars such as Evelyn Underhill when translated in 1926. The primitive Christian consciousness, Arseniev argued, "believed in the ultimate complete victory of life and the abolition of death, release from the dominion of sin and corruption, the glorification of all existing things, of the whole cosmos, of all creation in the kingdom of eternal life". From this sprang an all-encompassing conviction. "The resurrection is thus [to Orthodox] an event of cosmic significance, and the world, equally with man, is thereby already permeated by the radiance of the celestial glory, although as yet in hidden form, and has attained to a new and high worth; for it has already taken into itself the germ of immortality."[52] As we have seen, Ward had already encountered a material universe "permeated by the radiance of celestial glory"; the Orthodox conviction that physical matter – the human body, the physical world, all creation – would be (and in a sense already is) resurrected and transfigured by Divine Grace corroborated precisely to the sense of the psychic landscape of the Afterlife Ward had developed as a spirit medium.

Ward thus discovered in Orthodoxy a Christian faith, deeply rooted in the primitive jubilation of the apostles, martyrs and other early 'Church Fathers', which carried a keynote of joy at the victory over earthly death secured by Christ's Resurrection. This mystical theme (rather than the emphasis on Christ's suffering for humankind's sins dominant in Latin theology) is deeply embedded in the liturgy and practice of Eastern Orthodoxy. For Arseniev, the historical reality of Apostolic Succession, as Christ's apostles preserved the mystic revelation of His miracles and resurrection, infused the early Church with these supernatural themes. After all, the Apostles were witness to Christ's bodily survival of the grave and devoutly made this revelation the essence of their entire message and ministry. The result was that a "religious realism" became "thoroughly characteristic already of the earliest Christianity: the Incarnation, the Passion, and the Resurrection of the Son of God are not illusion, not deception, as the Docetists and other Gnostics taught, but reality".[53] This realism anchored the belief and teaching of early bishops and Eastern Church Fathers and provided the persistent and essential refrain in the basic tradition of the Eastern Church:

> This rejoicing of the Fathers of the Church over the resurrection of Christ and over His, and consequently also our, victory over death, finds perhaps its noblest expression in that wonderful sermon of Chrysostom which is up to the present day solemnly read on Easter night in the Eastern Church: ' . . . Enter ye all into the joy of your Lord . . . Let none fear death, for the death of the Saviour hath redeemed us. He hath stamped out death who was embraced by death, He hath made hell captive who went down into hell. He hath troubled it after it had tasted His body . . . O death, where is thy sting? O grave, where is thy victory? Christ is risen and the demons are fallen. Christ is risen and the angels rejoice. Christ is risen and life liveth. Christ is risen and of the dead there is none left in the grave: for Christ, risen from the dead, is become the first-fruit among them that sleep there! To Him be honour and dominion for ever and ever!'[54]

The mysticism preserved in Eastern Orthodoxy also contained a powerful eschatological principle. The Eastern Churches, that is to say, stridently taught that the consummation of history would occur in the Divine Advent, the return of Christ. Adherence to the doctrine of the second coming was a formulaic stance among the Orthodox Catholics of Ward's day. The *Orthodox Catholic Review* (another periodical emanating from Mar Georgius' see at Glastonbury), for instance, put it as follows: "The doctrine of the Second Advent of Christ is as much an article of the Catholic [i.e "universal"] Faith as that of the Incarnation or the Resurrection; and in Eastern Christendom due emphasis is still given to it. Let us, therefore, hold fast to it, and as so frequently admonished in Holy Scripture, let us pray earnestly for the hastening of that day, and prepare ourselves to meet the Lord should He be pleased to come in our day."[55] As we might expect, given his visionary

ANGLICAN OUTCASTS AND ORTHODOX CATHOLICISM

conviction that the return of Christ the King was imminent, Ward embraced the Orthodox conception of the Divine Advent with a fervour that surpassed even his colleagues in Orthodox Catholicism.

✵   ✵   ✵

Archbishop Sibley's church also offered Ward access to a living heritage of liturgy (the rites, sacraments and other forms of worship practiced in Orthodoxy) that was essential to the daily life of the Abbey of Christ the King. Ward's need to administer liturgical rites – ordaining his priests, conducting daily offices, celebrating the sacraments and so on – had prompted his suggestion about ordination in the Church of England to Bishop Furse in the first place. The richness of liturgical tradition he found in Orthodoxy after 1935 far outshone anything practised by the Anglicans.

In the Eastern liturgical tradition, words alone cannot sustain the full range of Christian communion in the 'Body of Christ'. Ceremonies, rituals and processions are as important to each gathering of the faithful as are prayers, hymns and passages from scripture. Orthodox services make use of symbols, icons, incense and ornaments, all of them in one way or another elements of the physical world: "Bread and wine, water and oil, fruits and flowers are but a few of the many elements taken up by the [Eastern] church in its worship. In blessing these things of the earth, the church affirms that the physical world has its origins with God, that it possesses intrinsic value, and that it can be a vehicle of divine presence."[56] The painted icon, in partic- ular, was inherent to Orthodox worship because the Incarnation was itself understood as essentially a process of 'image-making': "Through His Incarnation, God the Word 'being the brightness of his glory, and the express image of his (the Father's) person' (Heb. i, 3) reveals to the world, in His Divinity, the image of the Father", as Leonid Ouspensky put it.[57] Orthodox Catholics like Dr Overbeck understood that the excessive veneration of icons and relics was distasteful to many westerners unschooled in the Greek and Russian liturgy, and thus sought to explain them in detail.[58] He concluded:

> God endowed man with imagination, and as this faculty is His gift, He wished it to be appreciated and employed in the right way. Images are the instruments our imagination works with. Therefore they cannot be bad if employed in the right way. In fact, the corporeo-spiritual constitution of man cannot do without them. If we were angels we might dispense with them. The Puritan hatred of images was unreasonable barbarity . . . And as to the use of burning lamps before the icons and offering incense to them, every liturgical scholar knows that these are symbolic actions, denoting that the saints wish us to let our light shine before the whole

215

world in faith and good works, and that our prayer to them and their prayer for us may ascend like sweet-smelling incense to the throne of God.[59]

Ward's Confraternity adopted the spirit of such traditions enthusiastically. The traditional Anglican calendar of saints days and festivals that had previously dictated the rhythm of life in the Abbey at New Barnet was now modified to follow Orthodox practice. The place of icons and the aesthetic principle generally in Christian worship was already attractive to him, and as we have seen both the Abbey Church and the Abbey Folk Park were receptacles of religious art and ecclesiastical antiquities dedicated to the glorification of God, Christ and the Holy Spirit and their transfiguring power in the human condition. In his shift to Orthodoxy Ward was drawn by the most powerful rationale found in any Christian tradition for worship and spiritual education through visual art. As Ware explains, an icon "is not simply a religious picture designed to arouse appropriate emotions in the beholder; [for the Orthodox] it is one of the ways whereby God is revealed to man. Through icons the Orthodox Christian receives a vision of the spiritual world."[60] Such views – that the veneration of icons permitted worship with one's senses and emotions as well as the conscious mind – accorded precisely with the centrality of religious art to the work of Ward's Confraternity.

Finally, Orthodox Catholicism offered Ward a tradition of episcopal autonomy that matched precisely his organisational needs in New Barnet. Autonomous bishops had been intrinsic to the life of the Orthodox Church at least since the authoritative statements on the subject written in 107 AD by St Ignatius, Bishop of Antioch. Given the early Christian sense of the church as a localised fellowship of believers to celebrate the sacraments and in particular the Holy Eucharist, Ignatius conceived each rightful bishop as all-powerful and autonomous in his diocese: "The bishop in each Church presides in place of God." By his rightful ordination and consecration, a bishop in the Orthodox tradition was endowed with a "threefold power": the authority to guide and rule the flock committed to his charge, the gift of the Holy Spirit "in virtue of which he acts as a teacher of the faith", and the rightful power to celebrate the sacraments.[61] As we might expect, the modern prelates that embraced the promise of Orthodox Catholicism were specially enamoured of this notion. In Mar Georgius' description, for example, the bishopric was the "High Priestly Office of our Lord Jesus Christ". He elaborated on this theme in a homily after celebrating mass at Ward's Abbey Church in April 1948 on the tenth anniversary of his own consecration. "He pointed out that the Bishops of the Church on earth in exercising these offices", it was reported, "were in reality mirroring here on earth what our Lord Himself was doing in heaven, and that in the earthly

Bishop people should not see the man who held the office, but rather our Lord Himself acting through His chosen representative".[62]

* * *

In these ways Orthodoxy as a general tradition within Christianity had a whole complex of qualities that mirrored Ward's core convictions. Foremost was the strength of its mystical tradition, centred on the joyous message of victory over death that Ward found utterly seductive. Another was the fascinating depths of its liturgy – its rituals, ceremonies, iconography – that abounded with the kind of enduring esoteric symbolism that had so fascinated Ward in Freemasonry. A third was its fealty to a body of doctrine and observance based on a living heritage of faith rather than the interpreted evidence of scripture alone. Thus the basic stuff of Ward's personality – his mysticism, ritualism and antiquarianism – found direct correspondences in Eastern Orthodoxy, and we can see clearly the reasons for his eager embrace of Archbishop Sibley's offer of immediate consecration. It was a commitment from which he never resiled, and became the rock on which Ward erected his own version of Christ's earthly and transcendent church. In idealistic mood he could even imagine that Orthodox Catholicism might supply the universal framework for a revitalised Christian worship, bound by sacramental tradition but infused with an essential mysticism and spiritual creativity. He suggested that his re-unified Orthodox Catholic Church might inspire a new ecumenism as "a Centre Party in spiritual matters, wherein could be gathered all who adhere to the faith once delivered to the Saints, and yet this great Federation would recognise that men are free souls, and should use the intelligence God has given them, within broad but nevertheless definite limits, to comprehend the mysteries of life and all for which religion truly stands".[63]

These were high-flying ambitions, and in pursuit of them Ward seems to have been prepared to overlook smaller predicaments. He must have been aware, for example, that the Syrian Orthodox Patriarch (then in exile at Homs after fleeing Antioch and the Turks in 1920) had specifically disavowed the Vilatte line of succession in a series of statements. Perhaps the most explicit was contained in a letter the Patriarch's emissary in England, the Rev. Dr S. D. Bhabba, had written to the editor of the *Church Times* in November 1930. "I have been asked repeatedly of late", he wrote, "as to whether the orders of the American 'Archbishop' Lloyd and of his representative in England 'Archbishop' Sibley, are derived from the Jacobite or Syrian-Orthodox Church". Dr Bhabba sought to dispel this conclusion emphatically:

> I enquired of his Beatitude Mar Ignatios last May and was informed by him that our Jacobite or Syrian-Orthodox Church recognizes the Orders

neither of Archbishop Lloyd nor of any of the ministers of the Church which he has founded and altogether repudiates all connection with him and with that Church.

I might add that when in America in 1922, the legate of the Patriarch, Mgr. Severius Barshawm, Archbishop of Homs, told 'Archbishop' Lloyd personally that his claim to be in Jacobite Orders was rejected by all Bishops of the Jacobite or Syrian-Orthodox Church and protested against certain publications in which that surprising claim was set forward.[64]

In December 1938, three years after Ward had taken holy orders and been consecrated a bishop in the very same church founded on this "surprising" claim, another public statement was issued directly by Mar Ignatius Ephrem I himself as Syrian Orthodox Patriarch of Antioch since his election in February 1933. He had earlier recommended to his predecessor as Patriarch "that all connection with 'that Satan Villate' should be publicly denounced", along with the bishops that had been consecrated in his line of succession. He asked simply, "how can they be accepted as Syrians when the[y] openly accept *filioque* and seven councils? Moreover they are men of bad character, with an irregular manner of making bishops, contrary to all Syrian precedent".[65] His December 1938 statement contained an even more explicit denunciation. It warned

> that there are in the United States of America and in some countries of Europe, particularly in England, a number of schismatic bodies which have come into existence after direct expulsion from official Christian communities and have devised for themselves a common creed and system of jurisdiction of their own invention. To deceive Christians of the West being a chief objective of the schismatic bodies they take advantage of their great distance from the East and from time to time make public statements claiming without truth to derive their origin and apostolic succession from some ancient Apostolic Church of the East, the attractive rites and ceremonies of which they adopt and with which they claim to have a relationship.

London groups that claimed lines of succession through René Vilatte were specifically condemned in the statement. The Patriarch concluded: "We find it necessary to announce to all whom it may concern that we deny any and every relation whatsoever with these schismatic bodies and repudiate them and their claims absolutely. Furthermore, our Church forbids any and every relationship and above all intercommunion with all and any of these schismatic sects and warns the public that their statements and pretensions . . . are altogether without truth."[66] Such disavowals, even if received in official church circles or published in the Anglican press, did little to stem the enthusiasm or activities of the English *episcopi vagantes*. Father Ward, it seems, simply ignored them.

His embrace of Orthodoxy was problematic in other ways. If he happily appropriated the aspects of Eastern Orthodoxy that suited the needs of his personal spirituality and pentecostal ministry, he seemed willing to let other elements that were awkward or less useful fall quietly by the wayside. Ward never subscribed to the Orthodox conception of the Trinity, for instance, and continued to teach the feminine element that was distinctive to his Confraternity (with their conception of God the Mother, God the Father, and God the Son). This position was, frankly, heretical to the Orthodox tradition. Likewise, he blithely disregarded the Orthodox convention that a bishop should be unmarried or a widower, deferring, it seems, to the expectation that an Orthodox priest might be married, but only before his ordination. He also ignored the rule that a bishop must exercise his episcopal office in unity with his colleagues, *i.e.* as a member of an episcopal council (a synod). He also neglected, at least between 1935 and 1945, the canonical requirement that an Orthodox bishop be consecrated in the presence of two or three others. Sibley alone performed the rites of ordination in October 1935, but this requirement was sufficiently well-regarded for it to be followed obsessively by Mar Georgius, Archbishop Ward and the other Orthodox Catholic prelates who aligned with the Catholicate of the West in a series of mutual re-consecrations at Ward's Abbey Church in 1945 to unify their precious lines of succession.

In his own defence, Ward might have insisted that such traditions were unique to 'Patriarchal' Orthodoxy centred on the Oecumenical Patriarch at Constantinople, rather than the Syrian Orthodox Church through which he, Sibley and other bishops of the Vilatte succession claimed their episcopal legitimacy. But that would seem special pleading, particularly given they clearly were not in communion, in any meaningful sense, with the Syrian Orthodox Church. Such an argument only underlines the selectivity with which Ward embraced the traditions and principles of Eastern Orthodoxy. If he was opportunistic in this eastward turn, he was also increasingly hostile to the communion he left behind in Anglicanism. This antipathy focussed not just on figures like Furse but also on the English proponents of reunion such as Canon J. A. Douglas in the Anglican and Eastern Churches Association. To a man this group was dismissive of the claims of the Vilatte bishops whom they dismissed as irregular mischief makers, and in return Ward regarded them as stooges for Anglican xenophobia and intolerance. "The main work of Canon Douglas and his Association", Ward wrote in one of the darkly reflective moods of his last years in Cyprus, "was to try and discredit anyone in the West who claimed to have Priestly or Episcopal Orders derived from any of the Eastern Churches". He was convinced their antipathy was entirely based on ecclesiastical jealousy and Establishment arrogance. "Knowing these men really had valid Orders, which the Anglicans have not", Ward concluded,

> the high officials of the Established Church were always afraid that many 'Anglo-Catholic' or High Church clergy would get valid Orders and even their own Bishops from these 'Episcopi Vagrantes' [*sic*] and build up a ritualist Church within the Anglican Church, which having valid Orders, could come to terms with Rome and that this would disrupt the Established Church and lead to its disestablishment and disendowment. For this reason Canon Douglas and many other high Anglican officials were always trying to attack and discredit men like Archbishop Sibley, Bishop Herford and later, me.[67]

❋ ❋ ❋

We have seen that, most superficially, Orthodox Catholicism provided an institutional connection for the Confraternity. The fact that Ward sought this connection so swiftly after the rift with St Albans indicates the importance of external recognition to him. In a similar vein, when in 1941 the Confraternity was informed by the Ministry of Labour that its members were exempt from national service, Father Ward pounced upon this modicum of official recognition as a hungry man might seize a morsel of food. This, claimed a manuscript outlining the various lines of succession vested in Ward's ministry that later circulated within the Confraternity, was "Britain's Government Recognition". "The Ministry of Labour on July 28 1941", the notes expounded, "decided that the clergy of the Orthodox Catholic Church in Gt. Britain under the jurisdiction of Archbp. J. S. M. Ward every man in Holy Orders may be regarded outside the scope of National Service Acts 1939 1941 etc."[68]

This sort of external recognition enabled Ward to occupy a prominent position in the local community and aspire to a national profile. As head of the Abbey, and Director of its extraordinary Folk Park, Father Ward enjoyed a significant local standing. He delivered sermons to small but evidently loyal local congregations that were reported in the local press. We get a sense of this in a short newspaper report of a 1936 sermon at the Abbey Church, when Barnet was struck by a fierce rainstorm.

> When the service ended, the choir found that they were cut off from the vestry, which is in the house, by a veritable river which was rushing past the west end of the church and piling débris against the gate-house. The congregation also were practically marooned by floods. A few of the more intrepid crossed the flood by walking on fences; others, led by Father Ward, who kilted up his cassock to well above the knees, descended into

the basement of the abbey, which was flooded, and spent an exciting three hours in baling out the water.[69]

The following week special collections were taken among the congregation "on behalf of a near neighbour of the Abbey, who had suffered heavy loss on account of the flood". It was also announced that the collection on the following Sunday would be contributed to a local councillor's fund for local flood relief.[70] Ward evidently relished his stature as a pillar of the local community.

There were, however, as always with John Ward, deeper matters at stake. As a direct result of the Confraternity's embrace of Orthodox Catholicism in 1935, Ward's interpretations of Christian doctrine became more elaborate and pronounced. Liberated from the need for discretion within the Anglican fold and fired by a zeal born of his personal revelations, he was free to express his synthesised theology much more stridently. In writings and sermons at the Abbey Father Ward espoused a Primitive Christianity that upheld the literal truth of scriptural miracles (the Divinity of Christ, the Virgin Birth, the Transfiguration, the Resurrection, the Descent of the Holy Spirit and so on) as his pronouncements became increasingly dogmatic. "Any denomination", he wrote in his *The Psychic Powers of Christ*, "which repudiates the Virgin Birth and the physical Resurrection of Our Lord, and by implication, therefore, denies that He was God Incarnate, will cease to be a living branch either of the Catholic Church in its widest sense or indeed of anything which can be regarded as Christianity at all."[71]

After 1935, once their content was no longer answerable to the Anglican mainstream, Ward's addresses and sermons in services at the Abbey Church dealt explicitly with matters of reincarnation and the afterlife, scriptural miracles explained in the manner of *The Psychic Powers of Christ*, and biblical and personal prophecies of impending cataclysm. The first in a series of Sunday evening sermons delivered in early 1936, for example, was titled "Life After Death" and took the text from Ecclesiastes: "Or ever the silver cord be loosed". The *Barnet Press* reported that Father Ward "proceeded to show that this was not a mere poetic phrase, but referred to a real fact in the process which we call death – the freeing of the soul from the encumbrance of the physical body".[72] During the last sermon in the series, which enlarged on pentecostal themes, Ward gave an "interesting explanation [unfortunately unrecorded] of why ten days elapsed between the Ascension and the descent of the Holy Ghost, and also of the fact that each person in the crowd heard the message given by the Apostles as if it were spoken in his own native tongue".[73] Another evening service in June that year saw Ward take as his text the passage in Revelations ix, 3: "And there came out of the smoke locusts upon the earth." He was particularly drawn to the passage comparing the locusts as "like unto horses prepared unto battle", with tails like scorpions and "breastplates of iron, and the sound of their wings was as the sound of chariots of many horses running to battle".[74] His interpretation of this prophecy, reported in the local newspapers, reflected the apocalyptic trends of international events.

Father Ward suggested that . . . St. John had a vision of an attack by aeroplanes using poison gas and screened by a smoke screen. He pointed out that the locusts were like no locust that ever crawled upon this earth, and that, on the other hand, a man who had seen a vision of an aeroplane 1,900 years before they were invented would have to make use of similes to describe what he had seen.

The text lent itself to a characteristically fervent discussion of the impending apocalypse. "Father Ward", the report continued, "then went on to show the devastating effect of modern air war, its barbarity, and its peculiarly destructive effects upon civilization, such as the great cities, illustrating much of what he said by recent events in Abyssinia. He pointed out that we had reached our present terrible crisis largely because all nations had repudiated the very basis on which our civilization was built, namely, the Christian faith".[75]

Later sermons in this vein that year dwelt on a series of biblical prophecies "which he considered had already been fulfilled, or were in the process of fulfilment, and which indicated the coming of a great war – a war likely to shake civilisation".[76] The return of the Jewish people to Palestine featured prominently, as did reflections on modern parallels with the apocalyptic visions of scripture. In the final sermon in the series, in mid-July, Ward reflected on the likelihood of the British Empire's salvation in the impending catastrophe. Rarely was his mission to England and the West so clearly spelt out as he once again explained the convictions embodied in the work of his Abbey Folk Park. Pointing out that "civilizations rise and fall, that they have their spring, summer, autumn and winter", Ward pointed to history and the collapse of Roman authority to confirm that "there was always some country or area which survived the general collapse and became a sort of haven of refuge from whence the light of civilization was once more diffused among the surrounding nations". Illuminated in the brilliant light of stained glass, standing at his ornate pulpit, the scarlet-robed Reverend Father warmed to his theme, which many of his regular attendees surely found a familiar one:

In the threatened collapse of Western civilization, why should not Great Britain play the same part as Byzantium played when Rome fell? . . . If, however, she was to perform this important function, she must put her own house into order. There were many sides to the problem; there was the problem of defence; the problem of the preservation of examples of the art and literature of the age which was passing, but above all there was the need for a revival of the spiritual life of the country. For years Britain had been turning away from Christ and Christianity. Unless she turned back to the faith of her fathers she would certainly not be deemed worthy by God to serve as the basis of the new civilization which was destined to rise out of the wreckage of this mechanical age.[77]

✳   ✳   ✳

Orthodox Catholicism provided a refuge from where Ward could enlarge the sacramental and prophetic aspects of his pentecostal ministry. Previously, in the Confraternity's alignment with Anglicanism, Ward was not ordained and therefore could not 'minister the Word'. His status as an ordained priest (and better still, as a consecrated bishop) within Orthodox Catholicism provided him with the office to interpret the corpus of Christian belief and ritual as he himself understood it. He creatively interpreted a rich heritage of Orthodox worship with a freedom from doctrinal and canonical oversight that was not possible in mainstream religion. In blunt terms, Orthodox Catholicism legitimised his ministry; but it simplifies matters to suggest that (in a manner alleged by Brandreth and Anson, for instance, to be altogether typical of the modern *episcopi vagantes*) he simply desired ecclesiastical status for its own sake or through crass egotistical delusion. As an Orthodox Catholic bishop, Ward appropriated a tradition of belief and worship in which the relics, icons and artworks of his Abbey and its Folk Park were entirely at home, and that perfectly matched his ministry, which like Eastern Orthodoxy itself was indivisibly mystical, pentecostal and adventist.

As we have seen, Ward's religious outlook was infused with a lively anti-quarianism that saw in the dramas and patterns of human history a single continuous revelation of the cosmic truths of incarnation, reincarnation, spiritual evolution and the return to God, the Source of All. Other 'bishops at large' and Orthodox Catholics may well have shared, in a general way, his sense of historical drama. Many would have endorsed his strident claim that Orthodox Catholicism was truly a historic *rapprochement* between Christianity's two great warring factions, East and West.[78] But Ward took the utility of history in the service of revelation, worship and faith much further than this. He would have agreed utterly, for instance, with Dr Overbeck's shrill insistence upon the inherently historical character of Christian faith and observance. "Christianity is a *historical product*, and not simply a *philosophical system*", Overbeck wrote.

Hence the uppermost importance of Tradition, which, properly under-stood, is only another name for History . . . Thus our Historical or Traditional Christianity sprang from incontestable facts, far beyond the reach and beyond the cavil of our fashionable critics. If we will be Christians, we must take Christianity as a hard and stubborn fact, such as History, uncorrupted History, has handed down to us, and not as a soft, workable, and kneadable dough, from which the skilful hand of the workman or modeler can shape any fancy of his brain.[79]

In truth Ward wanted both these things. In its promise of a primitive Christianity surviving as a "hard and stubborn fact" through human history we find the fundamental reason for his utter surrender to the fantasy of Orthodox Catholicism. It offered him a living heritage of faith, a carriage for mystical revelation that, as it unfolded its treasures of cosmic knowledge and spiritual insight, participated in the essential processes of history itself. But it was also a kneadable dough, a supple mass of themes and principles through which he might shape his ministry as something truly singular.

11

Wartime Trials

Everything changed with the eruption of war in September 1939. As Londoners mobilised for a prolonged war effort, visitor numbers at the Abbey Folk Park dwindled. Soon it was closed to the public and its exhibits mothballed, and to replace the lost income the sisters of Ward's Abbey made clothes and embroidered cushions for sale to local shops. Their religious work of prayer, services and public lectures continued through the war years with renewed urgency. In April 1941 the Abbey was recognised by the Ministry of Labour as a religious institution, and its members as being in a reserved occupation and exempt from national service. But with wartime rationing, blackouts and the occasional appearance of German bombers over Barnet the mood at the Abbey settled into an uneasy rhythm that was rarely tranquil. After a while, Peter Strong remembered, "shrapnel during the long night of watches on the roof, or Nazi bombers hedge-hopping over the property while I was working in the garden, sometimes in broad daylight, ceased to be a worry".[1] Other worries soon arose to take their place.

For a start, ecclesiastical changes were in the air. Father Ward and his Orthodox Catholic Church in England were part of an unprecedented attempt in 1943–6 to unify the major strands of the *episcopi vagantes* in England, an effort that is perhaps unique in the tangled history of the independent sacramental movement. It was driven by the former bicycle salesman Hugh George de Willmott Newman, under the aegis of a new Catholicate of the West centred at Glastonbury.

In response to the disavowal of the Vilatte bishops by the Syrian Orthodox Patriarch at Homs, Newman and other itinerant bishops met in a gathering they called the Council of London in October 1943. Here representatives of the Ancient British Church, the British Orthodox Catholic Church, the Apostolic Episcopal Church, the Old Catholic Orthodox Church, the Order of Holy Wisdom and the Order of Antioch took a dramatic step. They formally declared the Syrian Orthodox (Jacobite) Church to be in schism, and that their own western half was therefore fully autonomous and would be re-constituted as 'The Western Orthodox Catholic Church'. "To the objective observer", Anson comments, "the so-called Council of London and its Acts are of the stuff that dreams are reminiscent of, an Arabian Nights tale. For none of the prelates who took part in its brief sessions could claim jurisdiction over more than perhaps a dozen followers, and some of the Churches had only a paper existence."[2]

In this context, Newman was consecrated a bishop in April 1944 by Dr W. B. Crow, the biologist, occultist and Theosophist who had taken the title Mar Basilius Abdullah III at the head of the new unified Western Orthodox Catholic Church. Newman, "in golden vestments powdered with white flowers", was raised to the episcopate under the title Mar Georgius, Archbishop and Metropolitan of Glastonbury (the 'Occidental Jerusalem'). The Catholicate's journal, the *Orthodox Catholic Review*, reported on the historic event with suitable gusto.

> A notable episode in Church history took place recently, when, as a consequence of reunion effected between The Old Catholic Orthodox Church, The Ancient British Church, The Independent Catholic Church, and the British Orthodox Catholic Church, THE WESTERN ORTHODOX CATHOLIC CHURCH was formally constituted by a Deed of Declaration and erected by His Holiness the Prince-Patriarch Basilius Abdullah III of Antioch into THE CATHOLICATE OF THE WEST, under a Catholicos whose chair was established at Glastonbury in Somerset, thereby elevating that hallowed and historic little town to the rank and dignity of premier Orthodox Catholic See of Western Christendom.[3]

20 John Ward, kneeling at right, is consecrated a bishop by Mar Georgius I in the Abbey Church, New Barnet, August 1945. *AMAA 3 WC 3/37.*

Crow and Newman had been consecrated in the line of succession emanating from Jules Ferrete, but as the new Patriarch of Glastonbury Newman had bigger ideas. "The present Ferrete succession is extremely active", reported Henry Brandreth, the Anglican expert on these matters, to the 1948 Lambeth Conference. "The leader of this activity is H. G. de Willmott Newman (otherwise known as 'Mar Georgius I, Patriarch of Glastonbury'). Newman has conceived the idea of uniting all the various *episcopi vagantes* in England under himself, and for this purpose has received conditional re-consecration from bishops of all other successions, whom, in turn, he re-consecrates. Since his own consecration in 1944 he has consecrated, or re-consecrated, some fifteen men."[4]

One of these fifteen was Father Ward, who was consecrated for a third time by the Patriarch of Glastonbury at the Abbey Church on 25 August 1945. Two weeks earlier, in preparation for the event, a meeting of the Holy Synod of the Orthodox Catholic Church in England (in other words, the members of Ward's Confraternity) had elected him to the "Archiepiscopal See of Olivet, which is hereby constituted as the Primatial See of the Orthodox Catholic Church in England".[5] This was an institutional preparation for Mar Georgius' visit, because Ward's re-consecration was more than simply an attempt to guarantee the lines of succession pertinent to his status as a bishop. It was, in fact, the first major alteration to the constitutional basis of the Confraternity and Ward's Orthodox Catholic Church in England as a whole.

Thus on 25 August, Mar Georgius I, Patriarch of Glastonbury, arrived in state at the Abbey in much the same way that Archbishop Sibley and Mar Kwamin had done ten years before. The *Orthodox Catholic Review* recorded the occasion for posterity under the heading 'RECENT UNIFICATIONS: Two Churches Affiliate to the Catholicate: Consecrations in the Abbey'.

The Orthodox Catholic Church in England and The Evangelical Church of India were solemnly received into union with The Catholicate of the West as autocephalous Rites by His Beatitude the Catholicos Mar Georgius on Saturday, the 25th August, in The Cathedral and Abbey Church of Christ the King, Park Road, New Barnet, Herts.

On the same occasion, His Beatitude assisted by His Grace John, Lord Archbishop of Olivet and Primate of The Orthodox Catholic Church in England, and Mar Johannus, Lord Bishop of S. Marylebone, consecrated sub conditione The Right Rev. James Charles Ryan D.D., Lord Bishop of North Madras, Primate of the Evangelical Church of India, whose previous consecration had been in the Armenian Uniate and Anglican lines. Then, Mar Georgius, assisted by Bishop Ryan and Mar Johannus, consecrated sub conditione the Archbishop of Olivet (The Most Rev. John Sebastian Marlow Ward, M.A., D.D.) whose previous consecration had been in the Syrian-Malabar line derived from the late Archbishop Vilatte. This accomplished, Archbishop Ward, assisted by Bishop Ryan, consecrated sub conditione both Mar Georgius and Mar Johannus.

The object of these conditional consecrations was in all cases to vest further lines of Apostolic Succession in the Consecrands, and not to impute any doubt as to their existing episcopal status.[6]

Dozens of photographs were taken of the elaborate ceremonies to verify that correct form and procedure had been followed. Appropriate office bearers and witnesses were carefully reported in Catholicate's journal. "At the ceremonies", reported the *Orthodox Catholic Review*, "The Rev. Father W. Martin Andrew, Protonotary Apostolic of the Catholicate, acted as Registrar, The Rev. Father C. M. Chamberlain as Master of Ceremonies, and the Rev. Fathers Peter and Ignatius as Deacon and Subdeacon of the Mass. The Rev. Mother Superior and Sisters of the Confraternity of the Kingdom of Christ were present." The certificates recording the various ordinations and consecrations were registered in the archives of the Catholicate at Glastonbury.

The significance of this ceremony to Father Ward and his followers was twofold. In the first place, it vested in him seven other lines of succession to bolster his claims to episcopal legitimacy. It also had the re-assuring effect of welcoming his Confraternity and Church into a broader communion without compromising his independence and autonomy. Thus for Ward this was much more than a naïve attempt to 'guarantee' the lines of succession. The ceremonies of 25 August at the Abbey were considered by the Confraternity as, in effect, an act of union. They meant that his Orthodox Catholic Church in England had been "received into full communion with the Catholicate of the West under Mar Georgius Catholicos", even as the latter reciprocated by recognising Ward's church "as a lawfully constituted autocephalous and autonomous Rite or Branch of the One Holy Catholic and Apostolic Church having valid orders mission and jurisdiction . . . "[7] In other words, Ward sought to bolster his ecclesiastical authority by the only means available to him, by aligning with the emerging centre of Orthodox Catholicism Mar Georgius had established at Glastonbury.

✸   ✸   ✸

Ward's alignment with Glastonbury came in the wake of a catastrophic sequence of events that had broken his health and shattered his reputation. Since mid-1943 he and his wife and their community had been swept up in a family dispute over Dorothy Lough, a local teenager known in the Abbey as Sister Terese. Dorothy, a strong-willed and pious girl, had attended services and classes at the Abbey and was often placed into the Wards' care during holidays and times of family difficulty. But as her relationship with her parents deteriorated and matters escalated into legal action, the Wards were accused of maliciously enticing Dorothy away from home as a recruit into their order. The quarrel climaxed in a sensational case before Justice Cassels in the High Court over two weeks in May 1945. In the common law, 'enticement' generally referred to seduction and the use of the term helped to cast the proceedings as a 'morals' case in the national press. The spectacle of an eccentric, other-worldly Reverend Father and Mother Superior, on trial (it seemed) for irregular behaviour behind the closed doors of a modern abbey admitting disaffected children and married couples alike was arresting. Readers of the daily newspapers were provided with ten days of courtroom drama in the 'Sister Terese Enticement Case': accusations and denials, claim and counter-claim. "Even in the meagre four-page newspapers of that year", wrote Cassels' biographer, "it commanded attention. There were photographs of Sister Terese in her robes . . . Other pictures showed the father and mother superior of her order smiling as they made their way into court."[8]

When called to give their testimony, the Wards could not help but appear deluded and self-important. They seemed to have little grip on reality. In the harsh light of courtroom scrutiny the Reverend Father and Mother were suddenly notorious: mocked and subjected to gossip, their community painted in a lurid light and their personal morality – and even their sanity – questioned. The press headlines followed one after another: "DAUGHTER 'ENTICED INTO RELIGIOUS SECT'" (*Evening News*, 30 April); "SISTER TERESE SEES HER FATHER – High Court Drama" (*The Star*, 1 May); "YOU LIAR, MOTHER CRIES TO SISTER TERESE IN COURT" (*Daily Mirror*, 3 May); "FATHER WARD CHANTS IN EVIDENCE" (*Daily Herald*, 5 May). The tabloid sensationalism that enveloped the court proceedings savaged Father Ward's reputation beyond repair.

In Justice Cassels' words, this unusual case began with "a crisis in a working-man's family, and . . . a determined, self-willed but undoubtedly religious girl".[9] The girl in question was the attractive Dorothy Lough, who listened intently to the judge's comments as a young woman aged eighteen. Under English law she was still a minor, albeit one that had reached an age of 'discretion', and so remained legally a child. Even in the thick of this bitter family dispute, Dorothy's mother did not doubt that her daughter "was a very religious person, honest in what she professed, and truthful", agreeing "that Dorothy had no wish for any worldly gain, and that she was wholly unselfish".[10]

Dorothy had first attended the Sunday School at the Confraternity when she was eight or nine in the mid-1930s. Her father, Stanley Lough, was a gasworks electrician and lived at nearby Bulwer Road.[11] He and his wife had first attended lectures at the Abbey in 1934 or 1935; Dorothy remembered going at a very young age, and having a haircut especially for the occasion. She had been baptised there in November 1936 in the presence of both her parents. The Loughs later claimed to be unaware that the Confraternity was by that time no longer affiliated with the Church of England. Dorothy, on the other hand, recalled that when she joined as a junior oblate in 1937 at the age of ten, with her mother's full consent and in her presence, "she had seen the notice outside the church on which the words 'Orthodox Catholic Church' appeared. Those words had been there as long as she had known the church."[12]

In the years that followed Dorothy became a fixture at the Abbey. When her mother was ill and hospitalised in 1937, Dorothy "was temporarily left at the abbey as she had no relative with whom she could stay".[13] She appears in photographs taken in July 1937 depicting mock-historical scenes in the Abbey Folk Park's quadrangle with Lorna and Maurice Cuffe, two other children living with their family at the Abbey.[14] She was again left with the Wards on the outbreak of war, as her father considered their home to be in a dangerous location – the Abbey, by contrast, had a good air raid shelter. Meanwhile, her mother had volunteered for service as a nurse, and consequently Dorothy remained with the Wards for some three months. After finishing at school for good in December 1940 she spent most of her time helping her mother with housework, continuing to visit the Abbey two or three times each week and living there for up to a fortnight over the Easter and Christmas periods.

She formally joined the Abbey of Christ the King early in the August of 1943 aged 16 ½, under circumstances later hotly disputed in court. It was a happy day, she told her mother as they left home on 4 August to visit the Abbey, because she had wanted to join the Wards in their religious work since she was twelve.[15] Mrs Lough, on the other hand, was certain they were only visiting the Wards to discuss Dorothy's desire to enter the Abbey in general terms. But when they arrived at Park Road, Mrs Lough later stated, "when the door of the Abbey was opened [Dorothy] dashed in and disappeared". In an interview with the Wards in Hadley Hall's common room, Mrs Lough agreed that her daughter was "in so distracted a condition" that she could remain there until the Loughs could discuss Dorothy's situation with the Wards that evening.[16]

These discussions were unproductive. With Dorothy refusing to visit her parents or leave the sanctuary of the Abbey – her new home, she was convinced, where she would follow her calling from God – matters were at an impasse. A resolution seemed to appear on 6 August, when Mrs Lough sent a letter stating: "you have made life very bitter for me, but as you have chosen the Abbey in preference to your home, I hope you will be happy. I will not bother you anymore. Goodbye."[17] On 19 August she and Mr Lough

21 Dorothy Lough, 1946. The photograph taken for her passport, issued under the name 'Lillian Knight' to enable her to leave England undetected when the Confraternity departed for Cyprus. *AMAA 4 WA 5/1.*

were informed that Dorothy had assumed the name 'in religion' of Sister Terese, and was now a nun of the Confraternity of the Kingdom of Christ. She had not, however, taken her final vows and was free to leave at any time.

In the months that followed, Sister Terese's parents made a number of attempts to convince their daughter, through letters and visits to the Abbey, to return to the family home. In the first instance, just a month after Dorothy had entered the Confraternity, a policewoman with a female probation officer interviewed Sister Terese together with the Wards "to try to persuade her to return to her parents".[18] This and other attempts were in vain. Sister Terese refused to visit her father when he fell sick with influenza; her brother Harold, on leave from the RAF in December 1944, visited Dorothy to invite her to his wedding but she declined without giving a reason. As these family overtures proved ineffective, the Loughs consulted with the Bishop of St Albans and the Barnet police. With the Wards refusing to eject Dorothy from the Abbey against her will, legal proceedings commenced to force her to return to her family.

Their first legal manoeuvre was to obtain a summons under s.64 of the *Children and Young Persons Act* of 1933 on the grounds that Dorothy was "out of control", and compel her to appear in the local juvenile court.[19] This was granted, and a policewoman knocked on the Abbey's door in early October to place Dorothy under arrest and escort her to the Hitchin Girls Remand Home. She went meekly enough, although distressed at the serious turn that events had taken and the prospect of a lonely and enforced detention. She spent a miserable week in the Remand Home waiting for the matter to be heard.

When Mrs Lough's application for an order compelling Dorothy to return home was considered in the Barnet Juvenile Court in October, proceedings were short and unexpected. The Loughs' solicitor presented their case in brief. Dorothy had joined the abbey, he stated, because she believed "that, as an inmate of the Abbey, she would not be called upon to work in a factory, and on August 3rd [1943] told her mother that she wanted to live there. In spite of her mother's protests the girl insisted upon going to the Abbey the next morning, and she had stayed there ever since". Despite the many letters her parents had written begging her to return, the solicitor continued, Dorothy had refused to leave the Abbey and they had not seen her in the intervening months.

The Wards, meanwhile, had engaged a barrister on Dorothy's behalf to oppose the application who tabled compelling evidence refuting the Loughs' case. He pointed out that Mrs Lough had allowed her daughter to spend much of her time at the Abbey, especially during the early months of the war. He was also able to produce letters to Dorothy from her mother: "You have chosen the Abbey instead of me. I would love to have you, but it is for you to decide." In light of this evidence, the chairman of the court refused the Loughs' application and ruled that no order should be granted.[20]

It was a significant victory for the determined Dorothy Lough, and had the effect of further estranging her from her family and drawing the Wards into her corner as the dispute spiralled out of control. Previously John and Jessie had attempted to act as brokers in this family squabble, but by engaging legal representation they demonstrated a willingness to argue Dorothy's case in a much more partisan manner. Father Ward wrote a letter to the Loughs some time later, reflecting on the proceedings in the juvenile court in a tone that he would later come to regret. Recalling how distressed Dorothy had been, he told the Loughs with an air of melodramatic finality: "Dorothy Lough perished for evermore in the courthouse at New Barnet. Her name forever now is Sister Terese. If you had suffered as she has suffered I think you would understand."[21] He later explained these words:

> in the ten days of agony of being arrested, taken to a remand home, charged, and acquitted, everything which bound Dorothy to the old life was destroyed. Every link that brought back memories of her past life was cut for ever, and the life of Sister Terese was dedicated to God in the Abbey.[22]

But the New Barnet juvenile hearing was not the end of the matter. The Loughs brought their case before the High Court in a civil trial, charging that they had been deprived of the services of their daughter – under law Dorothy was still a minor – following her 'enticement' into the Wards'

Abbey. When the case was heard in April and early May 1945, it made headlines all around the country and catapulted the Wards to national notoriety.

The Loughs' basic accusation was that John and Jessie Ward had used their influence to actively entice Dorothy into the Confraternity. They had played on her fears she was about to be recruited for war service, they suggested, and had induced in her "a kind of religious exaltation".[23] No evidence was tendered to substantiate these claims. The Wards' alleged motives also proved difficult to establish with any clarity. Their barrister, Ryder Richardson, pointed out that Dorothy "was not an heiress. She was not particularly well educated. She had no attainments such as that of being a fine singer. She was not allured by the promise of high reward."[24] The clear insinuation, however, that underlay the charges was that Ward was "eager to enrol young people into his confraternity"[25] to boost the numbers of his little group of followers. When the suggestion was put to Ward directly in the witness box, he dismissed it impatiently:

> It suited you for this girl to enter your abbey at 16 ½? – No, it did not, most certainly.
> You got her free services? – I got a lot of trouble.[26]

Relations between the Wards and Dorothy's parents deteriorated rapidly as the matter worked its way through the courts. The Loughs came to condemn the Abbey – where they had previously entrusted their daughter without hesitation – and the Wards as improper guardians as they sought to bolster their case. A Freemason himself, Stanley Lough was aware of Ward's Masonic background. Accordingly, he wrote to ask the support of the Grand Secretary in the dispute, using bilious language to describe "the ruthless & filthy work of this fiend & his wife". His letter made serious accusations:

> This man has been doing some filthy work under the cloak of religion, & has already broken up the homes of six families by enticing some of their members to join his religious sect, of which he & his wife are the heads: they eventually persuade these victims to go & live with them . . . One woman aged 53 years is a victim & has taken her two children (a boy, now a priest, aged 21 years & a girl 18 ½ years) to live in this place. Her husband has now obtained a divorce from her on grounds of desertion. A Brother Hopping (lodge not known) has also lost his daughter in similar circumstances, but is unable to take action as she is over 21 years. They next make and use every effort to poison the minds of these inmates against their families.[27]

Consequently he requested the Grand Secretary "to use your influence in the right quarters to get them to expel this man from the Brotherhood &

make him pay the penalty for breaking the vows taken at his initiation". Given that Ward was no longer a subscribing member of any Masonic lodge, the Grand Secretary was unable to assist.[28]

✳   ✳   ✳

On 30 April 1945, as Adolf Hitler ended his life in his Berlin bunker and celebrations marking the end of the war broke out across Europe, the dispute that threatened to tear Ward's Abbey apart commenced in the High Court of Justice, King's Bench Division. Sister Mary, Sister Bertha, Sister Gabrielle and of course Sister Terese accompanied the Reverend Father and Revered Mother into London that morning, along with Father Filius Domini, Father Ignatius and two other male members of the Confraternity. Press photographers snapped away as the eye-catching group chatted and smiled outside the High Court, their robes and habits attracting attention amid the busy traffic and pedestrians of the Strand. Few of the newsmen present could resist their outlandish appearance or the allure of the story about to unfold in court. The *News Chronicle* splashed pictures of the Wards and Sister Terese across page three the next day, and set the courtroom scene:

> Something of the mystic atmosphere of the Abbey of Christ the King, the abode of the Confraternity, entered the court when Father Ward, in clerical habit, the Mother Superior and four brown-robed sisters, followed by four young Canons Regular in their clerical collars and badges with celestial crowns, took their seats. The strange story of the founding of the Confraternity was outlined by Mr N. L. Macaskie, K. C., in his opening speech for Mr and Mrs Stanley Lough, the parents of Sister Terese.[29]

The unorthodox character of Ward's Abbey was clearly going to be central to the courtroom strategy pursued by the Loughs' counsel, just as it was irresistible to the news reporters with the scent of a good story.

In formal terms, Stanley Lough alleged that the Wards had deprived him "of the services of his daughter, Dorothy Bartola, an infant, by enticing her into and harbouring her in premises occupied by the defendants, styled 'The Abbey of Christ the King, Park Road, New Barnet, Hertford'". Macaskie described the Loughs' charge in his opening address to the court:

> Mr Lough's general allegation was that the defendants, in their respective capacities as Father Superior of the fraternity, and his wife as its Mother Superior, induced in the plaintiff's daughter a condition of religious exaltation. The kind of religion was not clear, but, at a time when most young people in England were looking forward to the prospect of being called

22 An example of the sensational press coverage of the 'Sister Terese Enticement Case': *Daily Mirror*, 1 May 1945.

up to work in factories or in the services, the defendants played on the girl's fears that she might have to mix with drunken women and girls in factories, and that the only escape for her was to enter the order of which the defendants were the superiors.[30]

"If this is true", Macaskie continued, "I ask your lordship to say that there could be no more subtle and wicked influence than the combination of playing on the fears of a young girl, coupled with a sort of mixture of religion apparently derived from the Buddhist, Christian and Confucian beliefs."[31] On this basis Stanley Lough claimed damages and an injunction against the Wards to force Dorothy to return to the family home.

There was no accusation whatsoever of inappropriate or immoral conduct made against the Wards. At one point, the suggestion was put directly to Mrs Lough in the witness box, and she rejected it firmly: "There was nothing in the Abbey of which you did not approve? – No. Nothing scandalous? – No, certainly not."[32] On the contrary, the Loughs were happy to acknowledge that their decade-long relationship with the Wards and their Abbey had been entirely positive. Stanley Lough testified that, prior to the events of August 1943, "he and his wife had received nothing but kindness from the defendants. At that time they gave [them] credit for being decent and honest people."[33] Indeed, in early 1943 they had agreed that Dorothy would join the order when she reached 21 and was no longer a minor. It was the Wards' alleged manipulation of his daughter after that time that they claimed was objectionable. Similarly, Mrs Lough agreed that prior to August 1943 she had received "nothing but kindness from Mr and Mrs Ward nor was there anything of which she disapproved in the way in which the abbey was carried on".[34]

But around that time, the Loughs alleged, their daughter had become tense and withdrawn, unnerved by the notion that she might be conscripted to undertake munitions work for the war effort. For the Loughs, her changed outlook and decision to join the Abbey was simply because "she was frightened of having to live with nasty people if she had to go to a munitions factory".[35] What was more, they claimed, it was Father Ward who had deliberately implanted this notion in her mind. Mrs Lough told the court that on 3 August 1943 Dorothy had returned from the Abbey looking gloomy and distressed. "She had seen some young girls drunk in the street", Macaskie explained, "and had been told by Mr Ward that that was the sort of girl she would be compelled to mix with when directed to work in an aircraft factory, 'where she would be little more than a slave'".[36]

Macaskie elaborated on this to the court. He suggested that a simple question lay at the heart of the dispute: 'Would Dorothy Lough have left her home if the defendants had not interfered?' His appeal to the judge's "common-sense" rested on suspicion and innuendo. "Both the Wards," he surmised, with their experience of teaching children, would be a pretty good combination if they wanted to play on the mind of a young girl. One of the most powerful means of enticement was the glamour and appeal of religion, on the one hand, and the fear complex which might be implanted in the mind of the person to be enticed. There was no question about the interest of the abbey, with its highly decorated chapel and exhibits from various ages, and it must have proved a most interesting place for Dorothy when she first went there. Enticement embraced persuasion and allurement, and one remembered the story of the archenticer, The Pied Piper of Hamelin, who led a number of children into the mountain.[37]

The defendants responded vigorously to these charges. Ward denied under oath that he had implanted the idea that Dorothy would be forced to mix with 'rough girls' and drunkards in the munitions factories, and stated he had said nothing to induce Dorothy to leave her home.[38] She was not held against her will, the Wards insisted, had not taken her final vows and thus was entirely free to return home at any time – but they would not force her to leave against her will. Dorothy calmly maintained under cross-examination from the presiding judge that "she was not afraid of any associates she might have met in a factory, and she had not said that her only way of escape was to go into the abbey".[39] Ward stated he had only agreed to take Dorothy in after her parents had agreed, and had signed papers, willingly and without duress, to the effect that the Confraternity would bear responsibility for her maintenance until she reached the age of 21.

Between these conflicting versions of events lay a number of issues. In the background was the Loughs' alleged misapprehension about the purposes of the Abbey. They maintained that they were unaware that the link to the Anglican Church had been broken soon after Dorothy began attending Sunday school classes and services there. They had her baptised at the Abbey in 1936, thinking (as they later stated) the service was endorsed by the Church of England. When in 1937 Dorothy applied to become a junior oblate of the Confraternity's Third Order – and thus a non-resident member of the Abbey community – her mother, as she later claimed, thought it was "something like the girl guides and that Dorothy was promising merely to pray and to do a good deed every day".[40] Mr Lough confirmed the family's fairly absent-minded understanding of the Wards' religious work. They had only attended the Abbey's services two or three times, he testified. "They are rather dramatic," he told the court. "There is a funny sort of ritual attached to them. I could not follow it. During the addresses the majority of the people were asleep." Macaskie remarked that the same applied in many churches.[41]

The events of 3–4 August 1943 were more central to the dispute. These had been brewing for some time, as Dorothy had been visiting the Abbey several times a week since finishing school at the end of 1940. In the spring of 1941 she became a senior oblate and was required to attend services at least once a month. By the middle of 1943, her visits were even more numerous. In court, Sister Terese testified that on 3 August she had asked her mother if she could join the Abbey as a full residential member. She had spent the previous day, a bank holiday, at the Abbey, and having heard on a radio transmission that girls her age were being called upon for factory duty, she feared she would be prevented from attending services there and that "the time had come for me to answer the call I had from God". She specifically stated that neither John nor Jessie Ward had in any way prompted this request. Despite her mother's assurances she would be able to "wangle her [Dorothy] out of factory work", her fears were not mollified. Sister Terese did her best to explain to the court her sudden resolution to enter the Abbey. "I felt something just seemed to break", she stated, "and that I wasn't going to work for her any more, but was going to work for God."[42] Her mother replied sharply that her duty was clear: to stay at home and look after her parents.

The following morning more words were exchanged. Dorothy had spent a sleepless night, praying for guidance, but remained determined to commence her life as a sister in religion at the Abbey. The two agreed to discuss the matter with the Wards. In Dorothy's mind the visit was to put her request to enter the Abbey into action: as she collected her clothes to leave, she remembered, her mother had told her to leave them behind as she had done nothing to deserve them. She also testified her mother told her "that if she went to the abbey neither her nor her brother Harold, of whom she was very fond, would have anything to do with her".[43] Her mother, on the other hand, still hoped that she and the Reverend Mother could convince Dorothy to remain at home.

At the Abbey they met with Jessie Ward, and later with her husband. According to Dorothy's testimony, after the two women had discussed the matter the Mother Superior "tried to persuade [Dorothy] to go home. Thinking that she would never get out again if she went home she said that she was not going", kneeling devoutly according to the Wards' account and declaring that she would never leave.[44] (Mrs Lough denied that Dorothy was even present during this interview.) But in the face of her daughter's obstinacy, Mrs Lough asked the Wards to speak with her husband as mediators. With Dorothy refusing to leave the Abbey, they returned without her to the Loughs' house. There the Wards and Dorothy's parents sat down to sort the problem out.

Two conflicting accounts of the discussion that followed were provided in testimony to the court. In Ward's testimony he denied that he insisted Dorothy should remain at the Abbey. On the contrary, he had felt helpless in the face of her obstinacy: his problem, he told the court, "was that

Dorothy had planted herself in the Abbey and would not go, and he did not know what to do". Macaskie suggested the proper thing would have been to tell Dorothy to go home. "I told her that in substance", Ward replied, "but could not get her out without great violence, and then the first person who would have blamed me would have been Mrs Lough."[45] When he and Jessie had visited the Loughs' house that night, he stated, he had told Stanley Lough: "I am in a fix. Dorothy won't go home. I can't throw her out in the street; what am I to do?"

The long conversation that followed was finally resolved, he told the court, when Mrs Lough accepted that "the best way out of it is to let her try the life".[46] Accordingly she wrote a letter:

> Dear Girlie – the Rev. Father has been pleading for you, and I am quite willing for you to live at the abbey if you would prefer that life, but I want you to come back just for a few days to talk it over. If you insist on being such a mule you will make everybody unhappy. Be a good girl and listen to reason. I shall wait patiently for you this evening. Don't disappoint me or you will spoil both our lives.[47]

Although this extract was read in court by the Loughs' barrister, it did not conflict with Ward's version of events and indeed tended to corroborate it. Given that Dorothy "had planted herself in the abbey and they did not know what to do", an offer was made (Ward testified) to maintain her there until she could take holy vows at the age of 21. The Wards maintained that Mr Lough had agreed; saying, "yes, I think that would be best". This exchange was denied by Mr and Mrs Lough. They also denied ever giving consent for Dorothy to remain at the Abbey. Their recollection, rather, was that their demand that Dorothy should remain at home *until* the age of 21 (after which she would legally be an adult and free to return to the Abbey if she wished) was clearly expressed to the Wards.

Yet in a dramatic courtroom moment, Mrs Lough could not adequately explain the letter she had written that night, now the only piece of evidence extant that related to the disputed conversation. A crucial phrase was missing, that was intrinsic to the Loughs' case:

> The letter [to Dorothy] which she wrote when the interview was in progress was an honest one [she told Mr. Richardson]. When she wrote: 'The reverend father has been pleading for you and I am quite willing for you to live at the abbey if you prefer that life' she forgot to add the words 'when you are 21'.

In any event, when this letter was delivered to Dorothy, she replied to it re-stating her desire to remain at the Abbey. She was also willing to accompany the Wards to her home to discuss matters with her parents. "You know I love you both, and I don't want to spoil your lives", she had written.

Further letters in the following days charted the deteriorating relationship between the Wards and Dorothy's parents. Mrs Lough wrote what was described in court as an "angry and distracted letter" to her daughter, telling Dorothy she had "made life very bitter for me as you have chosen the Abbey in preference to your home". She also wrote to the Reverend Mother, stating that as Dorothy had made up her mind further meetings would be a waste of time. This letter contained the first seeds of the case the Loughs would later present in court. The Wards, she wrote, had not helped to sway Dorothy as much as she would have liked. "I feel that you could have persuaded her to return if you had wished."[48] Attempting to mend fences, Mr Lough also wrote a beseeching letter that contained a firm parental instruction: "Both mummy and daddy are the same funny old dears. Think hard and think again." Dorothy's response to this was forthright. "I have a mind of my own", she wrote, "and am no longer a baby. If you really want to talk it over you can always come to see me." This letter, the Loughs later alleged, had been composed under coercion from the Wards. "It is a curiously cold and rigid letter for a daughter of 16 ½ to write", Macaskie submitted to the court.[49]

Sister Terese was called on the third and fourth days of the hearing to give her account of these developments. Her testimony was delivered in calm and measured terms, punctuated by smiles and demure nods at counsel and Justice Cassels. Asked if she would like to take a seat, she said she'd prefer to stand and leaned occasionally on the edge of the witness box. She presented so well, in fact, that when at one point counsel suggested she might be embarrassed and distracted by the "twittering" of the public gallery that was clearly hanging on her every word, Cassels observed: "The young lady seems perfectly composed".[50] Her replies to the Wards' barrister were forthright:

> Mr. RICHARDSON. – It has been suggested that someone told you what to write. Is that true? – Nobody told me. After all, I was 16 and a half.
> Did anybody influence you to stay at the abbey? – Nobody.
> Did you want to return home? – No.
> Were you willing to go home for an afternoon to have a cup of tea with your parents? – No.
> Why not? – I thought that I should not get out again.
> The witness said that she had no desire now to leave the abbey. If an order of the Court was made for her to leave the abbey she 'certainly would not go to live with her parents'.[51]

She felt her desire for independence was no different to that of her brother Harold, "about whom her parents did not 'kick up a fuss' when he left home at 16 to join the Merchant Navy", she pointed out.[52] Dorothy's testimony made plain the extent of her estrangement from her parents. Her time in the Hitchin Remand Home had been very distressing, especially when her mother had come to visit. "I went to kiss her", Dorothy testified, "but she turned away, and told me that when I got useful at home I left her. After the hearing at the Juvenile Court, my mother asked me if I was coming home, and I said I was not." On another occasion, her mother had knocked aggressively at the Abbey door, and had come inside "talking loudly, in an angry mood". "I did not want to see my mother", Dorothy continued, "after the way she had treated me by sending me to a remand home. I didn't feel very safe with her. I said I would see her if the Rev. Mother and the Rev. Father were with me. When I did see her she made a grab at me," pulling her veil. When her mother had "asked her to come home, as her father was seriously ill, she replied that she could hardly be expected to come home after the way she had been treated. Her mother then said, 'I won't bother you any more.'"[53] Asked by Macaskie if she was familiar with the Fifth Commandment – 'Honour thy father and thy mother' – Sister Terese responded quickly that the First Commandment ('Worship the Lord thy God') came first.[54] She was emphatic: she had no desire to leave the Abbey, and if compelled to do so would not go to live with her parents.

The 'Enticement Case' dominated the news pages of the London and national daily press through the turbulent week of VE Day and its joyous public celebrations. We can easily see why. Dorothy, with her good looks, strong-willed demeanour and "high-school-girlish voice"[55] presented an intriguing figure. "A pretty 19–year old girl wearing a silver cross on her nun's robes sat in the High Court yesterday", reported the *Daily Express* breathlessly on the first day of the case, "listening to the action brought by her father against the man and woman who founded the order to which she belongs."[56]

The exotic figures of John and Jessie Ward and their strange Confraternity added irresistible colour to the story. Their eccentric garb and claims of mystical enlightenment kept the public gallery, press reporters and newspaper readers enthralled. The morning after the first day of the case, for example, the racy *News Chronicle* ran photographs of the Wards and Sister Terese smiling on the steps of the High Court beside the headline "Vision led sect on mystical pilgrimage for abbey foundation". Macaskie, an experienced counsel, knew such claims would fatally undermine the Wards' credibility in the case. He asked Ward in cross-examination whether after his return from Burma he had dressed as a Buddhist priest and kept a meditation room in his house where he kept statuettes and idols of Indian gods. This evoked the Wards' studies and ritual in the Order of Indian Wisdom during the 1920s, but the suggestion was flatly denied. Mr Justice Cassels provided another headline when he observed in the closing stages of the case that the "strange character" of the Abbey was relevant to his consideration of the matter. Despite Richardson's protests that the character of the Abbey was not at issue and not relevant to the case, His Lordship wondered out loud whether it could possibly provide a proper home for Dorothy. "This so-called Confraternity", he continued,

> is a very strange organisation when you can almost number the whole crowd upon the fingers of both hands. They all have high-sounding names, and the head of the affair is an individual who was ordained priest one day and bishop the next, and then Archbishop, and still the members scarcely increased. The only title not used is that of Pope. That has to be considered when it is said that this is a proper place for the girl in spite of the parents' protest against Mr. and Mrs. Ward exercising control over her.

"ONLY TITLE NOT USED IS THAT OF POPE", shouted the *Morning Advertiser* in hearty agreement the following day.[57]

The derision directed at Ward's modern-day Abbey during the hearing was made sharper by the broader circumstances of Britain's Home Front effort as the war at last drew to a close. At a time when all members of society

23 Sisters of the Confraternity of the Kingdom of Christ working at embroidery, Hadley Hall, April 1945. *AMAA 3 WD 1/5.*

24 Procession of Confraternity members, April 1945; Sister Terese (Dorothy Lough) carries the crucifix. *AMAA 3 WD 1/8.*

were expected to demonstrate their patriotic contribution to an Allied victory, the peculiar aloofness of the Confraternity in New Barnet attracted an inevitable scepticism. "What is it you think you have done in the abbey which would be described as your war effort?" Cassels asked Dorothy on her second day of evidence. She replied equally directly: "Prayer is our war effort."[58] The newspapers caught the significance of this exchange, and some ran with it as a headline. More specifically, the suggestion that Sister Terese had entered Ward's Abbey to deliberately avoid working in a munitions factory carried tremendous weight in this heightened atmosphere of national service and the call of duty. Macaskie put the matter bluntly in his opening address: "This young woman was trying to escape from serving her country." "SECT CHIEF TALKED OF 'WORKS SLAVES' TO LURE GIRL" trumpeted the *Daily Mirror.*[59]

Another equally damaging suggestion ran through the questions posed and evidence tendered at the hearing. This was that the Wards (a childless couple, despite their elaborate religious titles) had made an "unwarrantable intrusion on the rights of a mother and father".[60] They had recklessly pursued young and impressionable recruits to bolster the contrived 'family' of their Confraternity, and seemed to care little for the genuine families that came into their orbit. A group of questions to Jessie Ward when she was called to give evidence expressed this theme neatly:

You have not, unfortunately, had the happiness of being a mother? – That is so.

Or of knowing what a daughter can be to a mother? – Quite.

So that perhaps you are not as well able to appreciate what that affection means? – It is an open question which I cannot answer.[61]

Similarly charged questions were put directly to Father Ward when he was called to give evidence. "What rights do you think you have over other people's children?" Macaskie asked, to which Ward responded that he didn't know. Cassels pursued the question further from the bench, asking, "Do you think you have any?" "I don't know," Ward again replied.[62]

Thus the suggestion that the Abbey had actually broken up a number of homes and disrupted marriages ran through the questions addressed to the Wards in the witness box. Ward made a number of damaging admissions on this front when the hearing resumed for its sixth day. He acknowledged that he had refused to meet with the father of one 31–year old recruit who was opposed to her entering the Abbey. He had replied, he said, to the effect that an interview would be a "sheer waste of time, as the decision in the matter rests with your daughter, who is old enough to make up her own mind".[63] Pursuing his theme, Macaskie then asked the Reverend Father if he was aware that the father of Monica Hopping ('Sister Gabrielle') had "bitterly resented his daughter going to live at the abbey before she was 21". Ward conceded that this had recently come to his attention. He also admitted that another father, the husband of another adherent who had come to the Abbey with her two children in 1940, had since obtained a divorce on the grounds of desertion.[64] "DIVORCED AFTER ENTERING ABBEY" observed the *Daily Herald* the following day.

The insinuation that the Abbey's founders had wilfully broken up local families to gain recruits was linked to Father Ward's alleged neglect of his own daughter Blanche. She had suffered a paralysis in 1932; unable to continue working as a teacher she drew benefits from a fund administered by the National Union of Teachers. Ward admitted he contributed only five shillings a week to her maintenance, insisting to the court that with his commitments to the Confraternity and the pooling of their assets in trust he simply had no more money to offer his daughter. The Lough's barrister interrupted sharply: "What was to prevent your doing at least the same for Blanche as you were willing to do for Dorothy? You took her in, why not your own daughter?" Simply because her character as a "bitter atheist" was not suited to the life, Ward answered, and because the chapter of the Abbey would not endorse her residence there.[65]

From another point of view, though, the Lough family's very public quarrel evoked the commonplace tensions of households throughout the country. The Loughs' counsel was keen to draw out this aspect of the dispute. After questioning Mr Lough on the second day of the hearing, he asked Dorothy (seated across the room among the members of the Confraternity) to stand up in her seat. It was a simple but effective ploy, because the pathos and symbolism of the domestic drama that lay at the heart of the case was irresistible. The Loughs had lost their daughter to the influence of surrogate parents, the self-appointed heads of an esoteric religious order, who now stood revealed (it seemed) of an unscrupulous violation of the sanctuary of the family home. "In her dark brown habit", reported the *Daily Telegraph*, "she rose from her place beside Mrs. Ward in the white robes of mother superior, and father and daughter faced one another across the court."[66]

In this context, Macaskie's tactics deliberately played on the lurid associations of the word 'enticement' throughout the hearing. Although no open accusations of immoral conduct were made against the Wards, the term subtly transformed the Loughs' case, especially as far as the press coverage and popular opinion were concerned. 'Enticement' was a prurient term, usually associated in common law with seduction and sexual impropriety. Thus a number of titillating suggestions crept into the court's deliberations at various points. "Quite apart from the anguish of losing an only daughter", Macaskie had stated in his opening address, for example, "a parent, wise and watchful, might be anxious about entrusting even if he were willing, a daughter of 16 ½ to such a confraternity where provision was made for both sexes to live in the same dwelling."[67] At another point in his cross-examination, Macaskie asked if *Who Was Hiram Abiff?*, one of Ward's Masonic books, had "a greater pornographic interest". Ward vigorously denied the suggestion, but counsel pursued the point. "Is this the sort of stuff that Dorothy Lough would come into contact with?" he asked, developing the suggestion the Abbey was an unsuitable environment for an impressionable young girl. "She never saw it", Ward responded bluntly, and stated the obvious: "She is not a Freemason."[68]

The courtroom and press coverage became a public arena where Ward's eccentric demeanour as the self-styled 'Father Superior' of a tiny, self-righteous esoteric sect was readily mocked. Macaskie's tone of snide derision became more pronounced in concluding his case. "The girl had been imbued with the theatrical atmosphere of the convent", he surmised, "Mr Ward in his scarlet robes and his title of Metropolitan Archbishop, and his wife in her white robes with her high-heeled white kid shoes and gold girdle."[69]

John Ward's health cracked in the face of this unrelenting scrutiny. During the trial he suffered numbness and a complete loss of strength in his right arm, likely symptoms of a minor stroke. He was a sensitive man at the best of times, and felt the injustice of the court proceedings and their reception in the public arena very deeply.[70] The unfolding court case also filled others at the Abbey with concern and trepidation. All knew Sister Terese well, and shared the view that she had been an unloved and lonely girl at home. The Wards maintained privately that the Loughs only sought the return of their daughter after she reached an age at which she could earn a wage and thus contribute to their household finances. Long after the court proceedings had ended, this version of the Lough dispute circulated through the Orthodox Catholic community. Mar Georgius, for example, later referred to the matter:

> When the young lady arrived at an age when she was able to earn money, and incidentally to do a certain amount of housework, her parents demanded that she be restored to their custody, only to be refused by the Archbishop [i.e. Ward] on the ground that they had signed a legal document surrendering her to the custody of himself and his wife within the Confraternity.[71]

The Wards' barrister cross-examined Mrs Lough to the effect that Dorothy was a lonely girl in an unhappy family environment. Her mother agreed she was the "masterful" one in her relationship with her husband, but denied that their home life was marred by quarrelling and threats.[72] In her testimony, Dorothy firmly presented an alternative view, stating

> She was as happy at home as it was possible to be when her parents were making rows with each other. She could give no reason for the rows, but her parents seemed less happy since 1940. If her father did something which her mother did not like she used to get awfully angry, and if she could not get her own way she used to say that she would commit suicide.[73]

The revelations of the Lough's home life heightened tension in the court-room. The *Daily Mirror's* report revelled in another moment of drama, as mother and daughter confronted each other across the room:

> Sister Terese . . . looked straight at her mother in the front row of the court and said: 'I was as happy as I could be at home when my mother and father were making rows between each other'. Dorothy paused, looked at the Judge with her brown eyes and declared firmly: 'I often thought my father and mother would separate'. Then, as the girl lowered her eyes, Mrs Lough cried: 'You liar, Dorothy', and smothered her sobs in a handkerchief.[74]

Counsel for the opposing parties re-stated their basic arguments in closing statements. They were in stark contrast. For Richardson and the Wards, there was "not one scintilla of evidence" that any enticement had occurred.

It was clear that Dorothy had left home of her own accord on 4 August 1943, and that within twenty-four hours she received her parents' permission to remain at the Abbey. As to legal precedents, the matter was unlike any other in the case books, he submitted, and that while a parent had a right to the custody of a minor there was no basis in law for a parent to enforce that right against another person in claiming damages. If Lough had desired the return of his daughter, he pointed out, a well-recognised legal path was available to him from the beginning of the dispute: for five shillings, Lough "could . . . have taken out an originating summons and the whole matter of custody could have been decided in private by a Judge of the Chancery Division".[75] What was more, the injunction asked for – that would prevent the Wards from having any contact with Dorothy whatsoever – "went beyond the wildest dreams of any lawyer, and could not be enforced".[76] In summing up, Richardson placed a particular emphasis on the innuendo and implicit suggestions that had figured so prominently in the case:

> There had been introduced into the case prejudicial matters, which were entirely unconnected with any proved facts, and he submitted that on these facts – uncoloured by prejudice – there was no evidence of entice-ment . . . No fraud could be alleged and no suggestion was made of anything improper or wrong in the Abbey. The whole background of the case was suspicion and prejudice.[77]

The question for decision, he concluded, was essentially "whether a servant had been enticed from her employment. That being the issue, it did not matter for the purpose of the action what kind of place the abbey was." The Wards had kept their promise not to offer Dorothy the chance to take her final vows until she was 21; and "their reason for fighting the case was that they earnestly believed that the wishes of the girl to remain in the abbey should be supported".[78]

For Macaskie, on the other hand, there was "overwhelming evidence of enticement" over four and a half years, climaxing at the moment "when they succeeded in clinching the matter by playing on her fears of being sent into a Government factory and offering, as the only way of escape, entrance into the Confraternity".

> Once having got her there they exerted all their influence most success-fully to turn her against her parents and to induce her to remain in the Abbey and to believe, up to the present moment, that the Abbey was the only place where she could find happiness. If they have achieved that, said counsel, the result is that they have committed the most wicked wrong that could be perpetuated by a stranger intruding into the family life of decent English people.[79]

On the relevant legal questions Macaskie continued to work this theme, saying "it was important that parents should know what their rights and duties were with regard to their children, and that strangers should not intrude, unless they had good reason, on the private relations of families". While many would have sympathy for "misguided Dorothy Lough", he went on, "the parents had inherent rights – not to be arbitrarily asserted – in respect of her. This was not a case in which the wishes of the girl should be consulted". Cassels interrupted at this point. "If the court has no right to interfere, how much less had the Rev. Father and Rev. Mother?" he wondered aloud.

Macaskie posed a simple question: "Would Dorothy Lough have left her home if the defendants had not interfered?" The answer could only be in the negative, he suggested, because the Wards and their fanciful Abbey with its heady atmosphere of medieval piety and curious museum were clearly powerful enticements. He argued a pattern of behaviour was clearly evident that betrayed the Wards' motive: "the defendants enveigled young women into the abbey to put them to domestic service, for which they paid no wages, nor anything except keep and clothing, and for the purpose of running a market garden, museum and publishing department at a small profit." An injunction preventing the Wards from contacting Dorothy was necessary, Macaskie insisted in closing his case. "[It] is not going to be an easy matter for the child who has been estranged from her parents so long, but it is a matter which has to be faced, and Mr and Mrs Lough as devoted parents will do their best to make the transfer, to win back their daughter who has been so cruelly parted from them."[80]

❋   ❋   ❋

The hearing adjourned on 15 May for Justice Cassels to consider his verdict, in a case for which there was no previous authority for the circumstances and legal points involved.[81] When the court resumed three days later, the Loughs were so sure the judgment would be in their favour that they had a car standing by to collect Dorothy from the Abbey to bring her home. On the other side, Father Ward and the members of the Confraternity were also confident. Their view was that the initial agreement between themselves and the Loughs would be upheld over the claims of enticement, especially as no direct evidence demonstrating the latter had been tendered to the court.

These hopes were dashed. Although Cassels agreed that Dorothy was not kept at the Abbey against her will and that she was certainly happy there, he found the Wards had enticed her away from home: "This girl Dorothy", he stated with patriarchal finality, "has left her father's service and control." The 'enticement' rested on whether the Wards had "persuaded, induced or incited" Dorothy to leave her parents' home on the night of 3 August 1943;

Cassels found that they had: "She left her home as the result of a state of mind induced by the defendants."[82] As to what the Wards' motives might have been, Cassels could not be sure, but wondered whether Dorothy's domestic services might have been a factor:

> The Confraternity purports to be self-supporting. It obtains its money not only from those who give it but also by conducting certain activities, such as gardening, the museum, publishing, and making children's clothing. Domestic work has to be done. A community of ten women and four men cannot be housed and fed without some domestic work being done. Another pair of working hands would be of use to such a community. Dorothy had been useful to her father at home in the house and in the garden. By this enticement she transferred herself and her services to the defendants for her keep.[83]

Other than this speculation, it was entirely a question of religious piety, and the court took a dim view of the intense personal piety of a sixteen-year-old when it contradicted the wishes of her father. Her time in the Abbey was always in the Wards' company, "the two superiors", Cassels observed, "the two leaders, the two teachers, in gorgeous raiment". In this respect, then, the Wards seemed directly culpable for the changes that had come over Dorothy. "The religious influence was a very dangerous and a very powerful one, and never so dangerous and so powerful as when it was exercised by superior and older minds over those which were inferior and younger."[84] There was also a principle of paternal authority. "I do not think a father is without rights as to his children", Cassels stated.

> On the contrary, the law of England is that the father is the head of the family and has control over his children, their persons, their education and their conduct, until they are 21 years of age or marry under that age. It is because he is the father that the law recognises that he has those rights . . . So far as the father's religion is concerned, many cases decide that it is the father who has the right to say in what religion his children shall be brought up.[85]

He awarded the Loughs damages of £500 with costs, "to indicate this court's disapproval of the defendants' conduct", – a "mere formality", Cassels observed pointedly, "because the defendants had put it out of their power to possess so sordid a thing as money. Their sense of their duties as citizens is not very high."[86] The court also granted an injunction – suspended to 30 May pending an appeal – that personally restrained the Wards from continuing to harbour Sister Terese, an injunction that actively disregarded her desire to remain at the Abbey.[87] Cassels' forceful language in framing his judgment added salt to these wounds. Describing the Wards as Dorothy's "enticers" and "inducers", he felt obliged to conclude:

> there is some force in the suggestion that they are a couple suffering from a form of megalomania, taking delight in high-sounding titles. They seem to me to be playing at keeping a nunnery and indulging in make-believe, forming their own rules, and extracting vows of obedience from their little band of followers, of whom Dorothy has been persuaded by them to become a very young member.[88]

The popular press drew stark conclusions from the verdict. "DOROTHY ENTICED - £500 DAMAGES", announced the *Daily Mail* the following morning. "JUDGE SAYS GIRL WAS ENTICED TO ABBEY", ran the headline in the *News Chronicle*, Saturday May 19, "£500 AWARD – Father has right to decide religion." "SISTER THERESE MUST PUT OFF HER NUN'S ROBES", announced the *Daily Express*.

The difficulty with the court's injunction was that Dorothy had pointedly refused to remain with her parents. She was encouraged to take up residence in a neutral house; either with her aunt in Southampton or another woman – a Mrs Kathleen Roberts, widow of a county court judge – who had approached Mrs Lough during the trial and volunteered to take Dorothy into her home at Horley in Surrey. "I have no power in these proceedings . . . to order her to go back into her father's home", concluded Justice Cassels, "but I do earnestly advise her so to do. If the defendants' religious vows permit them to consider the feelings of a real father and a real mother, they will add their advice to mine."[89] He rejected suggestions from the Wards' counsel that Dorothy might be driven to suicide.

Dorothy did not take up Mrs Roberts' offer. She remained at the Abbey for another fortnight, until the end of the suspension of the injunction awarded against the Wards. On 30 May, with no sign of an appeal from Ward's lawyers, the injunction came into force. If the Wards continued to harbour Dorothy they would be in breach of a court order.

The tabloid circus resumed. Accompanied by a reporter and a photographer from the *Daily Mail*, Mrs Lough stepped up to the door at Hadley Hall to collect Dorothy. "That was the beginning of scenes I witnessed at the door of the Abbey", the reporter wrote.

> For 15 minutes Mrs. Lough repeatedly rang the bell and pounded the knocker, demanding that her daughter should be returned to her. The door was opened by the Abbey chamberlain, though the chain was kept on it. Through the space we could see the chamberlain's wife in the black garb of the fraternity. Mrs. Lough kept on ringing the bell. Three times the chamberlain opened the door to the length of its chain. He said:

'Father Ward wishes me to tell you your daughter is not here, and that is all he has to say'.

A photograph of Mrs Lough speaking through a crack in the door illustrated the stand-off for the *Daily Mail's* readers. "For two years I have lived for this day", Mrs Lough told the reporter, "I have everything ready. My sister is here and was to take Dorothy to Southampton for a holiday. But I have no idea where Dorothy is now. All they would tell me at the Abbey is that she was gone."[90] Through an enquiry by their solicitor the Loughs learned from Father Ward that Dorothy had moved to a small three-roomed house in Lawrence Road, South Tottenham, the home of a Mr and Mrs Cooper. The Coopers were the grandparents of a girl who had previously stayed at the Abbey for several months. It is unclear whether rent was paid, but Dorothy helped Mrs Cooper with the cleaning and shopping.

Dorothy's lonely and increasingly anguished state was once more catapulted into the national spotlight when her parents visited the redbrick house the following evening, trailed by more press reporters, to persuade her to return home. Dorothy appeared briefly on the doorstep, wearing a simple brown dress. She and her father went inside. After a while Mrs Lough joined them, but left again at 8.15 pm, telling the assembled reporters, "It is terrible, Dorothy will not come home with us."[91] Even after the police were called Dorothy was resolute. "HER MOTHER WEPT", announced the *Daily Mirror* the next day alongside a photograph of Mrs Lough turning away from Dorothy, "BUT 'SISTER TERESE' SAID: 'I WON'T COME HOME WITH YOU'". The *Daily Herald* ran a front-page photograph of the Loughs talking with police outside the Coopers' home: "SISTER TERESE STAYS AWAY." In what was described by her solicitor as a "vulgar and disgusting exhibition", Dorothy later told a court that her mother "caught hold of my arm" during their conversation inside the house, "and tried to drag me towards the door".[92] After the police advised the Loughs to once more contact their solicitor, Dorothy's parents left and the onlookers dispersed. "There is nothing we can do", a police inspector told the *Mirror* reporter.[93] In response to reporters' enquiries a day later, Mrs Cooper said that Dorothy had moved to another house and had sent for her clothes.

A fortnight later Dorothy appeared in a North London courtroom alleging assault against her mother. When asked in court for her current address, Dorothy wrote it on a piece of paper as she didn't want her mother to find her again. Unfortunately for her application, as a minor Dorothy was therefore not able to commence a private prosecution. The application was dismissed and she slipped back to the anonymity of her new lodgings.[94]

With Dorothy fully estranged from her parents it is likely that the Confraternity and the Wards began paying the rent on her behalf. At the first available opportunity, however, she returned to the Abbey and was secretly admitted in defiance of the High Court injunction. A concealed apartment was built into the attic, and for more than a year she hid there whenever necessary. Repeated enquiries from the Loughs and police visits to the Abbey failed to uncover any trace of her. Four months later, in September 1945, Stanley Lough stated: "Although judgment was given at the hearing of this case in my favour, I have not the slightest knowledge or idea where my daughter is now or what she is doing". He was still convinced "by some means both [Ward] and his wife have a very strong influence over the child and have persuaded her not to return to us and her home."[95]

Stanley Lough and his wife never saw their daughter again. She remained hidden in the Abbey, adopting the name Sister Nina in later years to evade the notoriety she had gained during the enticement case. With the other members of Ward's Confraternity she left England for Cyprus in 1946 and then on to Australia in 1955. Sister Nina remained a dedicated member of the Confraternity of the Kingdom of Christ long after Father Ward's passing, until her own death in Brisbane, Australia in January 1963.

✳   ✳   ✳

John Ward's reputation, meanwhile, was beyond salvage in the immediate aftermath of the enticement case. Whatever prominence and public esteem he had gained as a Masonic scholar, in Orthodox Catholicism or as director of the Folk Park now counted for little.

Among the broader Orthodox Catholic community, the reaction to the Confraternity's ordeal in the High Court and in the popular press was mixed. Sympathy for the treatment Ward had received was expressed, but at a muted and careful distance. Acknowledging that "most of our readers will have read in the daily press more or less garbled versions of the trial", the *Orthodox Catholic Review* emphasised that Ward was "in no way associated with the Catholicate of the West, and that we are therefore in no way involved in these proceedings".[96] Insisting that the action should never have been brought to court, and that the "awarding of damages against [Ward] was an act of gross injustice", the *Review* reserved its greatest condemnation for the tactics of Stanley Lough's lawyer and the implications of the verdict for other religious communities.

> The tactics adopted by the Plaintiff's legal representative in Court are to be thoroughly condemned, . . . [especially] the scoffing and innuendoes concerning the Archbishop's Episcopal status, his election to the Archbishopric, his quitting the Church of England, and the ecclesiastical vesture of himself and The Rev. Mother. We may well ask ourselves what the learned judge was doing to permit such as display of caddishness in the Curia Regis.

But the matter does not rest there. As a result of the decision in this case it would appear to be a highly dangerous thing for any religious community to admit a minor, even with the parents' consent, for should that consent be subsequently withdrawn the unhappy Superior might find himself faced with an action for 'enticement' and be mulcted in the sum of £500. This is a matter that affects all Orthodox and Catholic bodies, and the only way of preventing a recurrence of this sort of thing is for them to show the pagan State in no weak manner, and with no uncertain voice, that they do not propose to tolerate it. Surely this is a matter in which Rome might well give a lead?[97]

. Meanwhile, the Loughs could do little in the face of their daughter's obstinate attachment to Ward's Confraternity. But when payment of their court costs was not forthcoming, formal proceedings to enforce the court's ruling were commenced. A bankruptcy notice of 29 June 1945 required Ward to settle the outstanding amount of £500 by 18 July. It was served on Ward at the Abbey by a clerk from Lough's solicitor's office on 10 July. By not complying, Ward was inviting bankruptcy proceedings. Once that date had passed, and with the amount still unpaid, Stanley Lough petitioned the High Court on 24 July. His petition described Ward as "known as Father Superior and Archbishop of the British Empire of the Orthodox Catholic Church, Publisher and Director of a Limited Company", and followed legal convention in stating:

> that the said John Sebastian Marlow Ward is justly and truly indebted to me in the sum of £500.0.0 being the amount due to me under a final Judgment of the King's Bench Division of the High Court of Justice dated the 18th day of May 1945 in a certain action the short title whereof is Lough v. Ward 1944 L. No. 320 for damages awarded to me by the said Court against the said John Sebastian Marlow Ward for enticement. The said Judgment also provides for the payment to me by the said John Sebastian Marlow Ward of the costs of and relating to the said action the taxation of which has not yet been completed.[98]

The hearing before the Registrar was originally set for 16 August, but given international events (it was VJ Day, and joyous crowds once again thronged the streets) the matter was postponed until 23 August, when after a short hearing the matter was again adjourned until 30 August. In the interim, Ward made no application to oppose the petition.

The total debt stood at £1,522.13.7d.[99] Given Ward's failure to comply with the bankruptcy notice, a receiving order against him was issued by the court on 30 August and a receiver appointed. Ward was thereby required to attend the Official Receiver, a Mr Leslie West, in the Bankruptcy

Buildings at Lincoln's Inn. He was required by that officer to draw up a detailed statement of affairs, which he completed on 5 September. This must have appeared an eccentric document, for Ward listed virtually no assets, no income and no liabilities outside that owed as a result of the court proceedings. He held ten one-pound shares in the Baskerville Press, "a private company which has never paid a dividend", on behalf of the Confraternity of the Kingdom of Christ. His solitary asset was a sum of £3.10.0 estimated as income from publishing royalties for *An Interpretation of the Masonic Symbols* [sic] from A. Lewis, publishers, in 1944–5, which he also maintained were to be paid over to the Confraternity as required by its constitution.[100]

On 6 September, the Registrar ordered that Ward's public examination would be held before the Court in late October. Four days later the Official Receiver issued a notice informing Ward and his creditors that the first meeting of creditors would be held on 19 September, a meeting Ward was required to attend or be held in contempt of court. In the event he was absent due to ill-health, but his solicitor produced receipts for his liabilities, and indicated that the costs and expenses of the bankruptcy proceedings had also been discharged. The Confraternity, in other words, had scraped together sufficient funds to pay the debt, and on this basis Ward intended to apply for a rescission of the receiving order.[101] Meanwhile, on 18 September, Ward's lawyers met to discuss his outstanding debts for their services. Noting that he had paid Lough "the full amount due to him in respect of the said action and Receiving Order", the partners signed a deed releasing John and Jessie Ward "from all further sums which may be owing to the Firm under the action [Lough v. Ward] and Bankruptcy proceedings and otherwise and from all actions proceedings claims and demands in respect thereof".[102] According to the Official Receiver, this released the Wards from a debt of £500 to their solicitors, after a total debt of £1,050 incurred during the enticement case had been reduced by a payment of £550 provided by members of the Confraternity prior to the commencement of the bankruptcy proceedings.[103]

Matters then proceeded to resolution fairly swiftly. On 5 October Ward swore an affidavit to the effect that his debts had been paid in full, and a successful application was made to rescind the Receiving Order.[104] Ward was free of the threat of bankruptcy. Almost immediately he commenced plans for his Confraternity's permanent departure from England.

✹   ✹   ✹

Despite the notoriety of the enticement case and the damage it had wrought on Ward's reputation, the decision to leave England emerged as a result of a convergence of broader factors. Ward's conviction that British civilization and Empire were in terminal decline synchronised in his mind with an acute sense of persecution at his public humiliation during the High Court proceedings. He probably realised his prized Folk Park, in mothballs since 1940 but with its buildings intact ready for re-opening, would be unlikely to recapture its pre-war eminence given the fallout from the court case. The museum had also provided an important source of income for Ward's community, whose finances were now in chaos by the damages and costs awarded to the Loughs.

England no longer offered a future for Ward and his followers. But where could they go? A destination arose at least partly by chance. During the late 1930s Ward had come into contact with Gerald Gardner, a compelling personality who shared many of his interests. Gardner was a former customs officer, like Ward a public servant with experiences in the Far East, who dedicated his later years to esoteric study. Antiquities, ethnography, historic weapons, folklore, Freemasonry, magic and the occult all occupied his attention at various times. After being initiated into a New Forest coven, Gardner leapt to prominence as a leading figure in the post-war witchcraft revival. His books *High Magic's Aid* and *Witchcraft Today*, published in 1949 and 1954, announced the revival of pagan ritual among small groups of adventurous-minded Englishmen and women.[105] It is unclear when the two men first met, but Gardner appears to have advised Ward on the interior fittings for the witch's cottage in the Abbey Folk Park. In early 1946, as plans were conceived to leave the Abbey and England, Ward and Gardner struck a deal. In return for the cottage and its artefacts, Gardner offered the Confraternity a piece of land and farmhouse he owned at Gastria in Cyprus.[106] The destination was ideal: Cyprus was an English territory in the heart of the Eastern Mediterranean, with a benign climate that had long seduced English travellers and expatriates. It was, moreover, rich in both the classical antiquities and traditions of Orthodox Christianity that had figured so powerfully in John Ward's scholarly and religious career.

Late 1945 and the early months of 1946 saw preparations undertaken in a spirit (at least as far as Ward was concerned) of pragmatic resignation. His participation in the consecrations and re-consecrations initiated by Mar Georgius at the Abbey Church from August 1945 brought some closure to the Confraternity's activities in England. His younger followers were excited by the prospect of an adventure overseas, but the outward resolve of their Reverend Father masked a deep personal despair. Fr Peter helped him sort through the records of the Abbey and its Folk Park, and boxes of documents, notes, business records and letters were incinerated. Ward's enormous collection of antiquities – approaching 50,000 separate items – was broken up. The more valuable pieces were sold to finance the move, and the remainder was boxed into crates and prepared for the departure. More heartbreaking still was the dissolution of Father Ward's large personal library. A lifetime of scholarly application was sold to dealers, the books tossed out the windows of Hadley Hall, piled on the lawns and shoved into sacks. As the lorry rolled out the gate, we might imagine Father Ward gazing from an upstairs window in the desolate emptiness of his study. It had all come to nothing.

12

Cyprus and Beyond

Plans for departure were finalized by July 1946. Two non-resident members of the Confraternity – Reginald and Grace Ball, known as Father Stephen and Sister Grace – would remain behind at Hadley Hall, and then move to Bournemouth once the sale was finalised to join the 'Daughter House' of the Abbey established there by the Hall sisters five years earlier. All the others were ready to accompany their Reverend Father into a Mediterranean exile. Sister Terese was not present for the photograph taken in front of the Abbey Church; the community's explosive secret was that she had been hiding in Hadley Hall's attic for a year, and would also be going with them. A passport had been secured for her using false identity papers.

The Confraternity departed in groups from New Barnet on 13 July, and boarded the *Athlone Castle* at Southampton before sailing the following day. The ship was chartered by the British military to convey a large contingent of RAF personnel. Most of the Confraternity, meanwhile, were either seasick or sunburnt as the vessel struggled down the coast of Spain to Gibraltar, its passage slowed by propeller faults. Making better time across the Mediterranean, the Confraternity celebrated a private Sunday service in two of their cabins linked by a connecting doorway. They disembarked at Port Said on 23 July, and two days later boarded the *Lucinda* to continue on through rolling seas to Cyprus. The passage was so rough that everyone except Father Ward was seasick. On Sunday 28 July they again celebrated the Eucharist on dry land, this time on the roof of their hotel overlooking the Limassol seafront.[1]

It was quickly apparent that Gardner's property would not be the new home they had hoped for: the farmhouse was derelict and the land totally unsuited for agriculture. Consequently the group's funds were reduced further by the purchase of an orange orchard with a small two-storey farmhouse, situated on the rocky coastline outside Limassol surrounded by olive groves and sparse farming land. They paid £2,500 to the owner, the widow of a Greek sailor, including £20 for the poultry and some furniture. Ward described it in his diary on 10 August, the day they took possession:

It is situated 'between the Church of St George and the Germasoya Bridge, in the Parish of Agios Athenasios on the Nicosia road, facing the sea.' Consists of 9 donums of land. Large hall 23 f[ee]t by 10 with 4 rooms opening out of it. From the N[orth] West room the kitchen opens out and in that room there is a staircase leading to an upper room same size as the hall. Fine balcony in front and a smaller one at back. In addition to W.C., pantry and chicken house there is a 'brick' oven for bread and the Gardener's Cottage of one large and one narrow room not connected with each other or with the house.[2]

Nearby, in an old well away from the house, a refuge was built for Sister Terese in case anyone came looking for her.

Here Ward's community remained for over eight years, a small tight-knit group of married couples, siblings and children, eking out a basic subsistence with farming and handicrafts. Their surplus produce was carried by a neighbour for sale in Limassol. The Reverend Mother and Sister Mary tried their hand at painting icons and a small income was made teaching English lessons to some of the children of the district. Otherwise circumstances dictated self-sufficiency: the gardener's shed was converted into a workshop for Fr Filius Domini, where he made shelves, wardrobes and other essentials. Oranges, figs and garden vegetables were grown, and chickens and goats kept to supplement the kitchen, but it was a difficult and precarious existence. Only rarely did they walk the two and a half miles to Germasoya village, or drive to nearby Limassol in the black Hillman Minx they purchased. Money was very scarce, and it was a very welcome boost when, in October, £4,300 was sent to them after the sale of Hadley Hall and their remaining furniture and carriages to the art dealer William Ohly, who thereafter ran the property as an artist's colony. In February 1947 Gardner's land and the derelict house on it were also sold for £300, another welcome addition to their funds.

One neighbour, Solomon Panagides, was a Greek priest and Father Ward lost little time in making an introduction. Five weeks after moving in, he and Jessie walked over to introduce themselves. They were very kindly received, he wrote in his diary that evening: "He said he was very pleased to learn I was a fellow priest; but puzzled about being Orthodox Catholic in the West. I explained our history." In the weeks that followed very warm relations developed: on 23 September Panagides collected Ward in his horse-drawn carriage to show him his church in Limassol, and after returning him in the afternoon stayed for tea and admired their vestments and makeshift chapel. But by early October their neighbour had begun to entertain doubts. Ward visited him one day,

and came away much perturbed because he told me he was going to write to the Archimandrite in London to enquire whether our Church

(Orthodox Catholic) was in communion with or recognised by him. I told him I felt sure it was not because we derived from the Syrian Jacobite Church which he said was not in communion with the Greek Orthodox Church. I inwardly feared the Archimandrite might make enquiries among the Anglicans and thus let them know we were in Cyprus. I could not however do anything to stop him.[3]

The psychic instructions from the angelic 'Master of the Work' continued as before. Ward's diary noted on 18 September, for example, that following their introduction to Pappas Panagides "we were warned by the M[aster] that the Greek Church was now being tested as the Anglican had been". The general pattern was that John and Jessie Ward would receive the visions as had occurred at New Barnet, which would then be conveyed to the others at a chapter meeting after the main Sunday service. The emphasis now, if we rely on the notes of Ward's diary, often descended to matters of simple nutrition. Another vision in early 1947 instructed them to lay in stocks of tinned meat and fish. "I told Rev. Mother to look out for oval shaped tins containing herrings and such-like fish", Ward noted, "the shape of the tin was a definite inspiration from the Master, for we had neither of us seen any tins of fish except a few tins of salmon. When she went into the grocer's by the market she saw at the back of the shop a pile of tins and asked the man, 'What are all those oval tins, are they fish?' He said, 'Yes, herrings.' So she bought 15 tins."[4]

The Confraternity and their Reverend Father remained deeply committed to their religious calling. Bolts of artificial silk in blue and white were purchased to make a new set of vestments in the Orthodox style as the others had been left behind in New Barnet. New cassocks in brown were also made up for the brothers and sisters, with white veils for the latter that "looked very nice", as the Reverend Father recorded in his diary.[5] Religious services continued to provide the daily routine, and were usually held in the upstairs room that was also used as the dining hall or refectory where Father Filius Domini had built a new altar and *iconostasis* or screen to display icons in the Orthodox manner. They had not long settled at the farmhouse before their Turkish neighbour, a Mr Enver, indicated a desire to join the community. Ward's response, that "he could not possibly be admitted under two years", was somewhat indignant: "1st: [he] must attend services, then if he still liked them, 2nd: be baptised and confirmed. 3rd be admitted to 3rd order [of the Confraternity]. Then after some long time in [the] 3rd order we might elect him to the First order."[6] Membership was a serious undertaking and not to be offered or taken lightly.

Their regular calendar of services, saints' festivals and holy days was punctuated by other celebrations. For Ward's birthday in 1946, for example, a new altar frontal was made in yellow silk for their chapel, with a figure of

Christ the King painted by Sister Mary; his gifts included an illuminated calendar of saints days, and books of stories written by Father Peter and Sister Gabrielle. "In the evening", Ward recorded with obvious delight,

> They arranged a kind of fête in Sister Bertha's room transformed into a sitting room with floral decorations and a kind of tent for the Rev. Mother and me to sit in. After various guessing games and refreshments it ended with them singing carols to the accompaniment of two violins played by S. Bertha and Fr. Ignatius. The members had previously dressed up to represent famous characters in history or fiction, e.g. the Curé de Ars, St John of the Cross, the Three Musketeers, etc.[7]

Sister Ursula and Father Ignatius were married during a Eucharist service on 25 November 1948 (the service repeated as a civil ceremony in the town registry in early December), as were Father Peter and Sister Mary in April 1949. A baby boy named John was born to the Cuffes, and for his christening everyone worked busily all morning preparing for the service, converting the refectory into a church by moving the furniture away, installing a temporary altar and font. "In front of the two 'Museum' cases we hung brown-gold curtains", Ward wrote in his diary, "and in front of these banners of the Virgin and St Michael. Behind the altar was the Banner of the Cross. The font was placed in the middle of the room and was made from the cover of our font at Barnet, turned upside down and stood in a wooden stand made for it by F[ilius] Domini and gilded. A bowl was fixed inside the upturned cover by a thin rim, and the whole thing looked very nice." His description of their service is one of the few extant:

> I took the ceremony assisted by Father Ignatius, and the Godparents were (1) Rev. Mother, (2) Sr Gabrielle, (3) Filius Domini, (4) Fr Peter. The R. M. was senior Godparent and took the largest part. The four Godparents, Ursula and the baby assembled in the smaller front room, on the east side, and entered in procession after the Baptismal water had been consecrated. The room was elaborately decorated with flowers and foliage. The acacia provided a mass of yellow blossoms for the occasions; Peter and Helena made of it four long ropes which formed an open canopy over the font. The ceremony followed the sequence laid down in our Liturgy except that I blessed a little gold cross and suspended it round his neck; this was just before vesting him with the 'white robe'. All the Greek children receive such a cross at their baptism.[8]

Antiquities remained a great fascination. An eight mile return walk took them to the classical site of Amathus (old Limassol, abandoned after being ransacked during the Crusades), where the ground was littered with fragments of pottery. At their first visit in October 1946 Ward recorded a complete sequence of fragments from 800 BC to the Byzantine period. His curiosity was a sharp as ever, piqued by the archaeological evidence of classical antiquity present all around. An erudite letter from Canon Wigram, giving suggestions for the range of antiquities and classical references in the local area, indicates that at least some of his former colleagues remained in touch. Day trips to historical sites were frequent, especially for birthdays and anniversaries. On Father Ignatius' 25th birthday, for instance, a group set out to visit the archaeological dig at the citadel of Curium where Ward happily explored the underground passages beneath the ancient baths.[9] He and Father Peter climbed Mount Castra near Phasoula to examine the remains of a Roman fortress there.

The magpie instinct remained as strong as ever. In January 1947 Ward commenced a collection of matchbox labels, "as they may be of interest to future generations". He also noted his collection of postage stamps of the Middle East was growing steadily: Cyprus, Egypt, Palestine, Syria, Lebanon, Transordan, Saudi Arabia, Iraq, Rhodes, Turkey and Greece were all represented.[10] Photographs, postcards and press cuttings were pasted into his diary as mementoes of a life now in its final chapter. But some interests remained as fresh as ever. With a view to re-establishing his museum several new purchases were made, including glass-fronted cases in Limassol within a fortnight of their arrival at the farmhouse. On their first visit to the museum at Nicosia Ward bought some more items for the collection: two Roman flasks, a Phoenician pottery head, a red vessel and a Byzantine bowl. A later visit yielded another Byzantine bowl, a bronze age sword and an early iron age palette for £5 from a dealer. He also commenced an inventory of the several thousand surviving artefacts from his beloved Folk Park.

At the same time, however, his demeanour – at least insofar as we can reconstruct it from diary entries – was turning increasingly wistful and despondent. He began his autobiographical recollections on his sixty-second birthday, for instance, with the following: "I was born in Belize, British Honduras in Central America on Dec. 22nd 1885. What terrible changes have taken place, since I was born, in world affairs. My lifetime has seen the decline and fall of Europe and of her leadership in the world, particularly is this true of her loss of control in Asia."[11] He interpreted international developments with unrelieved pessimism, a major preoccupation being the rapid postwar unravelling of Britain's empire. On the day Peter and Mary were married, for example, he noted ruefully that Ireland had officially declared itself a republic outside the British Commonwealth. Another entry lamented the surrender of Burma to independence, and reading Kipling's *Kim* again he could not help but reflect on recent developments. "Kipling depicts the real life of India – Hindoo and Muslim – truthfully and lovingly as it was in the 1880–ies", he wrote, "a better and a happier India than the strife-torn

India of today bereft of the guiding and impartial hand of British officials, despite the empty pomp of [the] Dominion States."[12] The entry of 18 November 1948 gives us particular insight into his troubled mind, and the bitterness and sense of persecution that had taken root there:

> World Affairs. No progress in the Berlin dispute nor in Palestine. Ireland yesterday introduced into its Parliament (The Dail) its Bill severing the last link with the British Empire and proclaiming Eire an independent republic under the title of The Republic of Ireland. South Africa: Yesterday the S.A. prime minister hinted that his Govt. would convert the Dominion of S. Africa into an independant [sic] Republic. India: Here also the Prime Minister made it clear India would do likewise. Burma: Has already gone and is now 'enjoying' freedom from all stable Government in short civil war with Communists attacking the nominal Government on the one side and the Karen tribe likewise attacking it from the other . . . Thus the break-up of the British Empire goes on apace. Where will it end? I expect Parkistan [sic] and Ceylon will soon follow suit. Cyprus is anxious to be united to Greece and our south and central American Colonies, although loyal enough, are threatened with annexation by the Spanish-speaking Republics who are their neighbours. All this has come to pass since the Sister Terese Case in 1945 as foretold by the Master.[13]

Ward's poor health also continued to dog him, and doubtless contributed to this deteriorating state of mind. The stomach disorder contracted years earlier in Burma flared up and proved a persistent complaint. A second stroke during the latter months of 1948 was much more serious than the one he had endured at the time of the enticement case, and rendered him virtually an invalid. He began dictating autobiographical reflections to Sister Mary in daily sessions by his bedside or in the study. Her notes were annotated and corrected in Ward's scratchy handwriting before they were copied out by Mary, who decorated the margins with flowing emblems and illustrations.

One mid-summer afternoon, after several hours spent working on the autobiography, Father Ward retired for his usual afternoon nap. His diary entry suggests he was preoccupied by his health, international affairs and by the Confraternity's legacy:

SATURDAY July 2nd 1949
On this date in 1946 we first heard we should be able to sail together for Cyprus. I am a little better and able to sit at a table in my room but am still far from well, neither is the R[everend] M[other]. India: Chandanagore, a small French possession, has by a plebiscite voted to join India.

He seems to have suffered a stroke, his third in fewer than five years. When his wife came to call him for tea at 3.45, he was "still lying as if asleep, but his head and neck were purple, although his pulse beat slightly". She called the others into the room, and they massaged his chest and limbs while Ignatius sped in the car to collect a doctor. Ward died shortly before they returned, as Filius Domini read prayers. "His sudden passing was a tremendous blow to us all", Jessie Ward wrote in her husband's diary that evening, "and not least of all to me, but God knows best – His will be done!"[14] A service was held that night, and members of the Confraternity took turns to watch his body in vigil throughout the night.

He was buried in Limassol cemetery the following day. A requiem mass was celebrated in the morning, followed by the funeral service proper in the mid-afternoon. The church was crowded and the procession to St Nicholas cemetery nearby was solemn and impressive. The clergy led the mourners, preceded by a large crucifix held aloft, and followed by the hearse. Members of the Confraternity brought up the rear, chanting the Litany of the Saints as their tears flowed freely. In words that Ward would have appreciated far more deeply than the speaker could have imagined, Pappas Solomon Panagides hailed him as an Orthodox priest of equivalent standing to the priests of the Eastern Orthodox Church. "Not only this, however, he was more"; Pappas Solomon continued at the graveside, "he was leader of the Fraternity of the Orthodox Faith of the West", who had repeatedly proven his dedication and fidelity to the interests of the Orthodox faith in Cyprus. His words, according to Panagides' son who noted them down for the Confraternity, were an attempt "to give to the by-standers in their own tongue, and in a few words, an outline of the life and character of the Rev. Father J. Ward, and to pray for his soul." They were told

> that Father Ward was a learned man, and knew many things in archeology and in religion. He also stressed his great nobleness and kindness, and said how much those that had had the good fortune to know him loved him, because of his kind and noble character. As proof that everyone loved and respected him, he said, even those that knew him from afar through his great interest in attending the services of the Greek Orthodox Church, were very sorry and could not believe the news of his death.[15]

Father Ignatius, who stood with the others of the Confraternity by Ward's graveside, recorded that Pappas Solomon was at times overcome with emotion as he delivered the funeral oration. "No-one can set down in words", he wrote, "the emotional strain under which the preacher was labouring, time and again the words simply would not come, and when they did they came from his heart, and told of his very deep affection for our dear Rev. Father Superior, and his sorrow at his sudden call."

Under the heading 'Death of an English Orthodox Priest', the Limassol weekly newspaper *Papatiritys* carried a brief notice marking his passing. Ward's status as the "Superior of a Christian Brotherhood of the 'Orthodox of the West'" was emphasized. "Their dogma is entirely orthodox", readers were assured, "but they hold in practise many customs of the West." Although resident in Limassol for only three years, there was a genuine note of affection in the notice, which was most likely written by one of the Confraternity's Cypriot *confrères*. "Father Ward had [a] most encyclopaedic knowledge and had thoroughly mastered archaeology" it continued. "His residence is an entire museum, especially Christian. He was loved and honoured by as many as knew him, for his kindness and goodness."[16]

Several of the Confraternity returned to his grave with the Reverend Mother before dawn the following day, bringing oil, a wick and a small vessel to use as a lamp. Some charcoal was lit in a pottery censer Ward had bought when they first arrived in Cyprus. He had been told that these fragrant little pots were used to drive away the evil eye, and usually burnt cypress resin or olive leaves. "The lamp was placed in a little box", Jessie Ward wrote that night, "and is [to be] lighted at sundown; on the charcoal we placed olive leaves which had been in church during the 40 days of Lent, and censed the grave." The next day she sat down to continue the work of sorting and cataloguing that had been her late husband's lifelong passion. "Commenced sorting the Museum objects today", she wrote in his diary. "It is a hopeless task."[17]

✳ ✳ ✳

The years that followed were difficult for Ward's Confraternity. Father Filius Domini, the senior male member, was elected Archbishop as Ward's successor, but Reverend Mother Jessie Ward continued to act as the senior figure. Sister Bridget and Sister Bertha both passed away in 1951, it seems at least partly due to chronic malnutrition, while several children were born to the Cuffes and Strongs. As order deteriorated and with EOKA nationalist guerrillas increasingly targeting British nationals, it became clear they could remain in Cyprus no longer.

Departing the island in late 1954, the community arrived in Colombo in December from where Reverend Mother, Father Peter, Father Ignatius and Sister Gabrielle travelled to Mysore in India to investigate whether they might settle there with the help of the Maharajah, one of Ward's old Cambridge associates. After some indecision they pressed on to Sydney, Australia, where they arrived on 20 January 1955. For a time they lived at Bondi, while members took on secular occupations to keep the community afloat. In time a larger house was bought at Blackheath in the Blue Mountains to the west, where the Confraternity established a knitwear business. In mid-

1958, in recovery from a bout of pneumonia, Jessie Ward moved north to Redcliffe, a bay-side suburb of Brisbane in south-east Queensland, along with Sister Terese and two children, John Cuffe and Michael Strong. The others remained in Blackheath but planned to follow as soon as funds allowed a full re-location. Tragedy struck in January 1963 when the stomach ulcers that Sister Terese had suffered since the rupture with her family began to haemorrhage. She was admitted to Brisbane General Hospital in acute pain and died during the night of 22–23 January after refusing a blood transfusion on moral and religious grounds. The hospital and local newspaper were told that her name was Mrs Lillian Knight, a widow from England with no children and no relatives in Australia.[18] She was buried in Redcliffe Cemetery under that name.

On 4 February 1965 Jessie Ward also passed away suddenly in her sleep during a visit to Blackheath. With Ward's community now led by Sister Mary and Father Peter (after Archbishop Chamberlain's death in 1964), a parcel of land was purchased just north of Redcliffe, near the rural town of Caboolture, as the site for a permanent Abbey. Most of the remaining members moved north to re-establish the community during 1965, with new buildings, livestock and crops to enable self-sufficiency. What remained of Ward's collection of antiquities came with them, boxed up and still only partly catalogued, although individual items were sold from time to time to raise income, including a set of rare Japanese prints and an illuminated Book of Hours bought by the State Library of New South Wales. A new Abbey Church was built and consecrated at Caboolture on 9 September 1967, replete with Ward's magnificent stained glass that had been faithfully carried around the world.

In time, as the younger members of the Confraternity grew to adulthood, the Abbey evolved towards its present character as a spiritual community in the Christian tradition that largely eschews narrow dogma. A small independent primary school, St Michael's College, was established in fidelity to the educational work of Ward's original Confraternity, and plans were aired to re-establish his museum. A committee was established, chaired by Michael Strong, and set about raising donations to build galleries to house the 5,000 items that remained of John Ward's collection. After nearly a million dollars was secured the new Abbey Museum of Art and Archaeology was built, opened by Sir Gordon Chalk in 1986. Today it continues to grow and prosper, a sophisticated local attraction that hosts Australia's largest medieval re-enactment tournament and festival.[19]

✳   ✳   ✳

In J. S. M. Ward we find, indisputably, a man of many parts. A historian with a strong sense of the romantic, a visionary with heightened spiritual sensibilities, he was a questing soul, curious until his last days about the human past, how we might comprehend its mysteries, and the life beckoning beyond that of everyday sense experience. Not all will be convinced by his claims for mystical insight, of course, gained as they were through transcendent experiences that resist objective verification. But we can certainly admire the remarkable edifice Ward built upon them, and the courage of his convictions displayed in a career marked, to a greater extent than most, by eccentric turns that invited the slings and arrows of outrageous fortune. At the Abbey Museum of Art and Archaeology, at the end of a quiet country road and shaded by Australian eucalypts, his legacy shines most strongly in the patient labours of those who continue to honour his name.

Notes

Preface

1 Francis King, *Ritual Magic in England: 1887 to the present day* (London: Neville Spearman, 1970), p. 179.

2 Peter Anson, *Bishops at Large* (London: Faber & Faber, 1964), pp. 282–90.

3 Philip Heselton, *Gerald Gardner and the Cauldron of Inspiration* (Milverton: Capell Bann, 2003), pp. 135–54; and Joanne Pearson, *Wicca and the Christian Heritage: Ritual, Sex and Magic* (London: Routledge, 2007), pp. 48–50.

4 Antony Baker, "The Scholar the Builders Rejected – the Life & Work of J. S. M. Ward", *Ars Quatuor Coronatorum* 116 (2004): 127–92.

5 William James, *The Varieties of Religious Experience* (New York: Triumph Books, 1991 [1902]), pp. 24–5

1 Recollecting the Child

1 *The Cambridge History of the British Empire* (Volume II: The Growth of the Empire 1783–1870), (Cambridge: Cambridge University Press, 1940), p. 741.

2 J. S. M. Ward, "Autobiography, vol. 3, 1896–7, Chapter 11, Religious Envirement" [*sic*], f. 2; ms. copy held in Abbey Museum of Art and Archaeology Library (AMAA).

3 Ward, "Autobiography, vol. 2, 1896–7, Chapter 8, Parks and Exhibitions", f. 35.

4 Ward, "Autobiography, vol. 2, 1896–7", f. 36.

5 Ward, "Autobiography, vol. 2, 1896–7, Chapter 7, Other Amusements", f. 5.

6 Ward, "Autobiography, vol. 2, 1896–7, Chapter 8, Parks and Exhibitions", f. 55.

7 Ward, "Autobiography, vol. 2, 1896–7", f. 68.

8 Ward, "Autobiography, vol. 2, 1896–7", f. 60.

9 Ward, "Autobiography, vol. 2, 1896–7, Chapter 9, The Earls Court Exhibitions", ff. 71–2.

10 John M. Mackenzie, *Propaganda and Empire: the manipulation of British public opinion, 1880–1960* (Manchester: Manchester University Press, 1984), p. 102.

11 Ward, "Autobiography, vol. 2, 1896–7, Chapter 9, The Earls Court Exhibitions", f. 77.

12 Ward, "Autobiography, vol. 2, 1896–7", f. 76.

13 London Exhibitions Limited, *Official Guide: Empire of India Exhibition, 1895. Earls Court London* (pamphlet), p. 13.

14 Ward, "Autobiography, vol. 2, 1896–7, Chapter 9, The Earls Court Exhibitions", ff. 89–90.

15 Ward, "Autobiography vol. 2, 1896–7", ff. 95–6.

16 London Exhibitions Limited, *Report of the Empire of India Exhibition, 1895* (London, 1895), p. 8; British Library India Office collection: L/E/7/368.

17 Ward, "Autobiography, vol. 2, 1896–7, Chapter 10, Various Exhibitions", f. 100.

18 Ward, "Autobiography, vol. 2, 1896–7", f. 100.

19 London Exhibitions Limited, *Report of the Empire of India Exhibition, 1895* (London, 1895), p. 11.

20 London Exhibitions Limited, *Official Guide: Empire of India Exhibition, 1895,* p. 16.

21 Ward, "Autobiography, vol. 2, 1896–7, Chapter 10, Various Exhibitions", f. 105.

22 Ward, "Autobiography, vol. 2, 1896–7", ff. 105–06. Ward's description of the Indian Village is at ff. 100–15.

23 Ward, "Autobiography, vol. 4, 1898–9, Chapter 18, Back at Dr Wells' House", ff. 40–1.

24 Ward, "Autobiography, vol. 3, 1896–7, Chapter 15, The Vicarage", ff. 130–1.

25 Ward, "Autobiography, vol. 4, 1898–9, Chapter 16, More About Wath Vicarage", ff. 9–16.

26 Ward, "Autobiography, vol. 3, 1896–7", f. 139.

27 Ward, "Autobiography, vol. 4, 1898–9, Chapter 18, Back at Dr Wells' House", ff. 47–9.

28 Ward, "Autobiography, vol. 2, 1896–7, Chapter 10, Various Exhibitions", ff. 132–3.

29 Ward, "Autobiography, vol. 6, 1900, Chapter 39, The Death of Victoria", ff. 44–5.

30 Ward, "Autobiography, vol. 3, 1896–7, Chapter 11, Religious Envirement" [*sic*], ff. 34–5.

31 J. S. M. Ward, *The Psychic Powers of Christ* (London, Williams & Norgate, 1936), p. 7.

32 Ward, "Autobiography, vol. 3, 1896–7, Chapter 13, Colet Court School", f. 96.

33 Ward, "Autobiography, vol. 6, 1900, Chapter 41, More Archaeological Discoveries", f. 69.

34 Ward, "Autobiography, vol. 6, 1900, Chapter 40, The Archaeology of London", ff. 51–2. Ward was not alone in this interest. One antiquarian wrote during World War I that a "recent proposal to pull [Cloth Fair] down and widen the thoroughfares [was] opposed on account of the interest

attaching to the street, being one of the oldest left in the city and retaining an appearance of antiquity". Henry Harben, *A Dictionary of London* (London: Herbert Jenkins, 1918), p. 154.

35 Sir John Betjeman, *Sir John Betjeman's Guide to English Parish Churches* (Nigel Kerr, ed.) (London: HarperCollins, 1993), p. 358. Pevsner considered St Bartholomew-the-Great as "the most important C12 monument in London"; Simon Bradley and Nikolaus Pevsner, *London: the City Churches* (London: Penguin Books, 1998), p. 62.

36 Royal Commission on Historical Monuments (England), *An Inventory of the Historical Monuments in London* (Volume IV: The City) (London: H. M. S. O., 1928), p. 123.

37 Ward, "Autobiography, vol. 6, 1900, Chapter 40, The Archaeology of London", ff. 63–4.

2 History, Marriage and the Afterlife

1 Christopher N. L. Brooke, *A History of the University of Cambridge* (Volume 4: 1870–1990) (Cambridge: Cambridge University Press, 1993), p. 61.

2 Charles Crawley, *Trinity Hall: The history of a Cambridge college 1350–1975* (Cambridge: Trinity Hall, 1976), pp. 144–83 (where Ward's "wayward" career is briefly outlined, based on Anson, on p. 179); Brooke, *A History of the University of Cambridge*, vol. 4, p. 63.

3 C. W. Previté-Orton (comp.), *Index to Tripos Lists 1748–1910, contained in the Historical Register of the University of Cambridge to the year 1910* (Cambridge: Cambridge University Press, 1923), p. 288.

4 P. R. H. Slee, *Learning and a Liberal Education: The Study of Modern History in the Universities of Oxford, Cambridge and Manchester, 1800–1914* (Manchester: Manchester University Press, 1986), pp. 135–141.

5 Trinity Hall Tutorial Records, University of Cambridge: C.109, n.p.

6 Trinity Hall Tutorial Records, C.109, n.p.

7 Maurice Powicke, "Three Cambridge Scholars: C. W. Previté-Orton, Z. N. Brooke and G. G. Coulton", *Cambridge Historical Journal* 9, 1 (1947), pp. 106–7. Previté-Orton edited the *Cambridge Medieval History* and (between 1926 and 1938) the *English Historical Review*. His published works included *Political Satire in English Poetry* (1910), *The Early History of the House of Savoy* (1912) and a foundational textbook *A History of Europe, 1198–1378* (1937 and later editions).

8 Antony Baker, "The Scholar the Builders Rejected – The Life & Work of J. S. M. Ward", *Ars Quatuor Coronatorum* 116 (2004), p. 186. The poem was one of five "Epistyles in Terza Rima" included in a volume of poems composed in 1902–6, held in St John's College Library, Cambridge.

9 Trinity Hall Examinations and Miscellania, 1903–1910: C.86, p. 152 and p. 122: "Examinations and Prizes, Trinity Hall, June, 1906".

10 J. S. M. Ward, *Freemasonry and the Ancient Gods* (second edition) (London:

Simpkin, Marshall, Hamilton, Kent & Co, 1926), "Preface to First Edition", p. v.

11 Isaac Newton University Lodge, "A Hundred Years of the Isaac Newton University Lodge, 1861–1961" (Cambridge, 1961), p. 10.

12 Baker, "The Scholar the Builders Rejected", p. 130. See also J. S. M. Ward, "Diary, vol. 5, October 1947–December 1947", autobiographical notes of 31 December 1947; ms. copy held in Abbey Museum of Art and Archaeology Library (AMAA).

13 Tim Dedopolus, *The Brotherhood: inside the secret world of the Freemasons* (Melbourne: Viking, 2006), p. 8.

14 Peter Clark, *British Clubs and Societies 1580–1800: The Origins of an Associational World* (Oxford: Clarendon Press, 2000), p. 311.

15 Colin Dyer, *Symbolism in Craft Freemasonry* (Hersham: Lewis Masonic, 2003), p. 13.

16 J. M. Roberts, *The Mythology of the Secret Societies* (London: Secker & Warburg, 1972), p. 21.

17 Clark, *British Clubs and Societies*, p. 311.

18 Jessica Harland-Jacobs, *Builders of Empire: Freemasons and British Imperialism, 1717–1927* (Chapel Hill: University of North Carolina Press, 2007), p. 283. See also Stephen C. Bullock, *Revolutionary Brotherhood: Freemasonry and the Transformation of the American Social Order, 1730–1840* (Chapel Hill: University of North Carolina Press, 1996) and Margaret Jacob, *Living the Enlightenment: Freemasonry and Politics in Eighteenth-Century Europe* (Oxford: Oxford University Press, 1991).

19 Roberts, *The Mythology of the Secret Societies*, p. 21.

20 Ronald Hyam, *Britain's Imperial Century, 1815–1914* (third edition) (Basingstoke: Palgrave Macmillan, 2002), p. 300.

21 Hyam, *Britain's Imperial Century*, pp. 298–99.

22 Harland-Jacobs, *Builders of Empire*, p. 284.

23 Joscelyn Godwin, *The Theosophical Enlightenment* (Albany: State University of New York Press, 1994), p. xii.

24 Joanne Pearson, *Wicca and the Christian Heritage: Ritual, Sex and Magic* (London: Routledge, 2007), p. 62.

25 James Webb, *The Occult Establishment* (La Salle: Library Press, 1976), p. 8. See also his *The Occult Underground* (La Salle: Open Court, 1974).

26 Webb, *The Occult Establishment*, pp. 9–10.

27 See Philip Almond, *The British Discovery of Buddhism* (Cambridge: Cambridge University Press, 1988).

28 James Lewis, 'Introduction' to his *Witchcraft Today: An Encyclopedia of Wiccan and Neopagan Traditions* (Santa Barbara: ABC-CLIO, 1999), p. xvii.

29 In fact the two prejudices were closely linked: see David Hilliard, "UnEnglish and Unmanly: Anglo-Catholicism and Homosexuality", *Victorian Studies* 25, 2 (1982): 181–210.

30 W. W. Westcott, *History of the Societas Rosicruciana in Anglia* (1900), cited in

R. A. Gilbert, "William Wynn Westcott and the Esoteric School of Masonic Research", *Ars Quatuor Coronatorum* 100 (1987), p. 10.

31 Cited in Gilbert, "William Wynn Westcott and the Esoteric School of Masonic Research", p. 12.

32 William Wynn Westcott, "A Further Glance at the Kabbalah" (1893), cited in Owen, *The Place of Enchantment: British Occultism and the Culture of the Modern* (Chicago: University of Chicago Press, 2004), p. 54.

33 Considered a founding figure of British automotive and aeronautical engineering, Frederick Lanchester was later elected a Fellow of the Royal Society; his papers are deposited at the Lanchester Library, Coventry University.

34 J. S. M. Ward, *Outline Notes on English History* (Redhill: W. A. Bell, 1910), p. vi.

35 Muriel Clayton, "Prefatory Note", *Catalogue of Rubbings of Brasses and Incised Slabs* (second edition) (London: Victoria & Albert Museum, 1929), n.p.

36 J. S. M. Ward, *Brasses* (Cambridge: Cambridge University Press, 1912), p. v.

37 J. S. M. Ward, *Gone West: Three Narratives of After-Death Experience* (London: William Rider & Son, 1917), pp. 1–2. A brief obituary for Henry Lanchester appeared in *The Times*, 7 January 1914, p. 9.

38 J. S. M. Ward, *A Subaltern in Spirit Land* (London: William Rider & Son, 1920), p. viii.

39 Ward, *Gone West*, p. 20.

40 Ward, *Gone West*, p. 2. This account is, of course, likely to have been edited and embellished by Ward prior to publication.

41 Ward, *Gone West*, p. 60.

42 Ward, *Gone West*, p. 17.

43 Ward, *Gone West*, p. 43.

44 Ward, *Gone West*, p. 142.

45 Ward, *Gone West*, p. viii. The "living person" was presumably Carrie.

46 Arthur Conan Doyle, *The New Revelation* (London: Hodder & Stoughton), pp. 65–6.

47 Ward, *Gone West*, p. xv.

48 Peter Anson, *Bishops at Large* (London: Faber & Faber, 1964), p. 283; cited in Baker, "The Scholar the Builders Rejected", p. 129.

49 J. S. M. Ward, *The Kingdom of the Wise, Life's Problems* (London: The Baskerville Press, 1929), p. 138.

3 To the East

1 J. S. M. Ward, "Some Masonic Experiences in India", *The Masonic Record* 1,4 (March 1921), p. 149.

2 R. Talbot Kelly, *Burma* (London: Charles Black, 1905), p. 2.

3 Talbot Kelly, *Burma*, p. 3.

4 J. S. M. Ward, *Fairy Tales and Legends of Burma* (Bombay: Blackie & Son, 1916), p. 6.

5 J. S. M. Ward, *Poems of the Empire* (London: John Marlowe, Savage & Co., n.d. [*c.*1924]), p. 9.

6 J. S. M. Ward, "Diary, vol. 5, October 1947–December 1947", entry of Tuesday 28 October 1947, f. 9; ms. copy held in Abbey Museum of Art and Archaeology Library (AMAA).

7 Ward, "Diary, vol. 5", autobiographical notes of 19 October 1947, f. 10.

8 Talbot Kelly, *Burma*, p. 6.

9 Talbot Kelly, *Burma*, pp. 23–6.

10 Ward, "Diary, vol. 5", autobiographical notes of 19 October 1947, f. 7.

11 My thanks to Emma Martin, Curator of Asian Collections at National Museums Liverpool for her detailed explanation of items in the museum's collection sourced from Ward's period in Burma.

12 Ward, "Diary, vol. 5", autobiographical notes of 26 October 1947, ff. 24–5.

13 Ward, "Diary, vol. 5", autobiographical notes of 26 October 1947.

14 Ward, "Diary, vol. 5", autobiographical notes of 19 October 1947, ff. 4–5.

15 Ward, *Fairy Tales and Legends of Burma*, p. 5.

16 Ward, *Fairy Tales and Legends of Burma*, p. 5.

17 Ward, *Fairy Tales and Legends of Burma*, pp. 150–6.

18 Ward, *Fairy Tales and Legends of Burma,* p. 157.

19 "Address delivered by Wor. Bro. Lt. Col. T. L. Ormiston . . . on Monday 29 July 1918", in *Reports of Proceedings of District Grand Lodge, Burma* (1904–1915), Library and Museum of Freemasonry, London, Appendix E, pp. 32–5; Clarke, F. C. P. C. (comp.), *Burma Masonic Diary 1899* (Maulmain: Maulmain Advertiser for District Grand Lodge, Burma), pp. 165–85. For the eighteenth-century globalisation of the Masonic network, including into India, see Jessica Harland-Jacobs, *Builders of Empire: Freemasons and British Imperialism, 1717–1927* (Chapel Hill: University of North Carolina Press, 2007), pp. 21–63.

20 Clarke, *Burma Masonic Diary 1899*, pp. 174–5.

21 Antony Baker, "The Scholar the Builders Rejected – The Life & Work of J. S. M. Ward", *Ars Quatuor Coranatorum* 116 (2004), p. 130.

22 District Grand Lodge, Burma, "Minutes of the Half-Yearly Meeting held . . . on 28 July 1915", in *Reports of Proceedings of District Grand Lodge, Burma* (1904–1915), Library and Museum of Freemasonry, London, pp. 1–2.

23 Ward, "Some Masonic Experiences in India", p. 149.

24 District Grand Lodge, Burma, "Minutes of a Regular Communication held . . . on Saturday 29 January 1916", in *Reports of Proceedings of District Grand Lodge, Burma* (1916–1933), Library and Museum of Freemasonry, London, pp. 3–4.

25 Ward, "Some Masonic Experiences in India", p. 148.

26 Ward, "Some Masonic Experiences in India", p. 150.

27 Harland-Jacobs, *Builders of Empire*, p. 15.

28 Harland-Jacobs, *Builders of Empire*, p. 230, pp. 237–9.

29 United Grand Lodge of England, "Report of the Deputation appointed by the M.W. Grand Master to visit the District Grand Lodges of India, Burma and Ceylon" (typescript, 1928), Library and Museum of Freemasonry, London, p. 4.

30 J. S. M. Ward, *Freemasonry, its aims and ideals* (London: William Rider & Son, 1923), pp. 146–7.

31 Ward, *Freemasonry, its aims and ideals*, p. 150.

32 Ward, "Diary, vol 5", autobiographical notes of 19 October 1947, f. 8.

33 Ward, *Freemasonry, its aims and ideals*, p. 152.

34 Ward, *Freemasonry, its aims and ideals*, p. 151.

35 Ward, *Freemasonry, its aims and ideals*, p. 151.

36 Cited in Harland-Jacobs, *Builders of Empire*, p. 238.

37 Ward, *Freemasonry, its aims and ideals*, pp. 154–5.

38 Ward, "Some Masonic Experiences in India", p. 148.

39 Ward, "Diary, vol. 5", autobiographical notes of 26 October 1947, f. 19.

40 Ward, "Diary, vol. 5", autobiographical notes of 26 October 1947, f. 21.

4 Gone West

1 J. S. M. Ward, "Diary, vol. 5, October 1947–December 1947", autobiographical notes of 18 November 1947, f. 56; ms. copy held at Abbey Museum of Art and Archaeology Library (AMAA).

2 Ward, "Diary, vol. 5", entry of 18 November 1947, f. 58.

3 J. S. M. Ward, "Introduction", *A Subaltern in Spirit Land* (London: William Rider & Son, 1920), p. vii.

4 Ward, *A Subaltern*, p. 1.

5 Geoffrey Nelson, *Spiritualism and Society* (London: Routledge & Kegan Paul, 1969), p. 155.

6 Nelson, *Spiritualism and Society*, pp. 155–6.

7 Modris Eksteins, *The Rites of Spring: The Great War and the Birth of the Modern Age* (London: Black Swan, 1990), p. 318.

8 Arthur Conan Doyle, *The New Revelation* (London: Hodder & Stoughton, 1918), pp. 48–9.

9 Ward, "Introduction", *A Subaltern*, p. ix.

10 J. S. M. Ward, *Gone West: Three Narratives of After-Death Experiences* (London: William Rider & Son, 1917), pp. 2–3.

11 Ward, *Gone West*, p. 8.

12 Ward, *Gone West*, p. xv.

13 J. M. Winter, "Spiritualism and the First World War" in R. W. Davis and R. J. Helmstadter (eds.), *Religion and Irreligion in Victorian Society: Essays in Honor of R. K. Webb* (London and New York: Routledge, 1992), p. 187.

14 Ward, *A Subaltern*, p. vii.

15 Winter, "Spiritualism and the First World War", p. 193. Winter specifically identifies Ward's books as "two examples among many", p. 199.

16 Ward, *A Subaltern*, pp. xi–xii.
17 Ward, "Dedication", *Gone West*, n.p.
18 Ward, *Gone West*, pp. vii–viii.
19 Ward, *Gone West*, p. viii–ix.
20 Ward, *A Subaltern*, p. viii.
21 Arthur Conan Doyle, *The Vital Message* (London: Hodder & Stoughton, 1919), p. 107.
22 Conan Doyle, *The New Revelation*, p. 16.
23 Winter, "Spiritualism and the First World War", p. 189.
24 Winter, "Spiritualism and the First World War", p. 188.
25 Conan Doyle, *The New Revelation*, pp. 66–7.
26 Oliver J. Lodge, *Raymond, or Life and Death* (London: Methuen & Co., 1917), p. 83.
27 Conan Doyle, *The New Revelation*, p. 88.
28 Lodge, *Raymond*, p. 194.
29 Ward, *Gone West*, p. 2.
30 Ward, *A Subaltern*, p. 1.
31 Conan Doyle, *The Vital Message*, p. 75.
32 Conan Doyle, *The Vital Message*, p. 80.
33 Cited in Renée Haynes, *The Society for Psychical Research 1882–1982: A History* (London: Macdonald, 1982), p. 184.
34 Lodge, "Interaction of Mind and Matter", *Raymond*, p. 319.
35 Conan Doyle, *The New Revelation*, p. 85.
36 Ward, *Gone West*, p. 28.
37 Ward, *A Subaltern*, pp. 31–3.
38 Lodge, *Raymond*, p. 203.
39 Ward, *A Subaltern*, p. 49.
40 Conan Doyle, *The New Revelation*, p. 87.
41 Ward, *Gone West*, p. 29.
42 Conan Doyle, *The New Revelation*, pp. 74–5.
43 Lodge, *Raymond*, p. 231.
44 Ward, *Gone West*, pp. 77–8.
45 Ward, *A Subaltern*, pp. 57–8.
46 Lodge, *Raymond,* p. 184.
47 Conan Doyle, *The New Revelation*, p. 97.
48 Ward, *Gone West*, p. 121.
49 Conan Doyle, *The New Revelation*, pp. 97–8.
50 Conan Doyle, *The New Revelation*, p. 98.
51 Ward, *Gone West*, p. 120.
52 Lodge, *Raymond,* p. 375.
53 Conan Doyle, *The New Revelation*, pp. 129–30.
54 Lodge, *Raymond,* p. 394.
55 Lodge, *Raymond,* p. 376.
56 Ward, *Gone West*, p. 18.

57 Ward, "Diary, vol. 5", entry of 18 November 1947, f. 59.

58 Ward, "Diary, vol. 5", entry of 7 December 1947, ff. 109–10.

59 Ward, "Diary, vol. 5", entry of 6 December 1947, ff. 109–10.

60 Ward, "Diary, vol. 5", entry of 31 December 1947, f. 179.

5 Opening the Guarded Door

1 J. S. M. Ward, *Gone West: Three Narratives of After-Death Experiences* (London: William Rider & Son), 1917, p. 17.

2 Arthur Conan Doyle, *The New Revelation* (London: Hodder & Stoughton, 1918), p. 99.

3 Ward, *Gone West*, p. 18.

4 Ward, *Gone West*, pp. 18–9.

5 Ward, *Gone West*, pp. 34–9.

6 See the discussion of "anti-Christian" spiritualism in Janet Oppenheim, *The Other World: Spiritualism and Psychical Research in England, 1850–1914* (Cambridge: Cambridge University Press, 1985), pp. 85–100.

7 Frank Podmore, *Modern Spiritualism: A History and a Criticism* (2 vols.) (London: Methuen, 1902).

8 Conan Doyle, *The New Revelation*, p. 67.

9 Cited in Podmore, *Modern Spiritualism*, vol. 2, pp. 163–4.

10 Conan Doyle, *The New Revelation*, pp. 96–7.

11 Ward, *Gone West*, p. 88.

12 William Stainton Moses, *Spirit Teachings Through the Mediumship of William Stainton Moses* (London: London Spiritualist Alliance 1907 [1883]), p. 26.

13 Ward, *Gone West*, pp. 45–6, p. 60.

14 Ward, *Gone West*, p. 116.

15 Ward, *Gone West*, pp. 175–6.

16 Ward, *Gone West*, p. 83.

17 Conan Doyle, *The New Revelation*, pp. 90–1.

18 J. S. M. Ward, *A Subaltern in Spirit Land* (London: William Rider & Son, 1920), p. 83.

19 Ward, *Gone West*, pp. 114–5.

20 Ward, *Gone West*, pp. 111–2.

21 Ward, *Gone West*, pp. 112–3.

22 Ward, *Gone West*, pp. 127–8.

23 Conan Doyle, *The New Revelation*, pp. 99–100.

24 Cited in Kelvin Jones, *Conan Doyle and the Spirits: The Spiritualist Career of Sir Arthur Conan Doyle* (Wellingborough: Aquarian Press, 1989), p. 154; see also Chapter 7, "A Missionary Zeal".

25 J. S. M. Ward, *The Psychic Powers of Christ* (London: Williams & Norgate, 1936), "Prologue", pp. 11–2.

26 Ward, *The Psychic Powers of Christ*, "Prologue", p. 12.

27 J. S. M. Ward, *Life's Problems* (London: Baskerville Press, 1929), pp. 6–7.

28 Ward, *The Psychic Powers of Christ*, "Prologue", pp. 7–8.

29 Ward, *The Psychic Powers of Christ*, "Prologue", p. 8.

30 Ward, *The Psychic Powers of Christ*, "Prologue", p. 10.

31 Ward, *A Subaltern*, p. 310.

6 Explorations in the Craft

1 J. S. M. Ward, "Diary, vol. 5, October 1947–December 1947", autobiographical notes of 31 December 1947, f. 179; ms. copy held in Abbey Museum of Art and Archaeology Library (AMAA).

2 Modern Records Centre, University of Warwick: Confederation of British Industries, MSS 200/F/3/D1/4/11, "Organisation of the F. B. I.", memorandum dated 3 March 1925, p. 3.

3 *Encyclopædia Britannica* (thirteenth edition) (London, 1926), supplementary vol. I, pp. 885–6. My thanks to Tony Baker for this reference.

4 *Encyclopædia Britannica* (thirteenth edition) (London, 1926), supplementary vol. II, pp. 25–6; supplementary vol. III, pp. 548–9.

5 J. S. M. Ward and N. E. Crump, *Financial Review of 1919* (London: Federation of British Industries, n.d. [*c.*1920]), p. 19.

6 J. S. M. Ward and N. E. Crump, *Financial Review of 1920* (London: Federation of British Industries, n.d. [*c.*1921]), p. 22.

7 J. S. M. Ward, *Can Our Industrial System Survive?* (London: William Rider & Son, 1921), p. 5.

8 Ward, *Can Our Industrial System Survive?* pp. 78–80.

9 Ward, *Can Our Industrial System Survive?* pp. 80–1.

10 Ward, *Can Our Industrial System Survive?* pp. 5–6.

11 *Masonic Record* 1, 2 (January 1921), p. 95.

12 J. S. M. Ward, "Diary, vol. 5", autobiographical notes' composed 31 December 1947, f. 179.

13 *Encyclopædia Britannica* (thirteenth edition) (London, 1926), supplementary volume II, pp. 110–11. Fort Newton, another Masonic scholar, contributed an article on American Freemasonry to this edition.

14 "Masonic News of the Month, The Industries Lodge, No. 4100", *Masonic Record* 3, 32 (July 1923), p. i. Ward's abilities as a Masonic speech-maker later resulted in a booklet course providing advice to fellow Freemasons on public speaking.

15 J. S. M. Ward, *An Outline History of Freemasonry* (The Masonic Handbook Series: studies in the growth of our order, No. 4) (London: Baskerville Press, 1924), pp. ii–iii.

16 J. S. M. Ward, *Freemasonry and the Ancient Gods* (second edition) (London: Simpkin, Marshall, Hamilton, Kent & Co., 1926), preface to first edition, p. viii.

17 "Freemasonry and the Ancient Gods" (review), *Masonic Record* 1, 8 (1921), p. 358.

18 Ward, "Diary, vol. 5", autobiographical notes of 31 December 1947, f. 180.

19 *Masonic Record* 4, 38 (January 1924), n.p. (notice printed inside back cover).

20 J. S. M. Ward, "Freemasonry and the Ancient East", *Masonic Record* 1,1 (December 1920), p. 13.

21 J. S. M. Ward, *The Moral Teachings of Freemasonry; incorporating Masonic Proverbs, Poems and Sayings* (London: Baskerville Press, 1926), n.p. ("No. 56").

22 J. S. M. Ward, *Freemasonry, its aims and ideals* (London: William Rider & Son, 1923), pp. 63–4.

23 Ward, *Freemasonry and the Ancient Gods*, preface to first edition, p. vii.

24 Ward, *Freemasonry and the Ancient Gods*, preface to first edition, p. vii.

25 Ward, *An Outline History of Freemasonry*, p. ii.

26 Ward, 'Freemasonry and the Ancient East', p. 13.

27 J. S. M. Ward, "Freemasonry, The Heir of the Ancient Mysteries", *Occult Review* 37, 6 (June 1923), p. 354.

28 Ward, *An Outline History of Freemasonry*, p. 78.

29 Ward, *An Outline History of Freemasonry*, pp. 12–14.

30 J. S. M. Ward, *An Interpretation of our Masonic Symbols* (London: Baskerville Press, 1924), p. 156.

31 See the pioneering essays in Eric Hobsbawm and Terrence Ranger (eds), *The Invention of Tradition* (Cambridge: Cambridge University Press, 1983).

32 Ward, *An Interpretation of our Masonic Symbols*, p. 154.

33 Ward, *An Interpretation of our Masonic Symbols*, p. 158.

34 Ward, "What the Ancient Sign Language Teaches Us", *Masonic Record* 1, 3 (February 1921), p. 112.

35 Ward, "Freemasonry and the Ancient East", p. 16.

36 Ward, "What the Ancient Sign Language Teaches Us", p. 113.

37 Ward, *Freemasonry and the Ancient Gods*, preface to first edition, p. vi.

38 *Transactions of the Masonic Study Society* 15 (1936–7), pp. 668–9; statement by W. L. Wilmshurst.

39 Sir John Cockburn, "Introduction", in J. S. M. Ward, *The E.A.'s Handbook* (Shepparton: Lewis Masonic, 1988 [1923]), p. 7.

40 *Transactions of the Masonic Study Society* 1 (1921–22), p. 2.

41 *Transactions of the Masonic Study Society* 1 (1921–22), p. 6.

42 See the appendices in Antony Baker, "The Scholar the Builders Rejected – The Life & Work of J. S. M. Ward", *Ars Quatuor Coronatorum* 116 (2004), pp. 182–3.

43 "Masonic Study Society", *Masonic Record* 1, 11 (October 1921), p. 443.

44 *Transactions of the Masonic Study Society* 4 (1925–26), p. 20.

45 A. G. Stevens, *Cyclopedia of Fraternities* (1907), cited in Noel P. Gist, "Secret Societies: A Cultural Study of Fraternalism in the United States", *University of Missouri Studies* 15, 4 (1940), p. 71.

46 Rudyard Kipling, "The Man Who Would Be King", in *Wee Willie Winkie and other stories* (London: Macmillan, 1912), pp. 231–3.

47 Gist, "Secret Societies", pp. 70–1.

48 Gist, "Secret Societies", p. 72.

49 J. G. Frazer, quoted in Robert Temple, "Introduction" to J. G. Frazer, *The Illustrated Golden Bough: A Study in Magic and Religion* (R. Temple abr.) (Sydney: Simon & Schuster, 1996), p. 6.

50 Ronald Hutton, *The Triumph of the Moon: A History of Modern Pagan Witchcraft* (Oxford: Oxford University Press, 2001), p. 113. See also Gillian Bennett, "Geologists and Folklorists: Cultural Evolution and the Science of Folklore", *Folklore* 105 (1994): 25–37 and Henrika Kuklick, *The Savage Within: The Social History of British Anthropology 1885–1945* (Cambridge: Cambridge University Press, 1991).

51 Ward, "Freemasonry, The Heir of the Ancient Mysteries", p. 348.

52 Ward, "Freemasonry, The Heir of the Ancient Mysteries", p. 348.

53 Ward, *An Outline History of Freemasonry*, p. 17.

54 Ward, "Freemasonry, The Heir of the Ancient Mysteries", p. 348.

55 Ward, "Freemasonry, The Heir of the Ancient Mysteries", p. 346.

56 Ward, *An Interpretation of our Masonic Symbols*, p. 25.

57 Ward, *An Interpretation of our Masonic Symbols*, pp. vii–viii.

58 J. S. M. Ward, *The Sign Language of the Mysteries* (London: Baskerville Press, 1928), vol. I, p. i.

59 J. S. M. Ward, "All the Degrees in Freemasonry: A Summary of their Meaning", *Masonic Record* 2 (1921–22), p. 794.

60 Ward, "All the Degrees in Freemasonry", p. 794.

61 Ward, "Freemasonry, The Heir of the Ancient Mysteries", p. 346.

62 Ward, "Freemasonry, The Heir of the Ancient Mysteries", p. 350.

63 Ward, "Freemasonry, The Heir of the Ancient Mysteries", pp. 349–50.

64 Ward, *An Interpretation of our Masonic Symbols*, p. 138.

65 Ward, *An Interpretation of our Masonic Symbols*, pp. 138–40.

66 Ward, *An Interpretation of our Masonic Symbols*, pp. 140–1.

67 "A Masonic Student", "An Endeavour to Make a Daily Advancement in Masonic Knowledge", *Transactions of the Masonic Study Society* 5 (1926–27), p. 57.

68 As Tony Baker points out, reviews of Ward's publications could descend to sarcasm: one reviewer commented that Ward's book *Freemasonry, its aims and ideals* might perhaps have been subtitled "The Aims and Ideals of Bro. J. S. M. Ward." Baker, "The Scholar the Builders Rejected", p. 140.

69 J. Walter Hobbs, "The Antiquity of Freemasonry", *Ars Quatuor Coronatorum* 35 (1922), p. 90.

70 Hobbs, "The Antiquity of Freemasonry", p. 91.

71 Hobbs, "The Antiquity of Freemasonry", p. 90.

72 Hobbs, "The Antiquity of Freemasonry", p. 90.

73 Hobbs, "The Antiquity of Freemasonry", pp. 93, 98.

74 Baker, "The Scholar the Builders Rejected", p. 160.

75 Hobbs, "The Antiquity of Freemasonry", pp. 98–9.

76 Hobbs, "The Antiquity of Freemasonry", p. 99.

77 Colin Dyer, *The History of the First Hundred Years of Quatuor Coronati Lodge*

No. 2076 (London: QC Correspondence Circle, 1986), p. 31, cited in Baker, "The Scholar the Builders Rejected", p. 162.

78 Hobbs, "The Antiquity of Freemasonry", p. 100.

79 Hobbs, "The Antiquity of Freemasonry", pp. 101–2.

80 Hobbs, "The Antiquity of Freemasonry", p. 102.

81 Hobbs, "The Antiquity of Freemasonry", p. 112.

7 Kingdom of the Wise

1 J. S. M. Ward, "Diary, vol. 5, October 1947–December 1947", autobiographical notes of 18 November 1947, ff. 59–60; ms. copy held in Abbey Museum of Art and Archaeology Library (AMAA).

2 P. G. Strong, *John Ward: The Prophet of These Times* (pamphlet) (Orthodox Catholic Church of Australia, 1999), pp. 11, 17.

3 Ward, "Diary, vol. 5", autobiographical notes of 31 December 1947, f. 180.

4 Comment by R. A. Gilbert in Antony Baker, "The Scholar the Builders Rejected – the Life & Work of J. S. M. Ward", *Ars Quatour Coronatorum* 116 (2003), p. 190. Quotations are from Waite's diary.

5 "Life After Death", in J. S. M. Ward, *Life's Problems* (London: Baskerville Press, 1929), pp. 138–9.

6 Strong, *John Ward: The Prophet of These Times*, p. 18. This testimony encapsulates the explanation that was later provided to the members of Ward's Confraternity.

7 Strong, *John Ward: The Prophet of These Times*, p. 18.

8 Strong, *John Ward: The Prophet of These Times*, pp. 18–9.

9 *The Confraternity of the Kingdom of Christ. What it stands for and how it came into existence* (pamphlet, n.d), p. 15; cited in Peter Anson, *Bishops at Large* (London: Faber & Faber, 1964), p. 283.

10 *The Confraternity . . . What it stands for*, p. 15. See also Lambeth Palace Library, Lang Papers: Vol. 131, 1935, A1–C4, f. 3.

11 *The Confraternity of the Kingdom of Christ, Its Message to the Nation and to the Individual* (pamphlet) (London: W.H Rickinson & Son, 1934), pp. 6–7.

12 E. Arbman and J. H. Austin, cited in David M. Wulff, "Mystical Experience", in Etzel Cardeña, Steven Jay Lynn and Stanley Krippner (eds), *Varieties of Anomalous Experience: Examining the Scientific Evidence* (Washington: American Psychological Association, 2000), p. 412.

13 William James, *The Varieties of Religious Experience* (New York: Triumph Books, 1991[1902]), pp. 294–5.

14 From H. F. Brown, *J. A. Symonds, A Biography* (London, 1895), pp. 29–31, abridged and cited in James, *The Varieties of Religious Experience*, p. 296.

15 Christopher Armstrong, *Evelyn Underhill: An Introduction to her Life and Writings* (Oxford: Mowbray, 1975), p. 109.

16 E. Underhill, *Mysticism: A Study in the Nature and Development of Man's Spiritual Consciousness* (New York: Meridian Books 1955 [1911]), p. 51. John Ruysbroek's "De Septum Gradibus Amoris" is cited in this quotation.

17 Underhill, *Mysticism*, p. 54.

18 Underhill, *Mysticism*, p. 55.

19 See Ward's comment on W. L. Wilmshurst, "The Fundamental Philosophic Secrets within Masonry", *Transactions of the Masonic Study Society* 4 (1925–6), p. 20.

20 Ward, *Life's Problems*, pp. 6–7.

21 Ward, *Life's Problems*, pp. 12–13, 2.

22 Ward, *Life's Problems*, p. 37.

23 *Hymns of the Church of Christ the King* (Margate: Herald Press, n.d.), Hymns 6 and 79. This hymnal of Ward's Confraternity of the Kingdom of Christ is known to members of the church as "The Black Book." In a typed commentary held at the Abbey Museum of Art and Archaeology Library, Father Peter Strong has identified those originally composed by Ward and those of a later date.

24 Ward *Life's Problems*, pp. 12–13.

25 Ward, *Life's Problems*, p. 35.

26 Ward, *Life's Problems*, p. 46.

27 Ward, *Life's Problems*, p. 13.

28 Ward, *Life's Problems*, p. 14.

29 Ward, *Life's Problems*, pp. 14–15.

30 Ward, *Life's Problems*, p. 16.

31 Ward, *Life's Problems*, p. 14.

32 Ward, *Life's Problems*, pp. 24–5.

33 Ward, *Life's Problems*, p. 40.

34 Ward, *Life's Problems*, p. 41.

35 Ward, *Life's Problems*, p. 45.

36 Strong, *John Ward: The Prophet of these Times*, p. 19.

37 Ward, "Diary, vol. 5", autobiographical notes of 31 December 1947, f. 181.

38 Ward, "Diary, vol. 5", autobiographical notes of 31 December 1947, f. 181.

39 Ward, "Introduction", *Life's Problems*, n.p.

40 "Law Report, 4 May: High Court of Justice, King's Bench Division", *The Times*, 5 May 1945.

41 Anson, *Bishops at Large*, p. 284.

42 Interview with Peter Strong, Wolvi, 25 April 2004.

43 J. Webster Kirkham, "Memories of a Loved Brother" [no further reference details], provided by Gillian Gear, Barnet Museum and Hertfordshire Association for Local History, November 2005.

44 AMAA Photograph Collection: 1 WD 2/6, Hadley Hall interior, undated [*c.* early 1930s].

45 "Law Report, 3 May: High Court of Justice, King's Bench Division", *The Times*, 4 May 1945; "Abbey Diary of Sister Terese", *Daily Express*, 4 May 1945.

46 Strong, *John Ward: The Prophet of these Times*, pp. 4–5.

47 "The Common Life in New Barnet: An 'Abbey' Organised on Primitive

Lines" unsourced newspaper clipping (*c.* October 1934), "Book of Centuries" (clippings books), vol. 1, AMAA.

48 Strong, *John Ward: The Prophet of these Times*, p. 3.

49 Lambeth Palace Library, Lang Papers: Vol. 131, 1935, A1–C4, f. 3.

50 Hertfordshire Archives and Local Studies Library (HALSL): DSA1/14/5, Act Books, 1923–1939, f. 170.

51 Cited in Anson, *Bishops at Large*, p. 285 note 2.

52 HALSL: New Barnet Parish Records, D/P15C 8/3, Vestry and Parochial Church Council Minutes, November 1930–January 1935, f. 37, Meeting of the Summer Sales Committee, 14 April 1931.

53 HALSL: New Barnet Parish Records, D/P15C 8/3, ff. 22–23, Annual Parochial Church Council meeting, Tuesday 27 January 1931. The "Free Will Offering Scheme" was a subscription contribution to parochial church funds that raised approximately £250 during 1931–2.

54 HALSL: New Barnet Parish Records, D/P15C 8/3, f. 57, Annual Report of the Parochial Church Council for 1931. The hangings were previously described as donated "for the East End of the [new] Chancel", f. 38.

55 HALSL: New Barnet Parish Records, D/P15C 8/3, f. 66, Minutes of the Annual Parochial Church Meeting of 10 January 1932.

56 HALSL: New Barnet Parish Records, D/P15C 8/3, f. 55, Minutes of the meeting of the Parochial Church Council, 12 January 1932.

57 "The Abbey of Christ the King", *Barnet Press*, 14 July 1934.

58 "Abbey Folk Park", *Yorkshire Herald*, 25 July 1934.

59 Interview at Wolvi, 25 April 2004.

60 "Hadley Hall Chapel", ms held by Barnet Museum, Barnet and District Historical Society. My thanks to Antony Baker for this reference.

61 "Hadley Hall Chapel", n.p.

62 AMAA Photograph Collection: 10 WA 1/1–53.

63 "Hadley Hall Chapel", n.p.

64 "Hadley Hall Chapel", n.p.

65 E. V. Lucas, "A Wanderer's Note Book: an Educational Abbey", *Sunday Times*, 9 September 1934.

66 "Hadley Hall Chapel", n.p.

67 Anson, *Bishops at Large*, p. 285.

68 "The Common Life in New Barnet", n.p.

69 "Hadley Hall Chapel", n.p.

70 Carol Coward, "A Woodcarver at Work on Christ the King", *The Catholic Fireside*, 15 August 1941, p. 105.

71 Confraternity of the Kingdom of Christ, *Message to the Nation and to the Individual* (pamphlet, 1934), p. 9.

72 Confraternity of the Kingdom of Christ, *Message to the Nation and to the Individual*, p. 1.

73 Confraternity of the Kingdom of Christ, *Message to the Nation and to the Individual*, p. 1.

74 Confraternity of the Kingdom of Christ, *Message to the Nation and to the Individual*, p. 7.

75 Ward, *Life's Problems*, p. 11.

8 An Ark for England

1 Abbey Museum of Art and Archaeology Library (AMAA): ms. receipt from Fenton and Sons Ltd, made out to J. S. M. Ward and dated 15 May 1933.

2 The illustrated guide *Unexpected Treasures: Highlights from the Abbey Museum* (Caboolture: Abbey Museum of Art and Archaeology, 2006) provides the most accessible summary of items remaining from Ward's collection, as well as more recent purchases and donations to the Museum. Typescript notes for a catalogue-style publication titled "A Mirror of the Passing World", evidently produced by Ward in the 1930s, are held in the Abbey Museum Library and provide fair detail on the artefacts assembled in his collection to that time.

3 "Prehistoric Man at Home", *Daily Telegraph*, 9 July 1934.

4 "A Unique Exhibition: A Wonderful Collection at New Barnet", *Barnet Press*, 30 June 1934.

5 "A Unique Exhibition", *Barnet Press*, 30 June 1934.

6 "A Unique Exhibition", *Barnet Press*, 30 June 1934.

7 "A Unique Exhibition", *Barnet Press*, 30 June 1934.

8 *The Times*, 6 July 1934.

9 "Prehistoric Man at Home", *Daily Telegraph*, 9 July 1934.

10 *The Times*, 23 August 1934.

11 "Prehistoric Man at Home", *Daily Telegraph*, 9 July 1934; "The Dwellings of Our Ancestors: Replicas of Prehistoric British Huts", *Illustrated London News*, 23 June 1934. See also "London 2,000 Years Before Christ", *Weekly Illustrated*, 18 August 1934.

12 "Councillors at the Abbey Folk Park", *Barnet Press*, 21 July 1934.

13 "Abbey Folk Park", *Yorkshire Herald*, 25 July 1934.

14 Geoffrey A. C. Ginn, "An Ark for England: Esoteric heritage at J. S. M. Ward's Abbey Folk Park, 1934–1940", *Journal of the History of Collections* 22, 1 (2010): 129–40 is to date the only major historical treatment of Ward's museum; see also Michael Strong, "John Ward: custodian of the past", *Australian Collectors Quarterly* (November–January 1991): 73–6.

15 For nineteenth-century visual spectacle and commercial entertainment, see Richard Altick, *The Shows of London* (Cambridge, MA: Harvard University Press, 1978).

16 "An Educational Abbey", *Sunday Times*, 9 September 1934.

17 See Raphael Samuel, *Theatres of Memory, Vol. 1: Past and Present in Contemporary Culture* (London: Verso, 1994), pp. 175–82; for the implications of interwar suburban expansion, see Alun Howkins, *The Death of Rural England: A Social History of the Countryside Since 1900* (London: Routledge, 2003), pp. 95–111.

18 "A Unique Exhibition: A Wonderful Collection at New Barnet", *Barnet Press*, 30 June 1934.

19 J. S. M. Ward, "Foreword", in his "A Mirror of the Passing World" (undated typescript catalogue), AMAA.

20 "Wonderful Out-of-Doors Museum", *Children's Newspaper*, 1 September 1934.

21 "Plea for Open-Air Museum", *Daily Telegraph*, 7 July 1934.

22 National Archives, Kew: PRO EB3/11, "Folk Museums", clipping from Hansard, 28 February 1938. The deliberations of the Board of Education committee remain obscure; the Hansard extract suggests that "in view of the financial situation then existing, the committee were of the opinion that no useful purpose would be served by proceeding with their reference, and no report was therefore submitted".

23 H. Balfour, "A National Folk-Museum", *The Times*, 3 January 1912, cited in Chris Wingfield, "From Greater Britain to Little England: The Pitt Rivers Museum, the Museum of English Rural life and their six degrees of separation", *Museum History Journal* 4, 2 (2011): 252. My thanks to Chris Wingfield for access to this article prior to publication.

24 National Archives, Kew: PRO EB3/11, "Folk Museums", typescript letter received from L. T. Davies of Rockfield Park, Monmouth, dated 2 May 1937, p. 5.

25 National Archives, Kew: PRO EB3/11, "Folk Museums", F. Bray (Under-Secretary, Ministry of Education), "Report of the Minister of Education on the Leicester Corporation Bill, 1955: Part XVII – Cultural Activities: Clause 251 – 'Power to provide Folk Museum'", 14 April 1955, p. 1. It was concluded that "the Minister does not think it would be a serious breach of the principle of a free public museum service if the Corporation were allowed to make a charge for admission to what, they claim is, a new and costly type of museum and therefore he does not wish to object to this clause" (p. 2).

26 "Councillors at the Abbey Folk Park", *Barnet Press*, 21 July 1934. For the 1929 Royal Commission, see House of Commons Parliamentary Papers, 1928–29 [Cmd. 3192] *Royal Commission on National Museums & Galleries: Interim Report*; [Cmd.3401] *Final Report Part 1* and [Cmd.3463] *Final Report Part 2* (London: H. M. S. O.).

27 "An English Folk Park", *Country Life*, 15 December 1934.

28 "Prehistoric Man at Home", *Daily Telegraph*, 9 July 1934.

29 Bridget Yates, "'Treasuring Things of the Least': Village Museums in the 1920s and 1930s", unpublished conference paper, November 2009. My thanks to Bridget Yates for providing a copy of this paper.

30 Peter C. D. Brears, "Kirk of the Castle", *Museums Journal* 80, 2 (1980): 90–2. The York Museums Trust holds the Kirk Archive; the finding aids for which include a summary of Kirk's life and work, "An Introduction to Dr Kirk" (5 pp. typescript).

31 "Councillors at the Abbey Folk Park", *Barnet Press*, 21 July 1934.

32 "Open-Air Museums", *New Statesman*, 24 June 1936.

33 "The Abbey Folk Park", *Women's Employment*, 3 July 1936.

34 Ward, "Foreword", in his "A Mirror of the Passing World", n.p.

35 Sheldon Annis suggests museums are at once a social space, a cognitive space and a "dream space"(see Gaynor Kavanagh, "Making histories, making memories" in Gaynor Kavanagh (ed.), *Making Histories in Museums* (Leicester: Leicester University Press, 1996), pp. 3–4). Ward's Abbey Folk Park is perhaps the forgotten pioneer of this theme in modern British museology.

36 "Diary of a Serious Woman", *Evening News*, 19 June 1936.

37 "Diary of a Serious Woman", *Evening News*, 19 June 1936.

38 *The Rover World*, September 1936.

39 J. S. M. Ward, "A Visit to the Folk Park", in his *The Tilie Family (A Story of Cockney Life)* (London: Herbert Jenkins, 1936), pp. 88–9.

40 Arthur Mee, *The King's England: Hertfordshire* (London: Hodder & Stoughton, 1939), pp. 76–8. For a contemporary reflection on Mee's life and work, see: Sir John Hammerton, *Child of Wonder: An Intimate Biography of Arthur Mee* (London: Hodder & Stoughton, 1946).

41 Ward, "Foreword", in his "A Mirror of the Passing World", n.p.

42 Abbey of Christ the King, *A Brief Guide to the Abbey Folk Park & Museum* (pamphlet) (London, 1935), p. 2.

43 "New Discovery of Stained Glass", *Daily Telegraph*, 10 August 1935.

44 "The Abbey 'Folk Park' at your Door: First and Only One in England", *Enfield Gazette*, 1 June 1935.

45 "Diary of a Serious Woman", *Evening News*, 19 June 1936.

46 "Visit to a Folk Farm", *St Pancras Gazette*, 27 July 1934.

47 "Antiquarians at Folk Park", *St Pancras Chronicle*, 27 July 1934.

48 Held at the Abbey Museum of Art and Archaeology Library.

49 *The Rover World*, September 1936.

50 Clough Williams-Ellis, *England and the Octopus* (London: Geoffrey Bles, 1926).

51 Abbey of Christ the King, *A Brief Guide*, p. 2.

52 *The Times*, 5 June 1937.

53 P. G. Strong, *John Ward: the Prophet of These Times* (pamphlet) (Orthodox Catholic Church of Australia, 1999), p. 24.

54 Strong, *John Ward: the Prophet of These Times*, p. 11.

55 Typescript dated "8.3.34" held at AMAA.

56 Undated ms. fragment held at AMAA.

57 "The Founders of Abbey Park . . . ", *American Weekly*, March 1936.

58 "The Founders of Abbey Park . . . ", *American Weekly*, March 1936.

9 A Walk in the Folk Park

1 "Recreating a Village Smithy", *Daily Telegraph*, 13 July 1934.

2 "An Open-Air Museum", *The Field*, 8 September 1934.

3 "Why Not An Open Air Rural Museum For Northants?", *Northampton Independent*, 23 November 1934.

4 "A Hampshire Folk Park?", *Hampshire Advertiser*, 2 January 1935.

5 "Arcade of Old-Time Shops", *Barnet Press*, 20 June 1936.

6 "Diary of a Serious Woman", *Evening News*, 19 June 1936.

7 *Rover World*, September 1936.

8 *The Times*, 31 March 1935.

9 "The Founders of Abbey Park . . . ", *American Weekly*, March 1936.

10 Trevor Allen, "You May 'Go Native' Out Here", *Star*, 19 June 1936.

11 "Wonderful Out-of-Doors Museum", *Children's Newspaper,* 1 September 1934.

12 "A Unique Exhibition: A Wonderful Collection at New Barnet", *Barnet Press*, 30 June 1934.

13 "You May 'Go Native' Out Here", *Star*, 19 June 1936.

14 "The Abbey Folk Park", *Women's Employment*, 3 July 1936.

15 J. S. M. Ward, "Foreword", in his "A Mirror of the Passing World" (undated typescript catalogue), Abbey Museum of Art and Archaeology (AMAA), n.p.

16 Ward, "A Mirror of the Passing World", caption to photograph, n.p.

17 "A Unique Exhibition: A Wonderful Collection at New Barnet", *Barnet Press*, 30 June 1934.

18 Ward, "A Mirror of the Passing World", n.p.

19 *Weekly Illustrated*, 18 August 1934.

20 Ward, "A Mirror of the Passing World", caption to photograph, n.p.

21 "Wonderful Out-of-Doors Museum", *Children's Newspaper*, 1 September 1934. The reconstruction was modelled on the illustration accompanying "The Dwellings of Our Ancestors", *Illustrated London News*, 23 June 1934.

22 J. S. M. Ward, *Prehistoric Man, His Dwellings and His Art (A lecture to accompany a series of lantern slides)* (London: Newton and Co., n.d. [c.1935]), p. 33.

23 AMAA Photograph Collection: 23 WG 1/1 B, printed caption on obverse.

24 "The Founders of Abbey Park . . . ", *American Weekly*, March 1936.

25 Trevor Allen, "You May 'Go Native' Out Here", *Star*, 19 June 1936.

26 "The Abbey Folk Park", *Finchley Press*, 10 May 1935.

27 *The Times*, 22 April 1935.

28 "Preserving Everyday Things of the Past", *The Illustrated Carpenter and Builder*, 21 December 1934.

29 "Footwear of Antiquity: Exhibition in an Abbey", *Footwear Organiser*, July 1934.

30 "Persian Exhibition at Abbey Folk Park", *Barnet Press*, 25 August 1934.

31 *Vauxhall Motorist*, July 1938; reproduced in AMAA Photograph Collection: 12 WA 8/2.

32 "Mystery of a Mummy", *Star*, 16 June 1937; "Its Tappings Bring Thoughts

of Nile's Dark Gods", *Daily Sketch*, 17 June 1937; "Crow's Homage to Mummy at Dawn", *Daily Mirror*, 17 June 1937.

33 "Riddle of the Crow and Egyptian Mummy", *Daily Express*, 17 June 1937.

34 "Four Centuries of Shops – Abbey Folk Park Extension", *Observer*, 14 June 1936.

35 "Old-Time Shops", *Illustrated Builder & Carpenter*, 3 July 1936.

36 "Nation of Shopkeepers", *Star*, 15 June 1936.

37 "Barnet People in a Film", *Barnet Press*, 17 October 1936.

38 *The Times*, 5 March 1936 and "Queen Mary's Gift to Museum", *Daily Telegraph*, 14 March 1936. It was suggested that over 800 items were received for the Victorian shop "from all over Britain, most of them accompanied with letters giving their complete histories"; "Ten Quaint Shops as a Museum", *News Chronicle*, 15 June 1936.

39 "A Wedding at the Folk Park", *Barnet Press*, 25 September 1936.

40 "A Year's Progress at the Abbey Folk Park", *Educational Handwork*, (July–September, 1935), p. 200.

41 "A Chinese Temple for Our Folk Park: Strange Room for London to See", *Children's Newspaper*, 20 July 1935.

42 "A Year's Progress at the Abbey Folk Park", *Educational Handwork*, (July–September, 1935), p. 200.

43 "Early Stained Glass at Abbey Folk Park", *Barnet Press*, 6 October 1934.

44 *The Times*, 25 January 1935.

45 After several weeks of reportage of the Abbey's purchases of stained glass, the Oratory was first mentioned directly in a press report just before Christmas; "An English Folk Park: History Made Visible", *Times Educational Supplement*, 22 December 1934.

46 "Diary of a Serious Woman", *Evening News*, 19 June 1936.

47 *The Times*, 25 January 1935.

48 J. S. M. Ward, "Where the Past Comes to Life: The Abbey Folk Park at New Barnet", *Overseas*, (April 1935), p. 33.

49 "You May 'Go Native' Out Here", *Star*, 19 June 1936.

50 J. S. M. Ward, "The Abbey Folk Park", *Educational Handwork*, (April - June, 1935), p. 29.

51 "The Common Life in New Barnet: An 'Abbey' Organised on Primitive Lines", unsourced newspaper clipping (*c.* October 1934), 'Book of Centuries' (clippings books), vol. 1, AMAA.

52 "Ancient Vehicles", *The Times*, 18 July 1934.

53 "The Abbey Folk Park and Museum", *Hertfordshire Mercury*, 27 July 1934.

54 "Procession of Victorian Carriages", *Finchley Press*, 1 September 1934.

55 *The Times*, 25 November 1936.

56 "East Barnet Smithy Makes a Journey", *Barnet Press*, 19 September 1936.

57 "The Abbey Folk Park, New Barnet – Valuable Addition to Museum", *Barnet Press*, 15 August 1936.

58 "New Discovery of Stained Glass", *Daily Telegraph*, 10 August 1935.

59 Interview with Peter Strong, Wolvi, 25 April 2004.

60 "The Founders of Abbey Park . . . ", *American Weekly*, March 1936.

10 Anglican Outcasts and Othodox Catholicism

1 "Programme of Lectures", printed bill *c.* 1934, copy held in Abbey Museum of Art and Archaeology Library (AMAA).

2 See W. R. Inge, *Christian Mysticism: Considered in eight lectures delivered before the University of Oxford* (London: Methuen, 1918 [1899]).

3 This chapter develops the initial ideas published as "J. S. M Ward, 'Bishop at Large': 'Orthodox Catholicism' and Church History in Interwar Britain", *Crossroads* 5, 1 (2010): 45–57.

4 Lambeth Palace Library, Lang Papers: Vol. 131, 1935, A1–C4, ff. 3–5.

5 J. S. M. Ward, "Diary, vol. 5, October 1947–December 1947", entry of 31 December, f. 183.

6 See Peter Anson, *Bishops at Large* (London: Faber and Faber, 1964), pp. 278–9.

7 Anson, *Bishops at Large*, p. 286.

8 Anson, *Bishops at Large*, p. 276.

9 J. S. M. Ward, "Diary, vol. 5", entry of 15 December, f. 133.

10 Anson, *Bishops at Large*, p. 286.

11 J. S. M. Ward, *The Orthodox Catholic Church in England (Showing its History and the Validity of its Orders)* (New Barnet: The Abbey of Christ the King, 1944), p. 39.

12 Ward, *The Orthodox Catholic Church in England*, p. 38.

13 A. J. Macdonald, *Episcopi Vagantes in Church History* (London: Society for Promoting Christian Knowledge, 1945), p. 30.

14 Henry St John, "Introduction", to Peter Anson, *Bishops at Large*, p. 15.

15 For recent overviews see John Plummer, *The Many Paths of the Independent Sacramental Movement* (Berkeley: Apocryphile, 2006), and Joanne Pearson, *Wicca and the Christian Heritage: Ritual, Sex and Magic* (London: Routledge, 2007), Chapter 2, "*Episcopi vagantes* and heterodox Christianity". See also the Arnold Harris Mathew Harris Centre for the Study of the Independent Sacramental Movement at the European-American University, a "diverse partnership of affiliated campuses located in Africa and Asia", with degrees validated by Universidad Empresarial de Costa Rica (www.thedegree.org/csism.html).

16 St John, "Introduction" to *Bishops at Large,* p. 15.

17 Lambeth Palace Library, Lang Papers: Vol. 49, "Old Catholics, 1930–1940", undated memorandum on "Episcopi Vagantes" by C. B. Moss, f. 282.

18 Lambeth Palace Library, Douglas Papers: Vol. 4, ff. 66–97, 'Lambeth Conference 1948, Report (Draft for 10/12/47) on Subject III [Formerly Subject II(a)], "Relations between the Anglican Churches and Foreign Churches", [L.C. (Subject II (a) C.16], Appendix II, Rev. H. R. T. Brandreth, "Memorandum on Episcopi Vagantes", [pp. 57–62], f. 97.

19 Brandreth, "Memorandum on Episcopi Vagantes", f. 96.

20 Lewis Keizer, "Preface" to his *The Wandering Bishops: Apostles of a New Spirituality* (privately published, 2000; earlier edition published by St Thomas Press, 1984).

21 Henry Brandreth, *Episcopi Vagantes and the Anglican Church* (London: Society for Promoting Christian Knowledge, 1947), p. 6.

22 Tixeront, *L'Ordre et les Ordinations*, cited in Brandreth, *Episcopi Vagantes*, p. 6.

23 Brandreth, *Episcopi Vagantes*, pp. 7–9.

24 St John, "Introduction" to *Bishops at Large*, p. 15.

25 For Vilatte himself, see Anson, *Bishops at Large*, pp. 91–129. Bishops and churches of the Vilatte succession are described in Anson, *Bishops at Large*, pp. 252–322, including Ward's Confraternity of the Kingdom of Christ (pp. 282–92).

26 Ward, *The Orthodox Catholic Church in England*, p. 32.

27 This brief overview of Eastern Orthodoxy is drawn from standard sources including Timothy Ware, *The Orthodox Church* (Harmondsworth: Penguin, 1964); "Eastern Christianity", *Encyclopedia of Religion* (second edition) Macmillan Reference, 2005, Vol. 4, pp. 2580–95; George Every, *Understanding Eastern Christianity* (London: SCM Press, 1980); Adrian Fortescue, *The Lesser Eastern Churches* (London: Catholic Truth Society, 1913).

28 Lambeth Palace Library, Douglas Papers: Vol. 27, ff. 20–6, notes by W. A. Wigram on "Orthodoxy and Anglicanism today", Nikaean Lecture delivered at King's College, 30 June 1930, f. 21. The patriarchates of Russia, Serbia, Romania, Bulgaria, Georgia, Cyprus, Greece, Poland, Albania, the Czech and Slovak republics and the two autonomous churches of Finland and Estonia are now numbered alongside the ancient bishoprics of the Eastern Mediterranean.

29 Ward, *The Orthodox Catholic Church in England*, pp. 4–5. It may be that the date provided is an error, or that Ward relied on an alternative tradition to date St Peter's arrival in Antioch.

30 David F. Abramtsov, "The Western Rite and the Eastern Church: Dr. J. J. Overbeck and his Scheme for the Re-establishment of the Orthodox Church in the West", M.A. dissertation, University of Pittsburgh, 1961, p. 4, citing Overbeck's paper in the *Orthodox Catholic Review* III 1–6 (January–June 1871), p. 45.

31 Abramtsov, "The Western Rite and the Eastern Church", pp. 6–7.

32 J. J. Overbeck, *A Plain View of the Claims of the Orthodox Catholic Church* (London: Trübner and Co., 1881), p. 114.

33 Overbeck, *A Plain View*, p. 19.

34 Ware, *The Orthodox Church*, pp. 203–4.

35 *Hieratika; or The Voice of the Hierarchy* 1, 7 (April 1949), pp. 37–8. This publi-

cation was a newsletter circulated to clergy and lay members of Mar Georgius' Western Orthodox Catholic Church.

36 Overbeck, *A Plain View*, pp. 52–3.

37 Overbeck, *A Plain View*, p. 18.

38 Overbeck, *A Plain View*, p. 19.

39 Overbeck, *A Plain View*, p. 17.

40 Overbeck, *A Plain View*, p. 17.

41 *Hieratika* 1, 8 (June 1949), p. 41.

42 Ward, *The Orthodox Catholic Church in England*, p. 3.

43 Wigram, "Orthodoxy and Anglicanism today", ff. 22–3. Some reconstruction of Wigram's notes has been undertaken here to re-establish the flow of his address.

44 Ware, *The Orthodox Church*, p. 217.

45 Wigram, "Orthodoxy and Anglicanism today", f. 23.

46 Cited in Ware, *The Orthodox Church*, p. 247.

47 Ware, *The Orthodox Church*, p. 245.

48 "Eastern Christianity", *Encyclopedia of Religion*, 4, 2590–1.

49 Cited in Ware, *The Orthodox Church*, p. 226.

50 J. S. M. Ward, *Life's Problems* (London: Baskerville Press, 1929), pp. 12–13.

51 Ware, *The Orthodox Church*, p. 240.

52 Nicholas Arseniev, *Mysticism and the Eastern Church* (Arthur Chambers trans.) (Oxford: A. R. Mowbray, 1979 [1926]), pp. 23, 27–8.

53 Arseniev, *Mysticism and the Eastern Church*, p. 22.

54 Arseniev, *Mysticism and the Eastern Church*, pp. 29–30.

55 "The Approaching Season of Advent", *The Orthodox Catholic Review* 1, 11 (September–November 1945), p. 52.

56 "Eastern Christianity", *Encyclopedia of Religion*, 4, 2591.

57 "The Meaning and Language of Icons", in Leonid Ouspensky and Vladimir Lossky, *The Meaning of Icons* (New York: St Vladimir's Seminary Press, 1989), p. 26.

58 Overbeck, *A Plain View*, pp. 119–28.

59 Overbeck, *A Plain View*, pp. 128–9.

60 Ware, *The Orthodox Church*, p. 214.

61 Ware, *The Orthodox Church*, pp. 21, 253.

62 *Hieratika* 1, 5 (April 1948), p. 30.

63 J. S. M. Ward, "Prologue" in his *The Psychic Powers of Christ* (London: Williams & Norgate, 1936), p. 9.

64 Lambeth Palace Library, Douglas Papers: Vol. 70, f. 74, typescript copy of letter dated November 1930.

65 Lambeth Palace Library, Douglas Papers: Vol. 70, f. 79, copy of letter from Canon Bridgeman of St George's Cathedral, Jerusalem dated 20 September 1932. The *filioque* and the question of the validity of the Ecumenical Councils were among the issues that generated the historical separations within Orthodoxy and the Great Schism itself.

66 Lambeth Palace Library, Douglas Papers: Vol. 70, ff. 117–18, "Church of England Council on Foreign Relations: Notice from the Syrian Patriarchate of Antioch and all the East" Homs, Syria (No. 629) (C. F. R. 181); also reprinted as Appendix A to Brandreth's *Episcopi Vagantes and the Anglican Church*.

67 Ward, "Diary, vol. 5", entry for 15 December 1947, ff. 134–5.

68 Untitled exercise book dated after *c*.1947 held in archives of the Confraternity of Christ the King, Caboolture; copy in AMAA, p. 15.

69 "The Abbey Church", *Barnet Press*, 27 June 1936.

70 "Can a Christian Fight?", *Barnet Press*, 4 July 1936.

71 Ward, "Prologue", *The Psychic Powers of Christ*, pp. 9–10.

72 *Barnet Press*, undated clipping, "Book of Centuries"(clippings books), vol. 3, AMAA.

73 "The Abbey Church", *Barnet Press*, 6 June 1936.

74 Revelations ix, 7–10.

75 "Bible Prophecy and Air Raids", *Barnet Press*, 20 June 1936.

76 "The Coming of a Great War", *Barnet Press*, 11 June 1936.

77 "Can This Civilisation Be Saved?", *Barnet Press,*18 July 1936.

78 Ward, *The Orthodox Catholic Church in England*, pp. 3–4.

79 Overbeck, *A Plain View*, p. 9.

11 Wartime Trials

1 Peter Strong, *John Ward: The Prophet of these Times* (pamphlet) (Orthodox Catholic Church of Australia, 1999), p. 14.

2 Peter Anson, *Bishops at Large* (London: Faber & Faber, 1964), pp. 242–3.

3 "A Notable Episode in Church History", *Orthodox Catholic Review* 1, 1 (April 1944), pp. 1–2.

4 Lambeth Palace Library, Douglas Papers: Vol. 4, ff. 66–97, "Lambeth Conference 1948: Report (Draft for 10/12/47) on Subject III [Formerly Subject II (a)], "Relations between the Anglican Churches and Foreign Churches" [L.C. [Subject II (a)] C.16], Appendix II, Rev. H. R. T. Brandreth, "Memorandum on Episcopi Vagantes" [p. 61, f. 97]. As Anson comments, "it is improbable that any bishop during the past nineteen centuries has been re-consecrated so many times as Hugh George de Willmott Newman"; *Bishops at Large*, p. 452.

5 The various certificates of ordination, consecration, and election are held in the archives of the Abbey of Christ the King; copies are held in the Abbey Museum of Art and Archaeology Library (AMAA).

6 *Orthodox Catholic Review* 1, 10 (June–August 1945), p. 43.

7 Untitled exercise book dated after *c*.1947 held in archives of the Confraternity of Christ the King, Caboolture; copy in AMAA.

8 Iain Adamson, *A Man of Quality: A Biography of The Hon. Mr Justice Cassels* (London: Frederick Muller, 1964), p. 224.

9 *All England Law Reports: Kings Bench Division* (*AELR*), Vol. 2 (25 August

1945 and 22 September 1945), "Lough v. Ward and another", p. 338; see also "Law Report, 18 May: High Court of Justice, King's Bench Division", *The Times*, 19 May 1945.

10 "Law Report, 2 May: High Court of Justice, King's Bench Division", *The Times*, 3 May 1945.

11 National Archives, Kew: PRO, B9/1409, Bankruptcy Acts, Ward, John Sebastian Marlow (No. 85 of 1945).

12 "Law Report, 2 May: High Court of Justice, King's Bench Division", *The Times*, 3 May 1945.

13 "Law Report, 30 April: High Court of Justice, King's Bench Division", *The Times*, 1 May 1945,

14 AMAA Photograph Collection: 11 WC 1/9 and 10.

15 "Law Report, 2 May: High Court of Justice, King's Bench Division", *The Times*, 3 May 1945.

16 "Father Says Girl Was Enticed Into Religious Order: 'Played On Her Call-Up Fears'", *Morning Advertiser*, 1 May 1945.

17 *AELR* (25 August 1945), p. 343.

18 "Father Says Girl Was Enticed Into Religious Order", *Morning Advertiser*, 1 May 1945.

19 "Father Says Girl Was Enticed Into Religious Order", *Morning Advertiser*, 1 May 1945.

20 "Girl Who Left Home", *Barnet Press*, 16 October 1943.

21 This extract from Ward's correspondence with Harold Lough was quoted in court, and appeared in several newspaper reports of the enticement case. See for example, *News Chronicle*, 1 May 1945.

22 "Local Girl in an Abbey – Enticement Allegation", *Barnet Press*, 2 June 1945.

23 "Father Says Girl Was Enticed Into Religious Order", *Morning Advertiser*, 1 May 1945.

24 "Law Report, 11 May: High Court of Justice, King's Bench Division", *The Times*, 12 May 1945.

25 Adamson, *A Man of Quality*, p. 225.

26 "Father Ward's Evidence in 'Enticement' Suit", *Manchester Guardian*, 8 May 1945; "Law Report, 7 May: High Court of Justice, King's Bench Division", *The Times*, 8 May 1945.

27 Library and Museum of Freemasonry, Freemasons' Hall: letter from Stanley Walter Lough dated 20 September 1945.

28 Library and Museum of Freemasonry, Freemasons' Hall: letter dated 30 October 1945. Other correspondence records the librarian's opinion that Hopping and his wife took "the sensible view that as she grows older (now only 22), she will see the tinsel for what it is worth and come home." My thanks to Antony Baker for these references.

29 "Vision led sect on mystical pilgrimage for abbey foundation", *News Chronicle*, 1 May 1945.

30 "Law Report, 30 April: High Court of Justice, King's Bench Division", *The Times*, 1 May 1945.

31 "Vision led sect on mystical pilgrimage", *News Chronicle*, 1 May 1945.

32 "'You Liar, Dorothy' – Mother to Daughter in Court", *Morning Advertiser*, 3 May 1945.

33 "Law Report, 1 May: High Court of Justice, King's Bench Division", *The Times*, 2 May 1945.

34 "Law Report, 2 May: High Court of Justice, King's Bench Division", *The Times*, 3 May 1945.

35 "Law Report, 1 May: High Court of Justice, King's Bench Division", *The Times*, 2 May 1945.

36 "K. C. Tells Court The Story of Sister Terese", *Daily Express*, 1 May 1945; see also "Father Says Girl Was Enticed Into Religious Order", *Morning Advertiser*, 1 May 1945.

37 "Law Report, 14 May: High Court of Justice, King's Bench Division", *The Times*, 15 May 1945.

38 "Confraternity Case – 'She Planted Herself at the Abbey: Would Not Go' – Mr. Ward", *Morning Advertiser*, 5 May 1945.

39 "Law Report, 3 May: High Court of Justice, King's Bench Division", *The Times*, 4 May 1945.

40 *AELR* (25 August 1945), p. 341.

41 "Girl Prefers Abbey to War Factory", *Daily Telegraph*, 2 May 1945; "Mother Says In Alleged Enticement Case – I called him 'dirty hypocrite'", *Daily Express*, 2 May 1945.

42 "Sister Terese Tells Court: 'Duty to God Comes First': Would Not Go Home If Ordered To Leave Abbey", *Morning Advertiser*, 4 May 1945.

43 "'Enticement' Case: Girl's Evidence", *Manchester Guardian*, 4 May 1945.

44 "Law Report, 4 May: High Court of Justice, King's Bench Division", *The Times*, 5 May 1945.

45 "Confraternity Case – 'She Planted Herself At The Abbey: Would Not Go' – Mr. Ward", *Morning Advertiser*, 5 May 1945.

46 "Law Report, 1 May: High Court of Justice, King's Bench Division", *The Times*, 2 May 1945.

47 "K. C. Tells Court The Story of Sister Terese", *Daily Express*, 1 May 1945.

48 *AELR* (25 August 1945), p. 343.

49 "K. C. Tells Court The Story of Sister Terese", *Daily Express*, 1 May 1945.

50 "'You Liar, Dorothy' – Mother to Daughter in Court", *Morning Advertiser*, 3 May 1945.

51 "Law Report, 3 May: High Court of Justice, King's Bench Division", *The Times*, 4 May 1945.

52 "Father Ward's Denials in Lough 'Enticement' Suit', *Manchester Guardian*, 5 May 1945.

53 "Local Girl in an Abbey – Enticement Allegation", *Barnet Press*, 2 June 1945.

54 "'Enticement Case': Girl's Evidence", *Manchester Guardian*, 4 May 1945.

55 "'You Liar', Mother Cries To Sister Terese In Court – retort to story of home rows", *Daily Mirror*, 3 May 1945.

56 "K. C. Tells Court The Story Of Sister Terese", *Daily Express*, 1 May 1945.

57 "Judge On 'So-Called Confraternity' – 'Only Title Not Used Is That of Pope'", *Morning Advertiser*, 12 May 1945.

58 "Sister Terese Wants To Stay At The 'Abbey'", *Daily Sketch*, 4 May 1945.

59 "Sect Chief Talked Of 'Works Slaves' To Lure Girl, Court Is Told", *Daily Mirror*, 1 May 1945.

60 "Father Ward's Denials in Lough 'Enticement' Suit", *Manchester Guardian*, 5 May 1945.

61 "End of 'Enticement' Case Evidence", *Manchester Guardian*, 11 May 1945.

62 "Father Ward's Denials in Lough 'Enticement' Suit", *Manchester Guardian*, 5 May 1945.

63 "Father Ward's Evidence in 'Enticement' Suit", *Manchester Guardian*, 8 May 1945.

64 "Father Ward's Evidence in 'Enticement' Suit", *Manchester Guardian*, 8 May 1945.

65 "End of 'Enticement' Case Evidence", *Manchester Guardian*, 11 May 1945; "Man sued in Sister Therese case discloses: Invalid daughter is barred in abbey", *Daily Express*, 5 May 1945.

66 "Girl Prefers Abbey to War Factory", *Daily Telegraph*, 2 May 1945.

67 "K. C. Tells Court The Story Of Sister Terese", *Daily Express*, 1 May 1945.

68 "Abbey girl recruits 'died,' court told", *Daily Express*, 11 May 1945.

69 "Abbey girl must wait", *Daily Express*, 15 May 1945.

70 Interview with Peter Strong, Wolvi, 25 April 2004.

71 *Hieratika* 2, 1 (January 1952), pp. 7–8.

72 "Law Report, 2 May: High Court of Justice, King's Bench Division", *The Times*, 3 May 1945.

73 "Law Report, 1 May: High Court of Justice, King's Bench Division", *The Times*, 2 May 1945.

74 "'You Liar', Mother Cries To Sister Terese In Court – retort to story of home rows", *Daily Mirror*, 3 May 1945.

75 "Law Report, 11 May: High Court of Justice, King's Bench Division", *The Times*, 12 May 1945.

76 "Judge Criticises Sister Therese – 'lacked love for parents'", *Daily Express*, 12 May 1945.

77 "Only Title Not Used Is That Of Pope", *Morning Advertiser*, 12 May 1945.

78 "Law Report, 11 May: High Court of Justice, King's Bench Division", *The Times*, 12 May 1945.

79 "Sister Terese Case – 'Overwhelming Evidence Of Enticement'", *Morning Advertiser*, 16 May 1945.

80 "Judgment Reserved in 'Enticement' Case", *Manchester Guardian*, 16 May 1945.

81 *AELR* (25 August 1945), p. 338, editorial note. It should be noted that after

a 1969 recommendation of the Law Commission in its "Report on Financial Provision in Matrimonial Proceedings", in which a husband's ability to sue for damages in cases of adultery was abolished, the actions of enticement, seduction and harbouring of a spouse or child were also abolished. It would not have been possible for the Loughs to commence an action for damages against the Wards if, hypothetically, the matter had been heard after that date. The Irish Law Reform Commission's paper on "The Law Relating to Seduction and the Enticement and Harbouring of a Child" (Working paper No. 6, 1979) cited *Lough v. Ward* in recommending similar reforms. In modern legal practice and family law, also, the expressed wishes of a minor in such a dispute is required to be taken into account by the court. Dorothy's desire to remain in the Abbey was expressly disregarded by Justice Cassels, and the court decided where her best interest lay. *AELR* (22 September 1945), p. 349. My thanks to Matt Foley, Barrister-at-Law, for these observations.

82 *AELR* (22 September 1945), p. 347.

83 *AELR* (22 September 1945), p. 346.

84 "Law Report, 18 May: High Court of Justice, King's Bench Division", *The Times*, 19 May 1945.

85 *AELR* (22 September 1945), p. 348.

86 *AELR* (22 September 1945), p. 350, and "£500 Damages in Abbey Enticement Case", *Manchester Guardian*, 19 May 1945.

87 "Law Report, 18 May: High Court of Justice, King's Bench Division", *The Times*, 19 May 1945.

88 *AELR* (22 September 1945), p. 350; "Law Report, 18 May: High Court of Justice, King's Bench Division", *The Times*, 19 May 1945.

89 *AELR* (22 September 1945), p. 350; "Sister Therese Must Put Off Her Nun's Robes", *Daily Express*, 19 May 1945.

90 "Sister Therese has left the 'Abbey'", *Daily Mail*, 31 May 1945.

91 "Sister Terese Stays Away", *Daily Herald*, 1 June 1945.

92 "'Sister Terese' – Assault Summons Against Mother Dismissed", *Manchester Guardian*, 15 June 1945.

93 "Her Mother Wept, But 'Sister Terese' Said: 'I Won't Come Home With You'", *Daily Mirror*, 1 June 1945.

94 "'Sister Terese' – Assault Summons Against Mother Dismissed", *Manchester Guardian*, 15 June 1945.

95 Library and Museum of Freemasonry, Freemasons' Hall: letter from Stanley Walter Lough dated 20 September 1945.

96 "Lough v. Ward", *Orthodox Catholic Review* 1, 9 (May 1945), p. 40.

97 "Lough v. Ward", *Orthodox Catholic Review* 1, 9 (May 1945), p. 40.

98 National Archives, Kew: PRO, B9/1409, Creditor's Petition of Stanley Walter Lough dated 23 July 1945.

99 National Archives, Kew: PRO, B9/1409, Affidavit as to Petitioning Creditor's Debt (Stanley Walter Lough), dated 14 August 1945.

100 National Archives, Kew: PRO, B9/1409, Statement of Affairs dated 5 September 1945.

101 *The Times*, 20 September 1945, p. 8.

102 National Archives, Kew: PRO, B9/1409, Deed of Release dated 18 September 1945.

103 National Archives, Kew: PRO, B9/1409, Official Receiver's report of 3 November 1945.

104 National Archives, Kew: PRO, B9/1409, High Court of Justice in Bankruptcy, order dated 8 November 1945.

105 For Gardner, see Jack Bracelin, *Gerald Gardner Witch* (London: Octagon, 1960); Philip Heselton, *Wiccan Roots* (Milverton: Capel Bann, 2000) and *Gerald Gardner and the Cauldron of Inspiration* (Milverton: Capell Bann, 2003); for his relationship with Ward see also Joanne Pearson, *Wicca and the Christian Heritage: Ritual, Sex and Magic* (London: Routledge, 2007), pp. 49–50.

106 Heselton, *Gerald Gardner and the Cauldron of Inspiration*, p. 151 and Chapter 7, "The Witches' Cottage in the Woods".

12 Cyprus and Beyond

1 J. S. M. Ward, "Diary, vol. 1, July 1946–March 1947", entries from 13–28 July 1946, ff. 1–2; ms. copy held in Abbey Museum of Art and Archaeology Library (AMAA).

2 Ward, "Diary, vol. 1", entry for 10 August 1946, f. 4.

3 Ward, "Diary, vol. 1", entry for 7 October 1946, ff. 12–13.

4 Ward, "Diary, vol. 1", entry for 3 January 1947, ff. 73–4.

5 Ward, "Diary, vol. 1", entry for 13 October 1946, f. 14.

6 Ward, "Diary, vol. 1", entry for 23 October 1946, f. 19.

7 Ward, "Diary, vol. 1", entry for 22 December 1946, f. 63.

8 Ward, "Diary, vol. 11, March 1949–May 1949", entry of 29 April 1949, ff. 84–5.

9 Ward, "Diary, vol. 11", entry for 10 May 1949, ff. 97–8.

10 Ward, "Diary, vol. 1", entry for 5 January 1947, f. 75.

11 Ward, "Diary, vol. 5, October 1947–December 1947", entry for 22 December 1947, ff. 151–2.

12 Ward, "Diary, vol. 5", entry for 7 November 1947, f. 45.

13 Ward, "Diary, vol. 10, November 1948–March 1949", entry for 18 November 1948, f. 34. A diary entry of 21 December 1946 strikes a similar note: "the Socialist Govt. intend[s] to allow *Burma to leave the British Empire* just as it had already agreed to let India do so. Thus the disintegration of the Brit[ish] Empire goes forward rapidly and the judgment of God on Gt. Britain, as declared by His messengers after the injustice of 'The [Enticement] Case' has alas started and is going forward rapidly." Ward, "Diary, vol. 1", f. 62.

14 Ward, "Diary, vol. 12, May 1949–July 1949", ff. 88–89.

15 "Outline of the address given by the Rev. Oeconomos S. Panagides, at the graveside of the Reverend Father"; ms. held at AMAA.

16 "Newspaper Article from the Limassol Weekly Paper" [transcribed by Daphnya Panagides]; ms. held at AMAA.

17 Ward, "Diary, vol. 12", entry for 5 July 1949, f. 90.

18 'Refused blood . . . she died', *Courier-Mail*, 24 January 1963, p. 1, and 'Adults have say on blood', *Courier-Mail*, 25 January 1963, p. 3.

19 See http://www.abbeymuseum.asn.au/.

Sources

Publications by J. S. M. Ward
Books and pamphlets

Outline Notes on English History (Redhill: W. A. Bell, 1910).

Brasses (Cambridge Manuals of Science and Literature) (Cambridge: Cambridge University Press, 1912).

Fairy Tales and Legends of Burma (Bombay: Blackie and Son, 1916).

Gone West: Three Narratives of After-Death Experience (London: William Rider & Son, 1917).

A Subaltern in Spirit Land: a Sequel to 'Gone West' (London: William Rider & Son, 1920).

Financial Review of 1919 (London: Federation of British Industries Intelligence Department, n.d. [*c.* 1920]) (with N. E. Crump).

Financial Review of 1920 (London: Federation of British Industries Intelligence Department, n.d. [*c.* 1921]) (with N. E. Crump).

Can Our Industrial System Survive? Being a treatise on the European Financial Crisis as indicated by the present rates of exchange (London: William Rider & Son, 1921).

Freemasonry and the Ancient Gods (London: Simpkin, Marshall, Hamilton, Kent & Co., 1921).

Freemasonry, its aims and ideals (London: William Rider & Son, 1923).

The E.A.'s Handbook (The Masonic Handbook Series: studies in the meaning of our ritual, No. 1) (London: Warrington Publishing, 1923).

The F.C.'s Handbook (The Masonic Handbook Series: studies in the meaning of our ritual, No. 2) (London: Warrington Publishing, 1923).

The M.M.'s Handbook (Masonic Handbook Series: studies in the meaning of our ritual, No. 3) (London: J. Page, Warrington Publishing, 1923).

An Outline History of Freemasonry (The Masonic Handbook Series: studies in the growth of our order, No. 4) (London: Baskerville Press, 1924).

The Higher Degrees Handbook (The Masonic Handbook Series: studies in the meaning of our ritual, No. 5) (London: Baskerville Press, 1924).

Poems of the Empire (London: John Marlowe, Savage & Co., n.d. [*c.*1924]).

Textile Fibres and Yarns (London: Ernest Benn, 1924).

An Interpretation of our Masonic Symbols (London: Baskerville Press, 1924).

The Hung Society (three volumes) (London: Baskerville Press, 1925) (with W. G. Stirling).

An Explanation of the Royal Arch Degree (London: Baskerville Press, 1925).

Ritual of IM with Explanation (London: Baskerville Press, 1926).

The Moral Teachings of Freemasonry; incorporating Masonic Proverbs, Poems and Sayings (London: Baskerville Press, 1926).

How to Make a Good Masonic Speech: A Course of Six Lectures (London: Baskerville Press, 1926).

Labour and Refreshment (London: Baskerville Press, 1926).

Told Through the Ages: a series of Masonic stories (London: Baskerville Press, 1926).

Who was Hiram Abiff? (London: Baskerville Press, 1926).

The Sign Language of the Mysteries (two volumes) (London: Baskerville Press, 1928).

The Masonic Why and Wherefore; being answers to 101 questions which perplex the average mason (London: Baskerville Press, 1929).

The Kingdom of the Wise: Life's Problems (London: Baskerville Press, 1929).

The Confraternity of the Kingdom of Christ: Its Message to the Nation and to the Individual (pamphlet) (London: W. H. Rickinson & Son, 1934).

The Confraternity of the Kingdom of Christ: What it Stands for and how it came into existence (pamphlet) (London: W. H. Rickinson & Son, n.d. [*c.*1934]).

Prehistoric Man, His Dwellings and His Art (London: Newton & Co., n.d. [*c.*1935]).

The World before the Coming of Man (London: Newton & Co., n.d. [*c.*1935]).

The Psychic Powers of Christ (London: Williams & Norgate, 1936).

The Tilie Family: A Story of Cockney Life (London: Herbert Jenkins, 1936).

A Brief Guide to The Abbey Folk Park & Museum (pamphlet) (New Barnet: Abbey of Christ the King, n.d. [*c.* 1936]).

The Orthodox Catholic Church in England (Showing its History and the Validity of its Orders) (New Barnet: The Abbey of Christ the King, 1944).

Articles

"Freemasonry and the Ancient East", *Masonic Record* 1, 1 (December 1920): 13–16.

"The Preserver and the Cross", *Masonic Record* 1, 2 (January 1921): 56–8.

"What the Ancient Sign Language Teaches Us", *Masonic Record* 1, 3 (February 1921): 112–15.

"Some Masonic Experiences in India", *Masonic Record* 1, 4 (March 1921): 148–51.

"The Hindoo Symbol of the Point Within the Circle", *Masonic Record* 1, 5 (April 1921): 193–5.

"Continental Freemasonry", *Masonic Record* 1, 6 (May 1921): 263–6.

"The Additional Degrees in Freemasonry" (part I), *Masonic Record* 1, 7 (June 1921): 290–2.

"The Additional Degrees in Freemasonry" (part II), *Masonic Record* 1, 8 (July 1921): 332–4.

"The Historic Origin of the Mark Degree", *Masonic Record* 1, 11 (October 1921): 446–8.

"The Meaning of Some Parts of our Ritual and the Universality of our Signs and Symbols", *Transactions of the Masonic Study Society* 1 (1921–22): 7–10.

"History and origin of the Knights Templar", *Transactions of the Masonic Study Society* 1 (1921–22): 11–15.

"The Meaning of Some Parts of our Ritual: The Tyler and the CT", *Transactions of the Masonic Study Society* 1 (1921–2): 37.

"The Knights Templar" (part I), *Masonic Record* 2, 14 (January 1922): 546–7.

"The Knights Templar" (part II), *Masonic Record* 2, 15 (February 1922): 593–4.

"All the Degrees in Freemasonry: A Summary of their Meaning" (Part I), *Masonic Record* 2, 22 (September 1922): 793–4.

"All the Degrees in Freemasonry: A Summary of their Meaning" (Part II), *Masonic Record* 2, 23 (October 1922): 819–20.

"All the Degrees in Freemasonry: A Summary of their Meaning" (Part III), *Masonic Record* 2, 24 (November 1922): 845–7.

"All the Degrees in Freemasonry: A Summary of their Meaning" (Part IV), *Masonic Record* 3, 25 (December 1922): 875–7.

"Our Illustrations", *Transactions of the Masonic Study Society* 2 (1922–3): 46–8.

"All the Degrees in Freemasonry: A Summary of their Meaning" (Part V), *Masonic Record* 3, 26 (January 1923): 902–3.

"All the Degrees in Freemasonry: A Summary of their Meaning" (Part VI), *Masonic Record* 3, 27 (February 1923): 934–6.

"All the Degrees in Freemasonry: A Summary of their Meaning" (Part VII), *Masonic Record* 3, 28 (March 1923): 965–6.

"The Aims and Ideals of Freemasonry: Why Men Enter Freemasonry", *Masonic Record* 3, 29 (April 1923): 991–2.

"The Aims and Ideals of Freemasonry: The Political Ideal", *Masonic Record* 3, 30 (May 1923): 1019–20.

"The Aims and Ideals of Freemasonry: The Social Ideal", *Masonic Record* 3, 31 (June 1923): 1047–9.

"Freemasonry: The Heir of the Ancient Mysteries", *Occult Review* 37, 6 (June 1923): 346–54.

"The Aims and Ideals of Freemasonry: The Social Ideal (continued)", *Masonic Record* 3, 32 (July 1923): 1078–9.

"The Aims and Ideals of Freemasonry: The Ritualistic and the Archaeological Ideals", *Masonic Record* 3, 33 (August 1923): 1109–11.

"The Aims and Ideals of Freemasonry: The Mystical Ideal", *Masonic Record* 3, 34 (September 1923): 1142–3.

"The Triad Society", *Transactions of the Masonic Study Society* 3 (1923–4): 5–13.

"Sprung from the Same Stock", *Transactions of the Masonic Study Society* 4 (1925–6): 59–60.

"Let Us All Endeavour to Learn the Necessary Signs", *Transactions of the Masonic Study Society* 4 (1925–6): 61–5.

"Dyeing, 1: The Industry in Great Britain", *Encyclopaedia Britannica* (thirteenth edition, supplement: Volume 1) (London and New York: The Encyclopaedia Britannica Company, 1926): 885–6.

"Fibres", *Encyclopaedia Britannica* (thirteenth edition, supplement: Volume 2) (London and New York: The Encyclopaedia Britannica Company, 1926): 25–6.

"Freemasonry", *Encyclopaedia Britannica* (thirteenth edition, supplement: Volume 2) (London and New York: The Encyclopaedia Britannica Company, 1926): 110–11.

"Secret Societies, Chinese", *Encyclopaedia Britannica* (thirteenth edition, supplement: Volume 3) (London and New York: The Encyclopaedia Britannica Company, 1926): 497–8.

"Silk", *Encyclopaedia Britannica* (thirteenth edition, supplement: Volume 3) (London and New York: The Encyclopaedia Britannica Company, 1926): 548–9.

"When in Distress", *Transactions of the Masonic Study Society* 5 (1926–7): 54–6.

"The Symbolism of the 2°", *Transactions of the Masonic Study Society* 6 (1927–8): 6–16.

"A Peculiar System of Morality", *Transactions of the Masonic Study Society* 6 (1927–8): 79–80.

"[Sir John Cockburn]", *Transactions of the Masonic Study Society* 7 (1928–9): 8–9.

"The Emblems of Morality", *Transactions of the Masonic Study Society* 7 (1928–9): 61–2.

"A Letter to a Young Mason", *Transactions of the Masonic Study Society* 11 (1932–3): 334–6.

"Interpretation of Trinity Boss in Peterborough Cathedral", *Transactions of the Masonic Study Society* 12 (1933–4): 422.

"The Hung or Triad Society", *Transactions of the Masonic Study Society* 13 (1934–5): 472–87.

"The Abbey Folk Park, New Barnet", *Museums Journal* 36, 6 (1936): 239–43.

"The Abbey Folk Park, New Barnet", *Transactions of the East Hertfordshire Archaeological Society* 9, 3 (1937 for 1936): 316–29.

Manuscript Collections

Abbey Museum of Art and Archaeology

J. S. M. Ward, "Diary" (manuscript), twelve volumes, 13 July 1946–2 July 1949 (photocopies of originals held in Abbey of Christ the King).

J. S. M. Ward, "Autobiography" (manuscript, written c.1947–1949), six volumes for period 1896–1900 (photocopies of originals held in Abbey of Christ the King).

J. S. M. Ward, "A Mirror of the Passing World", undated typescript, (c.1936).

"The Book of Centuries", clippings books, three volumes, 1934–1939.

Photographic Collection (three volumes, sourced from albums and private collections of Abbey of Christ the King).

Hymns of the Church of Christ the King (Margate: Herald Press, n.d.).

"Outline of the address given by the Rev. Oeconomos S. Panagides, at the graveside of the Reverend Father", undated manuscript, (*c.*1949).

"Programme of Lectures on The Decline of Christendom [and] The Writing on the Wall" (Abbey of Christ the King), copy of printed bill, 1934.

Michael Strong, "A Short History of the Abbey Museum", typescript, 1982.

"John Ward Biography", undated research notes by Richard Stephens.

"A Search for John Ward's Locations", undated typescript notes by Richard Stephens.

Peter Strong, "The Message of the Hymns", undated typescript.

Barnet Museum and Hertfordshire Association for Local History

"Hadley Hall Chapel", [manuscript, n.d. (*c.*1936)].

J. Webster Kirkham, "Memories of a Loved Brother" [typescript, n.d.].

British Library India Office Collection

Revenue and Statistics Department, Annual Files (1887–1921): IOR/L/E/7/336-379 (1894–1896) [papers relating to Empire of India Exhibitions, Earls Court].

Hertfordshire Archives and Local Studies Library

DSA1/14/5 Act Books, 1923–1939.

D/P15C 8/3 New Barnet Parish Records: Vestry and Parochial Church Council Minutes.

Lambeth Palace Library

Lang Papers (Cosmo Gordon Lang, Archbishop of Canterbury, 1928–1942):

Vol. 49: Old Catholics, 1930–1940; and memorandum on 'Episcopi Vagantes' by C. B. Moss.

Vol. 70: Archbishop of Canterbury's Committee on Spiritualism, 1936–1940.

Vol. 131: J. S. M. Ward and Confraternity of the Kingdom of Christ, 1935.

Douglas Papers (Canon J. A. Douglas):

Vol. 4: Papers on 'Episcopi Vagantes', 1923–1940; and report to Lambeth Conference on "Relations between the Anglican Churches and Foreign Churches" (1948).

Vol. 27: "Orthodoxy and Anglicanism today", Nikaean Lecture, King's College, 1930.

Vol. 70: The Church of England Council on Foreign Relations, report on Syrian Orthodox Church by Canon W. A. Wigram, November 1937; Notice from the Syrian Patriarchate of Antioch and all the East, 1938; and general correspondence regarding John Churchill Sibley.

Library and Museum of Freemasonry, Freemasons' Hall, London
Correspondence file: J. S. M. Ward.
District Grand Chapter of Royal Arch Masons, Burma, "Minutes of the proceedings of the Annual Convocations, 1910–1941".
United Grand Lodge of England, "Report of the Deputation appointed by the M. W. Grand Master to visit the District Grand Lodges of India, Burma and Ceylon", 1928, n.p. [typescript].

Modern Records Centre, University of Warwick
Federation of British Industries, MSS 200.

National Archives (Public Record Office and Historical Manuscripts Commission)
PRO: B9/1409 Court of Bankruptcy: Ward, John Sebastian Marlow (No. 85 of 1945).
PRO: HK2/6 Museums Association Council, Agenda Book 1930–1936.
PRO: EB3/11 Standing Commission on Museums and Galleries, "Folk Museums".

Trinity Hall, University of Cambridge
Examinations and Miscellania, 1903–1910, C.86.
Tutorial Records, C.109–10.

Newspapers and periodicals

Crockford's Clerical Dictionary 72 (1948).
Hieratika; or The Voice of the Herarchy 1, 1–13 (January 1947–July 1951).
Masonic Record 1–5 (1920–1925).
Orthodox Catholic Review 1–2 (April 1944–January 1954).
The Times, 1934–40, 1945.
Transactions of the Masonic Study Society 1–13 (1921–1935).

Contemporary Printed Sources

Abbey Folk Park, *Illustrated Souvenir of the Abbey Folk Park* (New Barnet: Abbey Folk Park, n.d. [*c.*1937]).
Anderson, Drysdale, "The Ritual Through Medical Eyes", *Transactions of the Masonic Study Society* 7 (1928–9): 35–49.
Arseniev, Nicholas, *Mysticism and the Eastern Church* (Arthur Chambers trans.) (Oxford: A. R. Mowbray, 1979 [1926]).
Blavatsky, H. P., *Studies in Occultism* (Pasadena: Theosophical University Press, 1987 [1887–1891]).
Brandreth, Henry, *Episcopi Vagantes and the Anglican Church* (London: Society for Promoting Christian Knowledge, 1947).
Chisholm, A. R, "Oswald Spengler and the Decline of the West", *Australian Quarterly* 27 (1935): 35–44.

Clarke, F. C. P. C. (comp.), *Burma Masonic Diary 1899* (Maulmain: Maulmain Advertiser for District Grand Lodge, Burma).

Clayton, Muriel, *Catalogue of Rubbings of Brasses and Incised Slabs* (second edition) (London: Victoria and Albert Museum, 1929).

Cockburn, John, *Freemasonry: What, Whence, Why, Whither* (London: Masonic Record, n.d. [*c*.1924)]

Collingwood, R. G., "Oswald Spengler and the Theory of Historical Cycles", *Antiquity* 1 (1927): 311–25.

Collingwood, R. G., "The Theory of Historical Cycles: II. Cycles and Progress", *Antiquity* 1 (1927): 435–46.

District Grand Lodge, Burma, *The Ceremony of Laying the Foundation Stone of Freemasons' Hall, Rangoon, January 18th, 1908* (Rangoon: American Baptist Mission Press, 1908).

District Grand Lodge, Burma, *Reports of Proceedings of District Grand Lodge, Burma* (1904–1915), Library and Museum of Freemasonry, London.

Doyle, Arthur Conan, *The New Revelation* (third edition) (London: Hodder & Stoughton, 1918).

Doyle, Arthur Conan, *The Vital Message* (London: Hodder & Stoughton, 1919).

Eckenstein, Kenneth, "The Hiramic Legend, or Freemasonry and Symbolism", *Transactions of the Masonic Study Society* 6 (1927–8): 43–58.

Fortescue, Adrian, *The Lesser Eastern Churches* (London: Catholic Truth Society, 1913).

Fox, Cyril, "Open-Air Museums (Presidential Address to the Museums Association)", *Museums Journal* 34, 4 (1934): 109–21.

Frazer, J. G., *The Golden Bough: a study in magic and religion* (third edition) (London: Macmillan, 1911–15).

Gardner, Gerald, *High Magic's Aid* (London: Michael Houghton, 1949).

Gardner, Gerald, *Witchcraft Today* (London: Rider & Co., 1954).

Garrett, Eileen J., *My Life as a Search for the Meaning of Mediumship* (Salem, NH: Ayer, 1986 [1939]).

Gist, Noel P., "Secret Societies: A Cultural Study of Fraternalism in the United States", *University of Missouri Studies* 15, 4 (1940): 9–176.

Harben, Henry, *A Dictionary of London* (London: Herbert Jenkins, 1918).

Harmer, F. G., "The Ancient Mysteries", *Transactions of the Masonic Study Society* 4 (1925–6): 27–41.

Hills, Gordon, "Women and Freemasonry", *Ars Quatuor Coronatorum* 33 (1920): 63–77.

Hobbs, J. Walter, "The Antiquity of Freemasonry", *Ars Quatuor Coronatorum* 35 (1922): 83–112.

Inge, W. R., *Christian Mysticism, considered in eight lectures delivered before the University of Oxford* (London: Methuen, 1918 [1899]).

James, William, *The Varieties of Religious Experience* (New York: Triumph Books, 1991 [1902]).

King, A., "Freemasonry – Symbolical, Mystical", *Masonic Review* 4, 42 (1924): 157–9.

Kipling, Rudyard, *Wee Willie Winkie and other stories* (London: Macmillan, 1912).

Lees, R. J., *Through the Mists, or, Leaves from the Autobiography of a Soul in Paradise* (Leicester: Eva Lees, 1952 [1898]).

Lodge, Oliver, *Raymond, or Life and Death* (London: Methuen, 1917).

London Dialectical Society, *Report on Spiritualism* (London: Longman, Green, Reader & Dyer, 1871), reprinted as Volume 4 of R. A. Gilbert (ed.), *The Rise of Victorian Spiritualism* (London: Routledge/Thommes Press, 2000).

London Exhibitions Limited, *Official Guide: Empire of India Exhibition, 1895. Earls Court London* (pamphlet) (London, 1895).

London Exhibitions Limited, *Report of the Empire of India Exhibition, 1895* (London, 1895).

Macdonald, A. J., *Episcopi Vagantes in Church History* (London: Society for Promoting Christian Knowledge, 1945).

Markham, S. F., *A Report on the Museums and Art Galleries of the British Isles (other than the National Museums)* (Edinburgh: T. and A. Constable, 1938).

Matthews, W. R., "Psychical Research and Theology", *Proceedings of the Society for Psychical Research* 46, 161 (1940): 1–15.

Mee, Arthur, *The King's England: Hertfordshire* (London: Hodder & Stoughton, 1939).

Murray, Margaret, *The Witch-Cult in Western Europe* (Oxford: Clarendon Press, 1921).

Overbeck, J. J., *A Plain View of the Claims of the Orthodox Catholic Church as opposed to all other Christian Denominations* (London: Trübner & Co., 1881).

Podmore, Frank, *Modern Spiritualism: A History and a Criticism* (two volumes) (London: Methuen & Co., 1902), reprinted as Volumes 6 and 7 of R. A. Gilbert (ed.), *The Rise of Victorian Spiritualism* (London: Routledge/Thommes Press, 2000).

Previté-Orton, C. W. (comp.), *Index to Tripos Lists 1748–1910, contained in the Historical Register of the University of Cambridge to the year 1910* (Cambridge: Cambridge University Press, 1923).

Rangoon Lodge, *Bye-Laws of the 'Rangoon' Lodge of Antient, Free, & Accepted Masons, No. 1268, E. C. held at Rangoon, British Burma* (Rangoon: Hanthawaddy Press, 1885).

Roebuck, G. E., "Masonic Research – Its Possibilities and Dangers", *Transactions of the Masonic Study Society* 7 (1928–9): 30–4.

Royal Commission on Historical Monuments (England), *An Inventory of the Historical Monuments in London* (Volume IV: The City) (London: H.M.S.O., 1928).

Simmel, Georg, "The Sociology of Secrecy and of Secret Societies", *American Journal of Sociology* 11, 4 (1906): 441–98.

Smith, Margaret, *Studies in Early Mysticism in the Near and Middle East* (Amsterdam: Philo Press, 1973 [1931]).

Wallace, Alfred Russel, *On Miracles and Modern Spiritualism: Three Essays*

(London: James Burns, 1875), reprinted as Volume 5 of R. A. Gilbert (ed.), *The Rise of Victorian Spiritualism* (London: Routledge/Thommes Press, 2000).

Watson, Samuel, *The Religion of Spiritualism, its Phenomena and Philosophy* (third edition) (Boston: Colby and Rich, 1889).

Webster, Nesta H., *Secret Societies and Subversive Movements* (London: Britons, 1964 [1924]).

Mortimer Wheeler, R. E., "Folk Museums", *Museums Journal* 34, 5 (1934): 191–6.

Wigram, W. A., "Masonry and the Ancient Mysteries", *Transactions of the Masonic Study Society* 2 (1922–3): 17–29.

Wigram, W. A., *The Separation of the Monophysites* (London: Faith Press, 1923).

Wigram, W. A., "Mithraism", *Transactions of the Masonic Study Society* 7 (1928–9): 10–29.

Williams-Ellis, Clough, *England and the Octopus* (London: Geoffrey Bles, 1926).

Wilmshurst, W. L., "The Fundamental Philosophic Secrets within Masonry", *Transactions of the Masonic Study Society* 4 (1925–6): 6–20.

Underhill, Evelyn, *Mysticism: A Study in the Nature and Development of Man's Spiritual Consciousness* (New York: Meridian Books, 1955 [1911]).

Underhill, Evelyn, *The Mystic Way: A Psychological Study in Christian Origins* (London: J. M. Dent & Sons, 1913).

Vibert, Lionel, "The Story of the Craft", *Masonic Review* 5, 60 (1925): 645–7, and 61 (1925): 676–7.

Secondary Sources

Abramtsov, David F., "The Western Rite and the Eastern Church: Dr. J. J. Overbeck and his Scheme for the Re-establishment of the Orthodox Church in the West", M.A. dissertation, University of Pittsburgh, 1961.

Ackerman, Robert, *J. G. Frazer: his Life and Work* (Cambridge: Cambridge University Press, 1987).

Adamson, Iain, *A Man of Quality: A Biography of The Hon. Mr Justice Cassels* (London: Frederick Muller, 1964).

Agnew, Neville, Michael Strong and Jennifer Webb, "The Abbey Museum Collection", *Australian Antique Collector* 33 (1987): 53–4.

Almond, Philip C., *The British Discovery of Buddhism* (Cambridge: Cambridge University Press, 1988).

Anson, Peter, *Bishops at Large* (London: Faber & Faber, 1964).

Armstrong, Christopher J. R., *Evelyn Underhill (1875–1941): An Introduction to her Life and Writings* (London: Mowbray, 1975).

Baker, Antony, "The Scholar the Builders Rejected – The Life & Work of J. S. M. Ward", *Ars Quatuor Coronatorum* 116 (2004): 127–92.

Bennett, Gillian, "Geologists and Folklorists: Cultural Evolution and the Science of Folklore", *Folklore* 105 (1994): 25–37.

Berger, Arthur S. and Joyce Berger, *The Encyclopedia of Parapsychology and Psychical Research* (New York: Paragon House, 1991).

Betjeman, John, *Sir John Betjeman's Guide to English Parish Churches* (Nigel Kerr, ed.) (London: HarperCollins, 1993).

Bowler, Peter J., *Reconciling Science and Religion: the debate in early-twentieth century Britain* (Chicago: University of Chicago Press, 2001).

Bracelin, Jack, *Gerald Gardner Witch* (London: Octagon, 1960).

Bradley, Simon and Nikolaus Pevsner, *London: the City Churches* (London: Penguin Books, 1998).

Brears, Peter C. D., "Kirk of the Castle", *Museums Journal* 80, 2 (1980): 90–2.

Brooke, Christopher N. L., *A History of the University of Cambridge* (Volume 4: 1870–1990) (Cambridge: Cambridge University Press, 1993).

Bullock, Stephen C., *Revolutionary Brotherhood: Freemasonry and the Transformation of the American Social Order, 1730–1840* (Chapel Hill: University of North Carolina Press, 1996).

Campbell-Everden, William Preston, *Freemasonry and its Etiquette* (New York: Weathervane Books, 1978 [1955]).

Cannadine, David, "War and Death, Grief and Mourning in Modern Britain" in Joachim Whaley (ed.), *Mirrors of Mortality: Studies in the Social History of Death* (London: Europa, 1981), pp. 187–242.

Capps, Donald and Janet L. Jacobs (eds), *The Struggle for Life: A Companion to William James's 'The Varieties of Religious Experience'* (West Lafayette: Society for the Scientific Study of Religion, 1995).

Cardeña, Etzel, Steven Jay Lynn and Stanley Krippner (eds), *Varieties of Anomalous Experience: Examining the Scientific Evidence* (Washington: American Psychological Association, 2000).

Clark, Peter, *British Clubs and Societies 1580–1800: The Origins of an Associational World* (Oxford: Clarendon Press, 2000).

Collinson, Patrick, "Religion, Society and the Historian", *Journal of Religious History* 23, 2 (1999): 149–67.

Crawley, Charles, *Trinity Hall: The History of a Cambridge College 1350–1975* (Cambridge: Trinity Hall, 1976).

Crow, W. B., *A History of Magic, Witchcraft and Occultism* (London; Sphere Books, 1968).

Cryer, N. B., "The Churches' Concern with Freemasonry", *Ars Quatuor Coronatorum* 95 (1982): 1–20.

Dedopulos, Tim, *The Brotherhood: inside the secret world of the Freemasons* (Melbourne: Viking, 2006).

Dyer, Colin, *The History of the First Hundred Years of Quatuor Coronati Lodge No. 2076* (London: QC Correpsondence Circle, 1986).

Dyer, Colin, *Symbolism in Craft Freemasonry* (Hersham: Lewis Masonic, 2003 [1976]).

Every, George, *Understanding Eastern Christianity* (London: SCM Press, 1980).

Galbreath, Robert, "Explaining Modern Occultism" in Howard Kerr and Charles L. Crow (eds), *The Occult in America: New Historical Perspectives* (Urbana and Chicago: University of Illinois Press, 1983), pp. 11–37.

Gilbert, R. A., "William Wynn Westcott and the Esoteric School of Masonic Research", *Ars Quatuor Coronatorum* 100 (1987): 6–32.

Gilbert, R. A., "To See Ourselves As Others See Us", *Ars Quatuor Coronatorum* 107 (1994): 1–7.

Ginn, Geoffrey A. C., "An Ark for England: Esoteric heritage at J. S. M. Ward's Abbey Folk Park, 1934–1940", *Journal of the History of Collections* 22, 1 (2010): 129–40.

Ginn, Geoffrey A. C., "J. S. M. Ward, 'Bishop at Large': 'Orthodox Catholicism' and Church History in Interwar Britain", *Crossroads* 5, 1 (2010): 45–57.

Godwin, Joscelyn, *The Theosophical Enlightenment* (Albany: State University of New York Press, 1994).

Hamill, J. M., *The Craft: a History of English Freemasonry* (Wellingborough: Aquarian Press, 1986).

Hamill, J. M., "The Sins of our Masonic Fathers", *Ars Quatuor Coronatorum* 101 (1988): 133–59.

Hammerton, John, *Child of Wonder: An Intimate Biography of Arthur Mee* (London: Hodder & Stoughton, 1946).

Harland-Jacobs, Jessica L., *Builders of Empire: Freemasons and British Imperialism, 1717–1927* (Chapel Hill: University of North Carolina Press, 2007).

Harris, Marvin, *The Rise of Anthropological Theory: A History of Theories of Culture* (Walnut Creek: AltaMira Press, 2001 [1968]).

Hazelgrove, Jenny, "Spiritualism after the Great War", *Twentieth Century British History* 10, 4 (1999): 404–30.

Heselton, Philip, *Wiccan Roots: Gerald Gardner and the Modern Witchcraft Revival* (Milverton: Capell Bann, 2000).

Heselton, Philip, *Gerald Gardner and the Cauldron of Inspiration* (Milverton: Capell Bann, 2003).

Hilliard, David, "UnEnglish and Unmanly: Anglo-Catholicism and Homosexuality", *Victorian Studies* 25, 2 (1982): 181–210.

Hoare, Philip, *England's Lost Eden: Adventures in a Victorian Utopia* (London: Harper Perennial, 2006).

Hobsbawm, Eric and Terence Ranger (eds), *The Invention of Tradition* (Cambridge: Cambridge University Press, 1983).

Holland Rose, J., A. P. Newton and E. A. Benians (eds), *The Cambridge History of the British Empire* (nine volumes) (Cambridge: Cambridge University Press, 1929–61).

Howkins, Alun, *The Death of Rural England: A Social History of the Countryside Since 1900* (London: Routledge, 2003).

Hutton, Ronald, *The Triumph of the Moon: A History of Modern Pagan Witchcraft* (Oxford: Oxford University Press, 2001).

Hyam, Ronald, *Britain's Imperial Century, 1815–1914* (third edition) (Basingstoke: Palgrave Macmillan, 2002).

Isaac Newton University Lodge, "A Hundred Years of the Isaac Newton University Lodge, 1861–1961" (Cambridge, 1961).

Jackson, A. C. F., "Rosicrucianism and its Effect on Craft Masonry", *Ars Quatuor Coronatorum* 97 (1984): 115–50.

Jacob, Margaret, *Living the Enlightenment: Freemasonry and Politics in Eighteenth-Century Europe* (Oxford: Oxford University Press, 1991).

Jacob, Margaret, *The Origins of Freemasonry: Facts & Fictions* (Philadelphia: University of Pennsylvania Press, 2006).

Jones, Kelvin, *Conan Doyle and the Spirits: The Spiritualist Career of Sir Arthur Conan Doyle* (Wellingborough: Aquarian Press, 1989).

Kavanagh, Gaynor, "Mangles, Muck and Myths: Rural History Museums in Britain", *Rural History* 2, 2 (1991): 187–203.

Kavanagh, Gaynor (ed.), *Making Histories in Museums* (Leicester: Leicester University Press, 1996).

Keizer, Lewis, *The Wandering Bishops: Apostles of a New Age* (St Thomas Press, 1984).

King, Francis, *Ritual Magic in England; 1887 to the present day* (London: Neville Spearman, 1970).

Kirby, Dianne, "Christianity and Freemasonry: The Compatibility Debate Within the Church of England", *Journal of Religious History* 29, 1 (February 2005): 43–66.

Kuklick, Henrika, *The Savage Within: The Social History of British Anthropology, 1885–1945* (Cambridge: Cambridge University Press, 1991).

Kuklick, Henrika, "The British Tradition" in Henrika Kuklick (ed.), *A New History of Anthropology* (Oxford: Blackwell, 2008), pp. 52–78.

Lewis, James, *Witchcraft Today: An Encyclopedia of Wiccan and Neopagan Traditions* (Santa Barbara: ABC-CLIO, 1999).

Lossky, Vladimir, *The Mystical Theology of the Eastern Church* (New York: St Vladimir's Seminary Press, 1976).

Louis, Wm. Roger (ed.), *The Oxford History of the British Empire* (five volumes) (Oxford: Oxford University Press, 1998–99).

Mathur, Saloni, "Living Ethnological Exhibits: The Case of 1886", *Cultural Anthropology* 15, 4 (2000): 492–524.

McGinn, Bernard, *The Foundations of Mysticism: Origins to the Fifth Century* (London: SCM Press, 1992).

McGinn, Bernard, John Meyendorff and Jean Leclerq (eds), *Christian Spirituality: Origins to the Twelfth Century* (London: SCM Press, 1989).

McLachlan, Jean, "The Origin and Early Development of the Cambridge Historical Tripos", *Cambridge Historical Journal* 9, 1 (1947): 78–105.

MacKenzie, John M., *Propaganda and Empire: the manipulation of British public opinion, 1880–1960* (Manchester: Manchester University Press, 1984).

Neher, Andrew, *The Psychology of Transcendence* (Englewood Cliffs: Prentice-Hall, 1980).

Nelson, Geoffrey, *Spiritualism and Society* (London: Routledge & Kegan Paul, 1969).

SOURCES

Oppenheim, Janet, *The Other World: Spiritualism and psychical research in England, 1850–1914* (Cambridge: Cambridge University Press, 1985).

Orel, Harold, *Sir Arthur Conan Doyle: Interviews and Recollections* (New York: St Martin's Press, 1991).

Ouspensky, Leonid and Vladimir Lossky, *The Meaning of Icons* (New York: St Vladimir's Seminary Press, 1989).

Owen, Alex, *The Place of Enchantment: British Occultism and the Culture of the Modern* (Chicago: University of Chicago Press, 2004).

Pearson, Joanne, *Wicca and the Christian Heritage: Ritual, Sex and Magic* (London: Routledge, 2007).

Piatigorsky, Alexander, *Who's Afraid of Freemasons? The Phenomenon of Freemasonry* (London: Harvill Press, 1997).

Plummer, John, *The Many Paths of the Independent Sacramental Movement* (Berkeley: Apocryphile, 2006).

Powicke. Maurice, "Three Cambridge Scholars: C. W. Previté-Orton, Z. N. Brooke and G. G. Coulton", *Cambridge Historical Journal* 9, 1 (1947): 106–16.

Roberts, J. M., "Freemasonry: possibilities of a neglected topic", *English Historical Review* 84, 331 (1969): 323–35.

Roberts, J. M., *The Mythology of the Secret Societies* (London: Secker & Warburg, 1972).

Samuel, Raphael, *Theatres of Memory, Vol. 1: Past and Present in Contemporary Culture* (London: Verso, 1994).

Slee, P. R. H., *Learning and a Liberal Education: The Study of Modern History in the Universities of Oxford, Cambridge and Manchester, 1800–1914* (Manchester: Manchester University Press, 1986).

Stocking, George W., *Victorian Anthropology* (New York: Free Press, 1987).

Strenski, Ivan, "The Spiritual Dimension" in Henrika Kuklick (ed.), *A New History of Anthropology* (Oxford: Blackwell, 2008), pp. 113–27.

Strong, Michael, "John Ward: custodian of the past", *Australian Collectors Quarterly* (November 1990–January 1991): 77–80.

Strong, Michael, "Queensland's Abbey Museum", *Australian Collectors Quarterly* (February–April 1991): 73–6.

Strong, Michael, *Unexpected Treasures: Highlights from the Abbey Museum* (Caboolture: Abbey Museum of Art and Archaeology, 2006).

Strong, P. G., *John Ward: The Prophet of These Times* (pamphlet) (Orthodox Catholic Church of Australia, 1999).

Tillett, Gregory, "Esoteric Adventism; three esoteric Christian Adventist movements of the first half of the twentieth century" in G. W. Trompf (ed.), *Cargo Cults and Millenarian Movements. Transoceanic Comparisons of New Religious Movements* (New York and Berlin: Mouton de Gruyter, 1990), pp. 145–78.

Ware, Christopher, *The Orthodox Church* (Harmondsworth: Penguin Books, 1964).

Webb, James, *The Occult Underground* (La Salle: Open Court, 1974).

Webb, James, *The Occult Establishment* (La Salle: Library Press, 1976).

309

Wingfield, Chris, "From Greater Britain to Little England: The Pitt Rivers Museum, the Museum of English Rural Life, and Their Six Degrees of Separation", *Museum History Journal* 4, 2 (2011): 245–66.

Winter, J. M., "Spiritualism and the First World War" in R. W. Davis and R.J. Helmstadter (eds), *Religion and Irreligion in Victorian Society: essays in honour of R. K. Webb* (London and New York: Routledge, 1992), pp. 185–200.

Wulff, David M., "Mystical Experience" in Etzel Cardeña, Steven Jay Lynn and Stanley Krippner (eds), *Varieties of Anomalous Experience: Examining the Scientific Evidence* (Washington: American Psychological Association, 2000), pp. 397–440.

Wynn, Catherine, *The Colonial Conan Doyle: British Imperialism, Irish Nationalism and the Gothic* (Westport: Greenwood Press, 2002).

Yates, Frances, *The Rosicrucian Enlightenment* (London: Routledge, 2002 [1972]).

Index